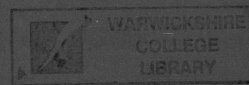
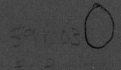

# DORLING KINDERSLEY
# ANIMAL
# ENCYCLOPEDIA

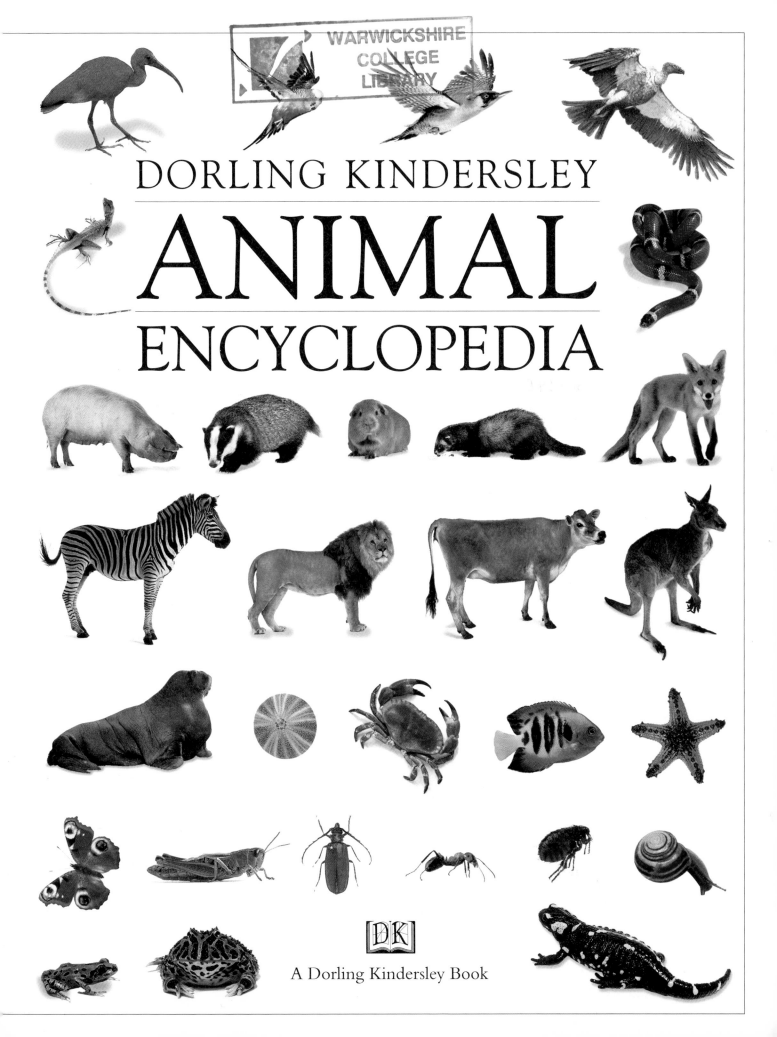

# DORLING KINDERSLEY
# ANIMAL
# ENCYCLOPEDIA

A Dorling Kindersley Book

# Dorling **DK** Kindersley

LONDON, NEW YORK, SYDNEY, DELHI,
PARIS, MUNICH, *and* JOHANNESBURG

PAGE *One*, Cairn House, Elgiva Lane, Chesham, Bucks HP5 2JD
**Creative director** Bob Gordon; **Editor** Charlotte Stock;
**Designer** Suzanne Tuhrim

*Harrison Research* and *Mason Linklater*
**General editor** James Harrison; **Art editor** Bill Mason

for Dorling Kindersley:
**Project editor** Kitty Blount
**Art editor** Sharon Grant
**Editors** Helena Spiteri, Sadie Smith,
Simon Holland, and Lucy Hurst
**Senior editor** Fran Jones
**Senior managing editor** Sue Grabham
**Deputy art director** Julia Harris

**Editorial consultant** Michael Bright

**Authors** Jonathan Elphick, Jen Green,
Barbara Taylor, and Richard Walker

**DTP design** Andrew O'Brien and Nomazwe Madonko
**Production** Orla Creegan and Kate Oliver
**Picture research** Michele Faram, Samantha Nunn,
and Rachel Hilford

First published in Great Britain in 2000
by Dorling Kindersley Limited,
9 Henrietta Street, London WC2E 8PS

2 4 6 8 10 9 7 5 3 1

A CIP catalogue record for this book
is available from the British Library

ISBN 0 7513 6256 5

Colour reproduction by
GRB Editrice, S.r.l., Verona
Printed by
Printer industria grafica SA

See our complete
catalogue at
**www.dk.com**

# Contents

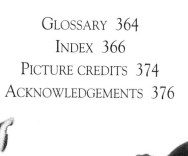

*Celine Philibert*
Age: 15
Bantam cock

*Kathleen Swalwell*
Age: 9
Turtle

**Overall winner:**
**Young Photographer**
**of the Year 1999**
*Raphaella Ricciardi*
Age: 11
King Charles spaniel

**Winner: Under 12 category**
*Montana Miles-Lowery*
Age: 10
Koi carp

**Runner-up**
*Josephine Green*
Age: 10
African elephant

**Young Photographer Awards**
In 1999, entrants in the DK Eyewitness/RSPCA Young
Photographer Awards came up with some real winners in both
the Under 12 years and 12–17 years categories. We are delighted
to show a selection of winners and runners-up on these pages.

*Jenny Moffat*
Age: 14
Pig in farmyard

*Keshini Ranasinghe*
Age: 17
Duck

# Foreword

On a sunny day in 1962, I crawled off a blanket onto the lawn and met a ladybird. Red, shiny, tickly, and perfect, it scurried over my tiny hand and, aged two years, I fell in love with life on Earth. That same hand is now scarred. A lion has left a slash, a griffon vulture a hole, and a viper a small puncture in a fingertip. But I think that hand is lucky – it has touched, stroked, held, and calmed a great diversity of animals and, despite its wounds, still stretches out for more. Today it safely turns the pages of this wonderful book, a beautiful catalogue of our animal life. There is so much colour, shape, texture, and surprise – and so much to learn, even for old folks like me!

Essential to the book's success are the brilliant photographs, so it is more than apt that in recent years Dorling Kindersley have been keen sponsors of the RSPCA's young people's photographic competition. Creatures from the garden, the farm, and the wilderness have become the subjects of the wonderful pictures, some of which are shown here. A turtle flies over sea-rippled sand, a bantam cock blazes, and weariness peers from the ancient eyes of an elephant. On the next pages you can admire the extraordinary shot of the goosander from underwater, its characteristic silhouette mounted in molten crystal, the inherent friskiness of the resting horse, and the lazing hippopotamus sculpture. These photographs are accomplished, artistic interpretations, but they are also reflections of each young

*Continued on next page*

photographer's passion. And the overall winner, a slumbering spaniel, is the epitome of this. You can feel its comfort, the warmth of the late afternoon sun that blends its soft fur into the shadows, and into the patterns of the blanket on which it rests. Most of all, you can feel how much he is loved.

I am often asked which is my favourite animal, but it is a question that is impossible to answer. Pick a page from the book! From the frill on that crazy lizard to the sleek beauty of the shark, or the shimmer from the wing cases of a beetle, so many are on my list. I suppose my favourite is the animal that I will next meet, but whichever it is, I hope it does not bite my hand too hard!

*Katie Budd*
Age: 11
Ring-tailed lemur

Chris Packham

**Winner: 12–17 category**
*James Lewis*
Age: 13
Hippopotamus

Sponsored by

The Young Photographer Awards 1999 were organized in conjunction with the RSPCA and were sponsored by Olympus Cameras. Chris Packham (TV presenter and wildlife photographer) was one of the judges, along with Peter Kindersley (Dorling Kindersley), Ian Dickens (Olympus Cameras) and Michaela Miller (RSPCA'S Animal Action Magazine).

The 1998 competition overall winner Keith Rae's photo of a leopard appears on pages 12–13; and 1999 runner-up Daniel Darby's photo of swans appears on pages 88–89.

**Runner-up**
*Oliver Thwaites*
Age: 17
Goosander

*Jonathan Ashcroft*
Age: 10
Ostrich

*Rebecca Noble*
Age: 11
Sheep in snowy landscape

*Anna Brownlee*
Age: 15
Horse

# How to use this book

THIS ILLUSTRATED ANIMAL ENCYCLOPEDIA is packed with information on the fascinating world of animals. The book is divided into two main sections, which are described on these pages. The first section, Animal Life, explains how animals behave and fit into their individual habitats. The main A–Z section is a guide to the animals themselves, arranged in easy-to-follow alphabetical order. There is also a glossary of new words and an index to guide you to the subject you want.

## Step-by-step

One of the many features of the encyclopedia is the step-by-step artworks and time-lapse photo techniques. These follow the various stages of, say, how a penguin moves through water, or how a duck flies. It allows you to see every step in a sequence of events.

## ANIMAL A–Z

The main part of the encyclopedia is organized alphabetically with entries from Aardvarks to Zebras. Each entry provides detailed information on individual members of the animal kingdom with photographs, artworks, and other special features that are described here. These animal entries vary in length from one to three pages.

## Fact box

Each entry in the A–Z section has a Fact Box that provides quick-reference information. You will find specific facts such as the family name for that group of animals, as well as details such as habitat, food, and number of eggs laid at one time. Facts listed will vary from animal to animal. If the Fact Box is for a mammal, for example, it would say number of live young rather than eggs.

### FACT BOX

**Family:** Spheniscidae

**Habitat:** Seawater, ice, rocky islands, coasts

**Distribution:** Oceans of the southern hemisphere

**Food:** Crustaceans, fish, squid

**Nest:** Stones, grass, mud, caves, or burrows

**Eggs:** 1–2

**Size:** 40–115 cm (16–45 in)

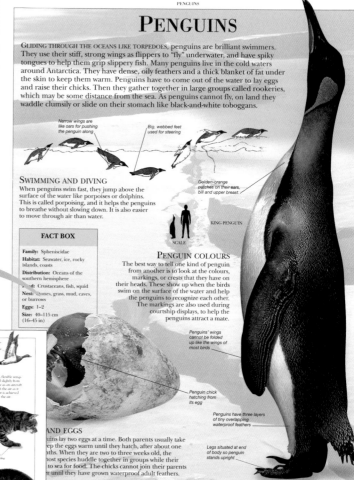

### PENGUINS

GLIDING THROUGH THE OCEANS LIKE TORPEDOES, penguins are brilliant swimmers. They use their stiff, strong wings as flippers to "fly" underwater, and have spiky tongues to help them grip slippery fish. Many penguins live in the cold waters around Antarctica. They have dense, oily feathers and a thick blanket of fat under the skin to keep them warm. Penguins have to come out of the water to lay eggs and raise their chicks. Then they gather together in large groups called rookeries, which may be some distance from the sea. As penguins cannot fly, on land they waddle clumsily or slide on their stomach like black-and-white toboggans.

Narrow wings are like oars for pushing the penguin along

Big, webbed feet used for steering

#### SWIMMING AND DIVING

When penguins swim fast, they jump above the surface of the water like porpoises or dolphins. This is called porpoising, and it helps the penguins to breathe without slowing down. It is also easier to move through air than water.

Golden-orange patches on their ears, bill and upper breast.

KING PENGUIN

SCALE

#### FACT BOX

**Family:** Spheniscidae
**Habitat:** Seawater, ice, rocky islands, coasts
**Distribution:** Oceans of the southern hemisphere
**Food:** Crustaceans, fish, squid
**Nest:** Stones, grass, mud, caves, or burrows
**Eggs:** 1–2
**Size:** 40–115 cm (16–45 in)

#### PENGUIN COLOURS

The best way to tell one kind of penguin from another is to look at the colours, markings, or crests that they have on their heads. These show up when the birds swim on the surface of the water and help the penguins to recognize each other. The markings are also used during courtship displays, to help the penguins attract a mate.

Penguins' wings cannot be folded up like the wings of most birds

#### AND EGGS

...ins lay two eggs at a time. Both parents usually take ...ep the eggs warm until they hatch, after about one ...ths. When they are two to three weeks old, the ...ost species huddle together in groups while ...to sea for food. The chicks cannot join their parents ...r until they have grown waterproof adult feathers.

Penguin chick hatching from its egg

Penguins have three layers of tiny overlapping waterproof feathers

Legs situated at end of body so penguin stands upright

276

## Movement

Animals need movement so that they can track down food, seek out a partner, or escape from the clutches of predators. To do this, some creatures have legs for running and jumping, while others have fins for swimming or wings for flying. Crawlers move overland without legs, such as the snail with its slimy foot and the earthworm that shortens and lengthens its body to burrow through soil. Some animals, known as drifters, have very little natural movement so they have to take advantage of any movement in their environment. Sea drifters float near the water's surface and move with the waves, while some small insects allow themselves to be carried along by currents of air.

### Holding on
Some lizards, such as geckos, have special ridges of scales on their feet that resemble sucker pads. These ridges are covered in millions of tiny hairs. They can grip onto almost any surface, enabling the gecko to walk along upright objects, such as tree trunks, and even to run upside-down on ceilings in houses.

### Duck flight
Like other birds, the mallard duck uses it light, flexible wings to move through the air. The wings are curved slightly from front to back, which give them the same profile as an aircraft wing. This shape lifts the bird upwards through the air as it flaps its wings. The forward movement in flight is achieved with the downward flap, which pushes against the air.

### Powerful pounce
Domestic cats do not have to hunt for their food. Even so, they are able to pounce and land with great accuracy, just like their wild relatives who use this skill when chasing prey. Before making a leap, the cat watches the movements of its prey carefully. It then uses powerful leg muscles to jump up in the air and pounce on its target. The cat's tail acts as a rudder to keep it on course and its front claws pin its prey to the ground.

### From side to side
The green anaconda moves by crawling - but it relies on the ground being uneven. Like all snakes, it has no legs. Instead, it moves on its ribs. The sides of the snake's body curve and bend around objects, such as rocks and plants. The waves created by this muscle movement pass back along the body and push against the rocks and plants. This allows the snake to glide forwards.

### Rudder action
The dogfish, like all sharks, moves by making an S-shaped wave through its body. The movement starts from the head which the fish swings from side to side. This pushes the body forward and then ripples down the body and into the tail. The pectoral (side) fins act like the wings of an aircraft and lift the dogfish as it swims forwards.

### Two at a time
The green tree frog of Australia, like all amphibians, sways its body from side to side in order to move. This is because the front and rear limbs on each side of the body move together as a pair. The tree frog's toes are equipped with sticky pads which help it to grip firmly when climbing among trees or walking across slimy leaf surfaces.

## ANIMAL LIFE

This first section of the book, which is not alphabetical, introduces a wealth of background information on animal life. You can learn about animal anatomy, including senses such as eyesight and hearing. Animal behaviour, on subjects such as communication and movement, is also described. Other pages bring to life the various animal habitats from grasslands to desert and oceans to outback.

## Scale

Every animal entry in the main A–Z section has a small artwork labelled "Scale". This gives you an idea of the average size of the animal compared to that of an average adult human male. For example, on the penguins entry, the size of the king penguin is shown. Where creatures are much smaller, such as the scorpion (right), then the size is compared to that of a human hand.

SCALE

## Animal groups

Slotted into the A–Z section there are pages that introduce you to the main animal groups – such as Amphibians, Birds, Fish, Mammals, and Reptiles. The pages on Fish, for example, will describe the various types and shapes of fish as well as identifying features, such as fins and skin. This entry also describes how fish use gills so they can breathe underwater.

### FISH

THERE ARE 25,000 DIFFERENT TYPES of fish worldwide. In fact, there are more types of fish than there are types of amphibian, reptile, bird, and mammal put together. Fish have spread throughout the world's oceans, from the ice-cold polar oceans to warm tropical seas. They also live in fresh waters, from huge rivers and great lakes to small pools, and even pitch-dark underground streams. Fish need oxygen to survive but rather than coming to the surface for air, they are able to take in oxygen underwater. They feed on plants and other sea creatures, moving through water using their powerful tails and body fins.

**FATHERHOOD**
Like pipefish, male seahorses have special egg-carrying pouches on their bellies. In the breeding season, the female lays her eggs in the pouch for safety. Several other groups of fish, called mouthbrooders, carry their eggs and newly hatched young in their mouths until they are ready to fend for themselves.

*Pouch carries and protects eggs*

*Dorsal fin helps fish to balance*

*YOUNG FRENCH ANGELFISH*

*CARIBBEAN NEON ROSE*

*Tail fin propels fish forward*

*Tail can grip onto plants and rocks*

*Water taken in contains dissolved oxygen*

*Gills enable fish to extract oxygen from water*

*Slimy coating helps fish to glide through water*

PARTS OF A FISH

**SCALES**
Most bony fish are covered with a layer of thin, flexible scales. Some have spiny scales that overlap one another, like tiles on a roof. Sharks and rays have very different kinds of scales called denticles. These are small toothlike structures sunk deep in the skin.

*SPINY SCALES OF PORCUPINE FISH*

*SHARK DENTICLE*

**OCEAN LIFE**
Fish are able to live in a range of water habitats and adopt different lifestyles. Many of them are cold-blooded and cannot alter their body temperature to adjust to changes in their environment. Some are docile grazers that feed on seaweed in warm tropical oceans, while others are fearsome predators that lurk in the cold weed fringes of northern lakes and rivers.

## Environment pages

Also in the A–Z section, there are dramatic full-page photographs that take you inside the environments, or living spaces, of some of the animals. A single paragraph of text describes that environment. You can admire the beauty of underwater worlds, feel the chill of icy landscapes, and experience the vastness of the great African grasslands.

**HUDDLING HERD**
Emperors are the biggest penguins. They huddle together for warmth to breed in the most hostile habitat on Earth – the pack ice of Antarctica. Their closeness to one another helps them survive freezing temperatures and winds of more than 160 kmh (100 mph).

*In the densest part of the huddle there may be ten adults to 1 sq metre (10.76 sq ft)*

*EMPEROR PENGUINS*

*Penguins on the outside of the huddle will get a turn in the middle where it is warmer*

*So much heat is trapped in the centre of the huddle that steam may rise*

*Emperors often turn their back to the constantly shifting wind*

*Chicks are carried on the parents' feet, kept warm by a fold of skin on the adult's belly*

**ROCKHOPPER PENGUIN**
The rockhopper gets its name from its skill and speed at climbing steep rocks to reach its clifftop nesting colonies. Instead of waddling like other penguins, it hops from boulder to boulder, its head thrust forward, flippers back, and feet together. It is the smallest of the penguins that breed in the islands around the Antarctic.

*ROCKHOPPER PENGUIN*

**CHINSTRAP PENGUIN**
Chinstrap (also called bearded) penguins are named for the narrow band of black feathers running from ear to ear. They are the most numerous of all penguins. They nest in huge colonies of hundreds of thousands on Antarctic islands and on the continent itself, on the Antarctic peninsula. They are among the most aggressive of all penguins, and drive off larger penguins if they try to nest near them.

*CHINSTRAP PENGUIN*

*Parent bird gently preens one of its two recently hatched chicks*

> **Find out more**
> ANTARCTIC 56
> BIRDS 115
> DOLPHINS AND PORPOISES 160
> OCEANS 74

> **Find out more**
> ANTARCTIC 56
> BIRDS 115
> DOLPHINS AND PORPOISES 160
> OCEANS 74

## Captions

These areas of text provide the main source of information to go with each photograph. They may tell you about where an animal lives, or describe its behaviour. On this page, the text explains why chinstrap penguins have that name, where they nest, and how they protect their eggs.

## Labels

To help you identify the animal that is being written about, each one has a label, in capital letters. This will tell you its common name.

CHINSTRAP PENGUIN

## Abbreviations

**Metric**

| | |
|---|---|
| m | metres |
| mm | millimetres |
| cm | centimetres |
| km | kilometres |
| sq km | square kilometres |
| kmh | kilometres per hour |
| °C | degrees Celsius |
| g | grams |
| kg | kilograms |

**Imperial**

| | |
|---|---|
| ft | feet |
| in | inch(es) |
| yd | yard(s) |
| sq miles | square miles |
| mph | miles per hour |
| °F | degrees Fahrenheit |
| oz | ounce(s) |
| lb | pound(s) |

CHINSTRAP PENGUIN

## Photography

Dramatic colour photographs throughout the book reveal specific facts about an animal or some aspect of that animal's life. Some of the photos highlight special close-up details. This penguin is shown caring for its young.

## Find out more

For each animal entry there is a Find Out More box. This directs you to other pages where you can read about a linked subject. For example, after you have finished the penguin pages, turn to the entry for Antarctic on page 56, and read more about where penguins live.

## Annotation

Many photos have annotations, printed in smaller lettering, that lead you to an extra detail about that animal.

*Parent bird gently preens one of its two recently hatched chicks*

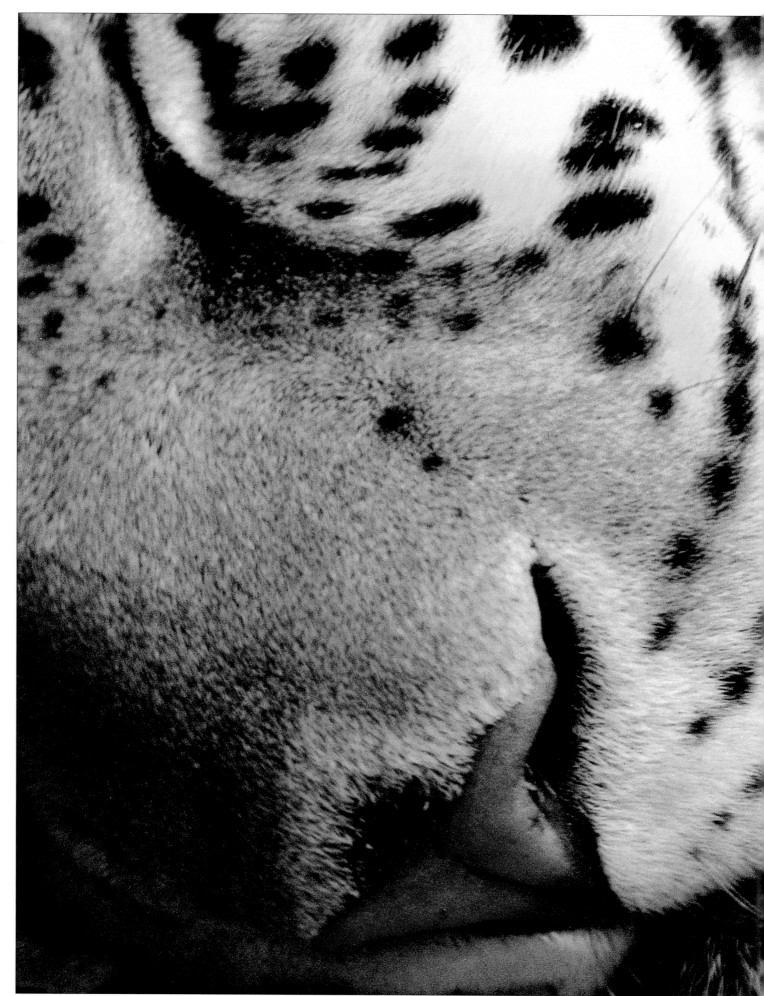

# Animal Life

The animal world is a weird and wonderful place. Sometimes we see it – a spider's web dangling in the morning dew. At other times, we miss it – a barn owl swooping down in pitch darkness on an unsuspecting harvest mouse. Animals, including humans, share this world either in harmony or with danger ever-present. Animal Life shows you the marvels and mysteries of the creatures of this planet and what is being done to protect threatened animals. This section also reveals where each beast belongs in the animal kingdom, what animals eat, how they communicate, move, attack other animals, and defend themselves. It discovers where they live and why they make the sort of homes they do. The photographs reveal the fascinating ways that animals mate, are born, develop as babies and youngsters, and survive into adulthood – or not, as the animal world can be savage as well as beautiful.

# Animal classification

There are dramatic differences as well as many similarities between animals. To understand how animals are related, they are arranged into groups. The more features that a group of animals share, the more precise the classification. So, all animals belong to the animal kingdom, but all cat-like animals are grouped in the cat family. Animals are given scientific names so that people all over the world are able to refer to the same creature no matter what language they speak. In the example below, the classification of the Manx cat is traced back to the animal kingdom.

## Kingdom

This is the most general grouping of animals – there are separate kingdoms for plants, bacteria, protists (mostly single-celled creatures), and fungi. All members of the animal kingdom have bodies made of many cells.

## Phylum

The animal kingdom is divided into 40 smaller groups called phyla (singular, phylum). Animals are allocated to a phylum according to their main features. For example, the Crustacea phylum (crustaceans) contains invertebrates (animals without backbones) with jointed legs and two pairs of antennae. Cats belong to the Chordata phylum (chordates) which contains all vertebrates (animals with backbones).

## Class

Phyla are subdivided into smaller groupings called classes. The chordates phylum separates out into fish, birds, mammals, amphibians, and reptiles. Cats belong to the class Mammalia (mammals), which contains all warm-blooded vertebrate animals that suckle their young.

## Order

Like other classes, mammals are divided into orders. Cats are placed in the order Carnivora because they are warm-blooded meat-eating animals. Other orders containing mammals include egg-layers, insect-eaters, marsupials, and rodents.

## Family

Within every order are families. Felidae (the cat family) includes big cats, such as lions and tigers, as well as small cats, such as pumas, bobcats, and lynxes. They are hunting animals, with flexible bodies, clawed feet, and long tails.

CAT FAMILY

## Genus

The cat family is further divided into genus or type. Animals that belong to the same genus are closely related but do not breed together. The domestic cat is grouped with 27 other types of small cat in the genus *Felis*.

DOMESTIC CAT GENUS

ANIMAL KINGDOM

CHORDATES PHYLUM

MAMMALS CLASS

CARNIVORA ORDER

*Sharp eyesight for*
*night vision and*
*detecting prey*

*Flexible backbone*
*makes cat agile*

MANX
SPECIES

*Typical*
*clawed feet*

## Species

The tail-less Manx cat is a domestic breed which has descended from the wild cat. The wild cat has the scientific name *Felis sylvestris* – the first name shows the genus, the second name indicating the species. The domestic cat, however, has the name *Felis sylvestris catus* – the third word indicates the sub-species. Animals in the same species or sub-species can breed together.

# Animal kingdom

All members of the animal kingdom are organisms that depend on foods, such as plants or other animals, in order to survive. Unlike plants, most animals are able to move freely through the air or water, at some stage in their lives, to find food or another animal to mate with. To know where they are or where they are going, all animals have sensory organs, and because they move frequently, they have nervous systems to co-ordinate their bodies. Many animals have circulatory systems that carry oxygen and food through their bodies and to take waste products away. Scientists divide the animal kingdom into smaller groups and families of animals that share the same body features. The whole kingdom divides into two types: those animals without backbones, called invertebrates; and those with backbones, called vertebrates.

## Invertebrates

There are 20 times more invertebrate types of animals than there are vertebrate types living on the Earth. Most invertebrates are insects – with more than one million described and catalogued. Several more million insects exist, but have not been identified. Living on a single tree in the Amazonian rainforest, for example, there might be 80 types of ant and more than 650 types of beetle, many of which scientists may not have seen before. The invertebrates group is made up of different phyla (animal types). These include insects, jellyfish and sea anemones, segmented and unsegmented worms, hard-bodied crustaceans and spiders, starfish, sea urchins, slugs, and snails, many of which have shells on the outside, and squid and cuttlefish which have shells on the inside.

## Insecta

Insects are arthropods with hard, protective outer skeletons and six, jointed legs. There are at least 5 million different insect species. They include beetles, cockroaches, wasps, ants, bees, butterflies and moths, and dragonflies and damselflies.

## Cnidaria

Cnidarians, such as corals and sea anemones, have jelly-like bodies. The stinging cells on their tentacles have the fastest moving parts of any known animal.

*Stinging tentacles*

SNAKELOCKS SEA ANEMONE

## Annelida

There are several phyla of worms – some are flat, others are long and round. Annelids include segmented worms, such as earthworms and ragworms.

COMMON EARTHWORM

*Body is divided into segments*

## Mollusca

All molluscs have soft bodies that are protected by a hard outer shell. They include land and sea slugs, squid, octopuses, chitons, clams, and freshwater snails.

*Soft body*

COMMON SNAIL

## Arachnida

Arachnids are hard-bodied arthropods (creatures with exoskeletons, segmented bodies, and jointed legs). They have eight pairs of walking legs, and include spiders and scorpions.

*Eight walking legs*

RAFT SPIDER

## Crustacea

Crustaceans are arthropods with crust-like casings around their bodies. They include marine creatures such as crabs, lobsters, shrimps, prawns, and barnacles, and land-living woodlice.

*Hard outer skeleton*

SHORE CRAB

## Echinodermata

These spiny-skinned animals have a circular body plan. They include mainly marine animals such as starfish, sea urchins, sea cucumbers, and feather stars.

*Body is arranged in a circle*

COMMON STARFISH

*Most insects have wings*

RED ADMIRAL BUTTERFLY

ANIMAL KINGDOM

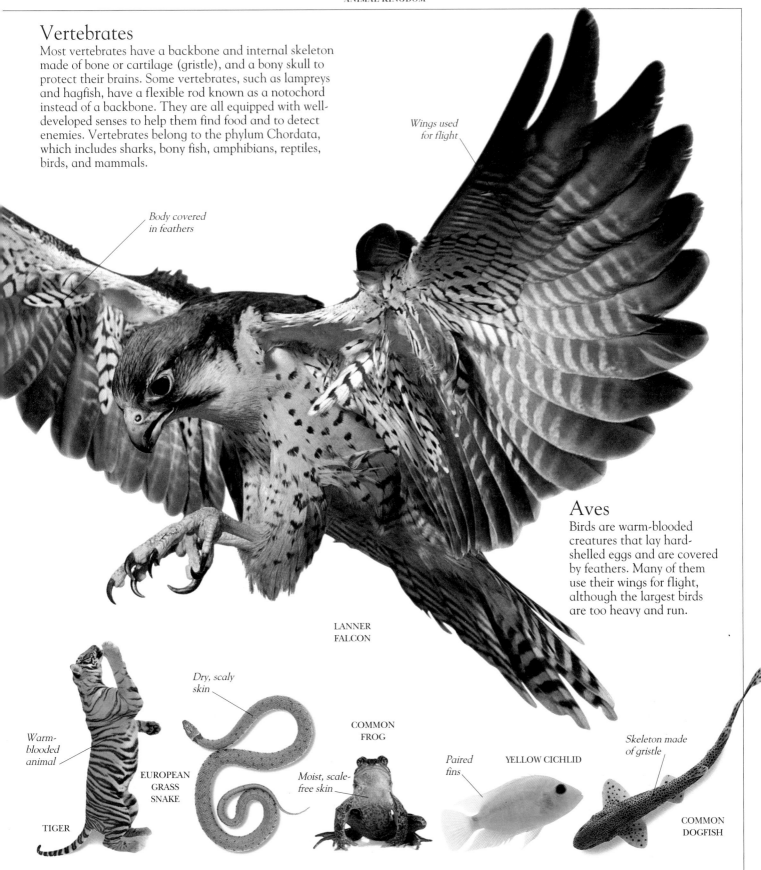

## Vertebrates

Most vertebrates have a backbone and internal skeleton made of bone or cartilage (gristle), and a bony skull to protect their brains. Some vertebrates, such as lampreys and hagfish, have a flexible rod known as a notochord instead of a backbone. They are all equipped with well-developed senses to help them find food and to detect enemies. Vertebrates belong to the phylum Chordata, which includes sharks, bony fish, amphibians, reptiles, birds, and mammals.

*Body covered in feathers*

*Wings used for flight*

## Aves

Birds are warm-blooded creatures that lay hard-shelled eggs and are covered by feathers. Many of them use their wings for flight, although the largest birds are too heavy and run.

LANNER FALCON

*Warm-blooded animal*

TIGER

*Dry, scaly skin*

EUROPEAN GRASS SNAKE

COMMON FROG

*Moist, scale-free skin*

*Paired fins*

YELLOW CICHLID

*Skeleton made of gristle*

COMMON DOGFISH

## Mammalia
All mammals are warm-blooded animals that feed their offspring on mother's milk. They include elephants, humans, and gorillas.

## Reptilia
Reptiles include snakes, lizards, crocodiles, turtles, and the tuatara. They have dry, scaly skin, and give birth to "live" young or lay eggs.

## Amphibia
Frogs, toads, newts, and salamanders have moist skin without scales. Most amphibians produce jelly-covered eggs.

## Osteichthyes
These are bony fish that vary in shape, from long, thin eels to spiny finned cichlids, and amphibian-like lung fish.

## Chondrichthyes
Sharks, rays, skates, and ratfish have a skeleton made of cartilage rather than bone. They also have up to seven gill slits that open separately.

# Skeletons

The skeleton gives shape and strength to an animal's body. It also provides attachments for muscles, which help to move bones into different positions, and a storage place for mineral salts. The internal skeleton of fish, amphibians, reptiles, mammals, and birds is made mainly from bone. The skeleton of sharks and rays is made of cartilage, a strong tissue that is more bendy than bone. Cartilage is also found at the ends of bones around joints, and it shapes some parts of the body such as the human nose and external ears. The shape of some animals, such as worms, is supported not by a solid structure but by an internal "skeleton" of water – a hydrostatic skeleton.

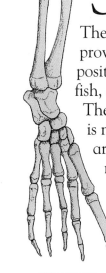

HUMAN FOOT          SEAL FLIPPER

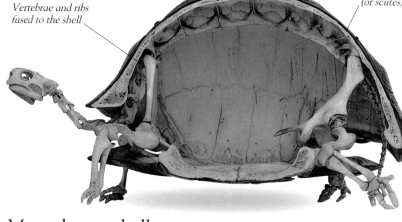

*Vertebrae and ribs fused to the shell*

*Horny plates (or scutes)*

## Legs and limbs

Human limbs and seal flippers are different shapes, yet they contain the same number of bones. The long leg bones and short toe bones of the human foot are adapted for running and walking, while the short leg bones and long toe bones in the seal's paddle-like rear flipper are used for swimming. These differences mean that humans are poor swimmers and seals are less agile on land.

*Tail is made up of 18 to 20 bones*

## More than a shell

Turtles, terrapins, and tortoises have an internal skeleton like other reptiles, but they also have an external "shell" (or carapace). The shell is made of bone covered by horny plates. It is joined to their backbone on top and breastbone below, forming a protective box around their vital organs. Some species of tortoise can pull their heads and legs inside their shells if danger threatens.

*Flexible backbone allows body to curve when moving*

*Leeches move using a sucker at each end of the body*

*Fluid-filled tube, or coelum*

## Water pressure

The leech has no backbone and lacks a solid skeleton. Instead, it keeps its shape by water pressure; in other words, it has a "hydrostatic skeleton". The animal is basically a water-filled tube surrounded by muscles. By flexing these muscles, it can squash or stretch its body in order to move. This is helped by suckers at each end of the body that can be attached to rocks or plants over which the leech is creeping.

COMMON LEECHES

*Back legs and spine meet at pelvic girdle*

SALAMANDER SKELETON

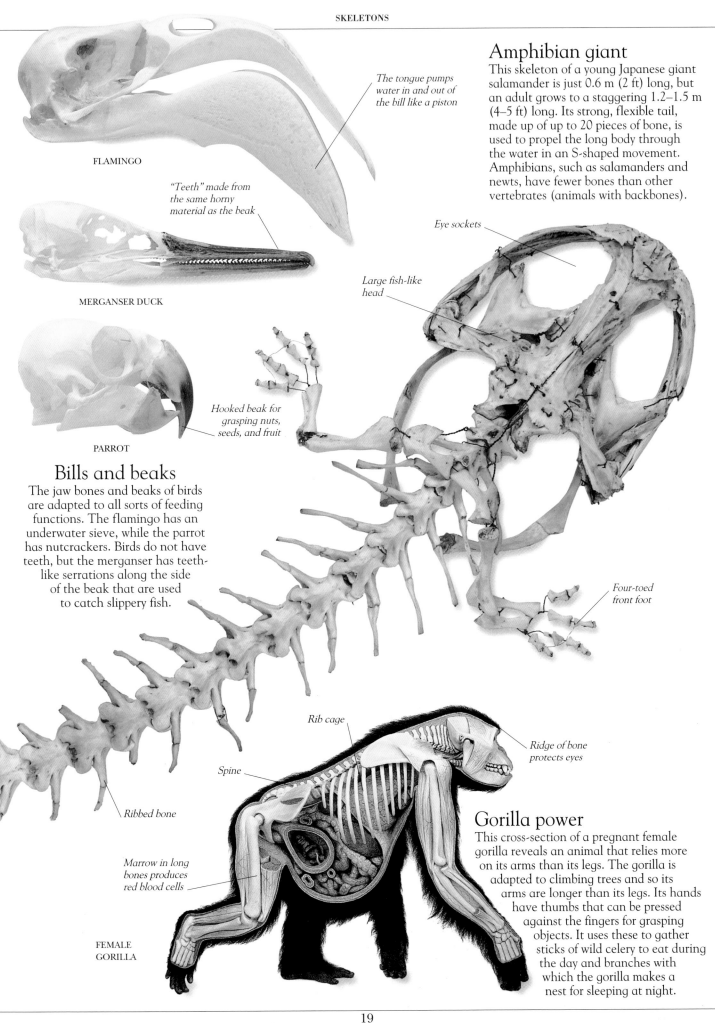

FLAMINGO

*The tongue pumps water in and out of the bill like a piston*

## Amphibian giant

This skeleton of a young Japanese giant salamander is just 0.6 m (2 ft) long, but an adult grows to a staggering 1.2–1.5 m (4–5 ft) long. Its strong, flexible tail, made up of up to 20 pieces of bone, is used to propel the long body through the water in an S-shaped movement. Amphibians, such as salamanders and newts, have fewer bones than other vertebrates (animals with backbones).

*"Teeth" made from the same horny material as the beak*

MERGANSER DUCK

*Eye sockets*

*Large fish-like head*

PARROT

*Hooked beak for grasping nuts, seeds, and fruit*

## Bills and beaks

The jaw bones and beaks of birds are adapted to all sorts of feeding functions. The flamingo has an underwater sieve, while the parrot has nutcrackers. Birds do not have teeth, but the merganser has teeth-like serrations along the side of the beak that are used to catch slippery fish.

*Four-toed front foot*

*Rib cage*

*Ridge of bone protects eyes*

*Spine*

*Ribbed bone*

*Marrow in long bones produces red blood cells*

## Gorilla power

This cross-section of a pregnant female gorilla reveals an animal that relies more on its arms than its legs. The gorilla is adapted to climbing trees and so its arms are longer than its legs. Its hands have thumbs that can be pressed against the fingers for grasping objects. It uses these to gather sticks of wild celery to eat during the day and branches with which the gorilla makes a nest for sleeping at night.

FEMALE GORILLA

# Exoskeletons

Several groups of invertebrate animals, including insects, snails, spiders, and starfish, have their skeletons on the outside like suits of armour. With this arrangement, the hard outer casing protects all of the delicate organs inside from being damaged by changes in the weather or environment, or from attacks by predators. For land-living animals the exoskeleton also helps to keep body fluids from being lost by evaporation. On the downside, a rigid exoskeleton presents an animal with problems when it wants to move. Insects and crabs have solved this by having jointed limbs. Snails have a single mobile foot which sticks out from the shell, and starfish have hundreds of tiny feet that squeeze out of holes in the exoskeleton.

*Worn-down spines*

*Markings in the shape of a five-pointed star*

*Holes for tubular feet*

SEA URCHIN SHELLS

## Hard ball

The living sea urchin is covered by spines. These are rubbed off by the waves when it dies, revealing the hard, round "shell" (or test). On its surface can be seen the places where the spines once were, together with the holes through which its tiny tube feet stuck out. The marks and holes are in a five-star pattern, which shows that sea urchins are related to starfish.

## Stag beetle

Insects produce a tough film of chitin, which is a strong, waterproof substance enclosing the entire body. The stag beetle even has hard wing covers to protect its fragile wings and abdomen, as well as a shield that protects the head and thorax. Its jointed legs are hollow tubes linked by peg-and-socket joints.

*Toughened wing cover*

STAG BEETLE

*Insect joints only move in one plane*

*Legs have irritating hairs for defence*

*Hard shield protects the brains and stomach*

TARANTULA

## Tarantula

Spiders also have exoskeletons made mainly of chitin (see above). Unlike insects, they have eight legs rather than six, and their bodies are divided into two sections rather than three. The tarantula is an especially large spider with a thick covering of tiny hairs all over its body. The hairs are sensitive to vibrations, and when broken off, they can irritate or sting attackers.

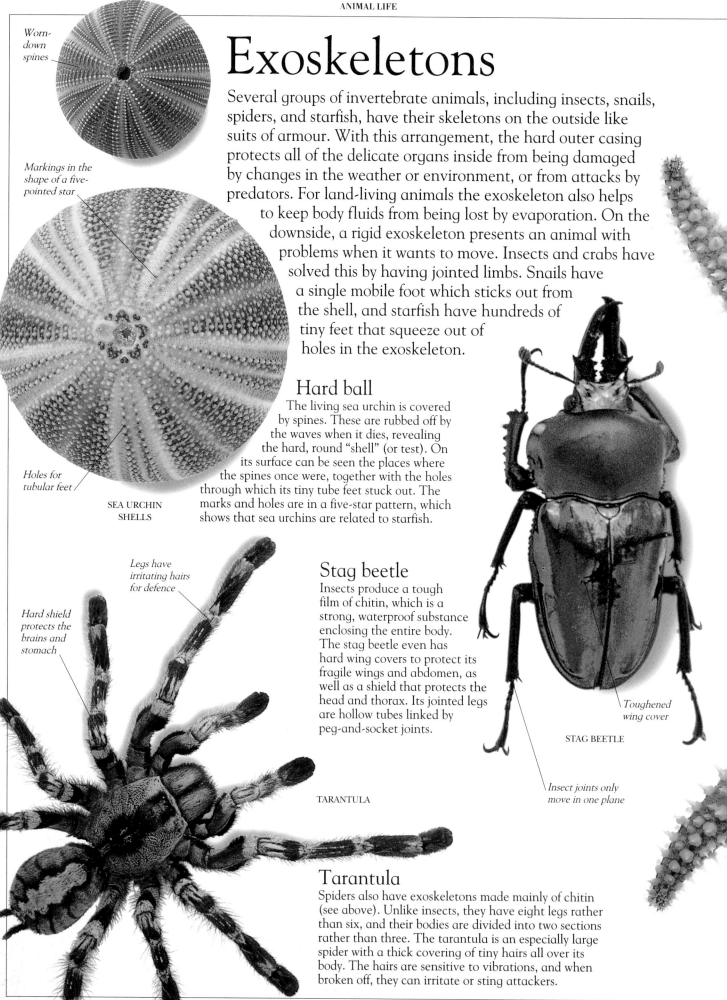

CHITON

*Sucker-like foot clings to rocks on the seashore*

## Suction pads

Chitons or coat-of-mail shells are protected by eight shell-like plates. The plates are connected by joints, allowing the chiton to roll into a ball if disturbed.

*Banded yellow shell is camouflaged in long grass*

COMMON EUROPEAN STRIPED SNAIL

## Snail home

Many species of snail live on land where they are in danger of drying out or being attacked by predators, such as birds. To prevent this happening, the snail encloses its soft body inside a protective, spiral-shaped shell. It is not always successful because some birds, such as thrushes, have learned how to break open the shells and eat the soft parts inside.

*Arms meet at central point*

SPINY STARFISH

*Sunstar has 12 rather than the usual 5 arms*

SUNSTAR

*Tough spines protect against other predators*

## Sea star

The spiny starfish has no front or back. Its body is made up of five or more arms that meet at a central disc, where its mouth and other vital organs are situated. On top, its arms are covered with chalky spines that help protect the starfish from attack. Underneath the body are lines of tiny tube feet that enable it to slither over the seabed.

# Organs

An organ is part of an animal's body that has a special function. Most animals have similar sets of organs in their bodies, the biggest of which is skin. Each organ has its own special purpose: there is a gut to help digest and absorb food, gills or lungs with which to breathe, a heart to pump the blood around the body, a kidney-like organ to get rid of unwanted material, muscles to make things move, and a brain to make the body's activities work together. The whereabouts of the organs within the body differ from animal to animal, since the size and shape of their organs relate directly to their lifestyle.

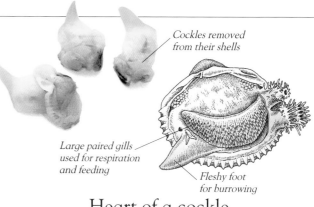

*Cockles removed from their shells*

*Large paired gills used for respiration and feeding*

*Fleshy foot for burrowing*

## Heart of a cockle

The cockle lives under the sand, sifting small pieces of food from the water at high tide. It rarely travels far, so its organs are adapted to moving water through the two halves of its shell, rather than moving the cockle itself through water. When the cockle wants to move, it uses its fleshy foot to burrow through the sand.

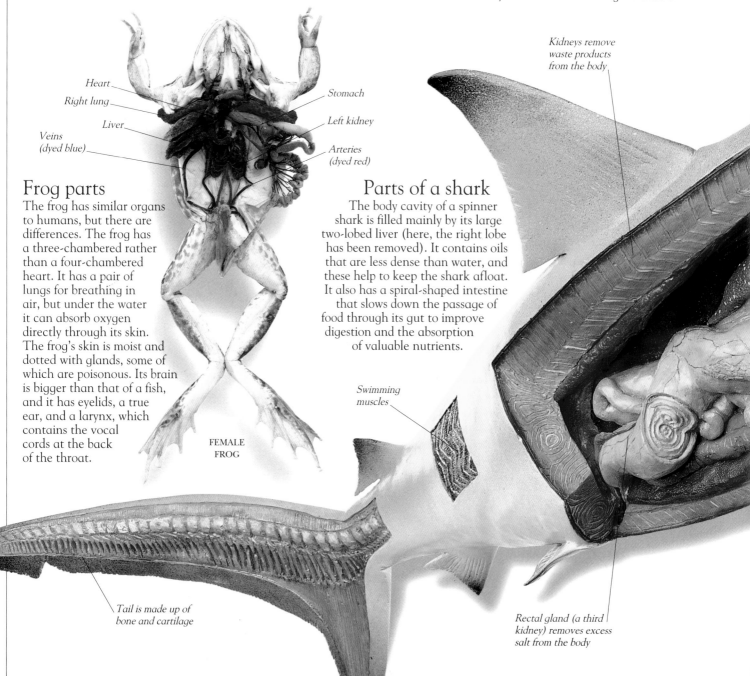

*Heart*

*Right lung*

*Liver*

*Veins (dyed blue)*

*Stomach*

*Left kidney*

*Arteries (dyed red)*

## Frog parts

The frog has similar organs to humans, but there are differences. The frog has a three-chambered rather than a four-chambered heart. It has a pair of lungs for breathing in air, but under the water it can absorb oxygen directly through its skin. The frog's skin is moist and dotted with glands, some of which are poisonous. Its brain is bigger than that of a fish, and it has eyelids, a true ear, and a larynx, which contains the vocal cords at the back of the throat.

FEMALE FROG

## Parts of a shark

The body cavity of a spinner shark is filled mainly by its large two-lobed liver (here, the right lobe has been removed). It contains oils that are less dense than water, and these help to keep the shark afloat. It also has a spiral-shaped intestine that slows down the passage of food through its gut to improve digestion and the absorption of valuable nutrients.

*Kidneys remove waste products from the body*

*Swimming muscles*

*Tail is made up of bone and cartilage*

*Rectal gland (a third kidney) removes excess salt from the body*

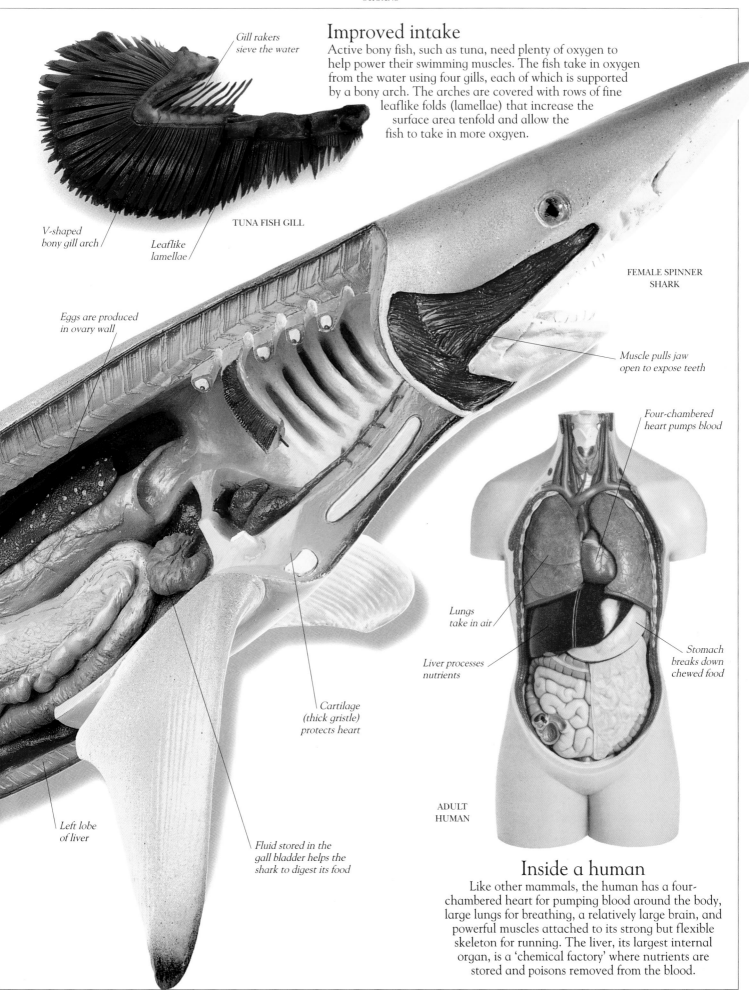

# Improved intake

Active bony fish, such as tuna, need plenty of oxygen to help power their swimming muscles. The fish take in oxygen from the water using four gills, each of which is supported by a bony arch. The arches are covered with rows of fine leaflike folds (lamellae) that increase the surface area tenfold and allow the fish to take in more oxgyen.

*Gill rakers sieve the water*

TUNA FISH GILL

*V-shaped bony gill arch*

*Leaflike lamellae*

FEMALE SPINNER SHARK

*Muscle pulls jaw open to expose teeth*

*Eggs are produced in ovary wall*

*Four-chambered heart pumps blood*

*Lungs take in air*

*Liver processes nutrients*

*Stomach breaks down chewed food*

*Cartilage (thick gristle) protects heart*

*Left lobe of liver*

*Fluid stored in the gall bladder helps the shark to digest its food*

ADULT HUMAN

# Inside a human

Like other mammals, the human has a four-chambered heart for pumping blood around the body, large lungs for breathing, a relatively large brain, and powerful muscles attached to its strong but flexible skeleton for running. The liver, its largest internal organ, is a 'chemical factory' where nutrients are stored and poisons removed from the blood.

*Fox-like snout indicates the bat's reliance on smell*

# Senses

Animals use a variety of senses to find out where they are, where they are going, where food is located, and what is likely to be attacking them. The combination of these five senses – sight, smell, touch, taste, and hearing – gives the animal an image of its world. Different animals "see" different worlds depending on which senses they use the most. For example, a human and a dog will observe quite different things when walking along a street, as the human relies mainly on what it can see but the dog gathers information from what it smells and hears. Some animals, such as sharks, even have a sense that detects the electrical field generated by the muscles of their prey.

*Small ears*

BORNEO FRUIT BAT

BRITISH SADDLEBACK PIG

## Sniffing fruit

Insect-eating bats rely on their highly sensitive hearing more than any other sense. In contrast, fruit-eating bats (here) are equipped with excellent eyesight, a keen sense of smell, but only small, simple ears. Their large eyes help the bats to find their way around in the dark, while their fox-like noses are able to sniff out ripe fruit or nectar.

*Convex shape of eye gives wide area of vision*

## Truffle hunting

The domestic pig has an extremely well-developed sense of smell – its snout is thought to be even more sensitive than a dog's to certain odours. In southern France and Italy, the pig is used to smell out small ball-like fungi known as truffles, which grow in the ground and are eaten as delicacies.

*Flattened nose for snuffling on the ground*

FLESHFLY

*Each optical unit has a lens to focus light*

SECTION OF COMPOUND EYE

## Compound eye

The fleshfly has enormous eyes that take up most of its head. Both eyes are made up of hundreds of "mini-eyes", each of which is fitted with its own tiny lens. The picture captured by the compound eye is like a blurred mosaic rather than the photographic image seen with a simple eye. This type of view means that the fly is unlikely to spot slow movements, but it will see quick movements such as the approach of a predator.

*Optical nerves pass information to the brain*

BUSHBABY

*Nimble claws grasp hold of prey*

*Large ears pick up night sounds*

# Night vision
To find its way around the dark forest at night, the bushbaby relies heavily on its senses of sight and sound. Its very large, forward-pointing eyes are able to cope with reduced levels of light, while its highly sensitive ears can detect even the sound of a flying insect. The bushbaby is able to grab things within reach with great accuracy and can run and leap through its nocturnal world at high speed, covering 10 m (33 ft) in less than five seconds.

*Nasal flaps direct water into the nostrils*

SNOUT OF AN
EPAULETTE SHARK

# Underwater smells
The epaulette shark has a pig-like snout with well-developed nostrils for detecting food, such as sea urchins and shellfish. It can pick up a faint odour at up to 3 m (10 ft) away and home-in on the target. It uses its tiny, spike-like front teeth to grab, then crushes it with its broad, flat hind teeth.

*Antennae normally fold back alongside the body*

# Feeling around
The antler-like antennae of the Indian beetle are sensitive to chemicals. For this reason, the beetle's view of the world is mainly made up from the patterns of smells and tastes that its antennae detect.

INDIAN
BEETLE

# Communication

Animals use many different ways of passing messages to their friends as well as sending out warnings to their enemies. Bird song, a flash of colour on butterfly wings, the unmistakable smell of a fox, and a touch of hands between two chimpanzees are just some examples of how animals make contact. There are those that mainly use sounds or vibrations, and others that rely on visual signals or smells. Certain types of fish have adopted a way of "talking" with electricity. Whatever the method, animals are not usually keen to draw attention to themselves in case predators are watching or listening. So, when they do speak out, it must be to say something very important indeed.

PAIR OF HAMADRYAS BABOONS

*"Groomer" picks out parasites, dead skin, and dirt from the other's fur*

## You scratch my back

Baboons spend time together simply grooming each other's fur. This touch signal from one baboon to another strengthens the bonds between these two members of the troop. It also underlines the social status each of them has in the group's hierarchy. In this case, the baboon being groomed has a higher position than its "groomer".

## Sky pirates

Skuas are seabirds that communicate with a loud, barking call. At nesting time, they perform an impressive 'raised wing' display in which they hold up their wings and thrust their heads forwards. This aggressive, visual signal warns intruders to keep away from their territory. When searching for food, a pair of skuas will exchange calls as they work together. One skua will harass a seabird to draw it away from its nest while the other skua snatches the exposed eggs.

*Raised wing warns away intruders*

BROWN SKUA

ANTARCTIC SKUA

*Thrust out neck*

## Sniffing dogs

Smell is a key means of communication in a dog's world, and is used to send messages that tempt or warn away other dogs. Smells are useful for marking territory, as they usually last for several days. Dogs communicate with one another by leaving scent marks at nose-level on trees and posts. Smells can also indicate the condition of the sender. For example, a female that is ready to mate will release an odour that invites would-be partners.

*Moisture on the nose helps to capture scent*

*Chin glands are used to mark possessions by scent*

*One dog learns a lot about another by the smell from its anal gland.*

MALE RABBIT

## Wild rabbit

Rabbits make quiet, short-range calls to each other in their burrows. Above ground, they reveal a white patch under the tail or thump the ground with their hind leg when they need to warn the rest of the warren of danger. A male rabbit has several female breeding partners. To make sure that other males realise that these females belong to him, the male rubs his chin gland against each female to leave a scent mark on her body – this signals possession. The male also marks his territory with droppings to warn other males to keep away.

*"Tummy rumble" calls come from the throat not the stomach*

## Rumbling tums

Elephants trumpet loudly when two meet each other or when the herd is nervous, but they also give out sound that we cannot hear. These very low frequency calls are called "tummy rumbles", and they can carry over great distances. Female elephants that are ready to mate will send out invitations to males by making these calls.

PAIR OF INDIAN ELEPHANTS

# Movement

Animals need movement so that they can track down food, seek out a partner, or escape from the clutches of predators. To do this, some creatures have legs for running and jumping, while others have fins for swimming or wings for flying. Crawlers move overland without legs, such as the snail with its slimy foot and the earthworm that shortens and lengthens its body to burrow through soil. Some animals, known as drifters, have very little natural movement so they have to take advantage of any movement in their environment. Sea drifters float near the water's surface and move with the waves, while some small insects allow themselves to be carried along by currents of air.

Hairy pads on toes "stick" to surfaces

TOKAY GECKO

## Holding on

Some lizards, such as geckos, have special ridges of scales on their feet that resemble sucker pads. These ridges are covered in millions of tiny hairs. They can grip onto almost any surface, enabling the gecko to walk along upright objects, such as tree trunks, and even to run upside-down on ceilings in houses.

Tail is used to "steer" the cat through the air

SEQUENCE OF A CAT'S POUNCE

## Powerful pounce

Domestic cats do not have to hunt for their food. Even so, they are able to pounce and land with great accuracy, just like their wild relatives who use this skill when chasing prey. Before making a leap, the cat watches the movements of its prey carefully. It then uses powerful leg muscles to jump up in the air and pounce on its target. The cat's tail acts as a rudder to keep it on course and its front claws pin its prey to the ground.

Eyes are fixed firmly on the prey

Powerful hind legs push against the ground

Tail moves in same direction as head, creating an S-shape

Pectoral fins work like aircraft wings

LESSER-SPOTTED DOGFISH

Body moves in opposite direction to head

## Rudder action

The dogfish, like all sharks, moves by making an S-shaped wave through its body. The movement starts from the head which the fish swings from side to side. This pushes the body forward and then ripples down the body and into the tail. The pectoral (side) fins act like the wings of an aircraft and lift the dogfish as it swims forwards.

SWIMMING SEQUENCE OF LESSER SPOTTED DOGFISH

Body moves to the left

Head moves to the left

Body starts to bend to the right

Head moves to the right

*Downward movement "powers" the flight forward*

SEQUENCE OF MALLARD DUCK IN FLIGHT

*Flapping wings "lift" the duck through the air*

## Duck flight

Like other birds, the mallard duck uses it light, flexible wings to move through the air. The wings are curved slightly from front to back, which give them the same profile as an aircraft wing. This shape lifts the bird upwards through the air as it flaps its wings. The forward movement in flight is achieved with the downward flap, which pushes against the air.

*Paws are ready to grab prey*

*Front legs take impact on landing*

## From side to side

The green anaconda moves by crawling – but it relies on the ground being uneven. Like all snakes, it has no legs. Instead, it moves on its ribs. The sides of the snake's body curve and bend around objects, such as rocks and plants. The waves created by this muscle movement pass back along the body and push against the rocks and plants. This allows the snake to glide forwards.

*Front and back leg move together*

*Sticky toe pads provide grip on smooth surfaces*

*Ribs run along the length of the body*

GREEN ANACONDA

## Two at a time

The green tree frog of Australia, like all amphibians, sways its body from side to side in order to move. This is because the front and rear limbs on each side of the body move together as a pair. The tree frog's toes are equipped with sticky pads which help it to grip firmly when climbing among trees or walking across shiny leaf surfaces.

SEQUENCE OF GREEN TREE FROG CLIMBING

# Plant-eaters

Trees, bushes, grasses, and herbs are available in most land habitats, and although they are the easiest foods for an animal to find, they are not the easiest to eat and digest. To protect themselves from plant-eaters, many plants have leaves laced with poison or thorn-lined stems. And, even if an animal manages to find a way around these defences and swallows a mouthful, its digestive system then has to tackle the problem of the plant's tough cell walls. These are difficult to break down without the help of microbes (tiny living creatures) to do the job for them. Plant-eaters as diverse as green turtles, manatees, and horses all have microbes in their guts. The gut is also quite lengthy, enabling the animal as long as possible to extract the nutrients from its plant food.

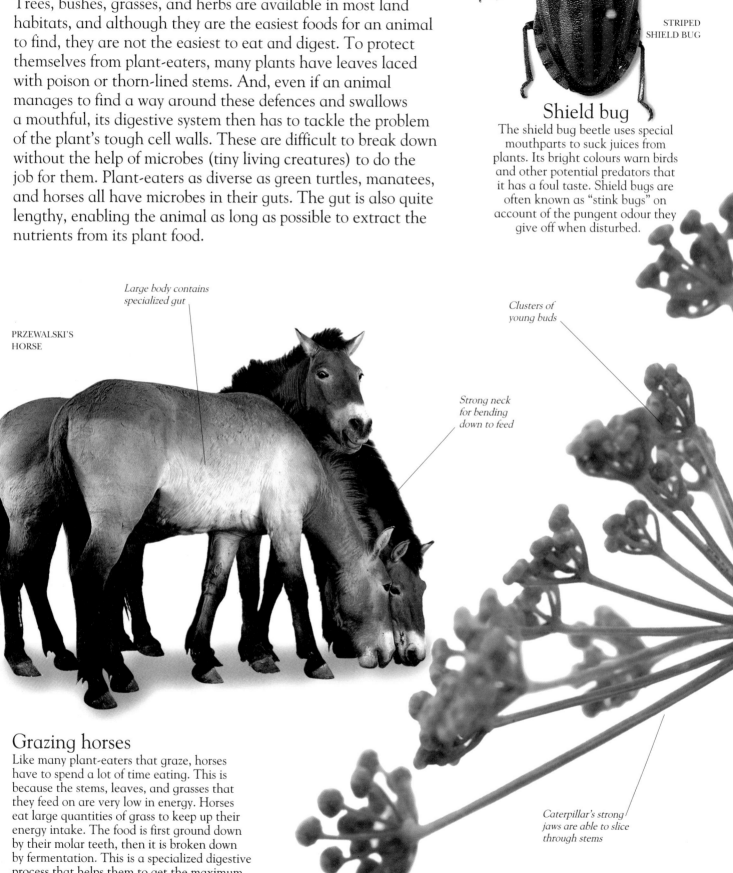

STRIPED
SHIELD BUG

## Shield bug

The shield bug beetle uses special mouthparts to suck juices from plants. Its bright colours warn birds and other potential predators that it has a foul taste. Shield bugs are often known as "stink bugs" on account of the pungent odour they give off when disturbed.

*Large body contains specialized gut*

PRZEWALSKI'S
HORSE

*Clusters of young buds*

*Strong neck for bending down to feed*

*Caterpillar's strong jaws are able to slice through stems*

## Grazing horses

Like many plant-eaters that graze, horses have to spend a lot of time eating. This is because the stems, leaves, and grasses that they feed on are very low in energy. Horses eat large quantities of grass to keep up their energy intake. The food is first ground down by their molar teeth, then it is broken down by fermentation. This is a specialized digestive process that helps them to get the maximum benefit possible from the grass.

KOALA BEAR
AND CUB

*Koala cub
feeds on part-
digested leaves
from its mother*

SKULL OF NORTH
AMERICAN BEAVER

*Incisors have a
chisel-like edge*

## Animal lumberjack

The skull of the North American beaver reveals a pair
of large incisor teeth (front teeth). As well as felling trees
with these chisel-like teeth, the beaver also uses them to
strip and feed on tree bark, its main diet. The beaver also
removes any new woody growth on the tree, some of
which it stores in a purpose-built larder. Like other
rodents, the beaver's teeth grow continuously but they
are worn down by constant gnawing.

## Up a gum tree

The koala bear is not a real
bear, but a marsupial. It has
a very specialized diet which
consists mainly of low-protein,
high-fibre eucalyptus leaves.
Although it eats about 500 g (1 lb)
per day, this diet does not provide the
koala with much energy. To avoid
tiring itself out, the koala moves slowly
and sleeps for 18 out of every 24 hours.

*Teeth strip off
loose coating
on nut*

CHIPMUNK

## Ground squirrel

Like its squirrel relatives, the
chipmunk feeds on nuts and
eats them in a particular way.
It takes a nut in its forepaws
and turns it around, gnawing
off any loose pieces. The
chipmunk then looks for a
weak point in the nut where
its teeth can crack it open.

*Powerful jaws bite
through plant*

*Clawed legs
hold on to food*

SWALLOWTAIL
CATERPILLAR

## Eaten away

Caterpillars are the "feeding stage"
in a butterfly or moth's life cycle.
Swallowtail caterpillars eat the
flowers of milk parsley, but other
species feed mainly on leaves. They
grasp the plant material between
their legs, stretching the head in
front, and then biting down
towards the body.

*Rear claspers
grip onto stalk*

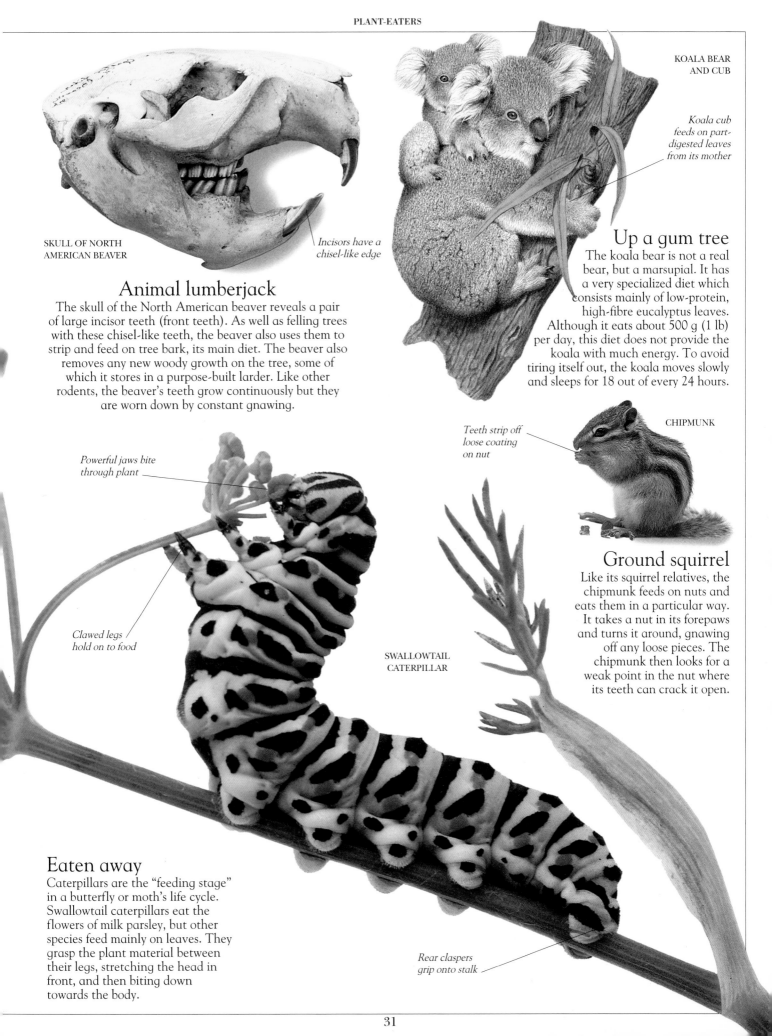

# Meat-eaters

Animals that eat meat are known as carnivores. Unlike plant-eaters and filter-feeders, which feed almost continuously, meat-eaters have distinct meal times. Each meal is dependent on how easily the prey can be found and caught, and how long it takes to eat. Most meat-eaters have specialized tools to help them capture and eat their prey. For example, big cats have well-developed canine teeth for grasping hold of their prey and special cheek teeth for slicing up meat. Sharks have pointed teeth to grasp slippery squid and fish, and triangular, saw-like teeth to cut through flesh and blubber. Likewise, birds of prey have long claws and hooked beaks for gripping or tearing meat.

OSPREY

Hooked beak for ripping flesh

Long claws grip prey firmly

Fish is snatched from below the water's surface

## Long fingers

The aye-aye, a shaggy, black lemur found on the island of Madagascar, uses its long middle finger to reach its food. In the same way that woodpeckers chisel through wood to reach prey, the aye-aye picks out wood-boring beetle grubs that tunnel into tree branches. The sharp curved claw on the tip of its middle finger hooks the grubs up and pulls them out.

Long middle finger picks out grubs from wood

Wrist bones

SKELETON OF AN AYE-AYE'S HAND

## Fish catcher

The osprey is a fish-hawk that feeds at lakes, rivers, and along the coast. It swoops down from the sky and snatches fish that are swimming just below the water's surface. The fish is held tightly in the osprey's long talons (claws), and is carried with its head pointing forwards to make it more streamlined in flight. The osprey eats its prey at a favourite perch or in the bird's nest, using its knife-like beak to tear through the flesh.

Smooth scales allow sandfish to dive into the sand like a fish in water

Fringed scales prevent feet from sinking in the sand

## Keeping warm

The sandfish lives on land in hot, dry deserts. In the early morning and late afternoon, it emerges from its cool burrow to feed on insects and small reptiles. The sandfish has to stay above ground to maintain its body temperature, so that the food can be digested. Once the meal is completed, it retreats into the cool of the sand to avoid overheating in the midday sun.

SANDFISH

## Spider-eating fly

The female small-headed fly lays her eggs on the bodies of tarantula spiders. When the maggots hatch out, they burrow into the spider's body and, while it is still alive, eat the spider from the inside out. This ensures that the maggot always has fresh meat, which gives it the nutrients it needs to pupate and emerge as a new adult fly.

*Feeding tongue*

SMALL-HEADED FLY

## Taking aim

The archerfish lives in tropical mangrove swamps in southern Asia and Australasia. It has earned its name from being able to spit accurately to distances of more than 1 m (3 ft). The archerfish uses this skill to fire drops of water at insects and spiders, knocking them down from swampside branches. It can also leap out of the water to grab its prey from branches, as well as to snatch low-flying insects that are passing by.

*Large eyes focus on spider*

LEAPING ARCHERFISH

*Large eye sockets indicate good vision*

SKULL OF BARRACUDA FISH

## Deadly jaw

The large, frightening teeth of the great barracuda fish confirm beyond any doubt that it is a meat-eating fish. The sharp, spiky teeth are designed to grab and hold slippery prey, such as squid and fish, as well as to tear through flesh.

*Dagger-like teeth for gripping prey*

*Lower jaw is longer than upper jaw*

*Eyes can be pushed down to help swallow large mouthfuls*

*Black and green markings help toad to blend in with forest floor*

*Tail end of a mouse*

ORNATE HORNED TOAD

## Toad's teatime

The ornate horned toad of South America is known as a "sit-and-wait" feeder. This means that it literally sits hidden among the leaf litter of the forest floor and waits for its unsuspecting prey to walk past. When a large insect, frog, or even mouse comes into view, the toad opens up its enormous mouth in an instant and grabs its victim. To help it swallow its enormous meal, the toad pushes its eyeballs down to increase the pressure in its mouth.

# Defence

Most animals are in constant danger of being attacked by other creatures that want to eat them. To avoid ending up as a predator's meal, some animals hide, keep very still, or run away as fast as they can. Others use a different kind of protection. They may be covered in sharp spines, hard shells, or tough scales, which act like suits of armour to protect them from attack. Some are poisonous and have brightly coloured bodies to warn other animals to leave them alone. Certain harmless animals even copy the warning colours of poisonous ones, to make it appear that they, too, are harmful to predators. Clever tricks, such as losing a tail, or showing off false eyes, are also used as defence against enemies.

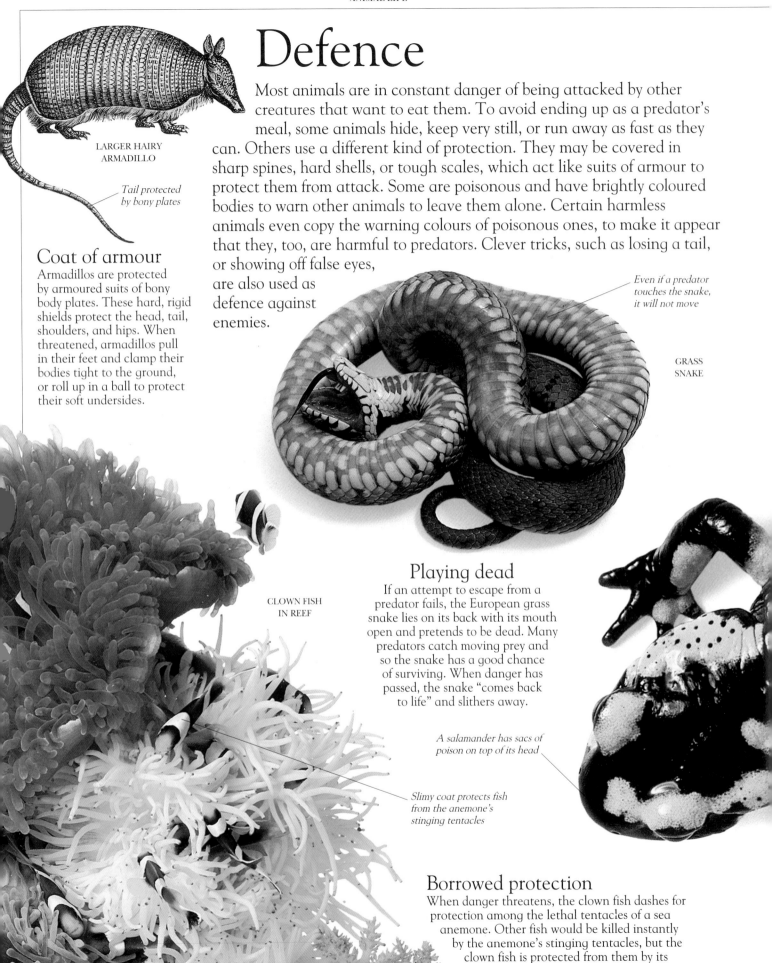

LARGER HAIRY ARMADILLO

*Tail protected by bony plates*

## Coat of armour

Armadillos are protected by armoured suits of bony body plates. These hard, rigid shields protect the head, tail, shoulders, and hips. When threatened, armadillos pull in their feet and clamp their bodies tight to the ground, or roll up in a ball to protect their soft undersides.

*Even if a predator touches the snake, it will not move*

GRASS SNAKE

CLOWN FISH IN REEF

## Playing dead

If an attempt to escape from a predator fails, the European grass snake lies on its back with its mouth open and pretends to be dead. Many predators catch moving prey and so the snake has a good chance of surviving. When danger has passed, the snake "comes back to life" and slithers away.

*A salamander has sacs of poison on top of its head*

*Slimy coat protects fish from the anemone's stinging tentacles*

## Borrowed protection

When danger threatens, the clown fish dashes for protection among the lethal tentacles of a sea anemone. Other fish would be killed instantly by the anemone's stinging tentacles, but the clown fish is protected from them by its special covering of slime.

*Frog's skin is highly poisonous*

POISON
DART FROG

*Spines on each scale or scute stick out when fish is inflated*

PORCUPINE
FISH

## Toxic skin

Poison dart frogs produce some of the most powerful poisons in the world in their skin. They have to be very poisonous because their predators, such as snakes and spiders, are not hurt by weaker poisons. Many of the frogs also have brightly coloured skin to warn away predators, and also to defend their territories from other males during the mating season.

## Spiny balloon

The porcupine fish has spines all over its body for protection. For added defence, however, it can make itself even more difficult to bite by swallowing water or air and swelling up like a balloon.

FIRE
SALAMANDER

## Warning colours

This fire salamander is poisonous and will not make a tasty meal. Its bright colours warn predators, such as shrews, birds, and snakes, to keep away. Predators learn that animals with these colours taste nasty and so do not attack them.

*The poison in the fire salamander's skin is strong enough to kill small mammals*

## Spines and armour

Slow-moving animals, such as hedgehogs, often rely on body armour for protection. A coat of sharp spines protects the hedgehog's soft body, especially when it rolls up into a tight ball. When the hedgehog is alarmed, it also raises its spines so they point in all directions.

*Yellow and black are warning colours to predators*

HEDGEHOG

# Camouflage

Some animals try to blend in with their background to escape predators, while others disguise their bodies so that they are invisible to their prey. This skill is called camouflage and can be used in self-defence or as a hunting aid. Camouflage can range from simple colour patterns that break up the body's outline to a more detailed deception, such as mimicry. Mimics can imitate droppings, leaves, flowers, and grass stalks, or they may even make themselves look like another animal that is more dangerous than themselves. Some animals can adjust their colour to suit their background. For example, Arctic foxes change from white fur in winter when they blend in with the snow-covered landscape, to brown fur in summer.

*Markings mimic leaf veins*

UNDERSIDE OF
LEAF BUTTERFLY

## Leaf mimic

The brown underside of the leaf butterfly from southeast Asia looks like a dead or decaying leaf. It even has a lookalike leaf stalk and veins. When resting on a twig or branch with its wings folded back, the butterfly looks no different from a real leaf on the tree and so escapes the notice of predatory birds.

*Patch of colour turns darker or lighter to make the fish "invisible"*

CAMOUFLAGED
PLAICE

## Flatfish

The plaice is able to make itself invisible to prey when it lies flat against the seabed. Whether hiding on a floor of lightly coloured shingle or on a bed of multicoloured pebbles and seaweed, the plaice can blend in perfectly. It simply changes the pattern of colours on its skin to achieve as close a match as possible to its background.

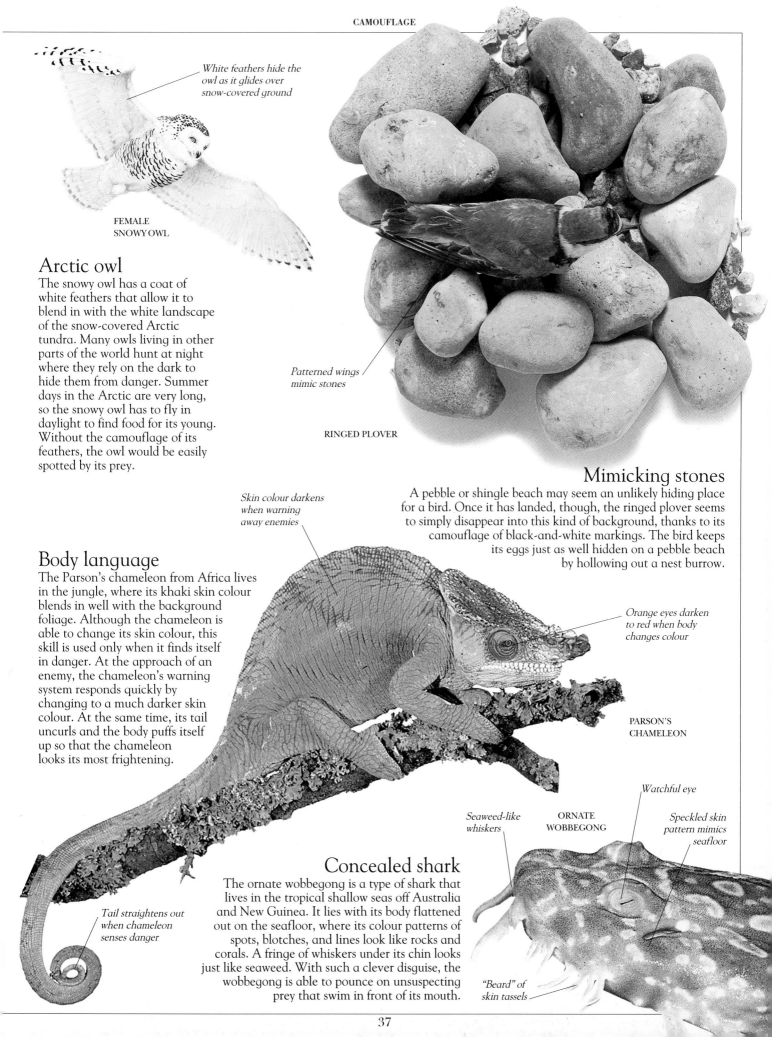

*White feathers hide the owl as it glides over snow-covered ground*

**FEMALE SNOWY OWL**

## Arctic owl

The snowy owl has a coat of white feathers that allow it to blend in with the white landscape of the snow-covered Arctic tundra. Many owls living in other parts of the world hunt at night where they rely on the dark to hide them from danger. Summer days in the Arctic are very long, so the snowy owl has to fly in daylight to find food for its young. Without the camouflage of its feathers, the owl would be easily spotted by its prey.

*Patterned wings mimic stones*

**RINGED PLOVER**

## Mimicking stones

A pebble or shingle beach may seem an unlikely hiding place for a bird. Once it has landed, though, the ringed plover seems to simply disappear into this kind of background, thanks to its camouflage of black-and-white markings. The bird keeps its eggs just as well hidden on a pebble beach by hollowing out a nest burrow.

*Skin colour darkens when warning away enemies*

## Body language

The Parson's chameleon from Africa lives in the jungle, where its khaki skin colour blends in well with the background foliage. Although the chameleon is able to change its skin colour, this skill is used only when it finds itself in danger. At the approach of an enemy, the chameleon's warning system responds quickly by changing to a much darker skin colour. At the same time, its tail uncurls and the body puffs itself up so that the chameleon looks its most frightening.

*Orange eyes darken to red when body changes colour*

**PARSON'S CHAMELEON**

*Tail straightens out when chameleon senses danger*

*Watchful eye*

*Seaweed-like whiskers*

**ORNATE WOBBEGONG**

*Speckled skin pattern mimics seafloor*

## Concealed shark

The ornate wobbegong is a type of shark that lives in the tropical shallow seas off Australia and New Guinea. It lies with its body flattened out on the seafloor, where its colour patterns of spots, blotches, and lines look like rocks and corals. A fringe of whiskers under its chin looks just like seaweed. With such a clever disguise, the wobbegong is able to pounce on unsuspecting prey that swim in front of its mouth.

*"Beard" of skin tassels*

# Courtship and mating

If animals lived forever, there would be no need for new ones to replace them. To make sure that their own species do not die out, all animals reproduce to create a future generation. Some animals reproduce asexually, that is without breeding with a partner, and can create exact copies of themselves. Others reproduce sexually, that is where two adults breed together to produce young. For sexual reproduction to take place, animals need to meet and pair up, so many of them perform special displays of courtship or make mating calls to attract a partner.

*Female's colours are more drab*

FEMALE ZEBRA FINCH

*"Crying" call is sung during courtship*

*Male's colourful chest feathers attract female*

MALE ZEBRA FINCH

## Battle of the giants
The competition between the bull (male) elephants to mate with a female becomes very intense during the breeding season. Driven by high excitement, bulls of equal size and strength fight together – a smaller male usually withdraws from a contest. Whichever bull wins the fight, earns the right to reply to the mating calls of a female.

## Finch couple
Like many birds, the male finch is more decorative than the female. The reason for this difference between the sexes is that the male needs to impress a female partner, but the female wants to avoid drawing the unwanted attention of predators when she is rearing her young. During courtship, the male finch sings a special song that sounds like a crying child and fans out his tail to reveal its white bars.

## Butterflies mating

Sweet oil butterflies are one of many butterfly species that are brought together by a special smell created during courtship. Known as "assembling", the female uses chemicals to produce a powerful scent that captures the attention of males looking for a mate. Once a pair has met, they will breed together on a plant that will provide enough food to cater for their offspring.

*Male (left) links his body with female (right)*

*Plant chosen as a suitable source of food for caterpillars*

PAIR OF SWEET OIL BUTTERFLIES

SULAWESI CRESTED MACAQUE

*Pink swelling around sitting pads*

## Attractive bottom

The Sulawesi crested macaque, like many female monkeys and apes, lets males know that she is ready to mate by displaying her bottom. It can be difficult to get yourself noticed or heard living in large troops or communities, so the pads of swollen pink tissue are used as an invitation to courtship.

## Grab a mate

The male common toad makes sure that he attracts female toads from the same species, by using a distinctive mating call. Once a female toad has been attracted, the male holds on to her in a tight, mating embrace. The special pads of rough skin on his thumbs give him extra grip on her slippery skin.

*Male grips female with special pads on his thumbs*

COMMON TOAD

*Males trumpet, flap ears, and lock tusks during combat*

*Trunks used to grab hold of rival's head*

BULL ELEPHANTS FIGHTING

Mother suckles
her kittens

MOTHER CAT
AND LITTER

# First life

Some baby animals develop inside their mother and are eventually born as tiny copies of their parents. Others develop inside protective egg cases. These eggs are either looked after in a nest by their parents or left in a safe place until they are ready to hatch. When a baby animal arrives, whether it is born or hatched, it is very vulnerable to attack by predators. The mother, or sometimes the father, looks after her young carefully until they can fend for themselves or she leaves the young in a protected space with food to hand, so that they are able to survive alone.

## Newly born

After spending about 63 days in the womb, a litter of usually four kittens is born. They are blind and defenceless at birth, and each weighs about 100 g (4 oz). At first, the mother cat hardly sleeps while she looks after her young. She makes sure that the kittens stay close to her stomach for warmth and that they are able to take milk from her whenever they are hungry. After nine days the kittens open their eyes, and they start walking at about 21 days.

Feathery gill
takes in oxygen
from the water

EIGHT-WEEK-OLD
NEWT LARVA

Body and tail
still undeveloped

Spindly
front leg

## Young newt

The development of a newt larva (young amphibian) into a fully grown adult is known as metamorphosis. This process is made up of a series of changes, in which a newt larva breaks out of an egg, and then takes on a completely new appearance when it becomes an adult. At first, the larva has feathery outer gills, large eyes, and not much shape. After 12 weeks, the body and tail will be longer and the legs more clearly defined. By 16 weeks, it will be a perfectly formed adult.

Baby snake may stay
in the hatched egg
for a couple of days

YOUNG RAT
SNAKE

Tongue is used
to "taste" and
"smell" the air

## Emerging snake

A young rat snake hatches out by breaking through the shell with a tiny egg tooth on its snout. This tooth drops off after a few days as it is no longer needed. The snake emerges with all the body parts of an adult. From the moment it hatches, the baby snake is on its own and has no parents to look after it. However, it has a set of built-in instincts that tell the snake how to find food and how to recognize danger.

YOUNG
CHIMPANZEES

## Beetle eggs

Young Mexican bean beetles chew their way out of individual egg cases. They emerge as tiny larvae that look quite unlike their parents – in fact, they look more like tiny caterpillars. The larvae then start to eat the leaves and shoots of the bean plant on which they live. After this period of intensive feeding, the larva turns into a hard-cased pupa, in which it lies dormant whilst its body goes through many amazing changes. Within three to four weeks, it emerges as an adult beetle.

*Sharp spines protect the larvae from being eaten by birds*

MEXICAN
BEAN BEETLE
LARVAE

*Red spots develop into eyes*

*Wrestling helps to build up muscles*

## Playful chimps

After they are born, common chimpanzees are totally dependent on their mothers for many months. During that time, they build up their strength and learn about the "rules" of their community. Part of this learning process is a behaviour known as "play", during which they chase each other around, go exploring together, have pretend fights, and learn how to communicate using sounds and facial expressions.

## Chicks galore

Like snakes, chicks have an egg tooth with which to crack open their hard shells from the inside. Partridge chicks are well-developed when they emerge from the egg and, within a couple of hours, their feathers dry and fluff up to form a warm jacket. The striped pattern across their bodies serves as camouflage in the open grasslands where they live. The chicks are also equipped with strong legs, which allow them to run quickly and hide from predators in the undergrowth.

PARTRIDGE
CHICKS

*Striped pattern blends in with grassland*

*Chicks are born in open nest built at ground level*

# Eggs and nests

Most egg-laying animals go to great lengths to help their developing offspring. Rather than abandon eggs or young unable to fend for themselves, a parent can adopt one of several methods to protect them. It might carry its eggs around, place them in tough protective cases, or gather them in a safe haven, such as a nest, over which they stand guard. A nest can be anything from a scrape in the sand or the underside of a rock to a complicated structure that the parents have taken many days to build. Whatever the method, the parents are trying to give their vulnerable offspring the best start in life by protecting them from the weather and from predators.

*Nest of soft down and leaves*

*Cylinder-shaped eggs*

HUMMINGBIRD'S NEST AND EGGS

## Perfect fit

Hummingbirds build a small cup-shaped nest to house their tiny, cylinder-shaped eggs. The female lays just two eggs at a time. She looks after the pair of eggs until the nestlings (young birds) hatch and leave the nest after just three weeks. The sturdy nest is made from stems, plant down, and feathers, which are held together with spiders' webs.

## Fish nests

While cod and herring produce millions of eggs and let them float away in the sea, other fish protect their eggs in temporary nest sites. For example, the female bullhead, or miller's thumb, lays her 250 eggs in scooped-out hollows on the bed of a lake or river. The male fish stands guard over the "nest". He uses his fin to fan water over the eggs, until the fry (young bullheads) hatch out after four weeks.

*Fin is used to fan water over the eggs*

MALE BULLHEAD AND EGGS

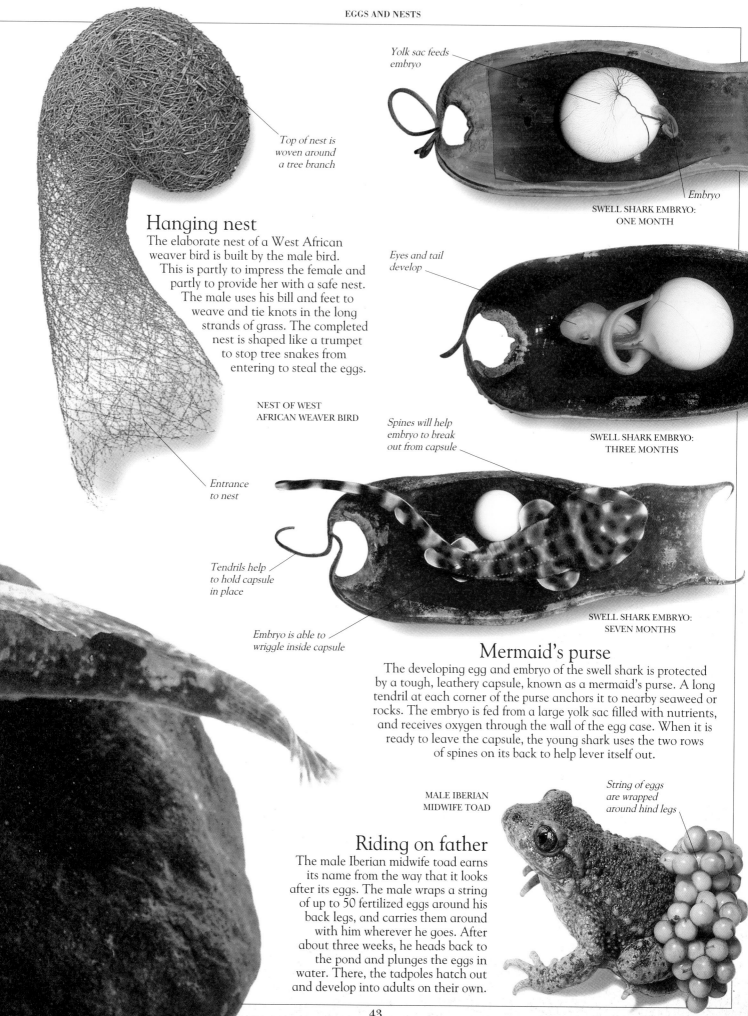

*Yolk sac feeds embryo*

*Embryo*

SWELL SHARK EMBRYO:
ONE MONTH

# Hanging nest

The elaborate nest of a West African weaver bird is built by the male bird. This is partly to impress the female and partly to provide her with a safe nest. The male uses his bill and feet to weave and tie knots in the long strands of grass. The completed nest is shaped like a trumpet to stop tree snakes from entering to steal the eggs.

*Top of nest is woven around a tree branch*

*Eyes and tail develop*

SWELL SHARK EMBRYO:
THREE MONTHS

NEST OF WEST
AFRICAN WEAVER BIRD

*Spines will help embryo to break out from capsule*

*Entrance to nest*

*Tendrils help to hold capsule in place*

SWELL SHARK EMBRYO:
SEVEN MONTHS

*Embryo is able to wriggle inside capsule*

# Mermaid's purse

The developing egg and embryo of the swell shark is protected by a tough, leathery capsule, known as a mermaid's purse. A long tendril at each corner of the purse anchors it to nearby seaweed or rocks. The embryo is fed from a large yolk sac filled with nutrients, and receives oxygen through the wall of the egg case. When it is ready to leave the capsule, the young shark uses the two rows of spines on its back to help lever itself out.

MALE IBERIAN
MIDWIFE TOAD

*String of eggs are wrapped around hind legs*

# Riding on father

The male Iberian midwife toad earns its name from the way that it looks after its eggs. The male wraps a string of up to 50 fertilized eggs around his back legs, and carries them around with him wherever he goes. After about three weeks, he heads back to the pond and plunges the eggs in water. There, the tadpoles hatch out and develop into adults on their own.

# Growing up

Some animals are born as fully formed tiny versions of adults, while others are quite undeveloped at birth. Whatever their start in life, young animals are at risk from changes in the weather, a lack of food or water, and predators. Many insects and amphibians are left to look after themselves. They survive this dangerous period by a process known as "metamorphosis" – larvae hatch from their eggs, later they change completely and emerge as adults. In contrast, young mammals and birds are fed and protected by their parents who teach them how to survive.

## Pond change

The damselfly nymph (young) lives in the water, where it feeds on small animals, including tadpoles and small fish. As it grows, the nymph changes its skin several times. When it is ready to turn into an adult, the nymph climbs out of the water, splits its final skin, and a fully developed damselfly emerges.

*Adult damselfly develops inside the nymph's skin*

*Skin splits open*

*Nymph's skin is shed to reveal adult damselfly*

DAMSELFLY LARVAE BECOMES AN ADULT

*Mother suckles the baby for up to a year*

FEMALE MONA MONKEY AND BABY

YOUNG MOOSE AND MOTHER

*Young moose has to gain weight in summer to survive cold winters*

## Young moose

During the summer, a baby moose feeds heavily to double its weight to provide it with a fat store to last the winter. The young moose stays with its mother for a year, learning essential survival skills.

## Fish change

The flatfish is a normal fish-shape at first – but as it grows and flattens, its left eye moves across the head so that both eyes are on the right side of its body. It then swims with its left side facing downwards.

*Fish now has a flat body like adult flatfish*

*Left eye moves to the other side of the head*

COMMON SOLE

*Pups usually keep out of the way of large males for fear of being trampled*

BULL STELLER'S SEA LION WITH PUP

## Sea lion pups

This sea lion pup is lying on the back of a large male, possibly its father. Its mother is away at sea where she is feeding. The pup is left, usually with other pups, on a secluded part of the beach. When the mothers return, they find their own pups by calling to them and detecting their smell.

*Helpless chicks with no feathers and eyes closed*

ONE-DAY-OLD BLUE TIT NESTLINGS

*Open mouths demand food from parents*

## Nest nursery

Blue tit nestlings are completely helpless and depend totally on their parents for food for their first few weeks of life. Fed mainly on caterpillars, they grow rapidly. After learning to fly, they still beg from their parents for several days, until they learn to fend for themselves.

THREE-DAY-OLD BLUE TIT NESTLINGS

*Nest becomes crowded as feathers sprout and bodies grow*

## Holding on

The baby mona monkey of West Africa clings tightly to its mother's fur as she moves swiftly through the trees. It even wraps its long tail around her body like an anchor. If the baby monkey lets go of its mother, it will fall to the ground and be killed. It suckles her milk when she stops to feed or rest, and is dependent on her for about a year.

*Mother uses her tail to balance on branches*

NINE-DAY-OLD BLUE TIT NESTLING

# Animal homes

Many small animals that live above the ground make their homes in trees or in thick undergrowth. The main reasons for their choice of homes is to avoid being caught by predators on the ground or in the air, to provide shelter from wind and rain, and to escape floodwaters when river banks burst. Some animals build homes simply to protect their young until they have learned how to survive in the wild. Others, such as wasps, build nests to house whole communities. Refuges are usually made from leaves, twigs, grasses, and mud, materials that are easily found in the local surroundings.

REED WARBLER'S
BASKET NEST

*Layers of mud are built up to form thick walls*

## Mud hut

This dome-like structure is the home of the ovenbird. When the bird is unable to find a suitable hole, such as a hollow tree trunk, for its home, it builds its own. Made from mud, plants, and droppings, the nest is placed in all sorts of places, from undergrowth to fence posts.

*Reed holds nest high above water so it stays dry*

OVENBIRD'S
MUD NEST

*Roof is added to the bird's abandoned nest*

## Tree house

Sometimes a squirrel will take over an old bird's nest and make its home there. Before moving in, the squirrel raises the walls and adds a roof using dried grasses, twigs, and leaves. This creates a rounded nest known as a drey. It is usually built in a tree fork near the trunk, where it is protected from high winds.

## On stilts

The cup-shaped nest of the reed warbler is slung between the upright stems of reeds. It is plaited from thin reed material, grasses, and flowers, and may be lined with soft plant down and feathers. The rim of the nest is softened by weaving in silk from spiders' webs. When the wind blows the nest sways with the reeds in the reedbed, but it does not fall.

GREY
SQUIRREL'S
DREY

# Hanging hive

Colonies of wasps build their nest from the top downwards. It is made from wood shavings that the wasps chew to make a papery material. The queen wasp is the first to start work on the nest, building the stem from which the nest hangs. Once she has finished the first few cells, she lays an egg in each of them. The eggs hatch into workers, who help the queen to complete the multi-storey structure with a central comb, several layers of outside wall, and an entrance at the bottom.

*Eggs laid in six-sided cells*

*Wasps paper over damaged walls*

*A network of silk threads draws the leaves together around the silkworm*

COMMON WASPS' NEST

OAK SILKWORMS (CATERPILLARS OF OAK SILKMOTH)

*Walls of paper are made from chewed wood*

## Leaf lodge

At the topmost branches of an oak tree, the oak silkworm builds its cocoon (shelter). To bind together the leaves, the silkworm uses fine threads of silk, produced from glands in its body. The leaves and silk form a strong, protective casing around the silkworm while it changes into a moth.

*Silkworm feeding on oak leaves*

# Shelters and burrows

One of the safest places to live is protected inside a well-made shelter or deep underground in a burrow. These homes hide animals from the prying eyes of many predators, and shelter them from the hot sun, cold wind, rain, or snow. Underground is also a good place to build a nest and raise a family. However, as a precaution, most subterranean homes have a back door so that animals can escape if a predator should finds its way in. Some animals, such as mole rats, live permanently below ground, nibbling at the underground parts of plants.

HERMIT CRAB
IN SHELL

## Shell squatter
Hermit crabs do not have shells to protect their soft bodies. Instead, they occupy the abandoned shells of other creatures, moving to larger shells as their bodies grow.

## Tunnel maze
Rabbits make their nests below ground in a maze of tunnels known as a warren. They emerge at dusk to feed on the upper parts of plants and this is when they are most in danger of attack. The rabbits remain close to their burrow entrance when feeding or playing so that they can dive down if a predator approaches.

RABBITS IN
WARREN

*Tunnels are just wide enough for rabbits to use*

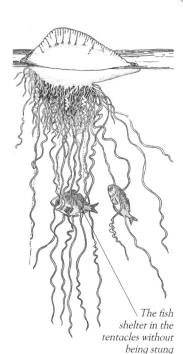

*The fish shelter in the tentacles without being stung*

FISH WITH
PORTUGUESE
MAN-O'-WAR

## Tentacle tease
Many fish are killed instantly if touched by the ends of the stinging tentacles of the Portuguese man-of-war. However, the young of some fish shelter in the tentacles to shield them from predators.

## Taking root

Some ants nest in the base of plants that grow on trees. The ants climb up through the roots and burrow their way through the plant. They settle in air spaces where they raise their young and cultivate gardens of fungus to feed on.

*Plant thrives on the compost created by the ants*

ANT HOME INSIDE PLANT

*Air spaces inside plant provide homes for ants*

*Entrance to rabbit warren*

*Above ground, rabbits stay close to the warren entrance in case danger threatens*

*Ants enter plant through the root system*

*Temperature inside den is 5°C (41°F) warmer than outside temperature*

POLAR BEAR DEN

## Cosy den

Female polar bears give birth to their cubs during mid-winter. To keep their young warm, the family shelters inside a snug, snow den where the temperature is warmer than outside. The family does not emerge until the early spring.

# World of habitats

Separated from each other by oceans and mountain ranges, each continent of the world has its own special types of animals and habitats. For example, egg-laying mammals, such as the duck-billed platypus, are only found in Australia. Such "primitive" mammals have survived because, isolated from other continents, they are able to escape competition from a wide range of other mammals. Animals that travel by sea or air between continents, such as seals or birds, are called "migrants". They journey in search of areas where food supplies are more plentiful at certain times of the year.

BHUTAN GLORY BUTTERFLY

*Dark colours absorb sunlight and so help butterfly to keep warm*

## Asia
The Bhutan glory butterfly lives in the mountain forests of Thailand, Bhutan, and India, where the climate can be cold and harsh. It makes short flights, keeping close to the land to avoid being blown away by strong winds.

ARCTIC OCEAN

*Large eyes for good night vision*

TAWNY OWL

EUROPE

ASIA

PACIFIC OCEAN

AFRICA

ATLANTIC OCEAN

INDIAN OCEAN

AUSTRALASIA

## Europe
There are owls of various types living on all continents except Antarctica. Tawny owls are residents of Europe, and are found from Scandinavia in the north to the southernmost parts of Italy. They live in woodland and open areas with large trees, and feed on mice and voles.

SOUTHERN OCEAN

*Markings blend in with the dead leaves and debris on the forest floor*

*Body forms an S-shape when it moves*

## Africa
Snakes live on all continents except Antarctica. The Gaboon viper is the largest viper in Africa. Its range stretches from southern Sudan to northern South Africa, where it lives in rainforests and thickets. It lies camouflaged in the leaf litter or partially buried in the peat on the forest floor. Using these hiding places, it can pounce on small creatures or shelter from predators.

GABOON VIPER

EQUATOR

TROPIC OF CAPRICORN

ANTARCTIC CIRCLE

## Antarctic
Surrounded by the Southern Ocean, Antarctica itself is home to very little. However, an extraordinary wealth of wildlife – including whales, seals, and penguins – feeds in the sea and breeds on the sub-Antarctic islands.

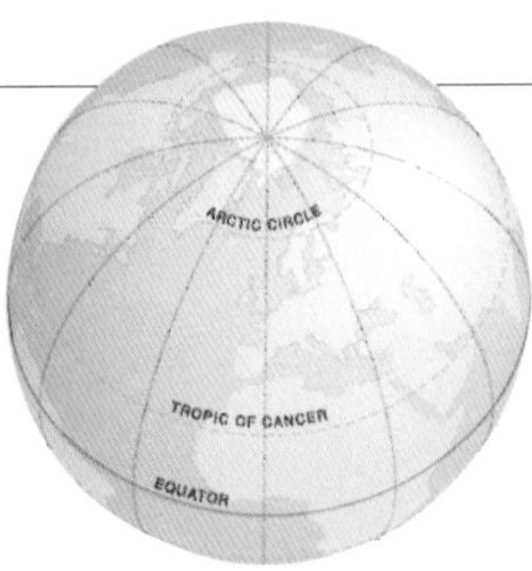

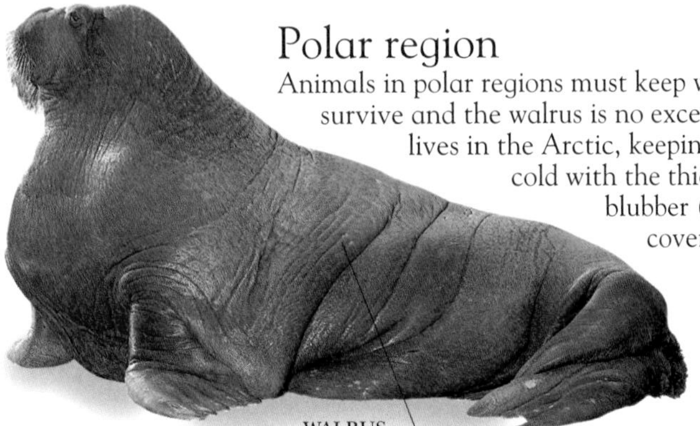

## Polar region

Animals in polar regions must keep warm to survive and the walrus is no exception. It lives in the Arctic, keeping out the cold with the thick layer of blubber (fat) that covers its body.

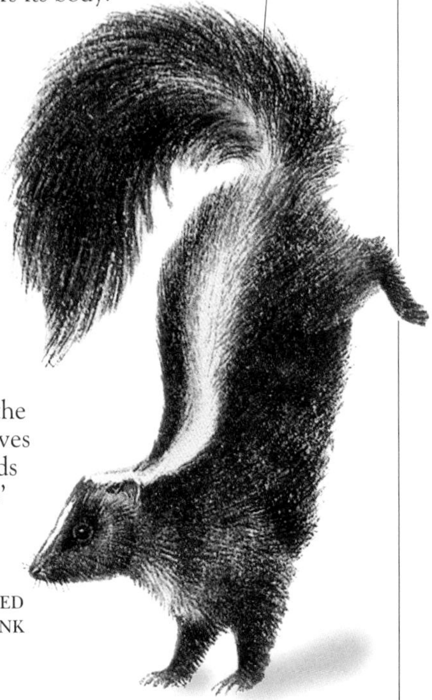

*Handstand is a warning to would-be attackers*

## Arctic

The Arctic is a vast, frozen sea surrounded by land. Very little survives on the solid ice itself, but at the ice edge, whales and polar bears thrive, and seals breed on ice floes.

WALRUS

*Layers of thick blubber*

NORTH AMERICA

ATLANTIC OCEAN

PACIFIC OCEAN

## North America

Skunks are found throughout the Americas. The striped skunk lives in underground burrows. It feeds on small animals, insects, birds' eggs, and fruit.

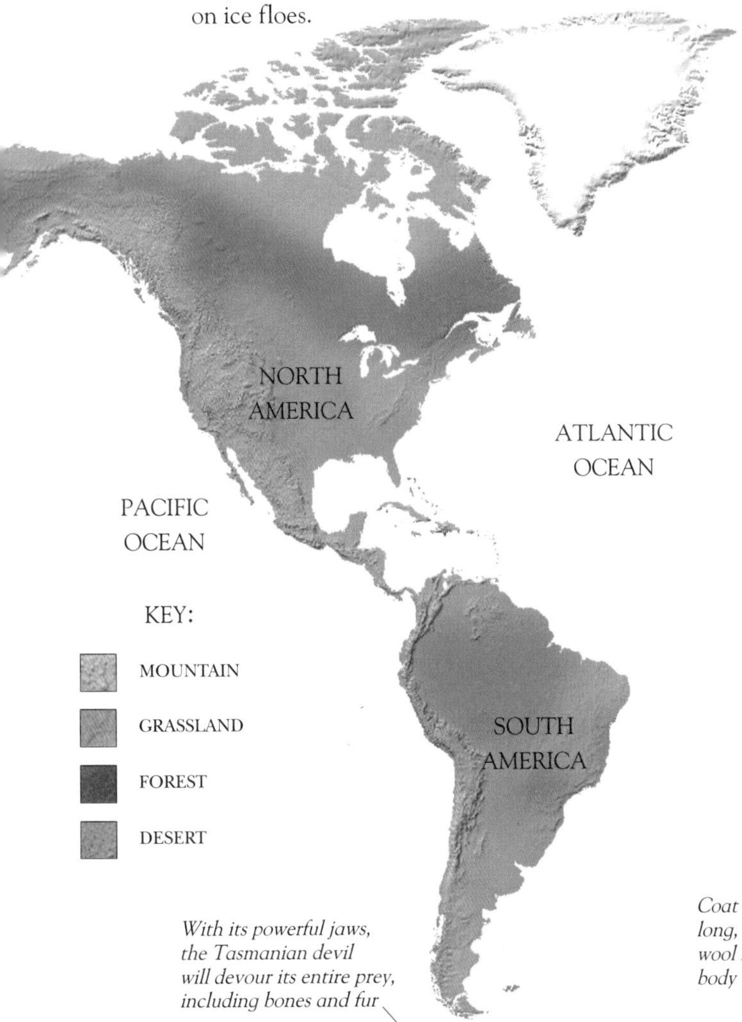

STRIPED SKUNK

KEY:

MOUNTAIN

GRASSLAND

FOREST

DESERT

SOUTH AMERICA

## South America

The guanaco is a South American camel without a hump. It lives in the foothills of the Andes mountains and on desert grasslands where its thick, woolly coat protects it from the fierce winds and low temperatures of winter. It feeds both on grasses and low bushes.

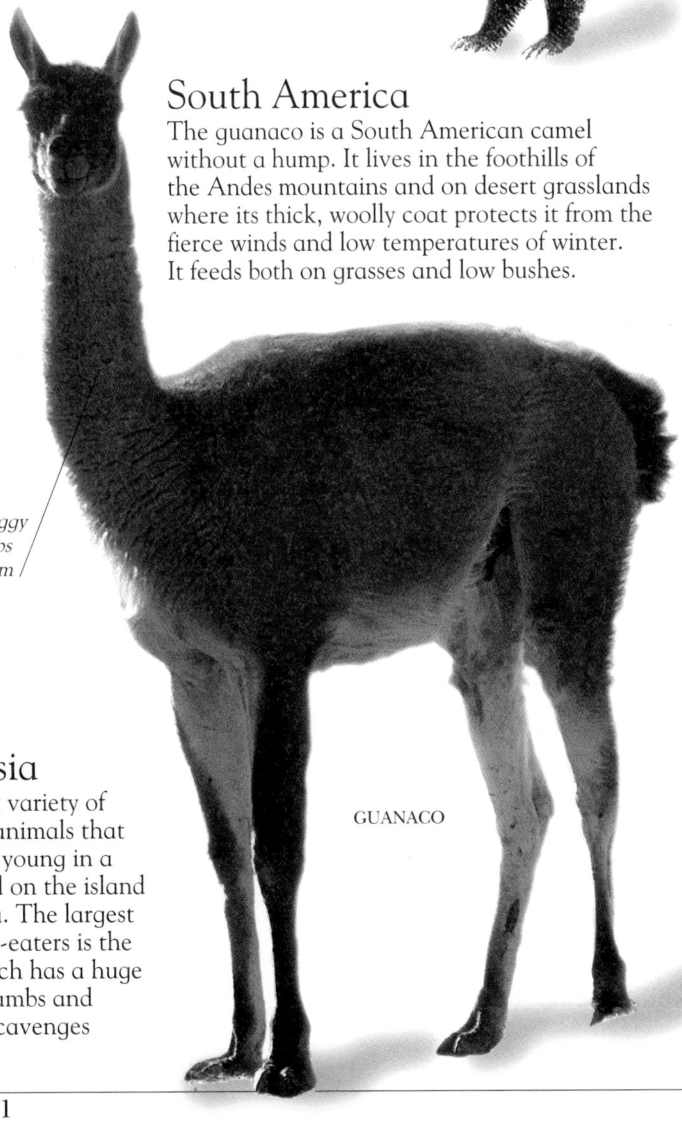

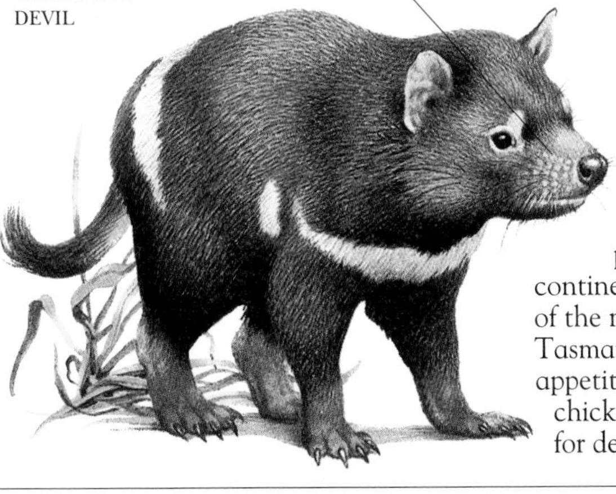

*With its powerful jaws, the Tasmanian devil will devour its entire prey, including bones and fur*

TASMANIAN DEVIL

*Coat of long, shaggy wool keeps body warm*

## Australasia

The greatest variety of marsupials (animals that bring up their young in a pouch) is found on the island continent of Australia. The largest of the marsupial meat-eaters is the Tasmanian devil, which has a huge appetite. It preys on lambs and chickens, and also scavenges for dead carcasses.

GUANACO

# Adaptation

Most animals are adapted to the habitats, or places, in which they live. These surroundings include polar regions, mountains, deserts, forests, grasslands, swamps, fresh water, and the sea. Some animals have such specialized needs that they can only survive in one particular habitat. The polar bear is so well insulated with fur that it would overheat if it lived anywhere other than the cold Arctic. The giant anteater would die if it was taken away from its grassland home where there are plenty of ants and termites for it to feed on. The monarch butterfly would be killed by predators if it could not find milkweed plants, which provide it with poison to keep enemies away. Other animals, such as the rat, fox, and cockroach, are able to survive in many different types of habitat because they are not specialists. Just like humans, they can adapt their behaviour to live almost anywhere.

ARCTIC FOX

## Ice fox

The Arctic fox keeps warm in the icy winter by growing a thick, double-layered winter coat. The heavy outer coat overlays a dense and woolly undercoat, trapping a layer of air warmed by its body close to the skin. Fur also lines the soles of its large feet which can run comfortably over snow. Its small rounded ears are also adapted to the cold, with an inner and outer lining of fur to reduce heat loss.

## Leaf-nosed bats

Bats that live in woodlands have large ears and face growths, or nose leaf. The leaf-nosed bat uses this face growth to sense sound waves (echolocation), which helps it to steer around obstacles such as tree branches.

Nose leaf detects sound waves

DAUBENTON'S BAT

Highly sensitive ears pick up sound echoes

## Velvet diggers

The European mole is well adapted to a life underground. Its shovel-like front paws and large claws are adapted for digging tunnels through the soil. Its sensitive snout can pick out the smells of prey, such as earthworms and burrowing insect larvae. Inside the snout, there is a small bone that helps with tunnelling. The mole has tiny eyes which are sensitive only to changes in light levels. Although it has no outer ear, the mole is able to detect sounds and vibrations.

EUROPEAN MOLE

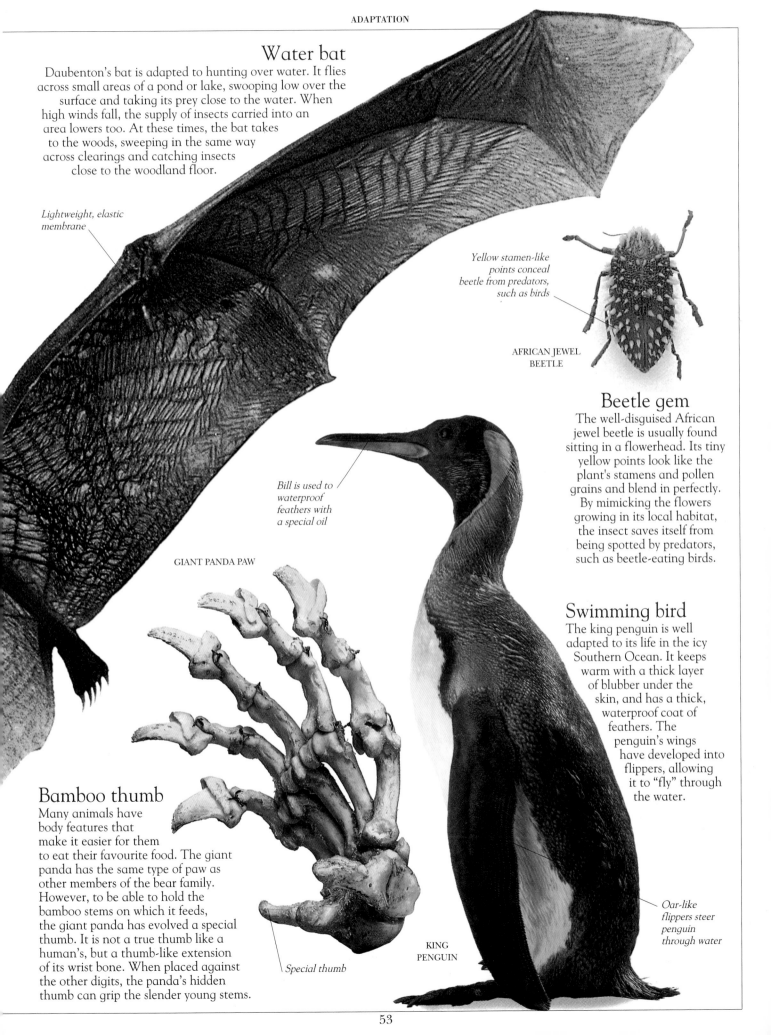

## Water bat

Daubenton's bat is adapted to hunting over water. It flies across small areas of a pond or lake, swooping low over the surface and taking its prey close to the water. When high winds fall, the supply of insects carried into an area lowers too. At these times, the bat takes to the woods, sweeping in the same way across clearings and catching insects close to the woodland floor.

*Lightweight, elastic membrane*

*Yellow stamen-like points conceal beetle from predators, such as birds*

AFRICAN JEWEL BEETLE

## Beetle gem

The well-disguised African jewel beetle is usually found sitting in a flowerhead. Its tiny yellow points look like the plant's stamens and pollen grains and blend in perfectly. By mimicking the flowers growing in its local habitat, the insect saves itself from being spotted by predators, such as beetle-eating birds.

*Bill is used to waterproof feathers with a special oil*

GIANT PANDA PAW

## Swimming bird

The king penguin is well adapted to its life in the icy Southern Ocean. It keeps warm with a thick layer of blubber under the skin, and has a thick, waterproof coat of feathers. The penguin's wings have developed into flippers, allowing it to "fly" through the water.

## Bamboo thumb

Many animals have body features that make it easier for them to eat their favourite food. The giant panda has the same type of paw as other members of the bear family. However, to be able to hold the bamboo stems on which it feeds, the giant panda has evolved a special thumb. It is not a true thumb like a human's, but a thumb-like extension of its wrist bone. When placed against the other digits, the panda's hidden thumb can grip the slender young stems.

*Special thumb*

KING PENGUIN

*Oar-like flippers steer penguin through water*

# Arctic

The Arctic consists of a vast frozen sea surrounded by tundra (treeless plains) at the top of the world. All of the animals that live there permanently are well-adapted to survive in the icy cold conditions. Those living on the ice, such as Arctic foxes and polar bears, have thick insulating fur outside their skin to keep them warm. Animals living under the ice, such as narwhals and walruses, are protected from the cold by a thick layer of blubber (fat) beneath their skin. Although the Arctic winters are dark and the sea freezes over, the summer days are long and the sea produces plenty of food, such as plankton and fish.

## Summer visitor

Snow geese migrate from the Gulf of Mexico to the Arctic in summer. The long hours of warm sunshine provide ideal conditions to breed and raise their young.

*Small rounded ears prevent heat loss*

FEMALE
POLAR BEAR

## Ice hunter

The polar bear's white coat blends in well with the ice- and snow-covered landscape of the Arctic. Hidden by its camouflage, the bear stalks seals across the ice and rushes at them before they can escape into the water. If the seals escape, the bear waits patiently by a hole in the ice made by seals for when they come to the surface to breathe.

*Male narwhals swim in deeper waters than females*

*Large clawed paws grab hold of prey*

## Polar whale

The unicorn whale or narwhal lives in remote, icy waters where there are plenty of fish to catch. The narwhal stays close to pack ice because its main enemy, the killer whale, dislikes touching the ice with its dorsal fins.

NARWHAL

*Hard tusk is an extra-long tooth*

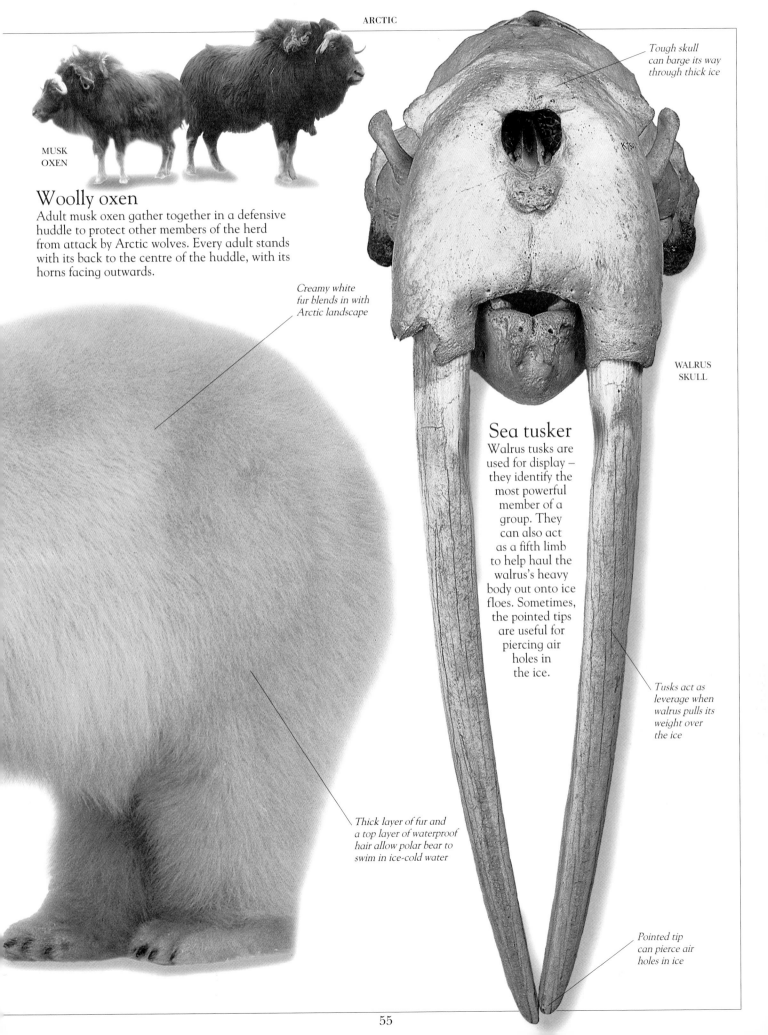

MUSK
OXEN

## Woolly oxen

Adult musk oxen gather together in a defensive huddle to protect other members of the herd from attack by Arctic wolves. Every adult stands with its back to the centre of the huddle, with its horns facing outwards.

*Tough skull can barge its way through thick ice*

WALRUS
SKULL

*Creamy white fur blends in with Arctic landscape*

## Sea tusker

Walrus tusks are used for display – they identify the most powerful member of a group. They can also act as a fifth limb to help haul the walrus's heavy body out onto ice floes. Sometimes, the pointed tips are useful for piercing air holes in the ice.

*Tusks act as leverage when walrus pulls its weight over the ice*

*Thick layer of fur and a top layer of waterproof hair allow polar bear to swim in ice-cold water*

*Pointed tip can pierce air holes in ice*

# Antarctic

The Antarctic consists of a vast frozen continent surrounded by the world's stormiest seas. The lowest temperature ever recorded here, -89°C (-110°F), makes it the coldest place on Earth. Even so, plenty of creatures manage to survive in these conditions. Like the Arctic, the Antarctic has 24 hours of sunlight in midsummer and this is when most creatures breed and raise their young. Seabirds, whales, and seals are influenced by conditions in the sea – they follow the pack ice which builds up at the edges of the ocean in winter and melts away in summer. The one exception is the emperor penguin, who stays on the continent the whole year round.

## Keeping warm

Male emperor penguins huddle together on land during winter, each balancing an egg on its feet. Using its thick blubber to keep warm, the penguin incubates the egg beneath a thick flap of skin. In the spring, the females take over the task of looking after the egg until it hatches.

KRILL

*Large, rounded eyes*

*Feathery feelers used for feeding*

## Food chain

Krill are an important source of food for whales, seals, and seabirds in the Antarctic. These small shrimp-like crustaceans feed on sea plants and small sea creatures, including other krill. When gathered together in great swarms, their massed bodies can make the ocean look red.

*Large eye for good vision in dark Antarctic waters*

*Short, bill reduces heat loss*

ANTARCTIC ICEFISH

*Slim body keeps body fluids to a minimum*

*Slimy coating helps fish glide through water*

MARBLE PLUNDERFISH

*Touch-sensitive whisker*

## Inner antifreeze

Antarctic icefish and marble plunderfish are just some of the fish that have adapted to living under the ice. Their bloodstream carries a type of antifreeze that stops the fluids in their bodies from turning to ice.

*Egg cannot survive on ice so it rests on the parent's feet*

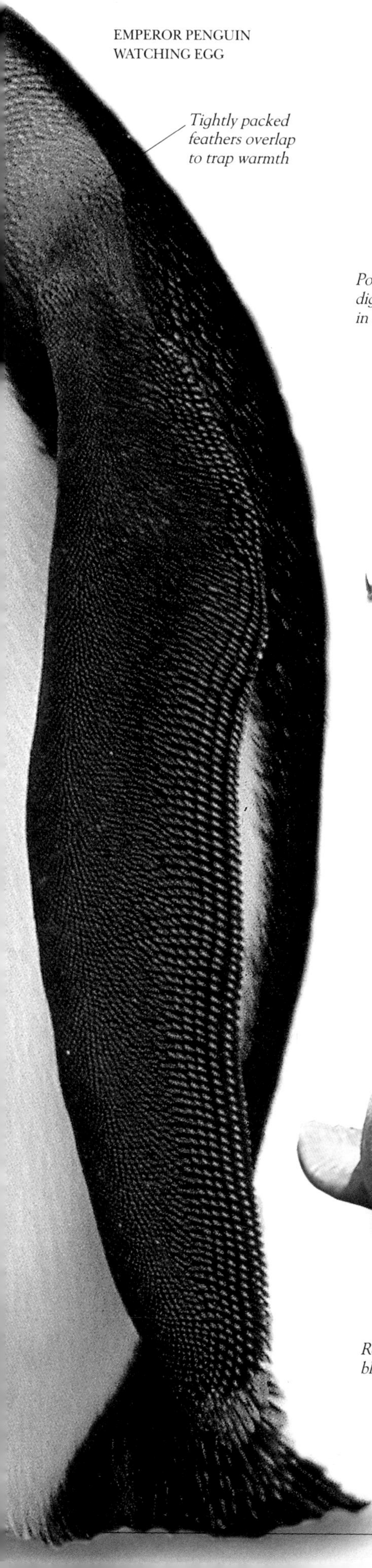

EMPEROR PENGUIN
WATCHING EGG

*Tightly packed
feathers overlap
to trap warmth*

## Southern traveller

The wandering albatross flies across the Antarctic seas in search of squid. Using little effort, it soars on the currents of air created by waves, and can cover up to 15,200 km (9,000 miles) in a month. It only settles on land in the breeding season, and makes its nests on one of the islands around the Antarctic tundra.

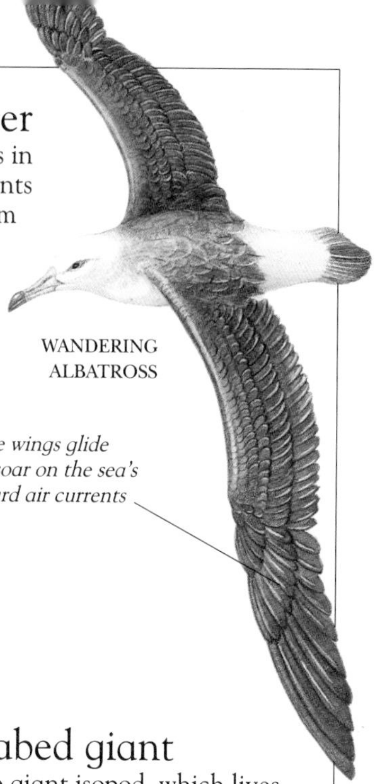

WANDERING
ALBATROSS

*Pointed tip
digs for food
in seabed*

*Large wings glide
and soar on the sea's
upward air currents*

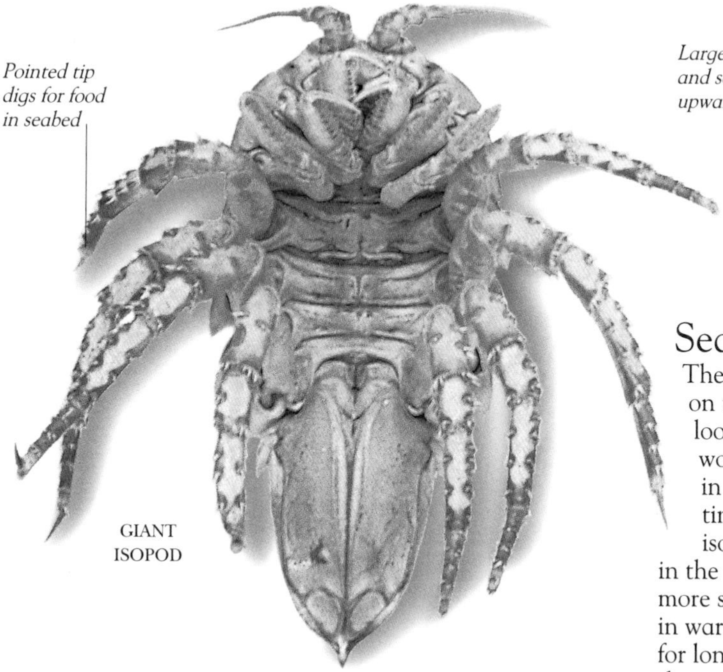

## Seabed giant

The giant isopod, which lives on the Antarctic seafloor, looks like an extra-large woodlouse. At 20 cm (8 in) in length, it measures three times bigger than any of its isopod relatives elsewhere in the world. Creatures grow more slowly in cold waters than in warm oceans and they live for longer, which means that they reach much larger sizes.

GIANT
ISOPOD

*Thick lining of
blubber is made
up of fat stores*

*Seal rolls on
the cold ground
to cool down*

YOUNG SOUTHERN
ELEPHANT SEALS

*Rolls of
blubber*

## Blubber store

To bring down its body temperature, the southern elephant seal pants, flaps its flippers, and comes up on land to roll on the ground. In summer, the elephant seal finds itself overheating because of the thick layer of blubber which keeps it so warm in winter.

# Mountain life

The tops of high mountains are cold places, where the temperature can drop to -20°C (68°F). Few animals live there permanently. The only visitors are tiny insects, blown there by fierce winds that can reach speeds of more than 300 kmh (186 mph). No food grows on the mountain tops, so the creatures must feed on pollen, plant spores, and other insects carried up from below. The snow fields below the summit are not barren, however, and are home to tiny worms and springtails. These creatures have antifreeze in their blood to prevent them from freezing, and feed on algae that colours the snow pink. Large animals, such as pumas, snow leopards, and mountain goats and sheep, live further down on the lower slopes. They inhabit the rocky crags and pastures during summer, escaping to the mountain forests and valleys below with the onset of winter. They need a thick insulating fur to survive the icy temperatures.

CHINCHILLA

## Furry nibblers
The chinchilla lives in the Andes mountain chain of South America. It is a small rodent with a long, soft, and dense fur that enables it to survive at altitudes of up to 5,000 m (16,400 ft).

*Well-developed hearing allows the puma to detect prey even when it is too dark to see*

*Eyes are able to look forwards as well as in a wide angle*

## Mountain zones
Different habitat zones occur at different altitudes on a mountain. On a European Alp, the very top may be permanently covered with snow, while a layer of scree below the peak drops to an alpine tundra of small, low-lying plants. Below this are grassy alpine meadows that lead down to coniferous forests. At the bottom are broad-leaved or deciduous woodlands.

Snow field to summit

4,200 m (14,000 ft)

Rocky scree

Alpine tundra

Alpine meadow

2,600 m (8,500 ft)

Deciduous woodland

# Blood and nectar

With so little food available, mountain insects must be alert to any opportunity to feed. A horsefly in the Himalayas has taken this need to an extreme. It has strong piercing mouthparts with which it punctures the skin of yaks and other mammals to suck their blood. This horsefly also possesses a long, thin proboscis or "tongue" to sip nectar from summer flowers.

*Long, thin proboscis*

HORSEFLY

# Low-level hunter

The merlin is found in northern America and Eurasia during summer. It is one of the top predators in the mountains of the region. It nests at the heads of steep, upland stream valleys, avoiding bare rocky areas and forests. The merlin prefers to hunt over open tracts of low, rough vegetation in the foothills. It flies close to the ground, taking small birds such as buntings and pipits. In the winter, the merlin leaves the mountains and heads for the milder coastal regions to the south and southwest.

MERLIN

# Fancy footwork

Mountain goats, known scientifically as goat antelopes, live on alpine meadows, where they feed mainly on mountain grasses. They have a surprising agility, thanks to their flexible, rubbery hooves, and can walk along very steep, rocky slopes. Their strong grip allows them to escape from predators by clambering onto narrow mountain ledges. Both male and female goats carry a pair of horns that slightly curve backwards.

MOUNTAIN GOAT

*Typical mountain coat of coarse, shaggy hair over a thick, insulating woolly underfur*

*Spongy pads under each hoof provide a strong grip*

# Puma – the mountain lion

The puma or cougar is a secretive cat found in the mountains from southern Canada to the tip of South America. It patrols a summer range of more than 200 sq km (80 sq miles), which shrinks to 100 sq km (40 sq miles) in the winter snows.

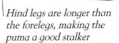

*Hind legs are longer than the forelegs, making the puma a good stalker*

PUMA

# Woodlands

Dense areas covered by trees and bushy shrubs are known as woodlands. Some temperate woodlands, found in Europe, North America, and New Zealand, feature mainly one type of tree, such as oak, conifer, or eucalyptus. Their presence influences which plants, animals, and insects choose to live there. Hot, dry woodlands provide year-round food and shelter for their residents. In contrast, deciduous woodlands are made up of trees that lose their leaves in winter, which means that the woodland community has to change its lifestyle with the seasons. Birds and small mammals raise their young in spring and summer, while leaf-eaters feed on the season's crop of fresh green leaves. In autumn, many insects nestle into the deep carpet of leaf litter and sleep through winter. Other creatures feed well before hibernating, while those that stay active in winter, store nuts and seeds for the hard times ahead.

PARASITIC CHACI WASP

## All in a gall

The small fruit-like globes seen on oak trees are called galls. When insects lay their eggs in buds and leaves, the plant wraps them in its tissues, forming a gall. Parasitic chalci wasps visit galls and lay their eggs on the tiny grubs inside.

## Woodland woodpecker

The green woodpecker is adapted perfectly to woodland life. Its stiffened tail helps it to perch on upright trunks and its tough bill is used to probe into bark for grubs.

*Tough beak can dig out insects*

GREEN WOODPECKER

*Stiff tail is used for support*

*Canopy: gets full strength of Sun*

*Shrub layer: tall bushes and small trees*

## Woodland layers

Different creatures live at the various levels provided by trees. Birds and caterpillars feed on the leaves and fruits in the topmost canopy. Birds and squirrels nest among branches and boughs. Snails, worms, and ground-living insects hide in the damp and dark leaf litter at the base of a tree.

*Herb layer: plants that can cope with low light levels*

*Litter layer: plants that enjoy moist, shady conditions*

*Topsoil*

*Subsoil*

*Bedrock*

## Wood owl

Tawny owls are nocturnal birds, which means that they are active at night. An adult tawny owl is equipped with silent flight, keen eyesight, and sharp hearing, which allow it to swoop on mice and voles. The markings on its feathers help the bird to blend in with the woodland background.

CENTIPEDE

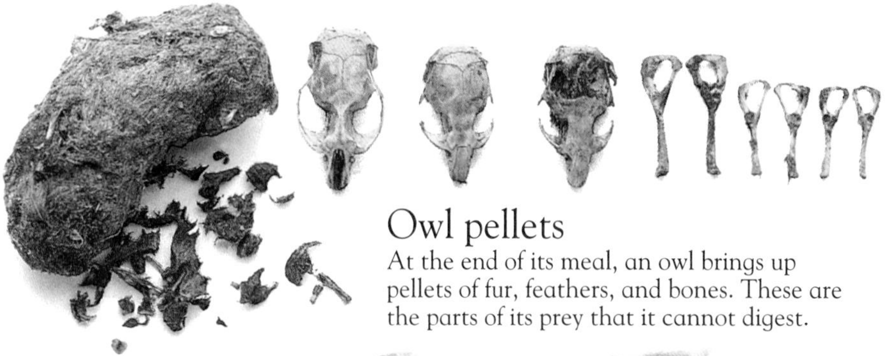

## Owl pellets

At the end of its meal, an owl brings up pellets of fur, feathers, and bones. These are the parts of its prey that it cannot digest.

## Multi-legged killer

Leaf litter is packed full of tiny members of woodland life that fall prey to the centipede. Unlike the millipede, which eats plants, the centipede dashes about the woodland floor in search of grubs, worms, and insects. Using its poisonous fangs to seize these small creatures, it sucks their bodies dry.

*Camouflaged wings*

YOUNG TAWNY OWL

*Feathered feet silence the approach of an owl about to pounce on its prey*

## Forest feast

Deer browse on fresh leaves, new buds, and young shoots in spring. During winter, they peel off and eat the bark on trees. They are creatures of habit, following well-trodden paths through the forest.

# Rainforests

Life exists at many different layers of the tropical rainforest. It is home to the richest and most diverse collection of animals to be found anywhere on the planet, and offers ideal growing conditions for plants, with year-round high temperatures and heavy rain. Most animals live in the forest canopy, or roof, bathed in sunlight about 50 m (164 ft) above the ground. Leaves, blossoms, and fruits provide food for some, while others hunt among the tree tops for their prey. By contrast, the forest floor is damp and dark, with the sunlight blocked out by the tangle of leaves and branches above. Mainly small, nervous mammals live in this twilight world. Food is limited on the forest floor, so they have to survive on nuts and fruits that rain down from the canopy above and on roots and tubers dug out from the ground.

MALAYAN FROG BEETLE

## Jumping beetle
Using its powerful back legs, the Malayan frog beetle can leap like a frog.

LEAF BEETLE

## Beetles galore
The leaf beetle lives in tropical forests and is just one of more than 300,000 types of beetle. Its bright metallic colours are caused by sunlight shining on its tough wing covers.

## Gliding gecko
Many tree-top animals glide between trees when looking for food or trying to escape being eaten. The flying gecko has loose flaps of skin along its body and limbs that spread out. These allow it to escape from its enemies by gliding to safety.

FLYING TREE SNAKE

## Lavish bird show
Only male birds of paradise are brightly coloured. The females are more dull, blending in with their forest background. To attract females, groups of males display their bright feathers in a special dance. Their performance takes place at a site called a lek, and is a noisy affair, filled with their loud whirs, chirps, and screams.

FLYING GECKO

*Loose flaps of skin make gliding possible*

*Camouflaged body blends in with tree bark*

*Flaps make body wider and flatter for gliding*

REINWARDT'S FLYING FROG

## Parachute feet
The long fingers and toes of Reinwardt's flying frog are linked by broad webs of skin, which make the feet and hands work like parachutes. When escaping from from danger, the frog leaps from its branch and floats down to a nearby tree. Then it clambers back up the trunk, returning to the canopy.

*Sting releases a paralyzing venom*

HUNTING WASP

## Low-flying wasp
The female hunting wasp flies close to the forest floor in search of crickets. She grabs the prey with her powerful jaws and uses her sting to inject a paralyzing venom. She then carries her victim to the burrow and deposits a single egg on its body. In this way, the female wasp makes sure that there is a fresh supply of food available for when the wasp larva hatches out.

*Snake "hangs" in the forest canopy by wrapping its body around branches*

## Flying snake

Snakes may seem too narrow to mimic flying, but the flying tree snake of southeast Asia can change its body shape and glide through the air. As it launches itself from a branch, it spreads out its ribs and flattens its body. In this way it can travel up to 50 m (164 ft) between the trees.

*Whitish bare skin reddens when the bird is excited or angry*

## Poison eaters

Macaws and parrots are able to eat the rainforest's poisonous seeds without any ill effects. They visit special river bank sites where they use their powerful beaks to break off chunks of soil. This contains medicinal minerals, such as kaolin, which neutralizes the poisons they have absorbed.

*Moveable ribs lets the flying dragon control its flight*

FLYING DRAGON

*Wingspan measures 30 cm (12 in) across*

GIANT ATLAS MOTH

## Dragon wings

The flying dragon has "wings" made from folds of skin stretched over its lengthened and moveable ribs. When the lizard wants to travel through the canopy, it spreads out these ribs and expands the folds on either side of the body like a fan.

## Giant moth

The atlas moth, a giant among moths, lives in the forests of tropical Asia. At night, it flies around in search of food, shielded from predators by the light-reflecting patches on its large wings. During the day, the moth hides itself away in plants.

*Light-reflecting patch*

# Grasslands

Hot savanna grasslands of East and southern Africa are just a small part of the grassland areas that cover one-quarter of the Earth's land surface. Large herds of plant-eating mammals, such as antelope and zebra, graze on the grasses, while groups of predators, such as lions and hyenas, prey on the slow, the weak, and the sick. Stands, or groups, of tall plants attract elephants, black rhinoceros, and giraffes, each of which feed on leaves at a different height. Acacia trees have deep roots that reach water underground. Their sharp, spiny leaves not only provide food but also much needed water in places where it is scarce. Some animals, such as wildebeest, travel great distances throughout the year in order to follow the seasonal rains that fall unevenly across the land. In this way, the migrating animals are always in the right place at the right time to feed on the new growth of grass.

*Skin markings blend in with background scrub and trees*

*Baby giraffes are able to run at just one-day old*

*Bony ridge protects the eyes*

*The patas is also known as the military monkey because of its smart red coat and soldier-like moustache*

PATAS MONKEY

*Powerful long legs allow the monkey to spring at speeds of up to 55 kmh (35 mph)*

## Giraffe herd
Giraffes live in loosely formed groups of about 12 animals. Some herds contain females and their young, while others are all bachelors (single males). When giraffes lie down to rest at midday, they keep an all-round watch for enemies. Each of the herd members takes up a look-out position holding its neck upright and pointing its head in a different direction to its neighbour.

## Grassland monkey
The patas monkey lives on the high grassy plains, wandering in troops of 15 to 20 individuals across a home range of up to 80 sq km (31 sq miles). It is active in the morning and late afternoon, spending much of the time on the ground looking for food. While the troop is feeding, an old male monkey stands guard and keeps a look out for danger.

Small horns

Long, narrow
tongue is used
for pulling leaves
and twigs into
the mouth

Stripes help zebras to recognize
each other within a herd

Sharp hooves
are used
for fighting

By stretching their
necks, giraffes can
feed on leaves up
to 6 m (20ft) high

Like other
mammals, giraffes
have just seven
neck bones

OSTRICH

Long, shaggy feathers

Twin-toed
foot helps
the ostrich
to run fast

## Feeding time

The giraffe is the tallest living
animal in the world. Its
height enables the giraffe to
reach leaves higher than any
other browsing animal, even
the elephant. Thanks to a
horny layer of skin inside
its mouth and very thick
saliva, the giraffe is not
injured by the sharp spines
on acacia leaves. It also
chews old bones for the
calcium they contain and
is a frequent visitor to salt
licks, where it eats large
amounts of soil for
essential minerals.

## Zebra herd

During the dry season, zebra families and wildebeest
migrate together. Unlike zebras, which prefer long grass,
wildebeest eat short grass so they can be certain of
finding a constant supply of food. For zebras, the
benefit of mixing with wildebeest is that
they are less likely to be attacked by
predators. Both species run away
when chased, but zebras are well
able to defend themselves with
their sharp hooves and teeth.

## Big bird

Like many animals that live on
the plains, the ostrich has long,
powerful legs and runs at great
speed. It is the fastest animal on
two legs, reaching up to 75 kmh
(45 mph). It is also the tallest bird
in the world at about 2.1–2.7m
(7–9 ft) high, and can weigh up
to 120 kg (260 lb). The ostrich
feeds on leaves, roots, flowers,
and seeds, as well as small
animals, including lizards,
snakes, and insects.

# Outback

A large area of isolated, barren land where the climate is typically hot and dry is described as outback. This type of habitat is commonly seen in Australia, and much of this island continent is made up of dry scrub and desert. Because Australia has been isolated for so long, the animals living here are unique. There are more pouched marsupials than anywhere else in the world, and the dominant predators are not mammals, but lizards and snakes. Many snakes in the outback are venomous and very dangerous to people, as are many of the spiders and scorpions. In fact, Australia has the greatest concentration of venomous animals in the world, and many of them are found in the sunbaked centre, the outback. With 3,500 hours of sunshine a year, Australia is the largest land mass in the world to receive such a scorching. Animals living there need to adapt to these long, dry seasons.

## Feral camels

Camels have nostrils and eyelashes that keep out sand, and they thrive on the tough and bitter leaves other animals reject. With adaptations like these, camels flourish in the wild in Australia.

*Distinctive dark eyestripe*

*Male kangaroos have deep russet-red fur*

*Tail helps the kangaroo to balance when hopping*

LAUGHING KOOKABURRA

## Laughing bird

The laughing kookaburra is the largest member of the kingfisher family. Typically, kingfishers are water-loving birds but this kookaburra chooses to live in the dry outback, far away from lakes and rivers. The bird uses a hollow branch or trunk as its nest, from where it swoops down to snatch grasshoppers, mice, lizards, and nestlings. The laughing kookaburra is named after the sound of its chuckling call, which it gives at dawn and dusk to mark its territory. A loud chorus can often be heard from a single territory in the outback because young birds stay with their parents for four or five years and help to bring up the next generations.

## Pouch baby

Kangaroos and wallabies are Australia's best-known marsupials. In the outback, they graze on plant material that is broken down by bacteria in their gut. During the long, dry season in the outback, food is short so the female raises her young one at a time, holding back any undeveloped embryos. Inside the female's pouch, the young, or joey, feeds on the mother's milk and is protected until it grows big enough to explore outside. Once the weather improves and food becomes more plentiful, the mother starts to raise the next of her young.

## Tree dwellers

Wherever there are trees in Australia, even in the outback, there are brightly coloured tree frogs. They are adapted for climbing, having large pads on their fingers and toes that are covered with sticky secretions. Even though they have made their homes in trees, these frogs still need to return to water in the breeding season, no matter how far away it is.

*Powerful hind legs*

*Claws provide grip when running*

DINGO

## Wild dog

Dingoes were introduced into Australia about 3,000 years ago. Today, they live in barren land and scrub, wherever there is a reliable source of water. Also known as Autralian wild dogs, dingoes generally hunt alone or in small family groups, but they will sometimes join together in an informal pack to bring down a large plant-eater, such as a kangaroo. Using their sharp teeth and powerful jaws, dingoes can crush a kangaroo's skull in one bite.

*Swollen tip of tail contains sacs of venom*

*Powerful pincers for grabbing hold of victims*

MARBLED SCORPION

*Forearms are used by males for "boxing" fights*

WESTERN GREY KANGAROO

## Sting in the tail

The marbled scorpion is just one of many poisonous animals to be found in the outback. It lives on the ground, hiding among the leaf litter, and under bark and stones. It darts out and grabs passing prey with its front claws, using its sting mainly for defence against bigger predators.

# Deserts

A hot desert has little water – less than 25 cm (10 in) of rain per year. The temperature can soar during the day and yet drop to freezing 0°C (32°F) at night. Even though it is a harsh place for living things, animals can and do survive here. They avoid the extremes of temperature by hiding in burrows or beneath boulders where it is cooler and shielded from the glare of the Sun. The air in these daytime shelters is damper than above ground, and so the animals lose less water. When the Sun goes down, desert mice and rats emerge to feed on tufts of grass and dead wind-blown vegetation. In turn, they fall prey to hungry snakes, hawks, and desert foxes, while lizards scamper across the sand in search of beetles. By sunrise all of the desert creatures disappear again.

DIADEM SNAKE

*Snake flicks its tongue out to "taste" the air*

GREY-BANDED KING SNAKE

## Venomous snake

Reptiles survive well in hot deserts. They lose little water through their scaly skin, because they do not sweat like humans do. Instead, they control their body temperature by gaining or losing heat from their surroundings. The red spitting cobra hides away in a burrow or among tree roots during the heat of the day, although the young are sometimes active. A mature snake comes out at night to catch small reptiles and mammals which it kills with its venomous fangs.

RED SPITTING COBRA

## Flicking tongue

A snake, like this diadem snake, flicks out its tongue repeatedly. It is using a chemical-detecting organ in the roof of its mouth to "taste" the air and to detect prey. The grey-banded king snake makes use of an additional sense, large eyes, that help it to seek out prey on the desert surface at night.

## Cool camel

The camel is adapted well to desert life, thanks to its hump. Most animals have fat beneath the skin all over the body, but this prevents them from cooling down. In a hot desert where heat retention is an unwanted problem, the best place to store fat is in one place – the hump.

HARRIS HAWK

Large broad
wings with
distinctive
chestnut patch

Hooked
beak for
tearing
flesh

Pincers are used
for burrowing

## Armoured diggers

Animals, such as scorpions, spiders, and
insects, have a built-in desert survival kit –
their hard exoskeleton (outer covering)
which reduces water loss. Those in the
hottest deserts still have to burrow deep
under rocks and roots to avoid drying up.
Using their claws, some species dig as far
down as 1 m (3 ft) into the sand.

## Co-operative killing

The Harris hawk of North American
deserts often hunts in pairs or even in
small groups. A breeding female may
be joined by several males to hunt at
dawn. While some of the group flush
out the prey, such as pack rats or jack
rabbits, from the undergrowth, the others
intercept the victim as it tries to escape.
The hunters share their prize.

Overlapping scales
make it possible for the
cobra to move rapidly

Snakes side-wind
across sand, moving
diagonally in an
S-shape

# Fresh water

Only three per cent of the water on Earth is fresh water. It varies in size from tiny puddles to lakes as big as seas, and from fast-flowing streams to slowly winding rivers that are several kilometres wide. When water falls as rain, it is almost chemically pure but as it runs across the land, the water gathers minerals from rocks and plants and, in time, contains enough nutrients to support living creatures. Each freshwater community has to adapt to the flow of the water where it lives. Animals in fast-flowing streams or mountain torrents have to protect themselves from being swept away, whereas those in a winding river or the still waters of a pond have to cope with low levels of oxygen and the hazard of water freezing over in winter.

## Fish watching

Scientists keep a watch on fish to help monitor stocks. Some fish are given an identity and are fitted with a numbered clip on their fin. Their progress can be recorded to find out where and how far they travelled between tagging and recapture.

CADDISFLY LARVAE

## Clean river

The small creatures living in streams and rivers help us to monitor water quality. Some are able to put up with pollution and thrive, while others simply die. For example, caddis fly larvae, mayfly nymphs, and water shrimps are known as positive indicators because their presence shows that a river is clean and healthy.

WATER SHRIMP

MAYFLY NYMPHS

## Middle waters

Where a river widens out, it becomes more winding and flows more slowly. As patches of mud and silt begin to build up at the water's edge, water plants grow and tiny aquatic creatures move in to live among the stems. These become food for bottom-feeding fish, like the minnow.

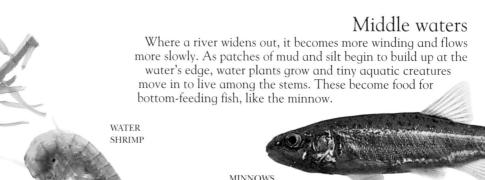

MINNOWS

*Slimy coating of mucus on body helps fish to glide through water*

TUBIFEX WORMS

FRESHWATER CRAYFISH

RAG-TAILED MAGGOT

BLOODWORM

## Dirty river

A river that lacks positive indicators and contains only rat-tailed maggots and tubifex orms (known as negative indicators) is in trouble. These creatures are adapted to living in polluted water with low levels of oxygen. The rat-tailed maggot (fly larva) has a special breathing tube that allows it to draw in oxygen from the air and the tubifex worm has a special ability to extract oxygen from the water.

## Crayfish shell

The freshwater crayfish chooses where it lives by the type of rocks found there. It only lives in ponds and lakes with hard water that flows over limestone or chalk. The calcium minerals in the water help to strengthen and protect the crayfish's hard outer shell.

*Eyes can look up and down*

## Oxygen rich

The rainbow trout is a
strong swimmer, able to cope
well with fast currents. The sources
of rivers draining the Rocky Mountains
of North America are fast flowing, well
oxygenated, and run over a clean gravel bottom.
They are the original home of the rainbow trout, which
is a fast-growing, short-lived member of the salmon family.
It has now been introduced by people to rivers all over the world.

*Pinkish-red rainbow sheen*

TENCH

BARBEL

YOUNG PIKE

## Fish preferences

Different sections of the river attract different
species. Tench prefer shallow lakes and slow
rivers, while shoals of barbels feed on the bottom
in clear waters. The pike is well-camouflaged
among the weeds, ready to ambush passing fish.

# Swamps

Mangrove swamps form in quiet tropical backwaters, where mud and silt pile up in river estuaries and lagoons. They create a half-way world between the land and the sea. The main plants growing here are mangroves, the only trees that can survive in salt water. Their tangled roots are home to an entire community of animals adapted to the rise and fall of the tides. As the tide goes out, sea snails, crabs, and mudskipper fish sift the damp mud for food, while hungry predators including a fish-eating snake and shrimp-eating frog, move down from the leafy canopy. Above the high-tide mark lives another group of animals. Birds nest in the branches, iguanas pluck fruits, monkeys feed on the leaves, and crabs climb the trees.

COMMON IGUANA

## Swamp lizard

The green iguana has long toes with sharp claws for climbing about in the branches of mangroves in Central America. Young ones catch insects, but older iguanas eat shoots, flowers, leaves, and fruits. Adults live alone, but young iguanas sometimes gather in groups. They rub chins and display to each other during the day. The young males fiercely guard their territories, often on branches overhanging water into which they can dive if danger threatens. For safety, the young iguanas all sleep together at night in the mangrove branches.

*Sharp-edged, hooked beak*

*Velvet, lettuce-like leave*

## Strong jaws

Slow-moving water in the swamps and creeks of the southern states of North America is home to the snapping turtle. It seldom swims but can clamber over the bottom by gripping plants and rocks with its long claws. The turtle generally lies on the bottom in shallow water, hidden by water plants and ready to snap at anything that looks edible.

SNAPPING TURTLE

## Floating plant

The water lettuce consists of a floating rosette of waterproof leaves. Each leaf is filled with air pockets to keep it above the surface. Underneath, its roots trail in the water. The lettuce spreads so rapidly that it can choke up waterways.

WATER LETTUCE

## Big-clawed crabs

At high tide, fiddler crabs remain in their burrows in the mud on the bottom of the mangrove swamp. At low tide, they emerge to feed. Females use both their claws to pick up mud and sift out food. Males can use only one because the other claw grows to an enormous size. Coloured bright blue, pink, purple, or white, this claw is used to send semaphore signals to other crabs. The crab waves its claw to attract females and frighten off rival males. If males enter into a fight, the giant claw can be used in one-arm combat.

## Extra roots

Mangroves are not alone in having special-support root systems. This Seychelles palm is found naturally only in the tropical rainforests covering the steep slopes of the Seychelles Islands. Here, it grows in the soggy ground at the bottom of wet river valleys or on the thin soils of the steep slopes. To anchor itself firmly in the difficult, wet conditions, the tree has stilted roots that splay out from the base of its trunk.

*Fine hairs protect the trunk*

*Emerging stilt-like root*

*Fiddler crab's long-stalked eyes keep watch for danger*

## Mangroves

The tangle of roots of the mangrove are home to many swamp creatures. The roots form an arch of scaffolding that sits on top of the mud like a raft. Mangroves take oxygen directly from the air. To do this, they have evolved patches of spongy tissue in the bark of special roots that project above the surface of the mud.

FIDDLER CRAB

# Oceans

The oceans cover 71 per cent of the surface of the planet, yet it is the least-explored habitat on Earth. Some of the largest living creatures are found here, together with a wide range of marine life that includes members of almost every known group of animals. Out in the middle of the ocean, high-speed hunters prey on slow swimmers, which live at the water's surface and graze on the blooms of tiny plants. More colourful creatures are found close to the shore, where their camouflage blends in with rocks and corals. Most of the creatures living deep in the sea rely on the dead bodies that sink down from above as their source of food. Other deep-sea dwellers are equipped with special light organs – these help them to find their way in the twilight world of the ocean's mid-waters.

## Flying ray

Skates and rays copy the movement of rippling waves to make their way through water. By beating their pectoral fins, or wings, up and down they seem to "fly" through the water.

RAY

BLACKTIP REEF SHARK

## Shark patrol

The blacktip reef shark is an aggressive and active hunter that grows to about 2.4 m (8 ft) long. It patrols the outer edges of coral reefs, grabbing small fish, squid, octopuses, and shrimps. Small groupers, or bottom-dwelling fish, are sometimes on the menu, but when groupers grow up the hunter may become the hunted. A large 36 kg (80 lb) grouper was once caught and in its stomach was a 46 cm (18 in) blacktip reef shark!

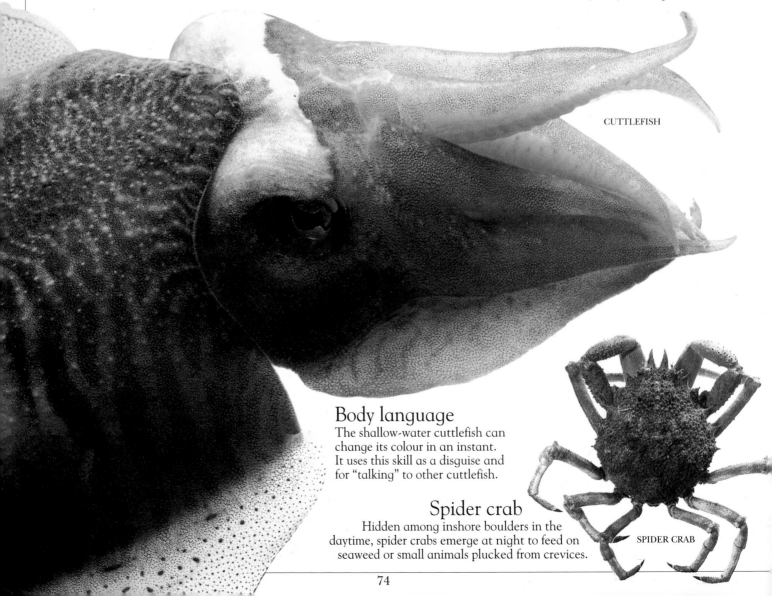

CUTTLEFISH

## Body language

The shallow-water cuttlefish can change its colour in an instant. It uses this skill as a disguise and for "talking" to other cuttlefish.

## Spider crab

Hidden among inshore boulders in the daytime, spider crabs emerge at night to feed on seaweed or small animals plucked from crevices.

SPIDER CRAB

GARFISH

## Ocean needles
The garfish, like flying fish, escapes predators by leaping from the water and skimming across the surface. It can leave the water with such a speed it has been known to spear people and even kill them.

*Long tail steers the shark through the water*

## Spring catch
The clown triggerfish lives in coral reefs. When asleep or being chased, the fish can lodge itself firmly into a crevice by raising its spines and locking them into place. The colourful patterns of the triggerfish break up its outline against rocks, seaweed, and corals, keeping it hidden from enemies.

*Spine can be locked upright*

CLOWN
TRIGGERFISH

*Zooplankton, or microscopic sea creatures*

GREY SEAL

*Hind flippers can be brought forwards for walking on land*

## Ocean drifters
The young of sea creatures, such as jellyfish, crabs, and marine worms, drift about on the surface of the open ocean. They feed on tiny plants floating on the water's surface.

## Blubber-wrapped
The grey seal keeps warm with a thick layer of fatty blubber under its skin. It spends much of its time in coastal waters, pulling itself out of the water occasionally to rest, moult, or breed on land. In the water, the seal uses its front flippers to propel its body and its rear flippers to steer it. In this way, it is able to make high-speed chases after fish, which it swallows whole.

# Islands

When volcanoes erupt from the bottom of the sea, some reach the surface and form new islands. Plants and animals are borne there on the wind or drift there on the ocean currents. As they establish themselves, an island community of unique animals is created. There are unexpected giants and dwarfs. Tortoises on Aldabra in the Indian Ocean grow to a gigantic size, and fruit flies on Hawaii are ten times bigger than those found elsewhere. The Hawaiian looper caterpillar has turned to flies as a source of food and is the only meat-eating caterpillar in the world. Some birds, such as New Zealand's kakapo, a giant parrot, have become flightless as there are no predators. On the downside, the isolation of island communities makes them vulnerable to pests – such as rats and cats, introduced by people – and they can be quickly wiped out.

*Coconut shell broken open by a robber crab*

ROBBER CRAB

*Powerful coconut-cracking claws*

*Strengthened shield protects the crab's rear*

VIOLIN BEETLE

*Long, flat wing covers*

## Violin beetle

The shape of this ground beetle has earned it the name of violin beetle. Its long wing covers are greatly enlarged and flattened. This enables the beetle to make its home between the layers of bracket fungi attached to the trunks of trees in rain forests on Indonesian islands.

## Coconut-eating crab

The robber crab of Pacific and Indian Ocean islands emerges from its burrow at night to eat the soft white meat of coconuts. It can climb trees, but more usually searches for coconuts that have fallen to the ground. It chips open the shell using its formidable claws. Although they are land crabs, the female robber crab lays her eggs in the sea. After the first growth stage, the larvae leave the water and occupy shells like hermit crabs. The shells are discarded and the miniature crabs emerge from the moist sand.

*Midrib mimics the central vein of a leaf*

LEAF
INSECT

## Leaf mimic

Leaves are a common feature of most habitats, so it is not surprising that some animals imitate them for protective camouflage. This leaf insect lives on the island of Java. Its body and skin have the same colour and pattern of a real leaf, including a midrib, veins, and a brown patch that resembles a dying leaf.

*Skin colour changes to match the background*

MADAGASCAN
CHAMELEON

SOUTHERN
CASSOWARY

*Tail is able to grip onto twigs and branches*

## Flightless

The cassowary is a formidable bird. One kick from its powerful legs and dagger-like claws can seriously injure an attacker. It is the largest land animal on the island of New Guinea where it lives in dense forests and feeds mainly on fruits that drop from trees. Like several other island birds it is flightless, using its long legs to run from danger rather than fly.

## Sticky tongue

This curious chameleon from Madagascar is a slow climber, holding on to twigs with its grasping feet and tail. Its stalked eyes move independently for all-round vision and are protected with scaly eyelids. To catch insects and spiders, chameleons send out their sticky-tipped tongue which can reach further than the length of their bodies.

# Migration

Animals need to be in the right place at the right time. For some, this means migrating, or moving home, to find warmer weather, new and plentiful supplies of food, or a safer environment in which to bring up their offspring. For example, birds journey back and forth across the world each year, while mountain goats might simply move to lower slopes because it is too cold for them to survive on the peaks during winter. It is still not known how these creatures know when and where to go. It is thought that some may use the Sun and stars to navigate, while others can detect and follow lines of magnetic force across the surface of the Earth.

MONARCH
BUTTERFLY

## Long flight

After spending the winter in Mexico, Monarch butterflies travel back to North America. There they lay their eggs on the milkweed plants on which their caterpillars feed. After pupation, the next generation of butterflies returns to the warm weather in Mexico.

*Sharp beak for pecking at caterpillars*

DIDRIC
CUCKOO

*Green colouring blends in with trees and grasses*

## Breeding season

Didric cuckoos from East Africa stay there all year. However, those from West and Central Africa live on the edge of the Sahara desert where food becomes scarce in the dry season. Flying mainly in the cool of the night, the birds migrate in October to the more fertile forests and papyrus swamps in Central Africa, where they can be certain of finding caterpillars, their main food. They return to the northern parts of West Africa at the start of the rainy season in March.

SPERM
WHALE

ATLANTIC
SALMON

## Warmer waters

Female sperm whales and their calves remain in warm waters throughout their lives. In contrast, the huge bulls (males) migrate to colder waters each year. There they feed on the large supplies of food available during the summer months. They also dive deep to catch large squid. As winter approaches, the bulls return to warm waters to breed.

*Only the sperm whale is able to dive deep enough to catch squid*

## Heading upstream

Salmon grow into adults in the ocean but when the time comes to breed, they return to the rivers where they were born. They head upstream, travelling against the current and overcoming rapids and waterfalls to reach the exact spot where they first hatched out of their eggs. It is thought they use the sense of smell to find the right place.

Wing colours
blend with
cave walls

BOGONG
MOTH

## Night flight

Bogong moths spend the hot, dry summer
months in caves in the Australian Alps,
a mountain range in southeast Australia.
When the weather starts to cool down in
autumn, the moths travel north to breeding
sites in the outback. On the way, they rest
out of the Sun by day and continue their
journey in the cool of dusk and night-time.

Head arches up
when the zebra
senses danger

Stripes provide
camouflage when
zebra runs across
grassland

Strong hind legs
are used to kick
out at predators
when threatened

PAIR OF ADULT
ZEBRAS

## Pastures new

Herds of zebra accompany the much
larger herds of wildebeest on their long
migrations across East Africa. Both
animals move on to find new pastures
of the lush, green grass that shoots up
after the rainy season. By staying close
to the wildebeest, the zebras gain
additional protection from attack
by predators during the journey.

# Ecology

Some animals live together in harmony, others live on or inside other animals and cause them harm. The study of these relationships is known as ecology. An animal cannot survive in isolation because it depends on plants or other animals for food or protection. In turn, the animal is often a source of food for other animals or even carnivorous plants. There are two types of food dependency – one is called a food chain, in which larger animals eat smaller animals, and the other is called a food web. This is a more complex network of animals that eat more than one type of food. Some plants may produce poisons or have thorns to stop them being eaten by animals, but many animals have found ways to overcome these defences.

PISTACHIO GALL

*Protective case forms around aphids*

HERMIT CRAB AND SEA ANEMONE

## Plants and animals

When the pistachio tree detects the presence of colonies of tiny aphids, its tissues form a protective case, known as a gall, around the aphids. The insects living there receive a steady supply of food from the tree. In return, they move or sow the tree's seeds to a place where they will make new plants. Many trees form this kind of partnership with insects.

*Cuckoo chick is raised by foster parents*

YOUNG CUCKOO

*Stinging tentacles deter predators*

## Animals together

The hermit crab and sea anemone live together in a relationship where they each benefit. The sea anemone is carried around by the crab, which enables it to feed in a variety of places. In return, the stinging tentacles of the sea anemone shield the hermit crab from attack.

## Crafty parent

When she is ready to lay her egg, the female cuckoo distracts a female bird of another species away from her nest. The cuckoo takes over the nest, throws out the other bird's eggs, and replaces them with her own single egg. She then leaves the nest and the original owner returns. When the cuckoo chick hatches out, the unsuspecting female raises the cuckoo's offspring instead of her own.

# Food chain

Some creatures depend on others as a source of food and are part of a feeding procession, or food chain. For example, the great white shark finds itself at the top of a food chain because it is rarely eaten. Next in line are seals, sea lions, and large fish, on which the shark feeds. In turn, these creatures eat smaller fish, which eat shrimps. The shrimps feed on tiny sea creatures known as plankton. Each of these animals depends on the existence of the others – without plankton, the shark would find itself without anything to eat.

PLANKTON

SMALL
FISH

LARGE FISH

GREAT
WHITE
SHARK

*Sharp, triangular
teeth tear up flesh*

*Crab moves along
on jointed limbs*

# Conservation

## Extinct?

Golden toads were last sighted in Costa Rica in 1990. Since then, the toads have vanished, presumed extinct, but the reason why remains is a mystery.

The protection of threatened environments, close monitoring of endangered species, and a determined effort to reduce pollution are just some of the ways in which conservation is helping the animal kingdom to survive the drawbacks of the modern world. Sadly, some species have already fallen victim to deforestation, excessive hunting, or pollution, but others have been saved from the brink of extinction thanks to our growing awareness of the hazards they face. The scope of conservation work lies not only in protecting the habitat and lifestyle of endangered species, but also in changing the ways in which we live so as to reduce their harmful effects on other animals. To this end, conservationists want industry to use resources such as glass and paper that are reusable, to replace depleted forests, and to restrict fishing to varieties that are quick to reproduce. Many governments are now actively encouraging people to be fuel conscious in their use of electricity or petrol, and place heavy fines on industries that generate excessive pollution.

ADULT
REINDEER
AND CALF

*Reindeer became contaminated after grazing on radioactive land*

## Radioactive

Pollution that originates in one place can affect plants and animals many thousands of kilometres away in another part of the world. When a nuclear reactor exploded at Chernobyl, Ukraine, in 1986, the radioactive fallout reached Lapland. Here the semi-domestic reindeer, feeding on contaminated lichens, became radioactive and their meat was banned for human consumption.
Constant monitoring of Arctic wildlife and the affected habitats need to be maintained from now on to ensure that the species survive this incident and recover their numbers in due course.

BOTTLE-NOSED
DOLPHIN

ORGAN PIPE
CORAL

## Banned nets

In the open ocean, large fishing boats set drift nets that are several miles long and float near the sea's surface. Dolphins, whales, seals, and sea turtles often become caught up in these invisible, floating traps and drown. To prevent any further unnecessary deaths, the United Nations has now banned the use of long, drift nets for fishing.

## Sea jewels

The fragile habitat of coral reefs provides an important home to a variety of marine species. Its use as jewellery and ornaments in South East Asia and the Caribbean threatens the survival of coral and its dependants. Many countries have now banned the collection, sale, and export of coral to help preserve this precious habitat.

*Unusual golden-coloured fur makes monkey very desirable to collectors*

LEOPARD

*Food becomes harder to find as farming takes over the leopard's hunting ground*

## Golden monkey

Today, golden lion tamarins are probably the most closely monitored animals on Earth. Thanks to a successful captive breeding programme that returned tamarins to the wild, the species was saved from certain extinction – their numbers were reduced to less than 100 in 1980. The cause of their decline was the growing trade in exotic animals. The tamarins were taken from their homes in the tropical forests of south-east Brazil, and sold on to wealthy pet collectors around the world.

VERVET MONKEY

GOLDEN
LION TAMARIN

## Shrinking habitat

The leopard is the most adaptable and widely distributed big cat, yet its living space is shrinking rapidly due to the demand for farmland. Only scattered populations survive today in the rest of Africa and Asia where it was once common. However, protected areas set up in East Africa have kept the number of leopards to an acceptable level.

# Animal records

Every type of animal has a remarkable and unique feature, such as the speed at which it can run, its ability to change colour, or simply its sheer size or strength. For example, fleas can survive 18 months without eating, sponges can regrow any part of their body that is damaged, and woodpeckers can move their heads at more than twice the speed of a bullet when searching for grubs in tree trunks and branches.

*Spiky crest runs along the length of the back and tail*

TUATARA

*Clawed feet used for digging daytime burrows*

## Longest life

The tuatara is the most ancient lizard-like reptile on Earth. It is almost identical to reptiles that were living 140 million years ago. Found only in New Zealand, it grows very slowly, often taking up to 50 years to reach maturity. An individual might live for 120 years or more.

*Fast-beating wings enable hummingbird to hover in mid-air*

*Long, thin bill sucks up nectar from flowers*

CUBAN BEE HUMMINGBIRD

## Smallest bird

The world's smallest living bird is the tiny Cuban bee hummingbird. At 57 mm (2.5 in) long, the male bird is smaller than the female and weighs less than a large moth.

## Longest snake

At lengths of up to 10 m (33 ft), reticulated pythons easily win the title of the world's longest snakes. They are found in Southeast Asia, where they live among the leaf litter on the forest floor. They feed on small mammals, lizards, and even other snakes.

# Highest jumper

Thanks to a special energy-storing protein in its body, the common flea can leap up to 34 cm (13.5 in) high in the air. It literally flies with its legs, and can do so 600 times an hour for up to three days when trying to find a new host on which it can feed.

COMMON
FLEA

*Head is held high on long, featherless neck*

*Long back legs provide lift-off*

ADULT
GIRAFFE

*Long neck contains just 7 neck bones*

# Biggest bird

The world's largest living bird is the African ostrich. Male birds stand about 2.4 m (8 ft) tall and weigh up to 127 kg (280 lb). Females are smaller. The ostrich is flightless but not defenceless. It can run at high speed, up to 48 kmh (30 mph), and has a powerful kick to fend off attackers.

*Long legs can run at high speed*

OSTRICH

# Tallest browser

The tallest animal is the giraffe. The male grows to about 5.3 m (17 ft) in height, although individual heights of 5.8 m (19 ft) have been recorded. Giraffes feed on thorny trees on the plains of Africa, using their long necks to reach the tastiest leaves that grow on the topmost branches.

# Detecting animals

Animals are very good at keeping out of sight and hiding themselves from enemies. However it is possible to find out whether they are present or have recently passed through an area by looking for the signs and tracks they leave behind. Hairs, wool, or fur may have caught on fence posts, moulted feathers tangled in bushes, droppings or pellets deposited on the ground, bones and shells left lying around, and footprints or tracks left in sand or soft mud. With each sign or track, you can identify the animal that was there, and in some cases you can also work out what it was doing there.

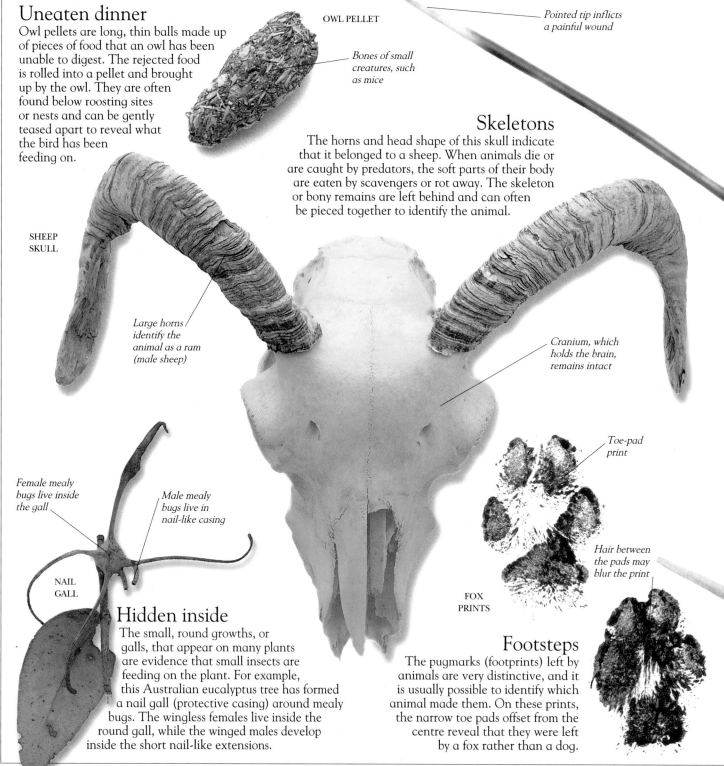

## Uneaten dinner

Owl pellets are long, thin balls made up of pieces of food that an owl has been unable to digest. The rejected food is rolled into a pellet and brought up by the owl. They are often found below roosting sites or nests and can be gently teased apart to reveal what the bird has been feeding on.

OWL PELLET

Pointed tip inflicts a painful wound

Bones of small creatures, such as mice

## Skeletons

The horns and head shape of this skull indicate that it belonged to a sheep. When animals die or are caught by predators, the soft parts of their body are eaten by scavengers or rot away. The skeleton or bony remains are left behind and can often be pieced together to identify the animal.

SHEEP SKULL

Large horns identify the animal as a ram (male sheep)

Cranium, which holds the brain, remains intact

Toe-pad print

Female mealy bugs live inside the gall

Male mealy bugs live in nail-like casing

Hair between the pads may blur the print

NAIL GALL

FOX PRINTS

## Hidden inside

The small, round growths, or galls, that appear on many plants are evidence that small insects are feeding on the plant. For example, this Australian eucalyptus tree has formed a nail gall (protective casing) around mealy bugs. The wingless females live inside the round gall, while the winged males develop inside the short nail-like extensions.

## Footsteps

The pugmarks (footprints) left by animals are very distinctive, and it is usually possible to identify which animal made them. On these prints, the narrow toe pads offset from the centre reveal that they were left by a fox rather than a dog.

# Abandoned shells

Empty shells can often be found among the shingle on seashores. They were once lived in by molluscs such as abalones. These shellfish have soft bodies that are protected by the hard, ridged shells. When the abalones die, their bodies fall away from the shells, which are then washed up on the seashore. By finding out which animal used to live in the shell, you can learn more about the creatures living below the sand or on nearby rocks.

*Rainbow-coloured lining is known as mother-of-pearl*

*Darker, wing feather*

ABALONE SHELL

*Inner flight feathers*

*Hollow quills give a warning rattle when shaken*

# Tell-tale feathers

Birds moult (lose) and replace their feathers regularly. The pattern on each feather reveals the type of bird that it has fallen from. For example, the pinkish colour of these feathers are typical of a flamingo. The colour comes from the dye in the shrimps and other crustaceans on which it feeds.

FLAMINGO FEATHERS

CRESTED PORCUPINE'S QUILLS

*Thrush pulls the snail's body out from the broken shell*

# Self-defence

Some animals deliberately leave reminders to warn away enemies. Porcupines run backwards into their enemy when threatened. Their sharp quills stab the attacker and detach themselves from the porcupine's body. Anyone coming across the discarded spines then knows that a porcupine has passed by.

BROKEN SNAIL SHELLS

# House break-in

These broken snail shells show that a thrush has been at work. The shells are usually found on a flat rock or hard surface. Known as the thrush's anvil, this is where the bird smashes the shell over and over again until it breaks apart. Using its sharp, beak, the thrush can then reach the soft parts of the snail inside and eat the tasty flesh.

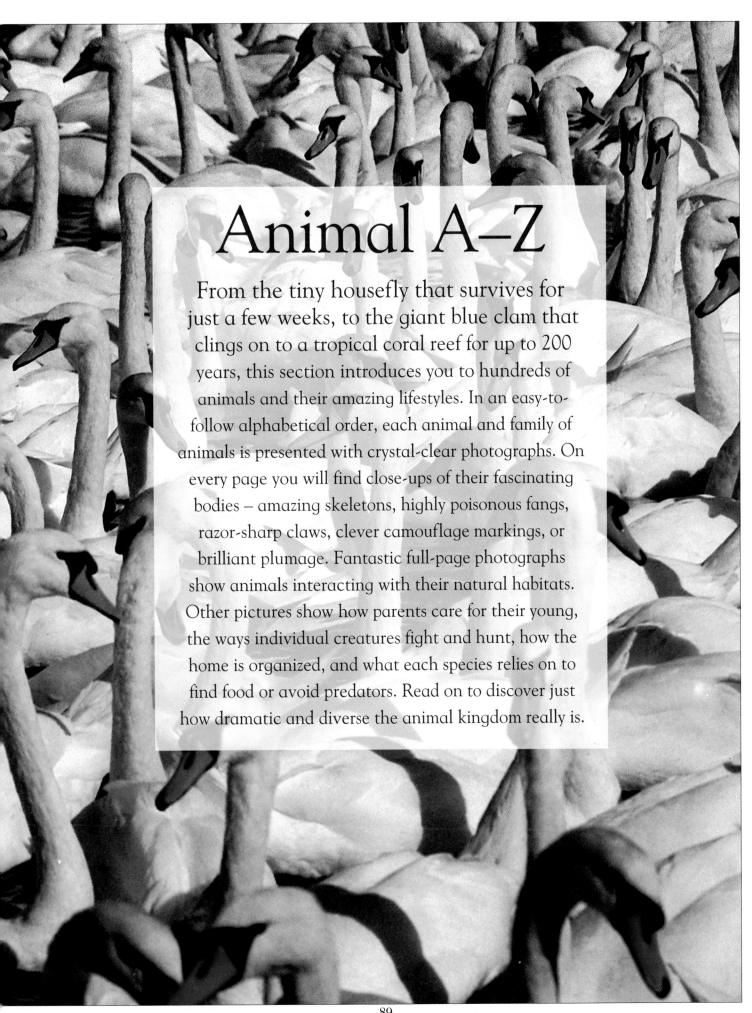

# Animal A–Z

From the tiny housefly that survives for just a few weeks, to the giant blue clam that clings on to a tropical coral reef for up to 200 years, this section introduces you to hundreds of animals and their amazing lifestyles. In an easy-to-follow alphabetical order, each animal and family of animals is presented with crystal-clear photographs. On every page you will find close-ups of their fascinating bodies – amazing skeletons, highly poisonous fangs, razor-sharp claws, clever camouflage markings, or brilliant plumage. Fantastic full-page photographs show animals interacting with their natural habitats. Other pictures show how parents care for their young, the ways individual creatures fight and hunt, how the home is organized, and what each species relies on to find food or avoid predators. Read on to discover just how dramatic and diverse the animal kingdom really is.

# AARDVARKS

Long, rabbit-like ears can be closed to keep out dust and insects

Stocky body has sparse covering of bristly hair

ADULT AARDVARK

THE BURROWING, PIG-LIKE animals known as aardvarks live on their own. They stay underground during the day, resting in burrows. At night, they travel long distances, using their super senses of smell and hearing to find termites and ants. They follow zigzag paths, with their long snout close to the ground to sniff out prey. If threatened by enemies, such as leopards or lions, aardvarks can dig very quickly and disappear below ground. They may also kick and slash the attacker with their claws.

## DUST FILTERS

Aardvarks have stout bodies with short, strong legs and feet armed with flattened claws. Their eyes are small, but they have long pig-like snouts. Hairs around the nostrils filter out any dust or small insects thrown up by the aardvarks when they dig. Their large ears are normally held upright but can be closed or folded to stop insects getting into them during feeding.

Termite nest forms a tall tower

SCALE

## DIGGING FOR FOOD

Termites, one of the aardvark's favourite foods, live in towering nests made out of earth. The aardvark rips the nest open using its powerful front legs and spoon-shaped claws. It laps up the insects using its 30-cm (12-in) long sticky tongue, and then demolishes another section of the mound to find more food.

Cheek teeth resemble short columns with flat tops

AARDVARK AND TERMITE MOUND

AARDVARK SKULL

### FACT BOX

**Family:** Orycteropodidae

**Habitat:** Grasslands, open woodlands, forests

**Distribution:** Africa

**Food:** Termites, ants

**No. of young:** 1 or 2

**Gestation period:** 7 months

**Lifespan:** Up to 20 years

**Size:** 1–1.6 m (3–5 ft)

## INSECT CRUSHERS

Aardvarks only have teeth in the back of their jaws. These flat, cheek teeth crush insects. They are constantly growing and never wear down. Unlike teeth in other mammals, an aardvark's teeth do not have a protective covering of hard, white enamel.

### Find out more

ANTEATERS 95
MAMMALS 239
MEAT-EATERS 32

# ALBATROSSES

THE 14 TYPES OF ALBATROSS belong to a group of birds known as tube-noses. This name comes from the distinctive tube-like nostrils that lie on each side of the birds' long, strongly hooked bills. Albatrosses are so big and heavy that they need a headwind to get airborne, either by making a long run across the ground or by launching themselves off the edge of a cliff. They spend most of their lives in the air and only visit land to breed. Occasionally, they are blown onto land by a severe storm.

WANDERING ALBATROSS

Bird is carried by air currents

## FLIGHT

Albatrosses save energy by soaring on the strong air currents above the waves of open seas. Soaring uses very little energy. It also allows the bird to search for food and travel long distances without constantly beating its wings to stay airborne.

SKELETON WING OF AN ALBATROSS

Finger bone

## WINGS

Albatrosses have extremely long wings for soaring and gliding. At up to 3.6 m (almost 12 ft), the wandering albatross has the longest wingspan of all the world's birds.

Large bill is sharply hooked to seize fish and squid

The chick is left alone in the nest for several days between feeds

Wing attaches to shoulder by a ball-and-socket joint

## NESTING

Most albatrosses build mounded nests made from huge piles of soil and plants. The birds breed mainly on small, remote islands, choosing cliff tops or ledges as their nesting sites. Some of them do not start producing their young until they are 15 years old. The parents take it in turn to look after the single egg, which hatches after about 11 weeks.

ALBATROSS CHICK

SCALE

## COURTSHIP

In the breeding season, albatrosses perform elaborate courtship displays. They stretch out their wings, dance, rattle their bills, bow deeply, or point their heads and necks skywards.

Head and neck stretches up towards the sky

Huge wings are held wide open

WANDERING ALBATROSSES

### FACT BOX

**Family:** Diomedeidae

**Habitat:** Open sea, except for visiting islands to breed

**Distribution:** Southern hemisphere and North Pacific

**Food:** Squid and fish

**No. of eggs:** 1

**Lifespan:** Up to 60 years

**Size:** 68–135 cm (27–53 in)

### *Find out more*

BIRDS 115
EGGS AND NESTS 42
OCEANS 74

# AMPHIBIANS

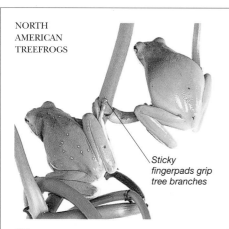

*Sticky
fingerpads grip
tree branches*

THE MAJOR GROUP OF ANIMALS called amphibians includes frogs, toads, newts, salamanders, and the less well-known caecilians. All amphibians have moist skin, but without the scales of reptiles. Some live entirely in water, but most live mainly on land, and only return to water to breed. Those that live on land need moisture to survive as their skins are not waterproof. Most lay jelly-covered eggs called spawn, but some amphibians give birth to live young.

## TREE LIFE

Some frogs living in warmer parts of the world have adapted to a life in the trees. They have toes equipped with large, disc-shaped suckers. These allow them to grip tightly to surfaces, including smooth, slippery leaves and branches, as they climb about.

*Round pupil
lets in plenty
of light*

MANDARIN
SALAMANDER

## SKIN COLOUR

Some amphibians, such as the Asiatic painted frog, camouflage themselves by using their green or dull skin colour to merge with leaves or other plants. Other amphibians are brightly coloured, often to warn enemies to stay away, as they can leak poison from special glands in their skin.

FEMALE ASIAN
PAINTED FROG

MARBLED
NEWT

## SENSES

Amphibians that live in water are able to detect movement. A series of lateral lines along their backs are sensitive to changes in pressure caused by moving objects. Many newts and salamanders also have a keen sense of smell and can detect food under water.

*Vertical pupil
adjusts quickly to
a change in light*

*Large, well-
developed
eyes provide
good vison*

RED-EYED
TREEFROG

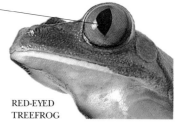

ASIAN TREE
TOAD

*Lateral lines
detect movement
in water*

AFRICAN
CLAWED FROG

## FACT BOX

**Class**: Amphibia

**Habitat:** Mainly in moist places, such as streamsides, marshes, and wet forests. Some can survive in deserts

**Distribution:** Worldwide, except for polar regions

**Food:** All adults are meat-eaters, feeding on insects, slugs, mice, and earthworms

## PUPIL SHAPE

Newts, salamanders, and some frogs have round pupils. Frogs that are active at night have vertical pupils which respond quickly to a change in light conditions. Horizontal pupils are common in frogs that are active during the daytime.

## CLOSE TO WATER
Like most amphibians, frogs need to return to water to breed in spring, often using the same site year after year. Here, common frogs are gathering together to mate in a pond, where they will also lay their eggs. Water is important for all amphibians, as it helps to keep their skin moist and prevent it from cracking and drying out.

# GETTING AROUND

Amphibians were the first vertebrates (animals with backbones) to develop limbs, emerge from the water, and live at least part of their lives on land. Salamanders and newts can run on land and some are also good swimmers. Some frogs are great jumpers, while others swim well or burrow into soil.

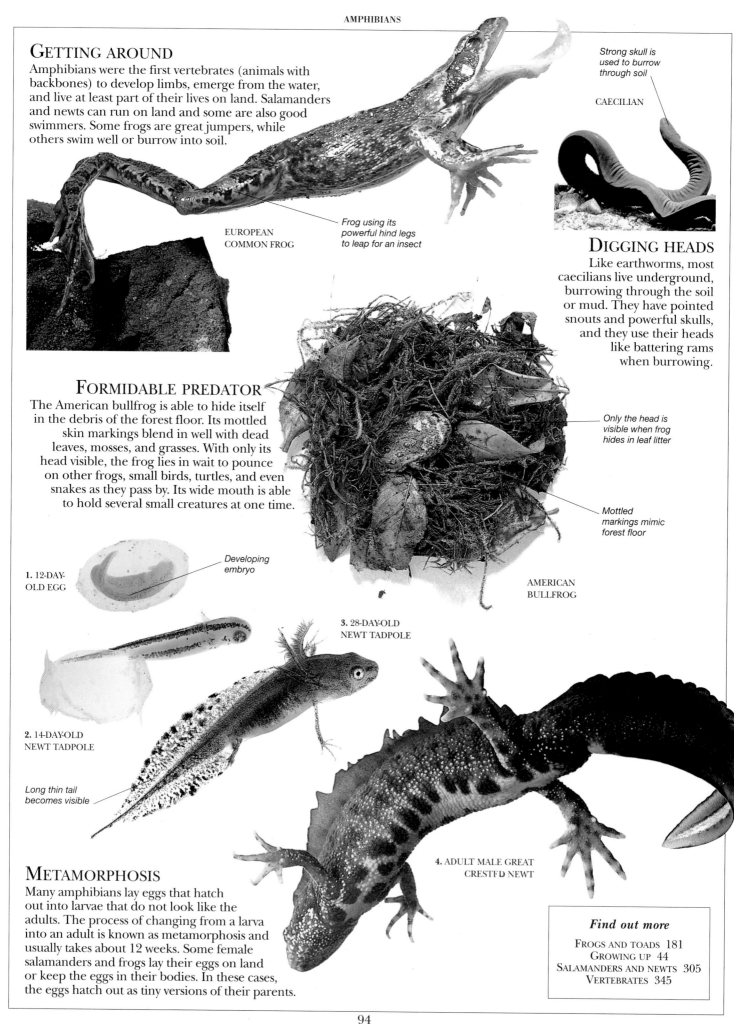

*Strong skull is used to burrow through soil*

CAECILIAN

EUROPEAN COMMON FROG

*Frog using its powerful hind legs to leap for an insect*

# DIGGING HEADS

Like earthworms, most caecilians live underground, burrowing through the soil or mud. They have pointed snouts and powerful skulls, and they use their heads like battering rams when burrowing.

# FORMIDABLE PREDATOR

The American bullfrog is able to hide itself in the debris of the forest floor. Its mottled skin markings blend in well with dead leaves, mosses, and grasses. With only its head visible, the frog lies in wait to pounce on other frogs, small birds, turtles, and even snakes as they pass by. Its wide mouth is able to hold several small creatures at one time.

*Only the head is visible when frog hides in leaf litter*

*Mottled markings mimic forest floor*

AMERICAN BULLFROG

**1.** 12-DAY-OLD EGG

*Developing embryo*

**3.** 28-DAY-OLD NEWT TADPOLE

**2.** 14-DAY-OLD NEWT TADPOLE

*Long thin tail becomes visible*

**4.** ADULT MALE GREAT CRESTED NEWT

# METAMORPHOSIS

Many amphibians lay eggs that hatch out into larvae that do not look like the adults. The process of changing from a larva into an adult is known as metamorphosis and usually takes about 12 weeks. Some female salamanders and frogs lay their eggs on land or keep the eggs in their bodies. In these cases, the eggs hatch out as tiny versions of their parents.

***Find out more***

FROGS AND TOADS 181
GROWING UP 44
SALAMANDERS AND NEWTS 305
VERTEBRATES 345

# ANTEATERS

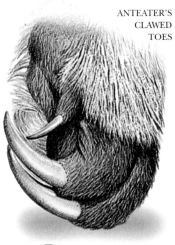

ANTEATER'S CLAWED TOES

GIANT ANTEATERS LIVE IN GRASSLAND and open woodland. They feed on ants and termites, which they grind between hard bumps in their mouths as they have no teeth. They have long, probing snouts, small ears and eyes, black-and-white shoulder stripes, and bushy tails. Anteaters use their powerful front legs and long claws to break open ant and termite nests. When threatened by a predator, they either run away with an awkward gallop, or grab their attacker and slash it with their strong claws. Some smaller types of anteater live in trees.

## STICKY LICKER

The giant anteater's tongue is an incredible 60 cm (2 ft) long. It has tiny backward-pointing spines, is covered with sticky saliva, and can be flicked in and out about 150 times a minute. This makes the tongue ideal for scooping up ants and termites from their broken nests. Giant anteaters can eat more than 30,000 insects, plus their eggs and larvae, each day.

GIANT ANTEATER'S TONGUE

Ants and termites captured by saliva and spines on tongue

### FACT BOX

**Family:** Myrmecophagidae

**Habitat:** Tropical forests, grasslands

**Distribution:** Central and South America

**Food:** Ants, termites

**No. of young:** 1

**Lifespan:** Up to 20 years

**Size:** 15–120 cm (0.5–4 ft)

## DIGGING TOOLS

The second and third toes of the anteater's front feet are equipped with long, curved claws. The anteater uses these strong claws, as well as its powerful front legs, to break open ant and termite nests, or anything else that might conceal insect prey. To protect its claws and keep them sharp, the anteater walks on its knuckles with its claws tucked inwards.

SCALE

GIANT ANTEATER

Anteater sniffs in search of food around rotting wood

## FOOD FORAGE

Anteaters use their excellent sense of smell to detect the faintest whiff of food. When an ant or termite mound is found, the anteater claws it open, pushes its snout into the hole, and starts to feed. They are careful not to destroy the nest and only feed for a short time, so that they can return to the same place to feed at another time.

### Find out more

AARDVARKS 90
ARMADILLOS 99
SLOTHS 321

# ANTS

BULLDOG
ANT

ANTS ARE INSECTS THAT LIVE in well-organized groups called colonies, which may contain hundreds, thousands, or even millions of ants. Many ants live in an underground maze of tunnels. Within the nest, one or several queen ants lay eggs, while workers carry out the day-to-day running of the nest. They fetch food for the adults and larvae (young ants), enlarge and clean the nest, and defend their home when danger threatens. When the colony is well established, young queens and males hatch out. These winged insects fly away and mate, so the young queens can produce new generations of ants.

Fierce jaws can
give a painful nip

## WELL-ARMED

Some species have large worker ants called soldiers, with huge heads and powerful jaws that bite. They squirt acid from a gland in their rear to make the wound more painful.

SCALE

Waist

Worker ants have
no wings

Jaws

WOOD
ANT

### FACT BOX

**Family:** Formicidae

**Habitat:** On land, ranging from rainforests to deserts

**Distribution:** Worldwide except Arctic and Antarctic

**Food:** Plants, leaf fungus, animals

**No. of eggs:** Up to 30,000

**Lifespan:** 25 to 30 years

**Size:** Up to 2.5 cm (1 in)

Hard body

## TINY BUT STRONG

There are more than 14,000 different kinds of ant. Most are dark in colour, and have hard bodies with very narrow "waists". The wingless worker ants are strong enough to lift up to ten times their own weight.

Jointed antennae
used for smelling,
touching, tasting,
and hearing

ANTS
LOOKING
FOR FOOD

Ants communicate
mainly through smell
and touch

## ANT ARMIES

Fierce armies of ants will march across the forest floor, killing and eating other insects, and even large animals that cross their path. When a colony of ants is threatened by predators or a rival nest, the workers swarm out to protect their queen and larvae. Some species even take young ants from other nests to use them as slaves.

### Find out more

BEES 111
DEFENCE 34
INSECTS 212
TERMITES 337
WASPS 351

# APES

THERE ARE TWO FAMILIES OF APES – the gibbons, or lesser apes, and the great apes, which include gorillas, orangutans, chimpanzees, and bonobos. Orang-utans live on their own, except for mothers with young, but the other apes all live in groups. Apes are large, intelligent creatures that live mainly in forests and are generally plant-eaters. The easiest way to tell an ape from a monkey is that only monkeys have tails.

## APE BODIES

Apes are tailless, have long arms and grasping hands and feet, with nails instead of claws. They are active during the daytime and have excellent eyesight. Their ability to see in colour helps them to find ripe fruit to feed on.

*Fur coat helps to keep apes warm and dry*

*Apes' arms are longer than their legs*

LOWLAND GORILLA

## MOVEMENT

An ape's arms are important for helping it to move about. Orangutans and gibbons use their arms to hold on to branches and swing through the trees. Chimpanzees and gorillas take their body weight on their strong arms as they travel along the ground.

SIAMANG GIBBON

*Legs are left to swing freely as gibbon moves through the trees*

*Chimpanzee is using a stick to collect termites*

CHIMPANZEE

## SMART APES

Apes have well-developed brains and are able to solve problems. They pass on their knowledge, such as how to use sticks and stones as tools, to their young.

### FACT BOX

**Family:** Great apes: Pongidae; Lesser apes: Hylobatidae

**Habitat:** Tropical forests, woodland, and grassland.

**Distribution:** Orang-utans and gibbons live in Southeast Asia; Africa is home to gorillas, chimpanzees, and bonobos.

**Food:** Gibbons and gorillas feed on fruits, shoots, and leaves; chimpanzees feed on plants, insects, and monkeys.

FEMALE LOWLAND
GORILLA AND
YOUNG

## PYGMY CHIMPANZEE

Bonobos can be recognized by
their small heads, distinctive
black faces, and slender,
graceful bodies. They are
slightly smaller than
common chimpanzees
and spend a lot more
time in the trees.
Within their close-knit
social groups, female
bonobos are held in
high respect.

BONOBO
OR PYGMY
CHIMPANZEE

Long,
slender
limbs

## CHILDCARE

Apes usually have just one baby at a time.
Mothers suckle and carry their young
around for several years, so they could
not manage more than one at a time.
The young apes have a long childhood,
during which they learn how to survive
in the forest and how to behave towards
other apes. Some are not fully grown
until they are about 10–15 years old.

ALBINO
GORILLA

Bright orange coat
turns dark brown or
maroon with age

## UNUSUAL COAT

Unlike most gorillas, who usually have
brownish-grey coats and black skins,
this gorilla is a rarity because it is an
albino. This is a condition, known
as albinism, that occurs in mammals
and produces white or colourless
hair as well as pink or blue eyes. The
thickness of fur on a gorilla's coat can
vary depending on the environment.
Gorillas living in cool, mountain areas
usually have longer, thicker hair than
those living in the warm lowlands.

## TREE DWELLER

Orang-utans have such big
appetites that if they lived
together in large, social
groups there would not be
enough food to go round.
For this reason, they spend
most of their time living
alone in the trees.

Strong, hook-
like hands and
feet are used to
grip branches
or pick fruit

ORANG-UTAN

### Find out more

BABOONS 100
CHIMPANZEES 139
GIBBONS 185
GORILLAS 192
ORANG-UTANS 258

# ARMADILLOS

ALL 20 SPECIES OF ARMADILLO are protected by an impressive coat of armour, which runs from their heads to their tails. They live in forests, deserts, and grasslands in the south of the USA and in South America. Most armadillos rest in burrows during the daytime and come out at night to feed on plants and small creatures. To find ants and termites, they dig into the big nests with their powerful front feet and then lap up the insects with their long, sticky tongues.

Hairs grow between bands of plating

Rings of tough plates form armour

HAIRY ARMADILLO

Protective head shield

Underside has no armour

## BUILT-IN SHOVELS
Armadillos use their powerful front limbs and long claws for scooping out burrows where they can rest or hide. They dig at an amazing speed, thrusting their snouts into the ground to avoid swallowing the soil being shovelled out.

Short, solid bones

SKELETON OF AN ARMADILLO'S FRONT LIMB

Strong fingers tipped with large claws

## BODY PARTS
The armadillo's body is covered with an armoured coat made up of bands of horn-capped scutes (plates). A narrow, flexible layer of skin between the bands of armour allows the armadillo to move its legs. A large shield protects the armadillo's head.

LARGER HAIRY ARMADILLO

Legs are pulled in and shell is pressed hard against the ground when threatened

## SELF DEFENCE
The armadillo's coat of armour does not cover its underside. This means that a skilful predator can flip an armadillo over on to its back to attack its soft belly. To defend themselves when a predator approaches, some armadillos pull in their legs so that their armour presses firmly against the ground. Others roll themselves up into a tight ball that cannot be pulled apart.

SCALE

### FACT BOX

**Family:** Dasypodidae

**Habitat:** Savanna, pampas, and other grasslands; a few in forests

**Distribution:** Southern USA, South America

**Food:** Insects, small lizards, snakes, baby birds, mice, plants

**No. of young:** Usually 2–4

**Gestation period:** 60–120 days

**Size:** 30–150 cm (12–60 in)

*Find out more*

ANTEATERS 95
COURTSHIP AND MATING 38
DEFENCE 34
GRASSLANDS 64
SLOTHS 321

# BABOONS

HAMADRYAS
BABOON

THE MOST WIDESPREAD MEMBERS of the group known as Old World (meaning from Africa and Asia) monkeys are baboons. They have large heads, cheek pouches for storing food, and long, dog-like muzzles. The adult males are twice the size of females and have capes of long hair over their shoulders. Baboons live mainly on the ground, moving around on all fours, but they hide in trees at the first sign of danger. The most typical are the Hamadryas, Savanna, and Guinea baboons, which live in dry savanna and rocky areas.

## WARNING CALL

Baboons pull faces, signal with their tails, and make calling sounds to "talk" to each other. When warning the troop of danger, they raise the alarm with a dog-like bark.

SCALE

Baboon assumes "lookout" duty for its troop

OLIVE
BABOON

Typical bent tail

Close-set downwards pointing nostrils

Seat pads

## OUT IN THE OPEN

When they are in open spaces, for example at a watering hole, baboons keep a careful watch for lions and other predators. At night, they move up to the trees or high rocks for safety. They sleep sitting upright on the cushions of hard skin on their bottoms.

ADULT AND
YOUNG
HAMADRYAS
BABOONS

Large, rounded brain case

## THE BRAIN CASE

A baboon's skull protects its large brain as well as sense organs, such as the eyes and nose. Eyesight is important, so the eye sockets are large and protected by a bony ridge. Male baboon's have a much bigger skull than females, with large, pointed, canine teeth.

Squared-off molar teeth for grinding

Shovel-shaped incisor teeth

FEMALE
BABOON
SKULL

## HAREMS AND TROOPS

Hamadryas baboons live in harems – these are small groups of up to 12 females, led by just one adult male. Other types of baboon live in troops – large, close-knit groups made up of males and females.

### FACT BOX

**Family:** Cercopithecidae

**Habitat:** Grassland, scrub, rocky desert, and rainforest

**Distribution:** Africa, south of the Sahara, and southwest Arabia

**Food:** Grass, seeds, fruit, roots, insects, small animals, gazelles

**No. of young:** Usually one

**Size:** 50–100 cm (20–39 in)

### Find out more

APES 97
COMMUNICATION 26
MONKEYS 252

## GRASSLAND TRAVELS

Baboons are social animals, staying close together in troops of up to 200 individuals. These communities share their food, care for the young, and keep a constant watch for enemies. Baboons spend their days travelling across the savanna of Africa. They may walk up to 11 km (4.5 miles) a day, stopping to rest in shade during the heat of midday, or to sleep in acacia trees at night.

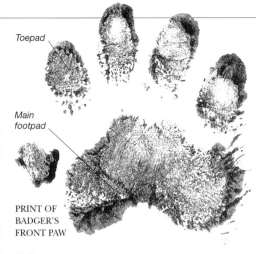

Toepad

Main
footpad

PRINT OF
BADGER'S
FRONT PAW

# BADGERS

TOGETHER WITH WEASELS AND OTTERS, badgers belong to a family of carnivores (meat-eaters). Badgers are nocturnal (night-time) animals, spending most of the day in their setts (underground burrows) and coming out at night to search for food. Their powerful jaws and crushing teeth are ideal for tackling a mixed diet of earthworms, fruits, roots, and small animals. They use their long snout and good sense of smell to find food.

## MAKING TRACKS

When badgers walk, the soles of their feet rest flat on the ground, leaving a paw print like this one. Both back and front feet have five toes, and each toe has a strong, sharp claw. These claws are useful when digging tunnels or grubbing around for food.

### FACT BOX

**Family:** Mustelidae

**Habitat:** Forests and woodland

**Distribution:** From Europe to China and Japan

**Food:** Earthworms, small animals, carrion, nuts, fruits,

**No. of young:** 2–6

**Lifespan:** Up to 12 years

**Size:** 56–90 cm (24–36 in)

Claws are raised
in defence

YOUNG
EURASIAN BADGER

## FAMILY LIFE

Badgers are playful animals. At dusk, both young badgers and adults often play near the entrance to the sett. Rolling on its back, a badger will raise its paws ready to strike out. Play helps to bond the family group together, and allows young badgers to practise the skills they will need to defend themselves as adults.

SCALE

## BADGER BASICS

The badger has a small head, a stocky body, and short legs. The body is covered with coarse guard (outer) hair and the head is patterned with black and white stripes that disguise the face at night.

Striped head
has a long
snout and
small eyes

Short,
hairy tail

EURASIAN
BADGER

Wedge-shaped
body covered by
long guard hairs

### Find out more

ERMINES, POLECATS, AND
MINK 173
OTTERS 264
SHELTERS AND BURROWS 48
WOODLANDS 60

# BATS

BATS ARE THE ONLY mammals that can fly. Most are active at night, or at dawn and dusk. During the day they rest by hanging upside down in roosts. Most bats – known as microbats – eat flying insects, but some feed on small mammals, fish, or even blood. Megabats, or fruit bats, include the largest bats and mostly feed on fruit. Female bats gather in a special nursery roost to give birth to their pink, naked babies.

AFRICAN EPAULETTED FRUIT BAT

Some young can fly within 20 days, others take up to 3 months

Large eyes can see in dim light

## NURSERY ROOST
Young bats huddle together for warmth while their mothers leave the nursery roost to hunt for food. On their return, the mothers can identify their own offspring from the huddle by the sound it makes.

Each infant bat makes a unique sound to identify itself

YOUNG COMMON PIPISTRELLE BATS

## FRUIT BAT
Whereas most bats use a kind of sonar, fruit bats use their keen sense of smell and large eyes to find food. Most fruit bats, also known as flying foxes, have fruit-only diets, while some species feed on flowers, nectar, and pollen.

SCALE

### FACT BOX
**Order:** Chiroptera

**Habitat:** Forests, woodland, and grasslands

**Distribution:** Worldwide except Antarctic

**Food:** Mainly insects, small animals, fish, flowers and fruit

**No. of young:** 1

**Lifespan:** 4–5 years

**Wingspan:** 15–200 cm (6–79 in)

GREATER HORSESHOE BAT

forearm bone

Wing membrane stretched tightly across arm and finger bones

finger bone

Sharp claws grab prey

## IN FLIGHT
The bat uses its wings to fly after and catch its prey. The wings are pulled downwards by muscles in the chest and upper arm, and raised by muscles on the back. They enable the bat to move through the air and turn at high speed. The wing membrane between the legs may be used to catch and hold insects until the bat is ready to eat its prey.

## CAVERN ROOST

As dusk falls, wrinkle-lipped bats emerge in search of food, leaving their regular roost, or shelter. This could be a cave, a tree hollow, or even the attic of a house. Inside the roost, bats hang upside-down, with their wings folded. They use their sharp, curved toes to grip the roof of the roost. Protected from danger there, they can sleep, wash, groom, and look after their young.

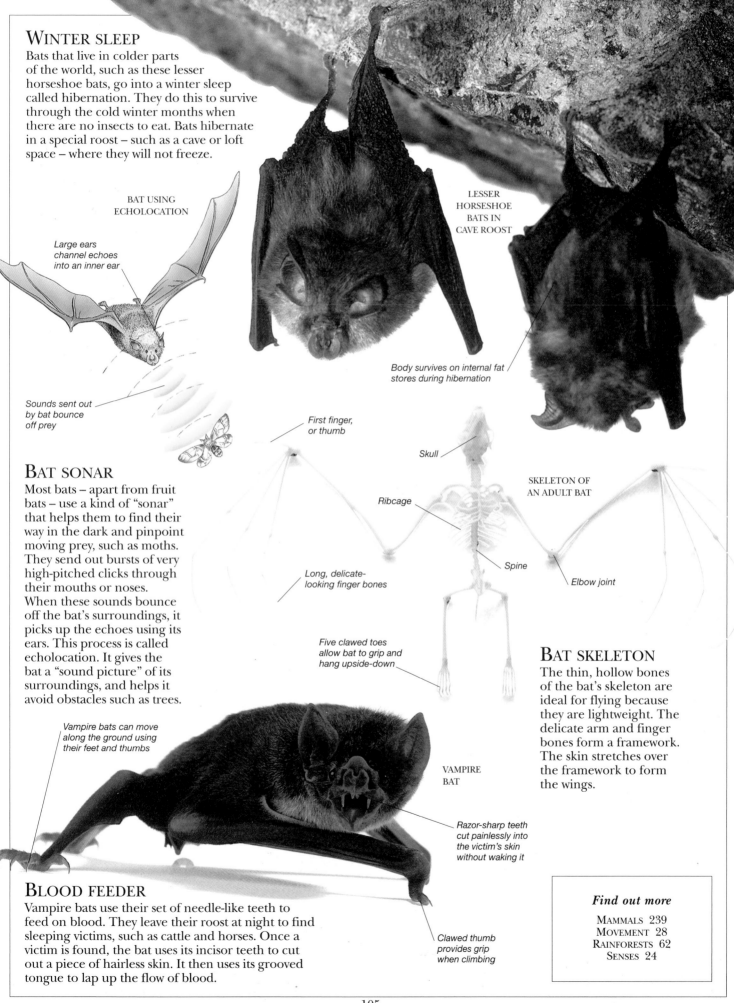

## WINTER SLEEP

Bats that live in colder parts of the world, such as these lesser horseshoe bats, go into a winter sleep called hibernation. They do this to survive through the cold winter months when there are no insects to eat. Bats hibernate in a special roost – such as a cave or loft space – where they will not freeze.

BAT USING
ECHOLOCATION

*Large ears channel echoes into an inner ear*

*Sounds sent out by bat bounce off prey*

LESSER
HORSESHOE
BATS IN
CAVE ROOST

*Body survives on internal fat stores during hibernation*

*First finger, or thumb*

*Skull*

*Ribcage*

SKELETON OF
AN ADULT BAT

## BAT SONAR

Most bats – apart from fruit bats – use a kind of "sonar" that helps them to find their way in the dark and pinpoint moving prey, such as moths. They send out bursts of very high-pitched clicks through their mouths or noses. When these sounds bounce off the bat's surroundings, it picks up the echoes using its ears. This process is called echolocation. It gives the bat a "sound picture" of its surroundings, and helps it avoid obstacles such as trees.

*Long, delicate-looking finger bones*

*Spine*

*Elbow joint*

*Five clawed toes allow bat to grip and hang upside-down*

## BAT SKELETON

The thin, hollow bones of the bat's skeleton are ideal for flying because they are lightweight. The delicate arm and finger bones form a framework. The skin stretches over the framework to form the wings.

*Vampire bats can move along the ground using their feet and thumbs*

VAMPIRE
BAT

*Razor-sharp teeth cut painlessly into the victim's skin without waking it*

## BLOOD FEEDER

Vampire bats use their set of needle-like teeth to feed on blood. They leave their roost at night to find sleeping victims, such as cattle and horses. Once a victim is found, the bat uses its incisor teeth to cut out a piece of hairless skin. It then uses its grooved tongue to lap up the flow of blood.

*Clawed thumb provides grip when climbing*

### Find out more

MAMMALS 239
MOVEMENT 28
RAINFORESTS 62
SENSES 24

# BEARS

Curved
claw

FRONT
PAW

## CLAWED PAW
Each paw has five toes with sharp, curved claws, used for tearing and digging, and to grip when climbing trees.

BEARS ARE BIG, STRONG MAMMALS THAT spend most of their time alone. Their eyesight and hearing are poor, so they rely on their sense of smell to find food. Although they are related to meat-eaters, such as lions and wolves, most bears will eat almost anything, including berries, roots, and insects. Bears that live in cooler places become less active in winter and will sleep in dens throughout to avoid the cold weather. In autumn they eat plenty to build up their fat reserves.

BROWN
BEAR'S HEAD

BROWN, OR
GRIZZLY, BEAR

Only brown bears
have a hump on
their shoulders

Sensitive
nose used for
finding food

SCALE

## FEATURES
Bears have large snouts and noses to help them sniff out food. As their small ears and eyes suggest, bears have poor eyesight and hearing.

### FACT BOX

**Family:** Ursidae

**Habitat:** Forests, grasslands, mountainous areas

**Distribution:** Europe, Asia, North and South America

**Food:** Fruit, roots, small animals, fish, insects

**No. of young:** 1–4

**Lifespan:** 25–30 years

**Size:** 1–2.8 m (3–9 ft)

## STRONG BODY
Bears may vary in size, but they all look similar to this grizzly bear. They have a strong body and powerful legs, covered with thick fur. The large head has strong jaws and teeth that can crush any type of food.

Sharp claws used
to dig up food and
attack other animals

## WOODLAND WANDERERS
Grizzly bears live in the open woodlands and meadows of north-western North America. They roam large distances feeding on berries, roots, small animals, or carrion (dead animals). During the summer, grizzlies wade into streams to catch salmon with their teeth and claws. When food becomes scarce in late autumn, they find or dig a den where they spend the cold winter asleep.

Bear shuffles along without hardly lifting its feet above the ground

## ON THE MOVE

Bears normally move around on all fours. When walking, they place their feet flat on the ground, lifting the heel and sole of the foot off the ground with each step. When searching for food, bears usually walk slowly with a shuffling movement, but when chasing prey they can run fast over short distances.

Mouth open to reveal large teeth

The bear walks on the soles of its feet, which are furry

Large paws ready to grab victim

SYRIAN BROWN BEAR

## BEAR CUBS

When bear cubs are born, they are tiny and helpless. They grow rapidly, spending a lot of time playing and learning to look after themselves. Even so, for the first year or so, they stay close to their mother, who protects them fiercely from danger.

Bear cub practise vital skills such as sniffing the air

GRIZZLY BEAR

ASIATIC BLACK BEAR CUBS

## REARING UP

Bears sometimes rear up on their hind legs. They do this when threatened – to make themselves look big and frightening – or to look round at their surroundings. When upright, a grizzly bear can be as much as 3 m (10 ft) tall. Grizzly is the name given to brown bears in north-western North America. They are called grizzly because they have white, or grizzled, tips to their hair.

# BEAVERS

AMERICAN
BEAVER

BEST KNOWN AS DAM BUILDERS, beavers are large, water-living members of the rodent order of animals. They are skilled engineers that build dams across streams to create calm ponds where they build nests called lodges. They feed on the bark and leaves of the trees in their surroundings. Beavers move awkwardly on land, but are fast movers in water. They have streamlined bodies with short legs, webbed hind feet for swimming, and small ears. Their dense fur keeps them warm in or out of water.

## FLAT TAIL

The beaver's broad, flat, scaly tail is a powerful tool in the water. When thrust up and down it pushes the beaver along at high speed. It also serves as a rudder, helping to steer the beaver as it moves along.

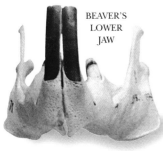

BEAVER'S
LOWER
JAW

## DAMS AND LODGES

Beavers dam their home stream using branches cut from trees, mud, and stones scrabbled from the bank using their front paws. The dam stops the flow of the water, and a deep pond forms behind it – this is where the beavers build their family home or lodge. Here they can shelter from cold weather and be protected from enemies.

Inner living
chamber and
underwater
entrance

Dam made of
sticks, mud,
and stone

BEAVER LODGE
AND DAM

## STRONG TEETH

Beavers have two large front teeth in their upper and lower jaws, just like other rodents. These teeth grow all the time, never wear down, and have sharp, cutting tips. Beavers use the combined strength of their jaw muscles and sharp teeth to cut down trees and gnaw through branches at high speed.

## AT WORK

Beavers live and work in close-knit family groups. They are active during the day, working together to fell trees and cut branches which they carry through the water in their mouths. If a beaver spots a predator, it slaps its tail on the water's surface to warn other family members to swim for safety.

SCALE

### FACT BOX

**Family:** Castoridae

**Habitat:** Streams, rivers, and lakes with wooded banks

**Distribution:** North America and northern Eurasia

**Food:** Inner bark, buds, leaves, and roots of trees; water plants

**Lifespan:** 13–20 years

**No. of young:** 2–4

**Size:** 105–120 cm (41–67 in)

BEAVER CHEWING
BRANCHES

### Find out more

## RIVERBANK HOME
The streams that flow through wooded
areas in North America and northern
Europe provide the ideal home for
beavers. The beavers cut down trees and
branches, and use them to build a dam.
This turns the stream into a lake in
which the beavers build a house or
lodge that protects them from enemies.
If the stream floods and breaks the dam,
the beavers quickly repair the damage.

# BEES

MOST TYPES OF BEES LIVE ALONE, but honeybees and bumblebees live in large nest colonies. The colony contains a single queen that lays eggs, hundreds of drones whose job is to mate with the queen, and thousands of worker bees who guard the nest and look after the young bees. All bees feed on nectar and pollen from flowers.

## BEE BODIES

Bumblebees have plump bodies covered in fine hairs that pick up pollen grains. Like other bees, their legs are fitted with special "baskets" which are used for carrying pollen back to the nest. Female bees are armed with a barbed sting that can inflict a painful, swollen wound.

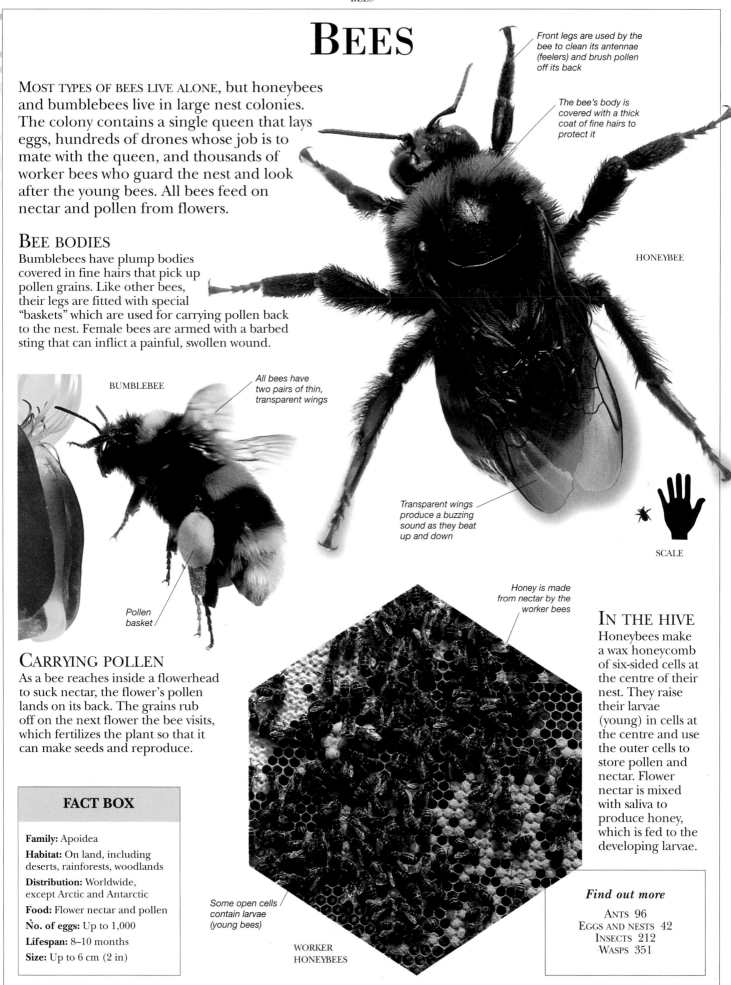

Front legs are used by the bee to clean its antennae (feelers) and brush pollen off its back

The bee's body is covered with a thick coat of fine hairs to protect it

HONEYBEE

BUMBLEBEE

All bees have two pairs of thin, transparent wings

Transparent wings produce a buzzing sound as they beat up and down

SCALE

Pollen basket

## CARRYING POLLEN

As a bee reaches inside a flowerhead to suck nectar, the flower's pollen lands on its back. The grains rub off on the next flower the bee visits, which fertilizes the plant so that it can make seeds and reproduce.

Honey is made from nectar by the worker bees

## IN THE HIVE

Honeybees make a wax honeycomb of six-sided cells at the centre of their nest. They raise their larvae (young) in cells at the centre and use the outer cells to store pollen and nectar. Flower nectar is mixed with saliva to produce honey, which is fed to the developing larvae.

### FACT BOX

**Family:** Apoidea

**Habitat:** On land, including deserts, rainforests, woodlands

**Distribution:** Worldwide, except Arctic and Antarctic

**Food:** Flower nectar and pollen

**No. of eggs:** Up to 1,000

**Lifespan:** 8–10 months

**Size:** Up to 6 cm (2 in)

Some open cells contain larvae (young bees)

WORKER HONEYBEES

*Find out more*

ANTS 96
EGGS AND NESTS 42
INSECTS 212
WASPS 351

## BEES' NESTS

Honeybees make their nests inside hollow trees, or they live in hives specially built for them by people. Other types of bee burrow into wood or live underground. In summer, the queen bee and many of her workers fly off in a swarm to make a new nest. The swarm shown here has landed on a tree branch while worker bees seek out a suitable place for nesting.

# BEETLES

BEETLES ARE THE LARGEST GROUP of insects. In fact, one in every four different animals on Earth is a beetle. They can be found all over the world, on icy mountains, scorching arid deserts, or in ponds, streams, and even hot springs. Members of the beetle family come in a variety of shapes and often jewel-like colours. They include long-nosed weevils, scurrying ground beetles, fierce stag beetles, aphid-eating ladybirds, and fireflies that glow at night.

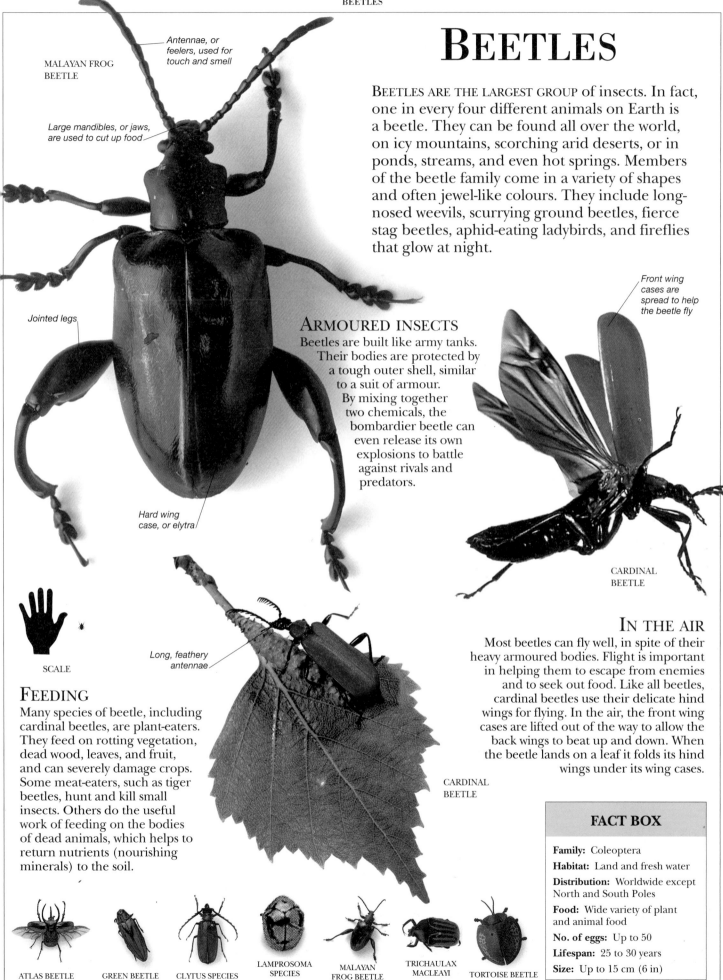

MALAYAN FROG BEETLE

Antennae, or feelers, used for touch and smell

Large mandibles, or jaws, are used to cut up food

Jointed legs

Hard wing case, or elytra

SCALE

Front wing cases are spread to help the beetle fly

CARDINAL BEETLE

Long, feathery antennae

CARDINAL BEETLE

## ARMOURED INSECTS

Beetles are built like army tanks. Their bodies are protected by a tough outer shell, similar to a suit of armour. By mixing together two chemicals, the bombardier beetle can even release its own explosions to battle against rivals and predators.

## IN THE AIR

Most beetles can fly well, in spite of their heavy armoured bodies. Flight is important in helping them to escape from enemies and to seek out food. Like all beetles, cardinal beetles use their delicate hind wings for flying. In the air, the front wing cases are lifted out of the way to allow the back wings to beat up and down. When the beetle lands on a leaf it folds its hind wings under its wing cases.

## FEEDING

Many species of beetle, including cardinal beetles, are plant-eaters. They feed on rotting vegetation, dead wood, leaves, and fruit, and can severely damage crops. Some meat-eaters, such as tiger beetles, hunt and kill small insects. Others do the useful work of feeding on the bodies of dead animals, which helps to return nutrients (nourishing minerals) to the soil.

### FACT BOX

**Family:** Coleoptera

**Habitat:** Land and fresh water

**Distribution:** Worldwide except North and South Poles

**Food:** Wide variety of plant and animal food

**No. of eggs:** Up to 50

**Lifespan:** 25 to 30 years

**Size:** Up to 15 cm (6 in)

ATLAS BEETLE     GREEN BEETLE     CLYTUS SPECIES     LAMPROSOMA SPECIES     MALAYAN FROG BEETLE     TRICHAULAX MACLEAYI     TORTOISE BEETLE

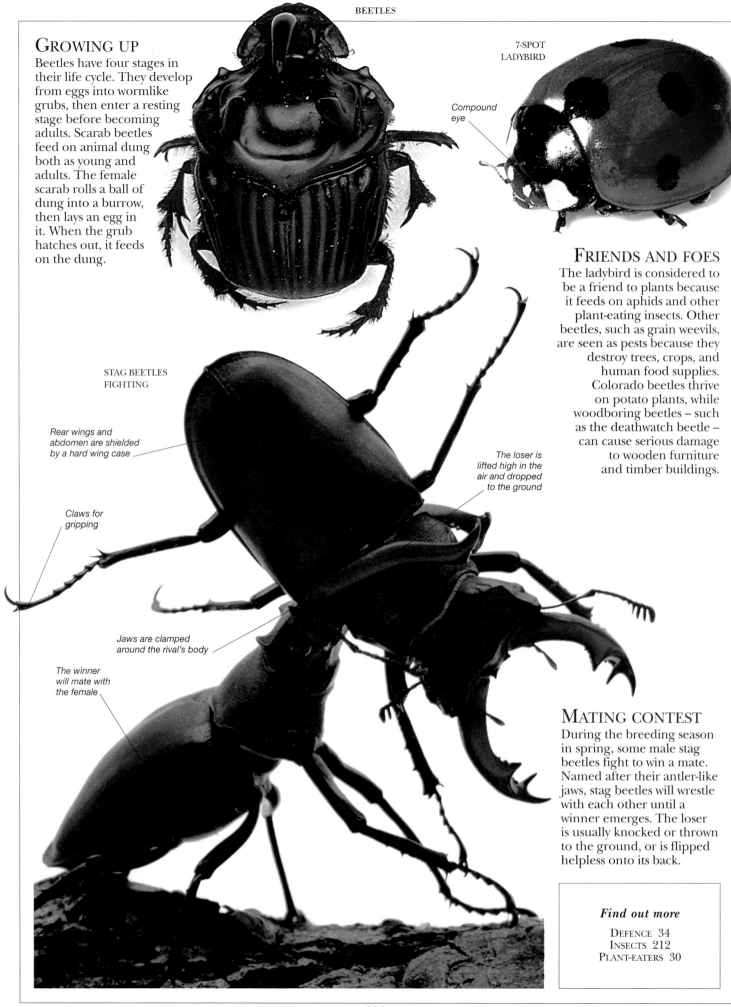

# GROWING UP

Beetles have four stages in their life cycle. They develop from eggs into wormlike grubs, then enter a resting stage before becoming adults. Scarab beetles feed on animal dung both as young and adults. The female scarab rolls a ball of dung into a burrow, then lays an egg in it. When the grub hatches out, it feeds on the dung.

7-SPOT LADYBIRD

Compound eye

# FRIENDS AND FOES

The ladybird is considered to be a friend to plants because it feeds on aphids and other plant-eating insects. Other beetles, such as grain weevils, are seen as pests because they destroy trees, crops, and human food supplies. Colorado beetles thrive on potato plants, while woodboring beetles – such as the deathwatch beetle – can cause serious damage to wooden furniture and timber buildings.

STAG BEETLES FIGHTING

Rear wings and abdomen are shielded by a hard wing case

The loser is lifted high in the air and dropped to the ground

Claws for gripping

Jaws are clamped around the rival's body

The winner will mate with the female

# MATING CONTEST

During the breeding season in spring, some male stag beetles fight to win a mate. Named after their antler-like jaws, stag beetles will wrestle with each other until a winner emerges. The loser is usually knocked or thrown to the ground, or is flipped helpless onto its back.

*Find out more*

DEFENCE 34
INSECTS 212
PLANT-EATERS 30

# BIRDS

ALL BIRDS HAVE FEATHERS and wings, even those that have lost the power of flight, such as penguins. The ability to fly has made it possible for birds to make long migrations in search of food supplies, and to colonize every part of the world. They have no teeth, but have horny bills, or beaks, which vary in shape according to the diet and lifestyle of each kind of bird. All birds reproduce by laying eggs.

*Small teeth-like ridges provide a tight hold on grass and slippery prey*

RED-BREASTED
GOOSE

## WATER BIRDS
Geese, ducks, and swans live in wetland habitats, where there are plenty of plants, invertebrates, and fish for them to eat. They all have webbed feet for swimming, and ridged beaks that are used for plucking grass or catching prey. The most highly adapted to life in and under water are penguins, which use their wings as oars to steer them through the water.

## MATCHING FEET
Each group of birds has feet that suit its lifestyle. Flamingos have narrow, webbed feet for walking on mud. Eagles have sharp-clawed feet for seizing prey. Ducks have wide, webbed feet for swimming. Warblers' feet are suited to perching.

FLAMINGO
FOOT

EAGLE
FOOT

DUCK
FOOT

WARBLER
FOOT

## WADERS
Waders, such as sandpipers and snipes, and unrelated birds like ibises, have long legs for wading in shallow water. They use their long bills to probe for prey, such as worms that live under the surface of the mud or sand.

*Long, curved bill probes into mud or cracks in hard earth*

*Long legs hold body above the water*

CONTOUR
FEATHER

DOWN
FEATHER

TAIL
FEATHER

WING
FEATHER

### FACT BOX

**Class:** Aves

**Species:** More than 9,500

**Habitat:** Every habitat, from high mountains, open oceans and polar ice, to deserts, grasslands, forests, lakes, farmland, and cities

**Distribution:** Worldwide

**Food:** Fish, birds, mammals, grasses, seeds, and nuts

*Long, spread-out toes with webbing stop feet from sinking into soft sand or mud*

SCARLET
IBIS

## FEATHER FUNCTIONS
Feathers keep birds warm and dry and, most important, allow them to fly. Contour feathers cover the body and provide a streamlined shape for flying. Beneath these are fluffy down feathers that trap air to form a warm layer above the skin. The feathers of the tail and wings are used in flight.

## PLUNGE DIVERS

Seabirds breed on sea-cliffs, outlying islands, and other sites. These gannets nest on top of a rocky islet and fly over the sea to feed. Their black-tipped wings span up to 1.8 m (6 ft) across. To catch their prey of fish, these dazzling white birds plunge like arrows into the water at speeds of 100 kmh (60 mph) or more. They eat the fish or carry it back to their young.

# HUNTING BIRDS

Most owls hunt by night to avoid competing with raptors (daytime birds of prey), such as hawks, eagles, and falcons. Both raptors and owls have keen eyesight and hearing to help them find prey. They also have powerful, sharp-clawed feet for seizing and killing, and sharply hooked bills, used by raptors mainly for tearing prey into bite-size pieces and by owls for killing.

Broad, rounded wings for slow, accurate flight between trees at night

Beak is used for killing prey

TAWNY OWL

Extra-soft flight feathers with comb-like fringes for silent flight to catch prey unawares

Large, heavy-looking bill has lightweight, honeycomb structure

TOUCAN

## FRUIT EATERS

Toucans have extremely long bills that allow them to reach up for fruits that grow at the tips of slender branches. If the birds tried to feed by sitting alongside a fruit, the branch would not support their weight. Most birds that live in tropical rainforests feed on fruit, because supplies are available all year round.

World's largest egg

## EGG VARIETY

Eggs vary in shape, colour, and size. A hummingbird's egg is no larger than a pea, whereas ostriches lay eggs up to 20 cm (8 in) long. Some female birds lay just one egg at a time, while others lay 20 or more. Many birds build elaborate nests in bushes or high in trees to protect their eggs. Others lay them into scooped-out holes or on bare cliff ledges.

ELEPHANT BIRD          OSTRICH     CASSOWARY    CHICKEN

# BOAS AND PYTHONS

SOME OF THE LONGEST AND LARGEST snakes in the world are boas and pythons. They are both known as constrictors because of the way that they kill their prey. They have a pair of tiny claws, called spurs, at the tail ends of their bodies. Pythons are found in Australasia, Asia, and Africa, whereas boas live in the Americas, as well as Africa and Asia, but not Australia. Pythons lay eggs to reproduce, while boas give birth to their young.

## TREE LIFE
To suit their treetop lifestyle, tree boas are longer, thinner, and lighter than ground-living boas. Their specially adapted bodies slide easily through trees, while their strong tails grip hold of branches.

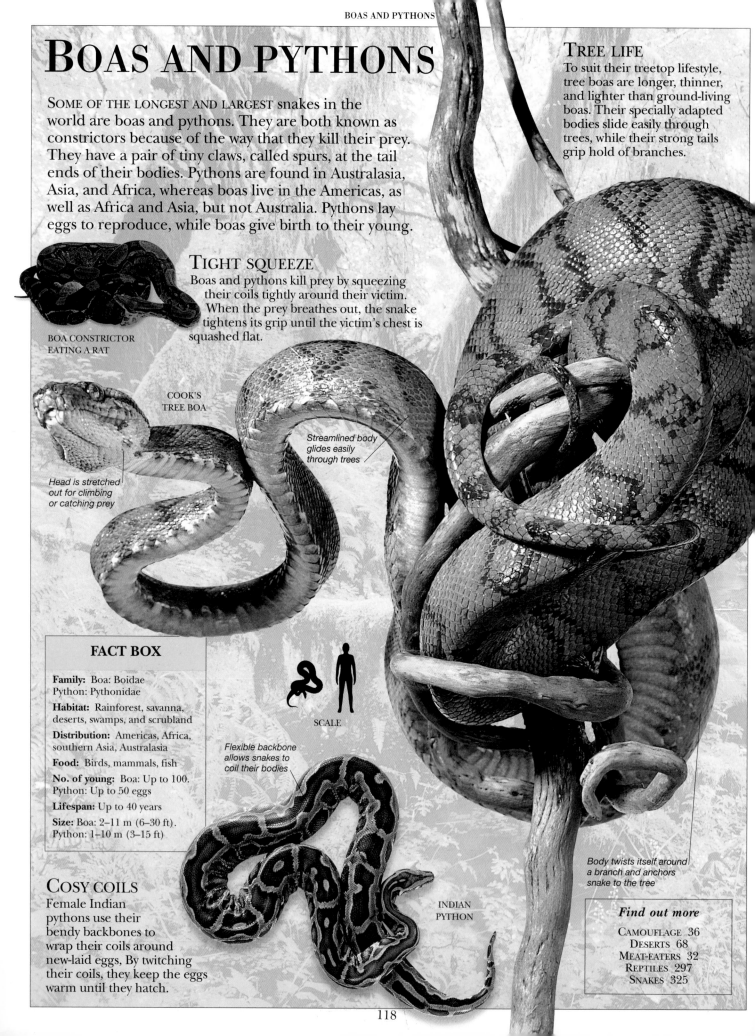

BOA CONSTRICTOR EATING A RAT

## TIGHT SQUEEZE
Boas and pythons kill prey by squeezing their coils tightly around their victim. When the prey breathes out, the snake tightens its grip until the victim's chest is squashed flat.

COOK'S TREE BOA

Streamlined body glides easily through trees

Head is stretched out for climbing or catching prey

## FACT BOX

**Family:** Boa: Boidae
Python: Pythonidae

**Habitat:** Rainforest, savanna, deserts, swamps, and scrubland

**Distribution:** Americas, Africa, southern Asia, Australasia

**Food:** Birds, mammals, fish

**No. of young:** Boa: Up to 100.
Python: Up to 50 eggs

**Lifespan:** Up to 40 years

**Size:** Boa: 2–11 m (6–30 ft).
Python: 1–10 m (3–15 ft)

SCALE

Flexible backbone allows snakes to coil their bodies

## COSY COILS
Female Indian pythons use their bendy backbones to wrap their coils around new-laid eggs, By twitching their coils, they keep the eggs warm until they hatch.

INDIAN PYTHON

Body twists itself around a branch and anchors snake to the tree

# BUDGERIGARS

THE DRY GRASSLANDS OF AUSTRALIA are the natural habitat of wild budgerigars, one of the smallest members of the parrot family. Despite their size, they are tough little birds, capable of flying great distances across the hot, dry landscape in search of water and food. They lead a nomadic life, which means that they never settle in one place but are always moving to new territories. Domestic budgerigars are bred in a variety of colours, but most wild budgerigars are green.

Long primary feathers used to steer and change direction quickly

Overlapping feathers create curved surface for smooth flight

BUDGERIGAR IN FLIGHT

## FLYING ACES
Budgerigars have a very fast, agile flight. They are able to twist and turn together when flying in a flock. This helps them to escape predators such as falcons, as the flock's sudden changes in direction confuse the enemy.

### FACT BOX
**Family**: Psittacidae (parrot)

**No. of species**: 330

**Habitat**: Dry grasslands

**Distribution**: Australia

**Food**: Seeds, especially those of grasses and weeds

**No. of eggs**: 4–8

**Lifespan**: 5–7 years

**Size**: 18–20 cm (7–8 in)

## MALE AND FEMALE
Male budgerigars develop a blue colour on the fleshy cere (base) around their bills. In females, the cere is brown. This is the only real difference in appearance between male and female budgerigars.

Blue fleshy base around bill

Full set of feathers develop after 21 days

MALE BUDGERIGAR

21-DAY OLD CHICK

## CHICKS
Most budgerigars produce their young when grasses start to seed. This means that they can be certain of enough food to feed the naked, helpless chicks when they are born.

"Necklace" of spots is puffed up in courtship

ADULT BUDGERIGARS ON A PERCH

Typical wavy lined pattern along back of head

Budgerigars perch close to their mates

SCALE

## SOCIAL BIRDS
Budgerigars are very social birds, and live together in large flocks (groups). They huddle close to each other for warmth and preen (clean) each other's feathers.

Long tail helps with steering and breaking in flight

### Find out more
BIRDS 115
EGGS AND NESTS 42
MOVEMENT 28
PARROTS 273

# BUGS

TRUE BUGS ARE A PARTICULAR group of insects with long feeding tubes that are designed to pierce and suck up liquid food. There are more than 23,000 different kinds of bug, including aphids, cicadas, hoppers, stink bugs, and bed bugs. Most live on land, but water boatmen, pond skaters, and water scorpions live in fresh water. Unlike many other insects, bugs do not reproduce by metamorphosis (a four-stage development from newborn to adult). They lay their eggs on plants, or glue them onto the hairs of animals. The young insects that hatch out look like tiny, wingless versions of the adults. Most are left to look after themselves rather than being sheltered by their parents.

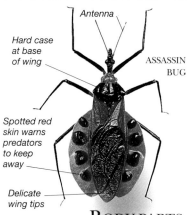

Antenna

Hard case at base of wing

ASSASSIN BUG

Spotted red skin warns predators to keep away

Delicate wing tips

## BODY PARTS

Bugs vary in size and shape. Most of them, like assassin bugs, have two pairs of wings, with tough, leathery bases and soft, delicate tips on the front pair. Many bugs are coloured to blend in with their surroundings.

Front legs for catching prey

Male cicada produces "song" by flexing muscles on its sides

CICADA

### FACT BOX

**Family:** Hemiptera

**No. of species:** 23,000

**Habitat:** Widespread on land and in fresh water

**Distribution:** All continents, except Antarctica

**Food:** Plants, animals, blood

**Size:** Up to 60 mm (Up to 2.5 in)

## MATING SONG

Cicadas are one of the noisiest insects to be heard in tropical forests. The loud clicking noises are made by the males to attract female cicadas during the breeding season. The songs, which can be heard up to 250 m (¼ mile) away, are produced by the males flexing the muscles on the undersides of their bodies.

WATER SCORPION

## BREATHING TUBE

Unlike the tails of land scorpions, which carry a poisonous sting, water scorpions' "tails" are actually breathing tubes. These air-breathing bugs make regular trips to the surface of the water to take in air through these long tubes.

Air is sucked up through the breathing tube

SCALE

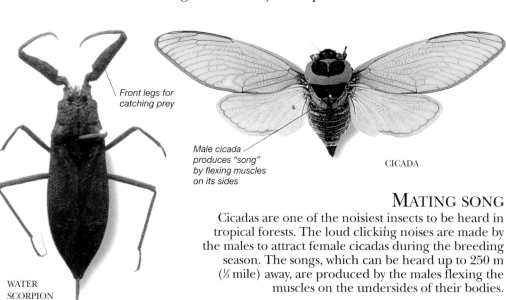

THORN BUGS

Footpad helps bug to grip smooth surfaces

## FEEDING

The thorn-like shape of thorn bugs helps to disguise them from predators while they feed on plant stems. Bugs feed on liquid foods which they suck up using their tube-like mouths. Aphids, hoppers, and shield bugs feed on plant sap, but assassin bugs and water boatmen hunt and suck the life juices from other creatures. Tiny bed bugs feed on the blood of animals.

Pointed spine makes bug look like a thorn on a stem

### Find out more

CAMOUFLAGE 36
COURTSHIP AND MATING 38
INSECTS 212

# BUTTERFLIES AND MOTHS

THE DELICATE-LOOKING INSECTS known as butterflies and moths are surprisingly tough. Most live in forests and meadows, but some survive in deserts and even in the Arctic. They feed on sugary liquids, such as nectar and fruit juices, that are high in energy. Their wings are covered in tiny scales. Butterflies and moths have different shaped antennae, but one of the easiest ways to tell them apart is to watch them resting. Butterflies rest with their wings held upright, but moths generally hold their wings flat.

*Male has the most brightly coloured wings*

MALE BIRDWING BUTTERFLY

*Long slender body; moths have short, hairy bodies*

## TROPICAL COLOURS

Many of the most colourful butterflies live in hot tropical areas. Butterflies are active during the day. They use their colours to attract a mate or to warn predators that they are unpleasant to eat. In contrast, moths are usually dull in colour and are active at dusk or during the night.

SCALE

*Butterfly's antenna has a small, rounded tip*

## FEEDING

Long, sensitive antennae help butterflies and moths to track down their food by detecting the scents of flowers. They also have long, hollow feeding tubes, like drinking straws. The insects stick their tubes into ripe fruit, stems, or flowers and suck out the juice, sap, or nectar.

*Speckled pattern blends in with woodland surroundings*

*Feather-like antennae*

## DISGUISES

The colouring and speckled pattern of peppered moths helps them to blend in with natural objects such as leaves and tree bark. This keeps them hidden from hunting animals such as birds and reptiles. In urban areas, the peppered moth has gradually developed dark colouring to blend in with its smokier surroundings.

BUTTERFLY HEAD

*Veins hold wing in position*

PEPPERED MOTH

## SCALE WINGS

Under a microscope, it is possible to see the intricate detail of a butterfly or moth's wing. They are covered with thousands of powdery scales that overlap each other to create beautiful patterns. Running through the wings are tough veins that hold the delicate scales together and keep the wings in shape.

*Feeding tube (proboscis) is coiled under head when not in use*

BUTTERFLY WING DETAIL

## FROM EGG TO ADULT

All butterflies and moths pass through four distinct stages in their lives. They hatch out from eggs into legless, wingless caterpillars that look nothing like adult insects. When fully grown, caterpillars spin a cocoon (protective case) to become a pupa. Inside, the insect's whole body is changing. Eventually the case splits open and the adult moth or butterfly struggles out.

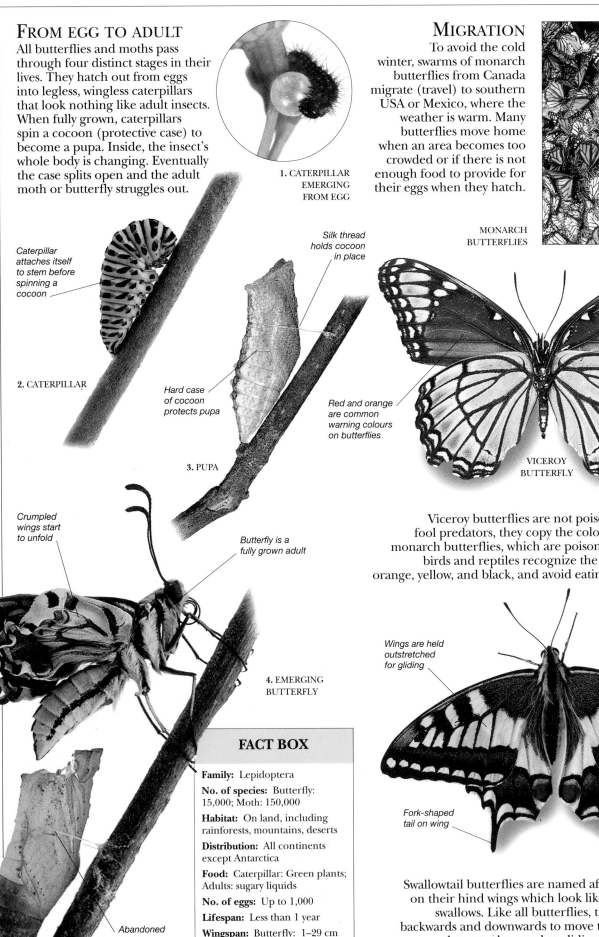

1. CATERPILLAR EMERGING FROM EGG

Caterpillar attaches itself to stem before spinning a cocoon

2. CATERPILLAR

Silk thread holds cocoon in place

Hard case of cocoon protects pupa

3. PUPA

Crumpled wings start to unfold

Butterfly is a fully grown adult

4. EMERGING BUTTERFLY

Abandoned cocoon

## MIGRATION

To avoid the cold winter, swarms of monarch butterflies from Canada migrate (travel) to southern USA or Mexico, where the weather is warm. Many butterflies move home when an area becomes too crowded or if there is not enough food to provide for their eggs when they hatch.

MONARCH BUTTERFLIES

Red and orange are common warning colours on butterflies

VICEROY BUTTERFLY

## COPYCAT

Viceroy butterflies are not poisonous. However, to fool predators, they copy the colours and patterns of monarch butterflies, which are poisonous to eat. Hungry birds and reptiles recognize the warning colours of orange, yellow, and black, and avoid eating these butterflies.

Wings are held outstretched for gliding

SWALLOWTAIL BUTTERFLY

Fork-shaped tail on wing

## WING SHAPE

Swallowtail butterflies are named after the pointed tips on their hind wings which look like the forked tails of swallows. Like all butterflies, they flap their wings backwards and downwards to move through the air, but they are also good at gliding on a current of air. Whenever the wings are used in flight, some of their dusty scales are shed and they become more ragged.

### FACT BOX

**Family:** Lepidoptera

**No. of species:** Butterfly: 15,000; Moth: 150,000

**Habitat:** On land, including rainforests, mountains, deserts

**Distribution:** All continents except Antarctica

**Food:** Caterpillar: Green plants; Adults: sugary liquids

**No. of eggs:** Up to 1,000

**Lifespan:** Less than 1 year

**Wingspan:** Butterfly: 1–29 cm (0.5–11 in); Moth: Up to 25 cm (up to 10 in)

## FALSE EYES

Peacock butterflies have markings on their wings that look like large eyes. For a moment, the markings may fool predators into thinking that a large, dangerous creature such as an owl is nearby. This gives the butterfly enough time to quickly escape before the predator realizes that is has been tricked.

PEACOCK BUTTERFLY

Large eye spots look like the eyes of an owl or leopard

BLUE MORPHO BUTTERFLY

Bright blue colour is produced by light reflecting off tiny ridges on the wing scales

Black-and-white stripes warn predators to keep away

## BLUE MALES

Male morpho butterflies have bright blue wings that help them to attract females in the breeding season. The females' wings have dull orange or brown colours, so they blend in with the background. This is important for the female while protecting her eggs. In many species of butterflies, males and females have different colours.

ZEBRA BUTTERFLY

OWL BUTTERFLIES FEEDING ON BANANAS

## WARNING SOUND

The zebra butterfly is armed with a bold warning pattern, and can release a nasty smell when threatened. If it hears an enemy, the butterfly can also wriggle its body to produce a creaking sound to frighten away predators.

## FOOD AND DRINK

Like other butterflies and moths, owl moths enjoy feeding on the juices of rotting fruit. In hot, dry countries, they drink from large puddles to replace lost salts.

*Find out more*

CAMOUFLAGE 36
CATERPILLARS 127
GROWING UP 44
INSECTS 212

# CAMELS

CAMELS ARE EXPERTS at surviving in dry, barren parts of the world. They can live for months without water, and survive by eating dry, thorny, or salty desert plants that no other animal will touch. The single or double hump on their back is a store of fat that is used to provide energy when food is scarce. The two types of camel – dromedary and Bactrian – have been domesticated (kept and used by people) for thousands of years. Desert people use camels for transport, and to provide them with milk, meat, and wool.

Single hump

## HUMPED BODY
Camels are hoofed mammals, like cattle and antelopes. They have long legs and a long neck. The dromedary has a single hump on its back, and a Bactrian camel has two humps.

Losing its coat makes the camel look ragged

BACTRIAN CAMEL

The camel's thick coat falls off in spring

## WINTER COAT
As winter approaches, Bactrian camels grow a thick coat to keep them warm. In spring, the winter coat is shed very quickly. This gives the camel a ragged appearance.

SCALE

Long legs raise the body above the intense heat at ground level

Thick pads protect the "knees" when kneeling

DROMEDARY CAMEL

### FACT BOX

**Family**: Camelidae

**Habitat**: Desert and dry grasslands

**Distribution**: North Africa, Middle East, central Asia

**Food**: Dry leaves, grasses, and thorny plants

**Gestation period**: 12–14 mths

**Lifespan**: Up to 50 years

**Size**: 1.8–2.3 m (6–8 ft) to the shoulder

This camel has not had any water for many weeks

The same camel a few minutes later after drinking water

BEFORE AND AFTER DRINKING

## LOSS AND GAIN
Unlike humans, camels can survive without water for weeks or even months. When there is no water, camels can lose over a quarter of their weight, so they look very thin. But when water is available, they drink large amounts very quickly to make up the loss.

## ARID SANDS

Dromedary camels live in the
deserts of North Africa and
Arabia. In the sandy, rocky
deserts, water is scarce and it is
very hot during the day. Most
mammals would not survive in
these harsh conditions. But
dromedary camels put up with
high temperatures, and can
wander for months without
water, filling up whenever they
arrive at an oasis, or water hole.

## SAND PROTECTION

Camels have large eyes and nostrils, which provide them with a good sense of sight and smell. In desert sandstorms, the camels' long eyelashes stop sand blowing into their eyes and the slit-like nostrils close to prevent sand getting up their noses.

Nostrils can be closed to stop sand blowing in

CAMEL'S FOOT

Leathery split upper lip allows camels to eat tough, thorny plants

Toughened toecaps

## TWIN TOES

A camel's foot has two-hoofed toes, linked by a piece of skin. When walking, the toes spread wide apart, stopping the camel from sinking into soft sand. A tough, bendy pad under the toes allows the camel to walk easily over rough, stony ground.

Goods and people are carried on a saddle fitted between the camel's humps

## PACK ANIMALS

Camels are the only animals able to carry heavy burdens across the desert and survive without food and water. Sometimes they cover long distances of more than 30 km (19 miles) a day. At night, when the temperature falls sharply, their fur keeps them warm. During the day, when the desert gets hot, camels are not affected by their body temperature increasing.

Camel bends its front legs first when kneeling

KNEELING DROMEDARY CAMEL

Hind legs bend to lower camel to the ground

### Find out more

COMMON MORMON
CATERPILLAR

# CATERPILLARS

CATERPILLARS ARE THE LARVAE (YOUNG) of moths and butterflies. This is the second stage in the life cycle of these insects, as they hatch from eggs into caterpillars, before becoming adults. Caterpillars look nothing like adult moths and butterflies. They are wingless and have long, plump bodies divided into 13 segments. They spend most of their time feeding and growing. When fully grown, the caterpillar spins a silken thread and attaches itself to a twig or leaf, ready to become a pupa and then an adult insect.

## HUNGRY FEEDERS

Caterpillars are big eaters and grow quickly. Each species likes a particular plant to eat. As the caterpillar grows, its skin gets too tight. So it moults (sheds) its outgrown skin to reveal a new, soft skin beneath with space inside for growing.

## DEFENCE

Caterpillars cannot fly, so they make easy prey for hungry birds and lizards. Some have sharp spines on their bodies to stop predators from eating them. Others are disguised to look like leaves or bark so enemies cannot spot them, or they have bright colours to warn that they taste nasty.

*Powerful jaws munch through the edge of a leaf*

CATERPILLAR WITH POISON SPINES

## FACT BOX

**Family:** Lepidoptera

**Habitat:** Deserts, rainforests, and mountains

**Distribution:** Worldwide, except North and South Poles

**Food:** Green plants

**Lifespan:** An average of 4 weeks as a caterpillar

**Size:** 1.5–10 cm (1–3 in)

SCALE

*Spiny bristles put off hungry predators*

*Claspers on the caterpillar's rear provide extra grip*

*Proleg*

CROW
SWALLOWTAIL

## GETTING ABOUT

Like adult insects, caterpillars have three pairs of legs. Several pairs of muscular stumps, or prolegs, on their rear segments help them to grip twigs and crawl about.

### Find out more

BUTTERFLIES AND MOTHS 121
CAMOUFLAGE 36
INSECTS 212

# CATS

CATS ARE INDEPENDENT, graceful, and secretive animals. They are one of the most successful carnivores (meat-eaters), equipped with sharp teeth for slicing up meat and strong claws for catching prey and climbing. The cat family is usually divided into two groups, known as big cats and small cats (which includes domestic cats). Wild cats live in forests, grasslands, or woodlands, but domestic cats are kept as pets worldwide.

ADULT TIGER

Big cats walk quietly on their toes

Rough tongue is used for grooming coat

## ODD CAT OUT

The markings on lions' coats are much fainter than the bold stripes or spots seen on other big cats. Lions also differ in their lifestyle because they live and hunt together in groups, known as prides.

Male lions are the only male cats with a mane of hair

## BIG CATS

Tigers, lions, jaguars, leopards, and snow leopards belong to the group known as "big cats". Of these, tigers are the largest and can reach up to 3 m (10 ft) in length. Most big cats lie down to eat, rest with their paws in front, and can roar, but not purr.

Flexible muscles allow neck to twist and stretch

LION AND LIONESS

## COMMUNICATION

Cats communicate by means of sounds such as roars, snarls, growls, yowls, mews, and purrs. They also tell other cats to keep out of their territory by scratching trunks, spraying urine, or leaving droppings at certain places. By licking and rubbing against each other, they exchange scent messages.

LEOPARD

Tail is made flexible by series of small bones

## BENDY BODY

A very flexible spine and a loose-fitting skin make it possible for cats to bend and stretch their bodies in many directions. This is useful when they pounce on prey and groom their fur.

BLACK LEOPARD OR PANTHER

## FACT BOX

**Family:** Felidae

**Habitat:** Forests, mountains, deserts, woodlands, and swamps

**Distribution:** Worldwide, except Antarctica

**Food:** Big cats: Mostly large mammals. Other cats: Small mammals such as mice, birds, fish, beetles, and reptiles

## CLAWS

All cats, except cheetahs, can retract (pull back) their claws into protective pockets in the skin of their feet. These pockets stop the claws from being worn down as the cats walk about and keep the claws sharp.

Claws hidden beneath protective pocket

OCELOT

FISHING CAT

Webbed feet

## WATER CATS

Some cats, such as the fishing cat, like the water and are good swimmers. The fishing cat even has webs between the toes of its front feet to help it swim.

Ears can rotate independently

CARACAL

## SENSES

Cats have excellent senses of sight, touch, and hearing, which help them to hunt at night. In the dark, a cat's pupils open really wide to let in as much light as possible. Cats have very flexible ears that can be turned in the direction of a sound. Their hearing is sensitive enough to detect the high pitched squeaks of small rodents.

Touch-sensitive whiskers help cats to navigate at night

Acute sense of smell picks up the scent of prey

Spotted coat acts as camouflage as serval creeps up on its prey

## HUNTING

A serval can leap twice its own body length to catch birds. Like other hunting cats, it first "sniffs the air" to pick up the scent of prey. Keeping its body low, the serval moves silently and slowly towards its victim – this is known as stalking. Once the prey is within reach, the cat makes a sudden pounce using its powerful hind legs, and holds on tight with its claws and sharp teeth.

SERVAL

Padded paws help cat to stalk silently

SIAMESE
KITTENS

*Kittens can
stand at three
weeks*

RED SELF
LONGHAIR

## LITTER OF KITTENS

Kittens are the young of small cats. There are usually
four in a litter and they cannot see or hear when first
born. Whereas kittens are able to look after themselves
by about eight weeks, cubs (the young of big cats) rely
on their mothers for food until they are 18 months old.

*Typical
flattened face*

*Paws covered
by tufts of
long fur*

*Fine hairs
on ears*

*Any whiskers
are brittle and
break easily*

SPHYNX OR
CANADIAN
HAIRLESS CAT

## LONGHAIRS

Persian cats, or Longhairs, are
domestic cats that are admired for
their thick, long fur. Although a
coat of long hair would keep a cat
warm in the wild, it would quickly
become matted and tangled.

## FUR-FREE

Some domestic cats, such
as this sphynx cat, have been
bred to have no fur at all. Their
bodies are covered only with a fuzzy
down. In the wild, a cat's fur coat helps
to keep it warm, especially in cold
climates. When the temperature
rises, the cat licks its fur to
lower its body heat.

*Pupils close to a
slit when angry*

SHORTHAIR
CAT

*Paw poised to
defend cat's
exposed body*

*Without fur, the
cat usually stays
indoors for warmth*

***Find out more***

CHEETAHS 136
JAGUARS 217
LEOPARDS 227
LIONS 231
TIGERS 339

## WARNING SIGN?

Domestic cats often lie down on their
sides and let themselves be stroked.
They learn this position as kittens,
when the mother cat gives them a
daily grooming by licking their fur.
However, this position is also used to
warn enemies to keep their distance.
When the cat feels exposed to danger,
it lies on its back and reveals its tummy.
With all four legs outstretched and
claws flexed, it bares its teeth and will
bite anything that gets too close.

# CATTLE

LIKE THEIR CLOSE RELATIVES, sheep and antelope, cattle have two-toed, hoofed feet, and they live in herds. They are large mammals with stocky bodies and wide heads that graze on grasses. The term cattle includes the domestic cattle seen on farms, as well as wild cattle such as yaks, bison, and buffaloes. Both bulls (males) and cows (females) have a pair of horns. These are used for defence against enemies, and by bulls to compete for cows in the herd. Cattle were first domesticated – used by humans – about 9,000 years ago to provide milk, meat, and leather.

YAK

## FURRY COAT

Yaks are the largest cattle. They live high up in the mountains of Central Asia where the weather is freezing. Their long, shaggy coats and thick underfur help to keep out the cold. Despite their size, yaks are sure-footed, and move easily over rough ground.

Horns curve outwards to the side of the head

## DOMESTIC BREEDS

All breeds of domestic cattle are descended from aurochs. These were wild cattle that once roamed the plains of Asia and Europe in large numbers. The last aurochs died out about 400 years ago. However, some breeds, like this long-horned cow and her calf, still carry the long shaggy fur and large horns of their ancestors.

LONG-HORNED COW AND CALF

SCALE

Distinctive hump and long hair make bison appear much larger

Strong legs enable bison to move quickly if in danger

AMERICAN BISON

Two-toed feet with hooves

## BODY SHAPE

Like other cattle, the American bison has a strong, sturdy body and horns that turn out from the side of its head. The bison uses its excellent sense of smell to detect enemies and to keep in touch with the whereabouts of other bison. It lives in herds in grassland and open woodland in North America.

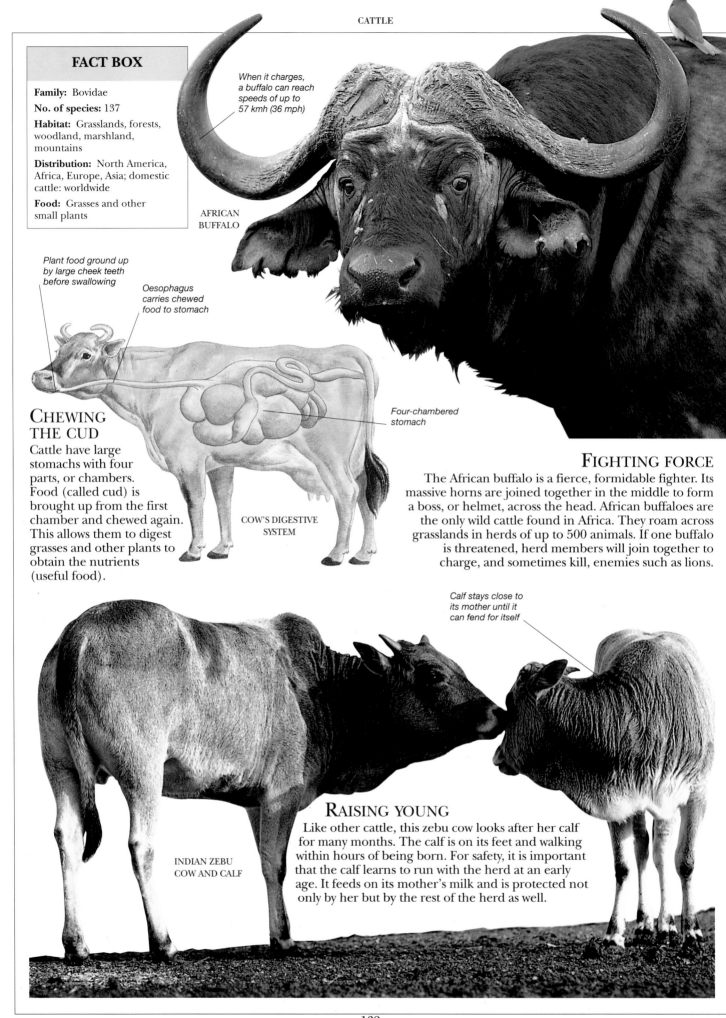

## FACT BOX

**Family:** Bovidae

**No. of species:** 137

**Habitat:** Grasslands, forests, woodland, marshland, mountains

**Distribution:** North America, Africa, Europe, Asia; domestic cattle: worldwide

**Food:** Grasses and other small plants

When it charges, a buffalo can reach speeds of up to 57 kmh (36 mph)

AFRICAN BUFFALO

Plant food ground up by large cheek teeth before swallowing

Oesophagus carries chewed food to stomach

Four-chambered stomach

## CHEWING THE CUD

Cattle have large stomachs with four parts, or chambers. Food (called cud) is brought up from the first chamber and chewed again. This allows them to digest grasses and other plants to obtain the nutrients (useful food).

COW'S DIGESTIVE SYSTEM

## FIGHTING FORCE

The African buffalo is a fierce, formidable fighter. Its massive horns are joined together in the middle to form a boss, or helmet, across the head. African buffaloes are the only wild cattle found in Africa. They roam across grasslands in herds of up to 500 animals. If one buffalo is threatened, herd members will join together to charge, and sometimes kill, enemies such as lions.

Calf stays close to its mother until it can fend for itself

INDIAN ZEBU COW AND CALF

## RAISING YOUNG

Like other cattle, this zebu cow looks after her calf for many months. The calf is on its feet and walking within hours of being born. For safety, it is important that the calf learns to run with the herd at an early age. It feeds on its mother's milk and is protected not only by her but by the rest of the herd as well.

Male bulls use their horns to fight rivals

## RIVAL BULLS

During the breeding season, bulls join the herd of cows and their calves. They challenge rival males to see who will mate with the cows. At first they stand stiffly and hold their head up to show rivals the full size of their horns. Then they snort and scrape the ground with their front hooves. If this display is not enough to drive rivals away, the bulls charge and fight with their horns until one of them gives up. Sometimes fighting can result in serious injury.

JERSEY COW
AND CALF

CAMARGUE
BLACK BULL

## MILK PRODUCER

Some breeds of domestic cattle are good dairy cattle (milk producers), while others are prized for their meat. Jersey cattle, one of the oldest dairy breeds, originally come from the small island of Jersey in the English Channel, but are now found worldwide. The cattle produce rich, creamy milk.

Typical red-and-white colouring and large, stocky build

Buffalo's hump is harnessed to the plough by a yoke

HEREFORD
BULL

Horns can measure up to 2 m (6.5 ft) across

## BEST FOR BEEF

Hereford cattle are easily recognized by their body shape and red-and-white coat. They are fed on grass and grain which makes their bodies produce high-quality beef. They are also popular with farmers because they grow quickly and need little protection from cold weather.

WATER
BUFFALO

## WATER LOVERS

The water buffaloes of southern Asia have been domesticated to provide milk and pull ploughs. They are massively built with huge horns that sweep backwards and upwards. When not feeding, they submerge themselves in water or wallow in mud. This keeps the buffaloes cool and protects them from biting insects.

### Find out more

CAMELS 124
DEER AND ANTELOPE 154
GAZELLES 183
PIGS 280

# CENTIPEDES AND MILLIPEDES

CENTIPEDES AND MILLIPEDES ARE many-legged minibeasts, with long bodies divided into segments (sections). Neither creature is very well named. The word centipede means "one hundred legs", but centipedes may have as few as 30 legs – or as many as 350. Millipede means "one thousand legs", but no millipede has more than 400. Centipedes and millipedes like damp, dark places. They live on the ground under leaves or stones, or in loose soil. They hide by day, and come out to feed at night.

GIANT TIGER
CENTIPEDE

Millipedes have two pairs of legs on each body segment

ARMOURED MILLIPEDE

Tough outer skin provides protection and helps keep the millipede moist

## RACING AHEAD
Centipedes are fierce, speedy predators. They race after worms, slugs, and insects, and bite their victims with their poisonous jaws.

Poison fangs catch prey

## FEEDING
Millipedes move slowly and do not hunt prey. They scour the woodland floor and soil, feeding on dead leaves and rotten wood.

When threatened, some millipedes curl up into a tight ball

## DEFENCE
Centipedes and millipedes have hard outer skins that deter predators from trying to eat them. When frightened, a millipede gives off an unpleasant smell to keep enemies away, or it may coil itself up.

### FACT BOX

**Family:** Centipede: Chilopoda Millipede: Diplopoda

**No. of species:** Centipede: 3,000+; Millipede: 10,000+

**Habitat:** Under stones, leaves and in loose soil

**Distribution:** All continents, except Antarctica

**Food:** Centipede: Worms, slugs, spiders, insects; Millipede: Dead plants, rotten wood

**No. of young:** 50–60

**Size:** Centipede: 0.5–30 cm (0.2–12 in); Millipede: 0.3–28 cm (0.1–11 in)

### Find out more
ANIMAL KINGDOM 16
INSECTS 212
MOVEMENT 28

## MOVEMENT
When centipedes and millipedes move forward, the legs on either side of their bodies move up and down in waves. Millipedes move between ten and 20 legs at once. The faster these minibeasts run, the fewer of their legs touch the ground.

COILED MILLIPEDE

SCALE

Centipedes have only one pair of legs on each body segment

GIANT TIGER CENTIPEDE

# CHAMELEONS

MEMBERS OF THE LIZARD FAMILY, chameleons live mainly in the tropical forests of Africa and Madagascar. They are well suited to living in trees, equipped with clawed feet and long, gripping tails for climbing. Their long sticky tongues are the same length as their bodies and tails combined, and are used to catch small insects. Chameleons live on their own most of the time. Males have long, drawn-out but fierce fights with each other to claim their territories in the forest. They puff up their bodies, wave special headflaps and even charge at each other, snapping their jaws.

MADAGASCAN
CHAMELEON

Extra long tongue
is bundled up
inside mouth

Eyes can look in
different directions
from each other

Males use
horns to fight
with rivals

Skin matches
the colour of
surrounding leaves

JACKSON'S
CHAMELEON

## STICKY END

To catch food, the chameleon flicks out its sticky-tipped tongue, which attaches itself to prey. The tongue can be flicked out and in so quickly that the victim is taken by surprise and has no time to escape.

Sharp-clawed toes
dig into branches

Two toes on each
foot go round one
side of a branch and
three toes go round
the other side

JACKSON'S
CHAMELEON

## SUPER GRIP

Chameleons climb along branches slowly and can hold on tightly with just their hind feet. The toes on each foot face in opposite directions so they can wrap around both sides of a branch. Sharp claws on the feet provide extra grip. Most chameleons also have a gripping tail, which can be coiled around twigs like an anchor.

Tail coils around
thin branches
to help chameleon
keep its balance

Pointed ridge
runs along
spine and
down the tail

SCALE

## CRAFTY COLOURS

The light green colour of the chameleon's body helps it to blend in well with its surroundings. Even its body has a leaf-like shape and provides extra camouflage. The mood of the chameleon can affect its colour. For example, when threatened by a rival the chameleon becomes angry and its skin changes to dark brown. The chameleon's skin colour also changes to make it more visible to a potential mate.

### FACT BOX

**Family:** Chamaeleontidae

**Habitat:** Tropical forests

**Distribution:** Madagascar, Africa, southern Asia, Europe

**Food:** Insects, spiders, scorpions; small birds

**No. of eggs:** 4–40; some species give birth to live young

**Lifespan:** 3–5 years

**Size:** 2–28 cm (1–12 in)

### Find out more

CAMOUFLAGE 36
RAINFORESTS 62
REPTILES 297

# CHEETAHS

ADULT
CHEETAH

THE FASTEST MEMBERS OF THE cat family, cheetahs are active during the day. This means they can survive in the same areas as lions and leopards, which are night-time hunters. The secret of the cheetah's super speed lies in its long, flexible backbone, which stretches out and closes up tightly like a coiled spring as it streaks across open grasslands. The females tend to live alone or with their young, whereas males keep together in small groups. Cheetahs are heavy enough to catch and kill gazelles and small antelope but small and lightweight enough to reach high speeds very quickly.

## SUPER SPEED

The cheetah is the fastest land animal over short distances. It can sprint across the savanna at speeds of more than 100 kmh (60 mph) but has to stop after about 20 seconds because it gets too hot.

Cubs stay close to their mother to learn survival skills

## AT THE KILL

When a cheetah catches up with its prey, it grips the victim's throat until it stops breathing. A cheetah cannot eat straight after a kill because it needs to get its breath back and cool down. Then, when it is ready, the cheetah eats the whole kill quickly before it is stolen by lions, hyenas, or vultures.

CHEETAH

ADULT
CHEETAH
AND CUBS

Teardrop line runs from each eye to the mouth

### FACT BOX

**Family:** Felidae

**Habitat:** Open grasslands, thick bush, semi-desert

**Distribution:** Africa, Asia, Middle East

**Food:** Gazelles, impalas, and other small antelope, small mammals, birds

**Gestation period:** 3 months

**Lifespan:** Up to 17 years

**Size:** 1.1–1.5 m (3–6 ft)

## HUNTING LESSONS

Cheetahs have between two and five cubs, which stay with their mother for their first 18 months. Under her care, they learn how to hunt by watching their mother and then practising on their own. A female cheetah with cubs has to kill every day to feed her family.

Polka dot markings help cheetah to blend in with dry grassland when it stalks its prey

SCALE

Striped rather than spotted tail

## CHEETAH FEATURES

A cheetah's running power comes from its powerful back legs and the large muscles along its flexible spine. It cannot pull in, or retract, its claws, so they grip the ground like spiked running shoes. The cheetah's long tail is used for balance and steering.

Clawed feet grip the ground

ADULT
CHEETAH

### Find out more

CATS 128
GRASSLANDS 64
LEOPARDS 227
LIONS 231
MEAT-EATERS 32

## OPEN HUNTING GROUND
Cheetahs hunt on the savannah grasslands, along with other predators such as lions and leopards. To avoid competition for food, cheetahs hunt and eat more during the daytime when other predators take shelter from the hot sun. They are also more likely to catch prey in an open area, then drag the kill to a hiding place so that rival meat eaters cannot steal their food.

# CHICKENS

BUFF SUSSEX
CHICKEN EGG

SILVER-GREY
DORKING
CHICKEN
EGG

TODAY, THERE ARE MORE CHICKENS in the world – more than 8,000 million – than any other kind of bird. Domestic chickens were originally bred from the wild red junglefowl of India and Southeast Asia. These birds live at the edge of rainforests and feed on small insects, seeds, and leaves. Together with domesticated turkeys, guineafowl, ducks, and geese, domestic chickens are known as poultry. They are kept on farms or smallholdings and fed mainly on grain and kitchen scraps. There are many different breeds of chicken, which are kept for their eggs or their plumage.

## EGG MEDLEY
Wild chickens build their nests in thick undergrowth, and sit on their eggs until they hatch. However, the eggs of domestic hens are removed as soon as they are laid, so the hens simply keep laying new ones.

## YOUNG CHICKS
As soon as they have hatched, chicks (baby chickens) follow the first moving object they see – usually the mother hen. Within a few hours of hatching, they can run about and find their own food. However, if a young bird helps itself to food before an adult has eaten, it will receive a sharp peck.

BUFF SUSSEX
CHICK

Loose, red skin is
called the comb

SILVER-GREY
DORKING CHICK

Domestic roosters look
similar to their wild
relatives, junglefowl

PEKIN BANTAM
ROOSTER

### FACT BOX
**Family:** Phasianidae
**Habitat:** Rainforests, fields
**Distribution:** Worldwide, except for Arctic and Antarctic
**Food:** Mostly grain and other seeds, fruit, leaves, worms, insects, and waste scraps
**Incubation:** 3 weeks
**Lifespan:** 3–5 years
**Size:** 42–75 cm (17–30 in)

## HEN BIRDS
Female chickens, called hens, are very protective of their chicks. If the hens sense danger or bad weather, they use a special call to tell their young to run and hide under their wings.

BRAHMA
HEN

Plumage is more
glossy and colourful
than that of hens

Sharp-clawed
feet scratch the
ground for food

## ROOSTER
The male chicken is called a rooster. Each flock of hens has a rooster who guards his hens from rival males and keeps a lookout for predators such as foxes.

SCALE

### Find out more

# CHIMPANZEES

CHIMPANZEES ARE INTELLIGENT and noisy animals that look and behave like humans in many ways. They are clever enough to solve problems and to make and use tools. Stones are used as hammers and leaves are adapted to sponge up water for drinking. Chimpanzees live in large communities of between 30 and 70 individuals, which move around in smaller groups of about four to eight chimpanzees. Each of these groups is headed by a male leader, noted for his strength.

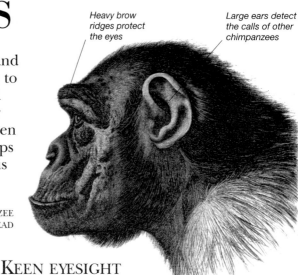

Heavy brow ridges protect the eyes

Large ears detect the calls of other chimpanzees

CHIMPANZEE HEAD

TWO-YEAR OLD CHIMPANZEE

SCALE

Pink face has no fur

Toes have nails rather than claws

## KEEN EYESIGHT

Like other apes, chimpanzees have good eyesight and are able to see in colour. Their eyes point forwards, rather than being set either side of the head, so they can focus on a single item.

## FINGERS AND TOES

The chimpanzee's long fingers and toes help it to pick up objects or hang onto branches, as well as pull leaves or fruit off plants. The thumbs and big toes can press against the tips of the fingers or toes, to form a grip that is very useful for grasping things.

### FACT BOX

**Family:** Pongidae

**Habitat:** Tropical forest, woodland, grassland

**Distribution:** West and Central Africa

**Food:** Fruit, leaves, nuts, seeds, eggs, termites, ants, monkeys

**No. of young:** Usually one

**Lifespan:** 40–45 years

**Size:** 70–92 cm (2–3 ft)

## NEST-BUILDING

Every night, the chimpanzee makes a sleeping nest up in the trees where it is safer from enemies. The nest is built from twigs and leaves in just five minutes, with a bunch of leaves to use as a pillow.

YOUNG CHIMPANZEE BUILDING A NEST

Young chimpanzees learn how to make a nest by watching their mother

## FOREST DWELLERS

Chimpanzees group together in communities of 30 or more individuals. They are not usually all together because they divide into smaller groups of eight or less for day-to-day living. Chimpanzees feed and sleep in trees but travel around their forest home, mainly on the ground, following a network of paths. Male chimps fiercely defend their area from rival groups.

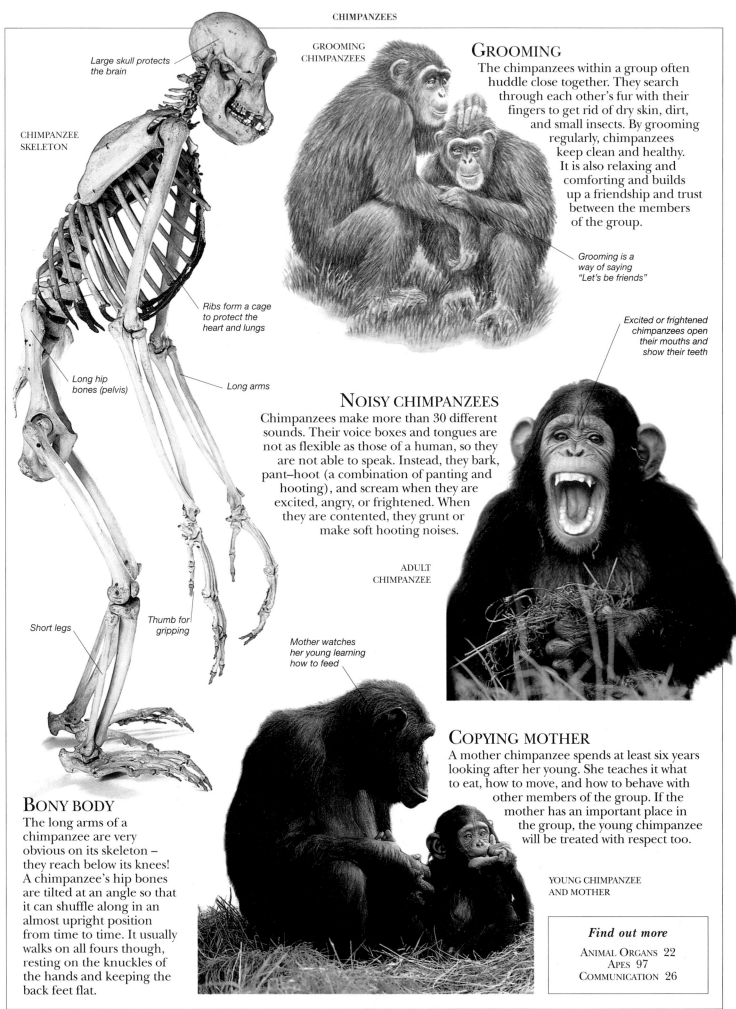

Large skull protects the brain

CHIMPANZEE SKELETON

GROOMING CHIMPANZEES

## GROOMING
The chimpanzees within a group often huddle close together. They search through each other's fur with their fingers to get rid of dry skin, dirt, and small insects. By grooming regularly, chimpanzees keep clean and healthy. It is also relaxing and comforting and builds up a friendship and trust between the members of the group.

Grooming is a way of saying "Let's be friends"

Ribs form a cage to protect the heart and lungs

Excited or frightened chimpanzees open their mouths and show their teeth

Long hip bones (pelvis)

Long arms

## NOISY CHIMPANZEES
Chimpanzees make more than 30 different sounds. Their voice boxes and tongues are not as flexible as those of a human, so they are not able to speak. Instead, they bark, pant–hoot (a combination of panting and hooting), and scream when they are excited, angry, or frightened. When they are contented, they grunt or make soft hooting noises.

ADULT CHIMPANZEE

Short legs

Thumb for gripping

Mother watches her young learning how to feed

## BONY BODY
The long arms of a chimpanzee are very obvious on its skeleton – they reach below its knees! A chimpanzee's hip bones are tilted at an angle so that it can shuffle along in an almost upright position from time to time. It usually walks on all fours though, resting on the knuckles of the hands and keeping the back feet flat.

## COPYING MOTHER
A mother chimpanzee spends at least six years looking after her young. She teaches it what to eat, how to move, and how to behave with other members of the group. If the mother has an important place in the group, the young chimpanzee will be treated with respect too.

YOUNG CHIMPANZEE AND MOTHER

### Find out more
ANIMAL ORGANS 22
APES 97
COMMUNICATION 26

# CIVETS AND GENETS

RELATIVES OF THE CAT FAMILY, civets and genets have slim bodies with short legs, and fur that is often striped or spotted. Their long faces have pointed snouts, pointed or rounded ears, long whiskers, and large eyes. Civets and genets are solitary animals that spend much of their time in trees. They are good climbers, using their sharp claws to grip tree trunks and branches, and their long tails to help them balance. They feed on small animals, such as birds and mammals, and also forage for fruit.

SPOTTED GENET

Strong, clawed feet for climbing trees

## NIGHT-TIME LONERS

Palm civets eat a lot of fruit, not only from palms but many other types of trees as well. They are cat-like animals that live alone in trees and bushes and are active at night. They feed both in the branches and on the ground, where they also catch insects and small animals.

COMMON PALM CIVET

## STEALTHY KILLER

By day, genets rest in tree branches or rock crevices. At night, they use speed and stealth to catch prey such as small mammals and birds, both in trees and on the ground. Genets have long, slim bodies and sharp, flesh-cutting teeth. Their large, forward-facing eyes enable them to see at night and pounce accurately on moving prey.

Coat of long, shaggy fur

SCALE

## GRIPPING TAIL

The binturong, or bear cat, has a prehensile (gripping) tail. It uses this as an extra leg when climbing, or to hold on when it grabs a branch laden with fruit. Binturongs spend most of their time in dense forests, moving slowly through trees in search of fruit and insects.

BINTURONG

### FACT BOX

**Family:** Viverridae

**Habitat:** Forests, grasslands

**Distribution:** Africa, Asia, southwest Europe, Madagascar

**Food:** Insects, frogs, lizards, birds and birds' eggs, small mammals, fruit, roots

**No. of young:** 1–4

**Lifespan:** Up to 20 years

**Size:** 33–95 cm (13–38 in)

### Find out more

# COBRAS

THE HIGHLY POISONOUS SPECIES known as cobras are related to the mambas of Africa, the coral snakes of the Americas, and the tiger snakes of Australia. They live mostly in tropical areas, feeding on birds, small animals, and other reptiles. Although snakes are meat-eaters, their teeth cannot rip or tear flesh so they have to swallow their kill whole. Cobras use their poison to stun prey and to defend themselves against predators, such as crocodiles and birds of prey.

RED SPITTING
COBRA

*Coloured ring
around eye looks
like a monocle
(eyeglass)*

*Long ribs support
the hood when
it opens out*

COBRA
SKELETON

## POISON FANGS

When threatened, spitting cobras fire a jet of poison into their attacker's eyes. All cobras have a pair of short fangs at the front of their mouths. The hollow fangs inject venom, a deadly poison, into the snake's prey, stunning the victim and breaking down its tissues to make it easier to digest.

## BENDY BODY

A cobra's skeleton has up to 400 bones in its backbone. A snake has loose joints in its backbone so that it can bend and coil its body in all directions. Curved ribs that join onto the backbone, protect the snake's internal organs and support its scaly body.

*Large eyespots,
horseshoes, or
bands decorate
cobra's hood*

## HOODED SNAKE

When a cobra is alarmed or angry, it rears up and spreads out a flap of skin behind its head to form a hood. This makes it look larger and threatening, and helps to frighten away enemies.

THAI
MONOCLED
COBRA

### FACT BOX

**Family:** Elapidae

**Habitat:** Woodland, grassland, fields, scrubland

**Distribution:** Africa and Asia

**Food:** Birds, small mammals, snakes and other reptiles

**No. of eggs:** Up to 40

**Lifespan:** Up to 30 years

**Size:** Up to 5.5 m (18 ft)

*Body bunches up
ready to attack if
necessary.*

***Find out more***

BOAS AND PYTHONS 118
DEFENCE 34
REPTILES 297
SNAKES 325

SCALE

# COCKROACHES

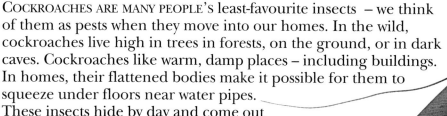

COCKROACHES ARE MANY PEOPLE'S least-favourite insects – we think of them as pests when they move into our homes. In the wild, cockroaches live high in trees in forests, on the ground, or in dark caves. Cockroaches like warm, damp places – including buildings. In homes, their flattened bodies make it possible for them to squeeze under floors near water pipes. These insects hide by day and come out to feed at night. They eat almost anything, including plants, animal carcasses and droppings, paper, books, and even soap. Fossils show cockroaches existed on Earth 300 million years ago, before the dinosaurs.

## WINGED INSECT

Cockroaches have flat, oval-shaped bodies that allow them to fit into narrow cracks. Most species have two pairs of wings. The tough, leathery front wings fold over and protect the delicate back wings while the insect is resting. Most cockroaches can fly, but they mainly escape from enemies by scurrying away on their long legs.

*Long antennae sweep back behind the insect's head*

*Tough front wings fold over back wings*

### FACT BOX

**Family:** Blattodea

**Habitat:** On land, from deserts to rainforests, also buildings

**Distribution:** Worldwide, except Arctic and Antarctic

**Food:** Plants, animal carcasses, rubbish, paper, soap

**No. of eggs:** 18

**Lifespan:** 2 years

**Size:** 1.3–10 cm (1–4 in)

*Feelers attached to the mouth detect the taste and smell of food*

## PRODUCING YOUNG

Female cockroaches lay their eggs in a tough case like a purse. The case protects the eggs until they are ready to hatch. Young cockroaches look like tiny versions of the adults, but have no wings. Different species take from six weeks to one year to mature.

SCALE

FEMALE AMERICAN COCKROACH

*Delicate hairs on the underside detect vibrations when other creatures are near*

*Long antennae help the cockroach find its way in the dark*

*Tough "purse" contains two rows of eggs*

## SENSES

The cockroach's main sense organs are its long feelers, or antennae. They are used for smelling and tasting, as well as touching. On the cockroach's legs are touch-sensitive hairs which can detect the slightest vibration. Many species have two large bristles on their abdomen which detect vibrations in the air.

### Find out more

INSECTS 212
GRASSHOPPERS AND CRICKETS 195
SENSES 24

# CORALS

SKELETON OF
MUSHROOM
CORAL

ALTHOUGH THEY LOOK LIKE STRANGE plants or fungi, corals are, in fact, animals. Each individual polyp (coral animal) looks like a miniature sea anemone. It has a ring of stinging tentacles surrounding a central mouth and stomach, which makes up almost all of the polyp's stalk. In most corals, polyps are connected by living tissue to form huge colonies. In stony or reef-building corals, millions of these tiny animals produce a hard, outer casing to protect them from damage and predators. When polyps die, their outer skeletons gradually build up to form a coral reef.

SCALE

## LIVING ALONE
Mushroom corals are made up of a single, large polyp. They are not attached to the rock like stony coral but rest loosely on it. They can even move about a little. Mushroom corals produce a sticky mucus containing stinging cells. These kill off the edges of colonies of other corals that intrude on their living space.

Long parallel tubes

Scallops shelter in the frills

SKELETON OF
ROSE CORAL

## FRILLED EDGE
The tightly packed frills of the rose coral provide a safe home for tiny algae and sea creatures. In exchange for the shelter and supply of nutrients that the coral provides, algae pass on some of their food to their host.

Feathery tentacles catch passing food

SKELETON
OF ORGAN-
PIPE CORAL

## PIPED CORAL
The long polyps of the organ-pipe coral live side by side, protected by a hard tubular casing. Most coral polyps open only at night, but the organ-pipe puts out its tentacles in the daytime to feed. The large tentacles overlap each other so that they cover as much area as possible to trap food.

### FACT BOX

**Group:** Cnidaria

**Habitat:** Warm, shallow seas, cool deep waters; stony corals: warm, clear, shallow water

**Distribution:** Indian and Pacific oceans, Caribbean

**Food:** Tiny sea creatures, plants

**Gestation period:** 6 months

**Lifespan:** 25–30 years

**Size:** 1 cm (0.5 in)

## FEATHERY FANS
Sea fans use their feathery tentacles to catch food. Their delicate branches grow facing the water current, so that they can trap any tiny sea creatures and plants being carried along.

Flexible skeleton allows branches to bend with the current

ORANGE
SEA FAN

### Find out more

CONSERVATION 82
EXOSKELETONS 20
INVERTEBRATES 215
JELLYFISH AND ANEMONES 219
OCEANS 74

## COLOURFUL KINGDOM
Coral reefs are among the richest of all habitats, and are as important in the sea world as tropical rainforests are on land. They thrive where the water is warm and kept free of pollution. The survival of coral reefs also depends on the strict protection of the many sea creatures that make their homes there. These include complex communities of fish and sea lilies.

# CRABS

LOBSTERS, PRAWNS, AND SHRIMPS are close relatives of crabs.
They are all crustaceans, with their bodies usually enclosed
in hard, protective casings and their legs jointed. As the crab
grows, it sheds its old shell to make way for a new soft shell
that gradually hardens up to protect its body. Crabs are
found worldwide, mainly in shallow coastal waters – although
some live on deep seabeds or in fresh water. Most crabs are
scavengers, feeding on the remains of other sea creatures
and debris found on the sea floor.

*Large pincers*

*Pointed foot used for digging in sand*

EDIBLE CRAB

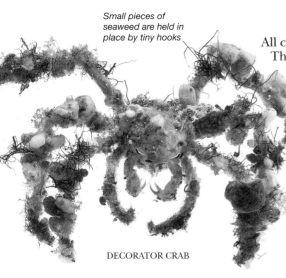

*Small pieces of seaweed are held in place by tiny hooks*

DECORATOR CRAB

## BODY PARTS

All crabs have five pairs of jointed legs.
The first pair have enlarged front joints
which form pincers (claws). The
other four pairs of legs are used for
walking. The soft main part of the
body is protected by a strong,
hard shell in typical crabs.

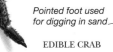

SCALE

## DRESSING UP

Unlike other crabs, decorator crabs avoid
predators by pretending to be something
else. They pick up pieces of seaweed or
small creatures such as sponges and place
them all over their bodies and legs. This
living coat of disguise soon grows over the
crab, hiding it from the eyes of predators.

## GETTING AROUND

Crabs move sideways, either walking
slowly or scuttling along at speed. Some
crabs can swim well, using their hind
pair of legs as oars. These are flattened
and fringed with hairs to increase
their surface area for rowing.

SHORE
CRAB

*Jointed walking legs*

## FACT BOX

**Class:** Malacostraca

**Habitat:** Seas and coastal waters,
fresh water, land

**Distribution:** Worldwide

**Food:** Mostly dead animals

**No. of eggs:** Typically 150,000

**Lifespan:** Up to 60 years

**Size:** Up to 1 m (3 ft)

## BEACH DWELLERS

Although most crabs spend all or much of their lives in water, some have mastered living on land. Coconut (or robber) crabs are typical land crabs, and scuttle across sandy beaches in the Indian and Pacific oceans. They will drown if submerged in water for a long time. Only the female crabs have any contact with water – when they go down to the sea to lay their eggs.

Antenna

Movable
stalked eyes

SWIMMING
CRAB

Large claws are
used to nip or
pinch enemies

BROWN
CRAB

## EYES ON STALKS

A crab has a pair of eyes set on short stalks, which can be
moved in different directions. Each eye is made up of
hundreds of tiny lenses which, together, build up a very
detailed picture. With such accurate eyesight,
crabs can detect the slightest movement.
Crabs also have a pair of
antennae (feelers), covered
in tiny hairs that help it to
touch, smell, and taste.

## SELF-DEFENCE

Crabs hold their large, powerful
pincers in front of them, ready
to defend themselves against
predators. Some crabs also hold
shells or leaves above them to
hide from enemies. The cunning
boxer crab wears a sea anemone
on each pincer, using the stinging
cells of its boxing gloves (the
anemones) to scare off attackers.

Shell is no longer
big enough for
the growing
hermit crab

Pincers are
are ready to
pull rival out
of shell

## STEALING A HOME

Unlike other crabs which grow their own
shells, hermit crabs have to find empty
ones in which to protect their soft
bodies. Shells that have been outgrown
and shed by other sea creatures can be
hard to find, so hermit crabs often fight
for the right to an abandoned shell.
Those that cannot find a shell run the
risk of being killed by a predator.

HERMIT
CRABS

### Find out more

CRUSTACEANS 153
DEFENCE 34
ISLANDS 76
LOBSTERS 237
OCEANS 74

Crab reverses
its body into
the empty shell

# CROCODILES AND ALLIGATORS

MEMBERS OF THE CROCODILIAN FAMILY include crocodiles, alligators, caimans (which are related to alligators) and gharials. They are all fierce meat-eaters, feeding on a wide range of animals from insects and frogs to fish, turtles, and birds. Alligators and caimans have wide, flat heads with rounded snouts, while crocodiles and gharials have more pointed snouts. They all live in the water but come out to bask in the sun during the daytime. Females lay their eggs on land, but the young enter water as soon as they have hatched out.

AMERICAN ALLIGATOR

CROCODILE TOOTH

## GIGANTIC JAWS
Alligators and caimans have short, wide snouts to catch larger prey while gharials and crocodiles use their long, pointy snouts to catch fish. They all have powerful jaws that can be firmly snapped shut to drive rows of knife-like teeth deep into prey.

## CONE TEETH
Crocodiles and alligators both have cone-shaped teeth. Unlike mammals, who have just two sets of teeth to last them a lifetime, crocodiles constantly shed and replace their teeth. New teeth grow below the old ones and push them out of place when they are fully developed.

Teeth are used to tear flesh as crocodiles and alligators cannot chew

SPECTACLED CAIMAN

Powerful tail is used to propel the caiman's body through water

Skin is tightly joined to the skull bones, without any muscular padding underneath

Only four toes on hind feet

Webbed feet

SCALE

## SCALY SUIT
Crocodiles and alligators, including caimans and gharials, control their body temperature by moving in and out of water to warm up or cool down. Their bodies are protected from sunburn and attack by an outer skin made up of toughened scales. These scales are also waterproof and help to stop the reptiles' bodies from drying out.

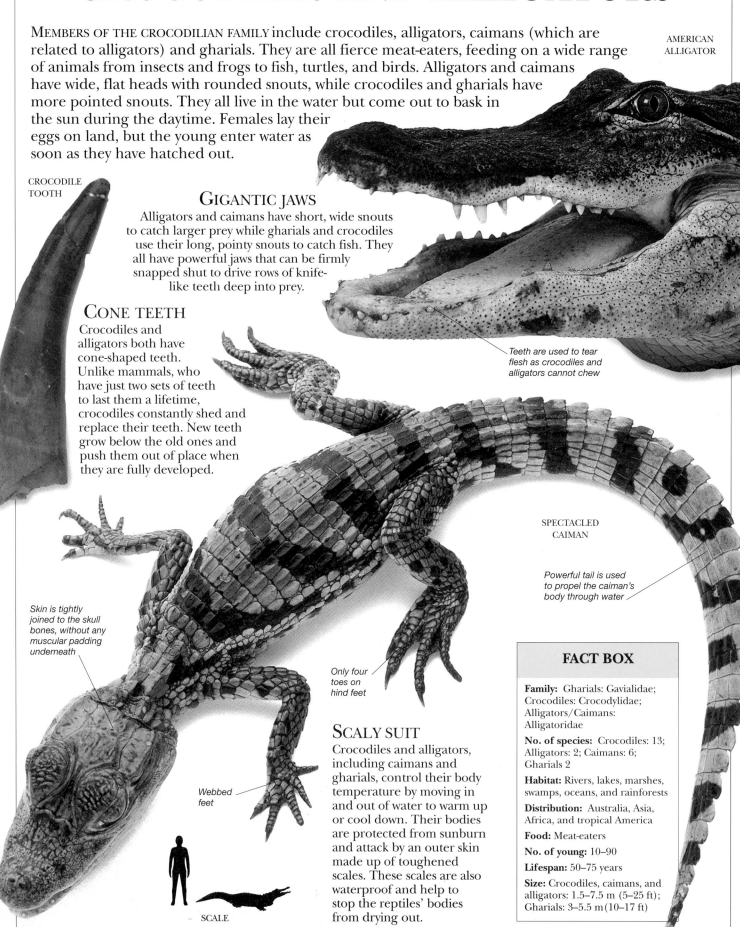

**FACT BOX**

**Family:** Gharials: Gavialidae; Crocodiles: Crocodylidae; Alligators/Caimans: Alligatoridae

**No. of species:** Crocodiles: 13; Alligators: 2; Caimans: 6; Gharials 2

**Habitat:** Rivers, lakes, marshes, swamps, oceans, and rainforests

**Distribution:** Australia, Asia, Africa, and tropical America

**Food:** Meat-eaters

**No. of young:** 10–90

**Lifespan:** 50–75 years

**Size:** Crocodiles, caimans, and alligators: 1.5–7.5 m (5–25 ft); Gharials: 3–5.5 m (10–17 ft)

## SWAMPLANDS

American alligators live in the shallow swamplands of the southeastern United States. There is plenty of food in this wetland, and they lie in wait for their prey, such as fish. There are also mud banks and islands on which they can bask in the sun or build nests. During the cold winter months, alligators retreat into a cosy den dug in the soil and sleep there until the spring.

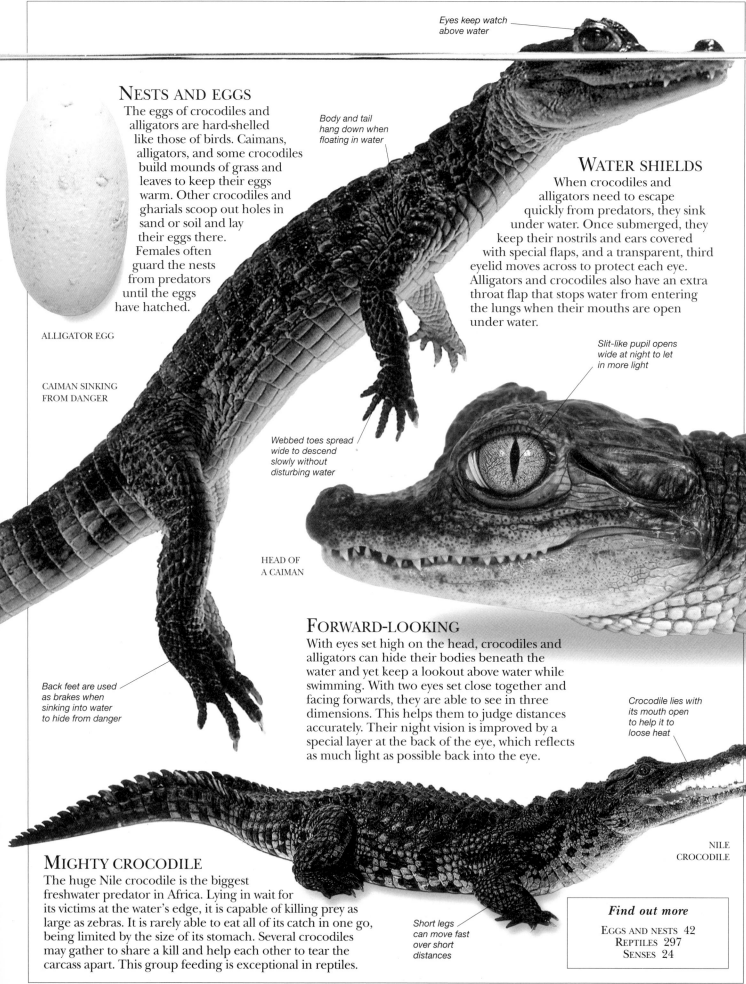

Eyes keep watch above water

## NESTS AND EGGS

The eggs of crocodiles and alligators are hard-shelled like those of birds. Caimans, alligators, and some crocodiles build mounds of grass and leaves to keep their eggs warm. Other crocodiles and gharials scoop out holes in sand or soil and lay their eggs there. Females often guard the nests from predators until the eggs have hatched.

Body and tail hang down when floating in water

ALLIGATOR EGG

CAIMAN SINKING FROM DANGER

## WATER SHIELDS

When crocodiles and alligators need to escape quickly from predators, they sink under water. Once submerged, they keep their nostrils and ears covered with special flaps, and a transparent, third eyelid moves across to protect each eye. Alligators and crocodiles also have an extra throat flap that stops water from entering the lungs when their mouths are open under water.

Slit-like pupil opens wide at night to let in more light

Webbed toes spread wide to descend slowly without disturbing water

HEAD OF A CAIMAN

## FORWARD-LOOKING

With eyes set high on the head, crocodiles and alligators can hide their bodies beneath the water and yet keep a lookout above water while swimming. With two eyes set close together and facing forwards, they are able to see in three dimensions. This helps them to judge distances accurately. Their night vision is improved by a special layer at the back of the eye, which reflects as much light as possible back into the eye.

Back feet are used as brakes when sinking into water to hide from danger

Crocodile lies with its mouth open to help it to loose heat

NILE CROCODILE

## MIGHTY CROCODILE

The huge Nile crocodile is the biggest freshwater predator in Africa. Lying in wait for its victims at the water's edge, it is capable of killing prey as large as zebras. It is rarely able to eat all of its catch in one go, being limited by the size of its stomach. Several crocodiles may gather to share a kill and help each other to tear the carcass apart. This group feeding is exceptional in reptiles.

Short legs can move fast over short distances

# CRUSTACEANS

THERE ARE ABOUT 40,000 different types of crustacean. These include crabs, lobsters, shrimps, prawns, barnacles, and woodlice. They range in size from tiny water fleas to giant spider crabs, but they are all protected by tough exoskeletons (outer skeletons). Most crustaceans live in the sea or in fresh water but a few, including some very specialized crabs and woodlice, are able to live on land. They all lay eggs; in most cases these develop, after several larval stages, into adults through a process called metamorphosis.

*Lid of shell opens to feed*

*Long antennae can detect prey's movements*

## STAYING PUT

Although most crustaceans can walk or swim well, barnacles – once they are adults – stay firmly fixed in one place. Barnacle eggs hatch into tiny larvae that drift in the sea until they find a place to settle. They then fasten themselves to rocks, boats, or even whales' skin, and grow shell-like cases. The shelled bodies of goose barnacles are held in place by their long, fleshy stalks.

*Large, powerful pincers for seizing, handling, and cutting up prey*

*Long, fleshy stalk*

COMMON GOOSE BARNACLES

COMMON LOBSTER

*Pair of short antennae – each pair divides into two branches*

*Exoskeleton made up of both separate and fused segments*

*Compound eye*

*Breathing gills at base of legs*

*Tail propels lobster through water*

*Four pairs of jointed walking legs*

## COMMON FEATURES

Crustaceans, like this common lobster, have jointed limbs and soft bodies that are protected by strong, rigid, outer skeletons. As their bodies grow, crustaceans shed these exoskeletons and grow new, larger casings. They all have two pairs of antennae, which they use to feel their way around and detect food.

## FACT BOX

**Class:** Fish lice: Branchiura; Water fleas, brine shrimps: Branchiopoda; Copepods: Copepoda; Shrimps, prawns, woodlice, sandhoppers, lobsters, crabs: Malacostraca; Barnacles: Cirripedia

**Habitat:** Oceans, coasts, fresh water, land

**Distribution:** Worldwide

**Food:** Small animals, plant matter; some are parasites

## LAND DWELLERS

Woodlice hide away by day in damp, dark places to stop their bodies from drying out. They come out to feed at night, when it is cooler and damper. Woodlice are among the few crustaceans that are able to live on land.

*Woodlice feed on rotting leaves and wood*

WOODLICE

### Find out more

CRABS 147
FRESH WATER 70
INVERTEBRATES 215
LOBSTERS 237
OCEANS 74

# DEER AND ANTELOPE

THE DEER AND ANTELOPE FAMILIES belong to the large group of even-toed animals. This group includes cattle, pigs, and camels. Both animals are plant-eaters, either grazing on grassland or browsing on trees and leaves. Deer and antelope are shy, fast-moving animals that often live in herds for safety. They are preyed upon by larger mammals and rely on their ability to run quickly to escape. Male deer (and all reindeer) grow antlers every year, while antelope have permanent horns.

*Antlers stop growing and velvet peels off*

*Antlers are covered in velvet (soft skin)*

*Antlers break off in winter*

*Antler buds start to grow in spring*

**SEQUENCE OF ANTLER GROWTH**

SPRING

EARLY SUMMER

AUTUMN

*Large eyes for all-round vision*

*Reddish-brown coat blends in with woodland background*

## ANTLERS
Deer are the only mammals that have antlers (bones at the top of the head). Male deer grow a new set every year, and use them to fight with rivals when looking for female mates in the breeding season.

**FEMALE RED DEER**

*Short tail*

## CHEW THE CUD
Antelopes and deer are plant-eaters. They can swallow food quickly, then bring it up later for "chewing the cud" to get all the goodness out of the food.

*Three- or four-chambered stomach allows food to be brought back up*

*Spotted markings blend in with woodland*

*Spindly legs*

**FAWN**

## BABY DEER
Many fawns or calves (young deer) have spotted coats to camouflage them from predators. They stay hidden in dense undergrowth for the first few weeks, coming out to drink milk from their mother when she visits.

*Two-toed hoof*

### FACT BOX

**Family:** Deer: Cervidae
Musk deer: Moschidae
Antelope: Bovidae

**No. of species:** Deer: 40
Antelope: 73

**Habitat:** Tundra, forest, woodland, grassland, mountains

**Distribution:** All continents, except Antarctica

**Food:** Grass, shoots, twigs, leaves, flowers, fruit, seeds, bark

**No. of young:** 1–3

**Lifespan:** Up to 30 years

**Size:** 0.4–2.3 m (3–8 ft)

SCALE

## SMALLEST ANTELOPE
The delicate royal antelope lives in the tropical forests of West Africa. No larger than a rabbit, it is the smallest hoofed mammal with horns. It has an arched back and short neck, which allow it to move quickly through dense vegetation. Royal antelopes are shy, timid animals that hide during the day and come out at night to feed.

**ROYAL ANTELOPE**

## WOODLAND COVER
Deer make their homes in woodlands. They feed on the wide variety of grasses and leaves, shoots, twigs, flowers, and fruits from bushes and trees that grow in the habitat. In woodlands, deer can shelter from bad weather and protect their young from danger. Their brown or spotted coats make them surprisingly difficult to see among a mass of tree trunks.

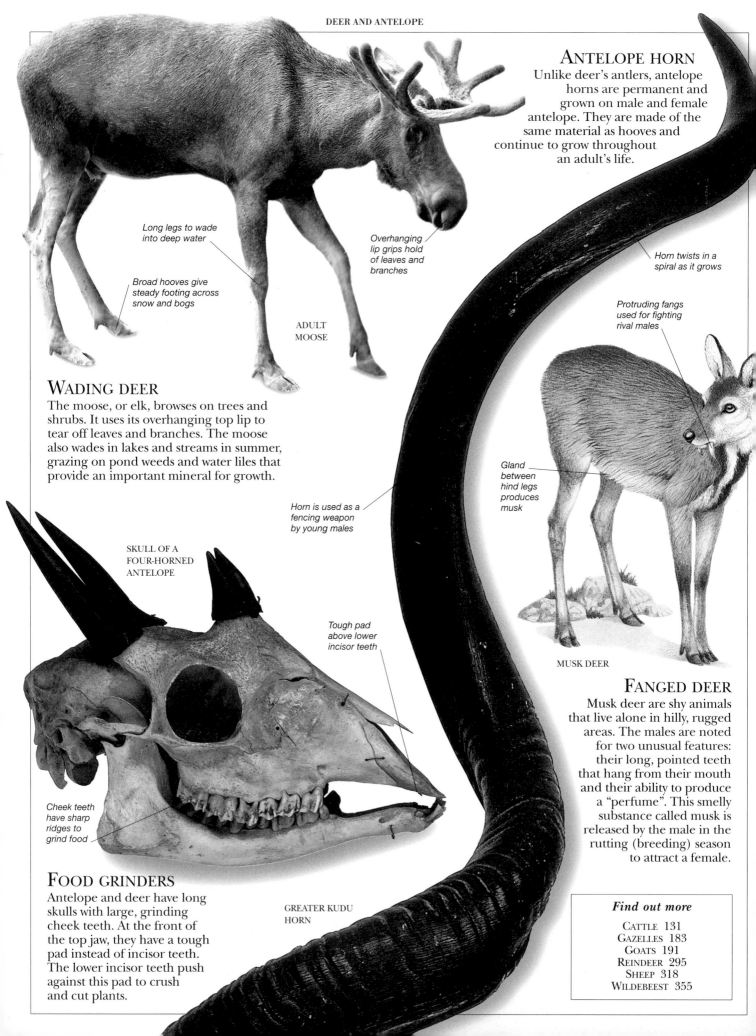

## ANTELOPE HORN

Unlike deer's antlers, antelope horns are permanent and grown on male and female antelope. They are made of the same material as hooves and continue to grow throughout an adult's life.

*Long legs to wade into deep water*

*Broad hooves give steady footing across snow and bogs*

*Overhanging lip grips hold of leaves and branches*

ADULT MOOSE

*Horn twists in a spiral as it grows*

*Protruding fangs used for fighting rival males*

## WADING DEER

The moose, or elk, browses on trees and shrubs. It uses its overhanging top lip to tear off leaves and branches. The moose also wades in lakes and streams in summer, grazing on pond weeds and water liles that provide an important mineral for growth.

*Horn is used as a fencing weapon by young males*

*Gland between hind legs produces musk*

SKULL OF A FOUR-HORNED ANTELOPE

*Tough pad above lower incisor teeth*

MUSK DEER

## FANGED DEER

Musk deer are shy animals that live alone in hilly, rugged areas. The males are noted for two unusual features: their long, pointed teeth that hang from their mouth and their ability to produce a "perfume". This smelly substance called musk is released by the male in the rutting (breeding) season to attract a female.

*Cheek teeth have sharp ridges to grind food*

## FOOD GRINDERS

Antelope and deer have long skulls with large, grinding cheek teeth. At the front of the top jaw, they have a tough pad instead of incisor teeth. The lower incisor teeth push against this pad to crush and cut plants.

GREATER KUDU HORN

### Find out more

# DOGS

THE DOG FAMILY INCLUDES wild species such as wolves, foxes, jackals, coyotes, and bush dogs plus about 200 breeds of domestic dog. Wild dogs are fast-running hunters with long legs, keen senses, and sharp teeth for killing prey. Some wild dogs live and hunt on their own, while others, such as wolves and African wild dogs, hunt together in packs. Domestic dogs are related to wolves and treat their owners as if they were members of their "pack". They are broadly divided into three groups: pet or toy (such as poodles), working, and hunting dogs.

*Large, pointed ears used to signal to other wild dogs and to control body temperature*

## PACK POWER

African wild dogs live and hunt in large family packs on the African grasslands. They prey on zebra, gazelle, and wildebeest, usually choosing young or weak animals. Once the dogs have eaten the meat, they return to the pack and bring up half-digested pieces of food to share with the young.

AFRICAN HUNTING DOG

*White tail tuft is used to signal to pack members*

*Four-toed front paw*

*Canines grip and kill prey*

## DOG ANCESTOR

The wolf is the ancestor of all domestic dogs. This skull reveals the wolf's long muzzle. Its strong jaws contain 42 teeth, including cheek teeth for tearing flesh and molars for crushing bone.

SCALE

SKULL OF WOLF'S HEAD

*Molars for crushing bones*

*Incisors gnaw bones*

*Small, rounded ears*

PAIR OF ADULT BUSH DOGS

## BUSH DOG

The bush dogs of Central and South America do not share the wolf-like features of most dogs. They have small heads with rounded ears, short legs, and stumpy tails. However, they are good hunters and can bring down large prey. They live in open country near water (bush dogs are good swimmers) and dig out burrows as homes.

*Large claws for burrowing*

Jackal pairs use the scent of their urine to mark their territory

## FAMILY TIES

Jackals live in close-knit family groups. They all share the duty of looking after the young cubs and providing food for them. When a male and female golden jackal become a pair, they stay loyal to each other for life. The pair will scent-mark their territory and patrol it together to prevent other jackals from trespassing.

Mane can be raised to make wolf look larger

Long, flexible ears "catch" sounds and channel them down to the eardrum

PAIR OF
GOLDEN JACKALS

ADULT
COYOTE

## PRAIRIE HUNTERS

As their name suggests, prairie wolves, or coyotes, live in the prairies and desert canyons of North America. They hunt mainly in the evening and early morning when the temperature is cool. During the winter, when food is scarce, they will hunt both day and night.

MANED WOLF

## WOLF ON STILTS

The maned wolf of South America is named after the thick black mane on its back. Its black-booted legs are longer than the length of its body – it is sometimes called the stilt-legged fox because of its long legs and red-haired coat.

Long legs hold wolf's body above tall grass

### FACT BOX

Family: Canidae

Habitat: Grasslands, forests, tundra, deserts, urban areas

Distribution: Worldwide, except Madagascar, New Zealand, and Antarctica. Bush dogs: South America. Coyote: North America. Domestic dogs: All continents

Food: Mostly mammals; also birds, lizards, carrion, and fruit

TEAM OF SIBERIAN
HUSKY DOGS

## TEAM WORK

Husky dogs are able to withstand the harsh, cold conditions of the Arctic. Like their ancestor, the Arctic wolf, huskies rarely bark but when in a pack, they take part in communal howling.

CAVALIER KING
CHARLES SPANIEL

## TOY DOGS

Most toy dogs are smaller versions of large domestic dogs, such as terriers and spaniels. Toy dogs were probably first bred by the Romans and were kept as status symbols by wealthy people in the Middle Ages.

Strong jaws form a "perfect" bite

Loud bark deters would-be attackers

## HELPER DOGS

German shepherds, or Alsatians, are intelligent domestic dogs that respond well to training. Their keen sense of smell and defence skills are used for police work and to guard people and buildings.

GERMAN SHEPHERD DOG

ST BERNARD DOG
OR ALPINE
MASTIFF

## MOUNTAIN RESCUE

One of the largest and heaviest domestic dogs, St Bernards, have always been known as mountain rescue dogs. They have an excellent sense of smell and are very strong. They are able to make trails through snow and are trained to rescue people who have been buried by avalanches.

Mane of long white fur

BORDER
COLLIE

## FARMER'S FRIEND

Some domestic dogs are important farmworkers, helping to protect and herd farm animals. Most herding dogs are light coloured or have large patches of white in their coats. This allows them to be seen more easily by the shepherd during bad weather or in the dark.

Dense, short fur protects against cold

### Find out more

DESERT 68
FOXES 179
GRASSLAND 64
MEAT EATERS 32
SENSES 24
WOLVES 356

# DOLPHINS AND PORPOISES

THE WHALE FAMILY INCLUDES dolphins and porpoises, as well as killer, false killer, and pilot whales. Most dolphins and porpoises live in ocean and coastal waters and can swim extremely fast. They are very social animals, living in schools or small groups. Members of a school look after one another – for example, if a dolphin is sick or injured, one of the school will push it to the water surface so that it can breathe. Dolphins are among the most intelligent of all animals, with a highly developed system of communication that uses a language of squeaks, grunts, and clicks.

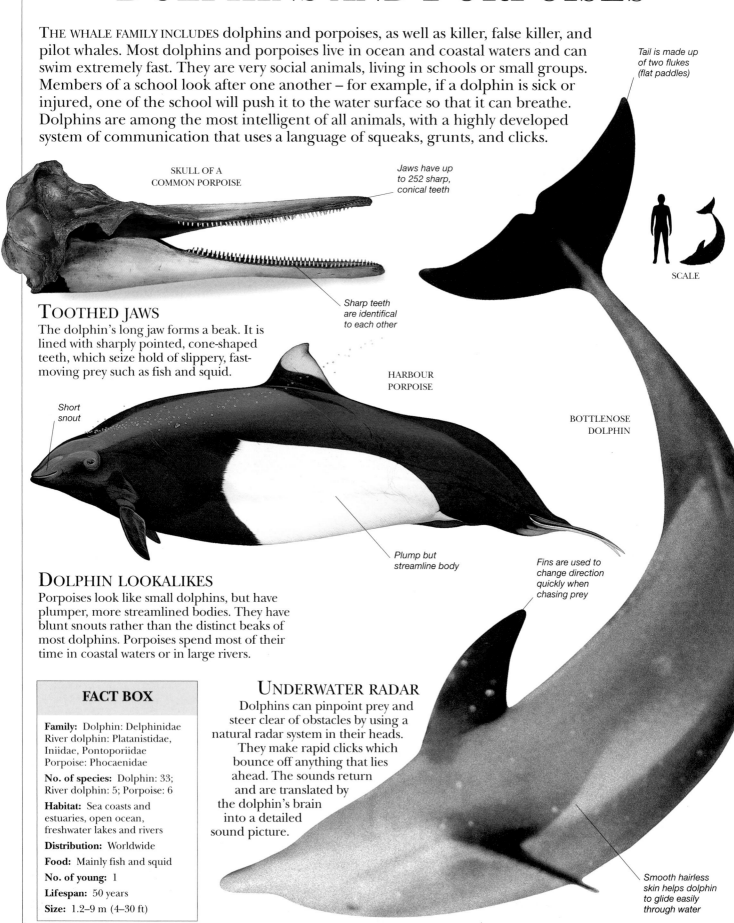

*Tail is made up of two flukes (flat paddles)*

SKULL OF A COMMON PORPOISE

*Jaws have up to 252 sharp, conical teeth*

SCALE

*Sharp teeth are identical to each other*

## TOOTHED JAWS
The dolphin's long jaw forms a beak. It is lined with sharply pointed, cone-shaped teeth, which seize hold of slippery, fast-moving prey such as fish and squid.

*Short snout*

HARBOUR PORPOISE

BOTTLENOSE DOLPHIN

*Plump but streamline body*

*Fins are used to change direction quickly when chasing prey*

## DOLPHIN LOOKALIKES
Porpoises look like small dolphins, but have plumper, more streamlined bodies. They have blunt snouts rather than the distinct beaks of most dolphins. Porpoises spend most of their time in coastal waters or in large rivers.

## UNDERWATER RADAR
Dolphins can pinpoint prey and steer clear of obstacles by using a natural radar system in their heads. They make rapid clicks which bounce off anything that lies ahead. The sounds return and are translated by the dolphin's brain into a detailed sound picture.

*Smooth hairless skin helps dolphin to glide easily through water*

### FACT BOX

**Family:** Dolphin: Delphinidae
River dolphin: Platanistidae, Iniidae, Pontoporiidae
Porpoise: Phocaenidae

**No. of species:** Dolphin: 33; River dolphin: 5; Porpoise: 6

**Habitat:** Sea coasts and estuaries, open ocean, freshwater lakes and rivers

**Distribution:** Worldwide

**Food:** Mainly fish and squid

**No. of young:** 1

**Lifespan:** 50 years

**Size:** 1.2–9 m (4–30 ft)

# OPEN SEAS

Dolphins and porpoises live in coastal waters and oceans. Along with their larger relatives, the whales, they are more at home in the water than any other mammals in the world. They even sleep, mate, and give birth underwater. But, like all mammals, dolphins and porpoises breathe air into their lungs, and have to visit the surface regularly to do this.

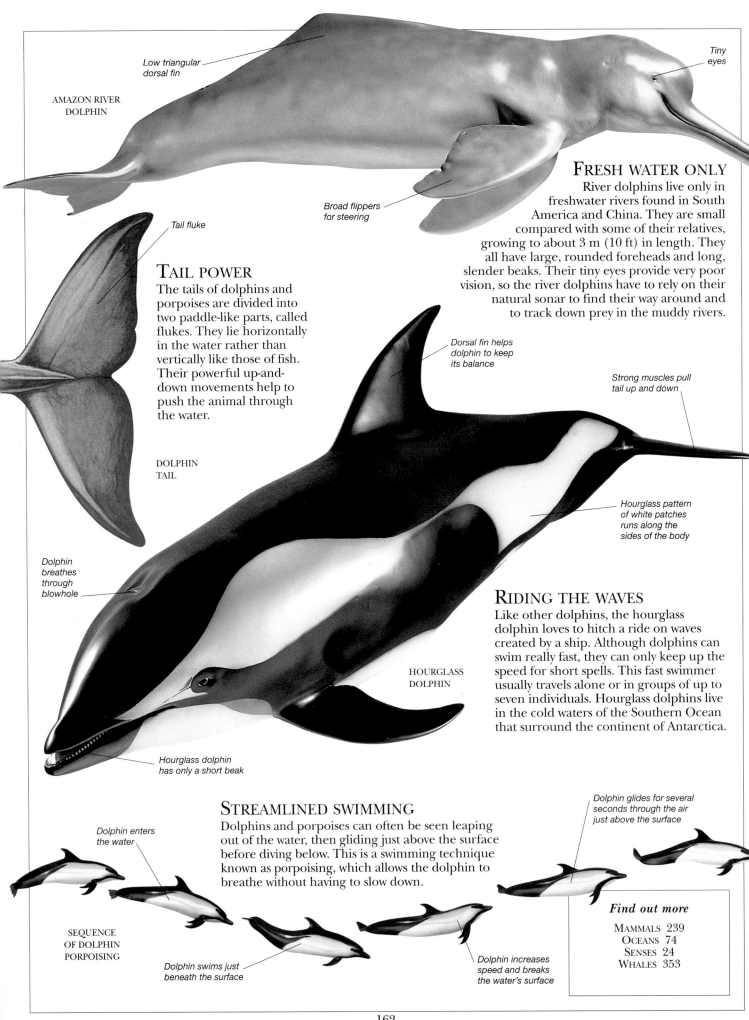

Low triangular
dorsal fin

AMAZON RIVER
DOLPHIN

Tiny
eyes

Broad flippers
for steering

## FRESH WATER ONLY

River dolphins live only in
freshwater rivers found in South
America and China. They are small
compared with some of their relatives,
growing to about 3 m (10 ft) in length. They
all have large, rounded foreheads and long,
slender beaks. Their tiny eyes provide very poor
vision, so the river dolphins have to rely on their
natural sonar to find their way around and
to track down prey in the muddy rivers.

Tail fluke

## TAIL POWER

The tails of dolphins and
porpoises are divided into
two paddle-like parts, called
flukes. They lie horizontally
in the water rather than
vertically like those of fish.
Their powerful up-and-
down movements help to
push the animal through
the water.

DOLPHIN
TAIL

Dorsal fin helps
dolphin to keep
its balance

Strong muscles pull
tail up and down

Hourglass pattern
of white patches
runs along the
sides of the body

Dolphin
breathes
through
blowhole

## RIDING THE WAVES

Like other dolphins, the hourglass
dolphin loves to hitch a ride on waves
created by a ship. Although dolphins can
swim really fast, they can only keep up the
speed for short spells. This fast swimmer
usually travels alone or in groups of up to
seven individuals. Hourglass dolphins live
in the cold waters of the Southern Ocean
that surround the continent of Antarctica.

HOURGLASS
DOLPHIN

Hourglass dolphin
has only a short beak

Dolphin glides for several
seconds through the air
just above the surface

## STREAMLINED SWIMMING

Dolphins and porpoises can often be seen leaping
out of the water, then gliding just above the surface
before diving below. This is a swimming technique
known as porpoising, which allows the dolphin to
breathe without having to slow down.

Dolphin enters
the water

SEQUENCE
OF DOLPHIN
PORPOISING

Dolphin swims just
beneath the surface

Dolphin increases
speed and breaks
the water's surface

***Find out more***

MAMMALS 239
OCEANS 74
SENSES 24
WHALES 353

# DONKEYS AND ASSES

ASIATIC WILD
KULAN ASS

Short, upright
mane

ASSES ARE MEMBERS of the horse family. They are smaller than horses, with heavier heads and longer ears. Like horses, they are social animals and prefer to live in herds or family groups. Wild asses live in dry grasslands, deserts, and mountains in parts of Africa and Asia. Donkeys are domestic asses that have been bred all over the world for their ability to carry heavy loads, often over great distances.

Long,
horse-like
tail

Short, donkey-
like mane

Broad, heavy
head

## WILD ASSES

Sure-footed wild asses are able to gallop on their slender legs at speeds of up to 48 kmh (30 mph). They all have long ears, short manes, no forelocks (fringes), and wispy tails. In the dry season, they travel across the plains and deserts in search of a new territory that offers a good supply of fresh grass and water.

HINNY

Sharp hooves are used for kicking enemies and rivals

SCALE

## CROSS-BREEDING

A mule is produced when a male donkey breeds with a female horse. The offspring has both the stamina (power to carry on) of a donkey and the strength of a horse. When a female donkey breeds with a male horse, the young is called a "hinny".

### FACT BOX

**Family:** Equidae

**No. of species:** More than 35

**Habitat:** Warm, dry places, rocky deserts

**Distribution:** Worldwide, especially in China, India, Africa, Central and South America

**Food:** Mainly grasses and hay

**Gestation period:** 12 months

**No. of young:** One

**Lifespan:** 40–50 years

**Size:** 1–1.5 m (3–5 ft)

Deep,
shaggy fur

Long,
rounded
ears

## DONKEYS

The Poitou donkey has a shoulder height of 142 cm (56 in), making it the world's largest. All donkeys descend from the African wild ass, which can travel long distances without much food or water.

White belly

Typical
white
muzzle

FAMILY OF
POITOU DONKEYS

### Find out more

# DRAGONFLIES AND DAMSELFLIES

DRAGONFLIES AND DAMSELFLIES are large, flying insects that are often seen darting along the riverbank in search of food. Dragonflies are the speed champions of the insect world, capable of flying at up to 95 kmh (60 mph). Damselflies are closely related, but smaller and slower than dragonflies. Dragonflies and damselflies are meat-eaters. They prey on other flying insects, which they grab in mid-air with the help of their spiny legs. The legs are held out in front to make a little catching basket.

*Compound eye*

SOUTHERN HAWKER DRAGONFLY

*Strong jaws make short work of captured insects*

ADULT DRAGONFLY

*Dragonflies rest with their wings outstretched. (Damselflies hold their wings above their bodies.)*

## BEADY EYES

Dragonflies have the largest eyes of any insect, covering most of the head and often touching at the back. These eyes, like those of damselflies, are called compound eyes. They are particularly good at detecting movement, and the insects rely on them to track down prey.

*Delicate, transparent wings are supported by a network of fine veins*

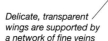

SCALE

## BUILT FOR FLYING

Both the dragonfly and the damselfly have bodies that are divided into three sections: head, thorax (middle section, to which the wings are fixed), and abdomen (rear). The slender shape of the abdomen is ideal for swift and skilful flying. It is used for balance and steering during flight.

*Mating damselflies link their bodies together to form a heart shape*

AZURE DAMSELFLIES

*During mating, the male clasps the female's neck with his abdomen*

*The female arches her body up to collect the male's seed*

## REPRODUCTION

Female dragonflies and damselflies lay their eggs in fresh water. Each egg hatches into a wingless nymph, which spends up to five years in water. When fully grown, it climbs out of the water and sheds its skin to emerge as a winged adult.

### FACT BOX

**Family:** Odonata

**No. of species:** 5,000

**Habitat:** Streams and wetlands in warm and temperate lands

**Distribution:** Worldwide, especially in the tropics

**Food:** Insects and other minibeasts

**Lifespan:** About 5 years

**Size:** 2–20 cm (1–8 in)

***Find out more***

INSECTS 212
SENSES 24

## RIVER-BANK HOME

Adult dragonflies live near streams and in wetland areas where their young develop. Many of them set up a home territory along the river bank where they hunt their prey, flying insects. They will chase away any intruders that try to invade their patch. During the mating season, each dragonfly fiercely defends its territory, to protect its eggs from being eaten by other hunters.

# DUCKS

MALLARD

Like swans and geese, their close relatives, ducks are good swimmers and strong flyers. Some of them spend most of their lives on the water, only visiting land to breed. Their thick plumage has a layer of soft downy feathers next to the skin, which traps air and keeps them warm even if the water is very cold. The birds keep their outer layer of feathers covered with plenty of oil, produced by their bodies, to make them waterproof. Most ducks nest on the ground near water, hiding their nest among undergrowth.

*Row of ridges sieves through water*

*Hard, slightly hooked tip grasps food*

## FOOD STRAINER
Mallards and many other ducks have rows of spiny, comb-like ridges along the edges of their bills. They use these to sieve or strain out food such as seeds or tiny water animals, whenever drinking water. Sawbilled ducks use their stronger, sharper ridges for seizing and holding slippery fish.

## SOCIABLE BIRD
Whistling ducks often live in flocks (large groups) of about 2,000 birds. Living in large numbers helps the ducks to avoid predators, as the more eyes looking out for danger the better. It also increases their chances of finding a mate in the breeding season.

*Typical humped back*

PLUMED WHISTLING DUCK

FEMALE TROUT RUNNER DUCK

*Males have more colourful plumage to attract females*

## TYPICAL FEATURES
Runner ducks have upright bodies and long legs that allow them to run, rather than waddle like other ducks. They are a popular domestic breed because they lay more eggs than other ducks – up to 300 per year.

*Females have duller plumage than the males*

*Short wings*

*Boat-shaped body makes duck buoyant when swimming*

MALE TROUT RUNNER DUCKS

*Long legs allow ducks to run on land*

*Webbed feet for paddling through water*

SCALE

### FACT BOX

**Family:** Anatidae

**Habitat:** Freshwater lakes, open sea, ponds, rivers, streams

**Distribution:** Worldwide, except Antarctic

**Food:** Seeds, water plants, grass insects, small water creatures

**No. of eggs:** 4–18

**Lifespan:** 20 years

**Size:** 30–100 cm (1–3 ft)

*Find out more*

BIRDS 115
EGGS AND NESTS 42
GEESE 184
SWANS 334

# EAGLES

RELATED TO HAWKS, KITES, harriers, and vultures, eagles are large, daytime birds of prey. They are superb flyers, with very long, broad wings that help them to stay airborne for hours. Eagles catch and eat a wide range of prey, from rabbits, ducks, and snakes to geese and small antelopes. They are attentive parents, patiently tearing up prey and passing small, easy-to-swallow pieces to their nestlings.

BALD-
HEADED
EAGLE

*Sharp talons pierce flesh*

GOLDEN
EAGLE
EGG

## EXTRA LARGE

Some eagles' eggs are pure white, but others are blotched or spotted to help camouflage them in the nest. Eagles' eggs are more rounded than hens' egg and about four times as large.

*Rust-coloured blotches help disguise egg*

## HUNTING SKILLS

Eagles are fierce hunters. They swoop down on prey spreading out their large, strong feet, tipped with razor-sharp talons (claws). Once caught, the victim is crushed by the eagle's powerful feet and stabbed to death by its talons. The eagle then tears apart the flesh using its large, hooked bill.

*Named after its golden collar of feathers*

*Sharp, hooked bill for tearing up prey*

SCALE

GOLDEN
EAGLE

### FACT BOX

**Family:** Accipitridae

**Habitat:** Mountains, moorlands, grasslands, deserts, marshes, seacoasts, fresh waters, woods,

**Distribution:** Worldwide, except Antarctic and New Zealand

**Food:** Mainly live animals

**No. of eggs:** 1–4

**Lifespan:** 60 years

**Size:** 45–105 cm (18–42 in)

## LOOKOUT POINT

Eagles often use a high cliff top or treetop branch as a watch tower when looking for prey. Once a suitable victim has been spotted, the golden eagle uses its well-known technique of giving chase by flying fast and low to ground until the prey is completely exhausted and unable to escape.

Outstretched wings provide balance

Courting pairs reach out for each other's feet

PAIR OF
BALD-HEADED
EAGLES

## COURTSHIP

During the breeding season, eagles use their graceful flight to impress their partners. Eagles mate for life, and each spring the pairs perform dances in the sky. They create roller coaster and figure-of-eight patterns or they tumble down through the air in cartwheels, sometimes grasping each other's feet.

## FEATHERS

The eagle's wings are made up of layer upon layer of different-shaped feathers. The outer feathers are the strongest and power the bird's flight. The inner feathers reduce air resistance allowing the eagle to glide and soar easily, while the soft, down feathers trap air to keep the eagle warm.

Strong, outer feathers provide flying power

Inner feathers help keep the bird aloft

Forward-facing eye

Down feathers keep eagle warm

GOLDEN
EAGLE

BATELEUR
EAGLE

## EAGLE EYES

An eagle's eye is larger than that of an adult human and provides extremely good vision. The eyes face forwards so that the eagle can judge distances accurately. Eagles have telescopic sight which means that they can spot prey far away and then catch them by surprise.

### Find out more

# EELS

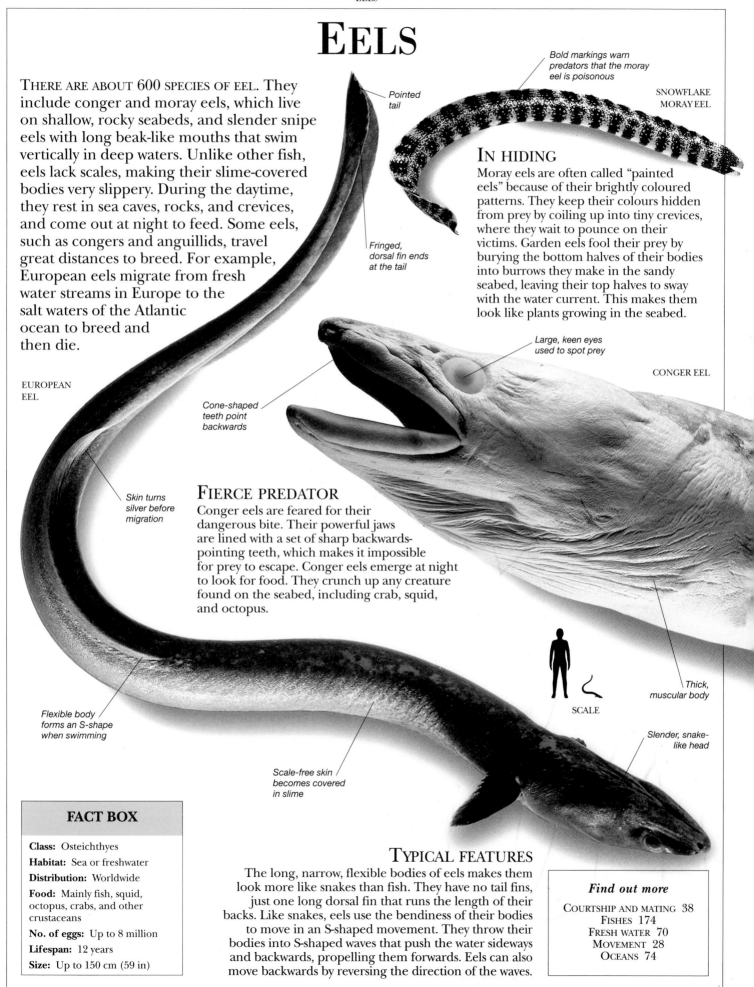

THERE ARE ABOUT 600 SPECIES OF EEL. They include conger and moray eels, which live on shallow, rocky seabeds, and slender snipe eels with long beak-like mouths that swim vertically in deep waters. Unlike other fish, eels lack scales, making their slime-covered bodies very slippery. During the daytime, they rest in sea caves, rocks, and crevices, and come out at night to feed. Some eels, such as congers and anguillids, travel great distances to breed. For example, European eels migrate from fresh water streams in Europe to the salt waters of the Atlantic ocean to breed and then die.

*Pointed tail*

*Fringed, dorsal fin ends at the tail*

EUROPEAN EEL

SNOWFLAKE MORAY EEL

*Bold markings warn predators that the moray eel is poisonous*

## IN HIDING

Moray eels are often called "painted eels" because of their brightly coloured patterns. They keep their colours hidden from prey by coiling up into tiny crevices, where they wait to pounce on their victims. Garden eels fool their prey by burying the bottom halves of their bodies into burrows they make in the sandy seabed, leaving their top halves to sway with the water current. This makes them look like plants growing in the seabed.

*Large, keen eyes used to spot prey*

CONGER EEL

*Cone-shaped teeth point backwards*

*Skin turns silver before migration*

## FIERCE PREDATOR

Conger eels are feared for their dangerous bite. Their powerful jaws are lined with a set of sharp backwards-pointing teeth, which makes it impossible for prey to escape. Conger eels emerge at night to look for food. They crunch up any creature found on the seabed, including crab, squid, and octopus.

*Thick, muscular body*

SCALE

*Slender, snake-like head*

*Flexible body forms an S-shape when swimming*

*Scale-free skin becomes covered in slime*

## TYPICAL FEATURES

The long, narrow, flexible bodies of eels makes them look more like snakes than fish. They have no tail fins, just one long dorsal fin that runs the length of their backs. Like snakes, eels use the bendiness of their bodies to move in an S-shaped movement. They throw their bodies into S-shaped waves that push the water sideways and backwards, propelling them forwards. Eels can also move backwards by reversing the direction of the waves.

## FACT BOX

**Class:** Osteichthyes

**Habitat:** Sea or freshwater

**Distribution:** Worldwide

**Food:** Mainly fish, squid, octopus, crabs, and other crustaceans

**No. of eggs:** Up to 8 million

**Lifespan:** 12 years

**Size:** Up to 150 cm (59 in)

### *Find out more*

# ELEPHANTS

THERE ARE TWO KINDS OF ELEPHANT in the world – the African elephant and the Asian elephant. These plant-eating mammals are intelligent, sociable animals that live in family groups of between eight and 12 female elephants with their offspring. The bulls or male elephants tend to live alone or in male-only herds. The elephant's great size and strength protects it from all predators, apart from humans.

SCALE

## AFRICAN VERSUS ASIAN

The African elephant is the larger of the two, has big ears, and a dip in the middle of its back. The Asian elephant has smaller ears, a domed forehead, and a straight or humped back. The African elephant's trunk ends in two "fingers", the Asian elephant's in one.

*Pillar-like legs support great weight*

AFRICAN ELEPHANT

## TEETH AND TUSKS

An elephant has four huge molars, which have sharp ridges for grinding up tough plant food. Its front teeth are its tusks, which are mainly used for digging up roots and stripping bark from trees.

ELEPHANT'S MOLAR TOOTH

*Each molar tooth weighs more than a house brick*

*Asian elephant has fewer rings on its trunk than an African elephant*

ASIAN ELEPHANT

## HANDY TRUNK

The elephant's trunk is an extension of the nose and the upper lip. It can grasp and break off a leafy branch, then carry it back to the mouth. It can also be used to suck up water to pour into its mouth or throw over its body to keep cool. Elephants also use the trunk to communicate with other elephants through touch and smell.

### FACT BOX

**Family:** Elephantidae

**Habitat:** Grasslands, forests, marshes, deserts

**Distribution:** Africa, India, Sri Lanka, Southeast Asia, Malaysia, Indonesia, southern China

**Food:** Grasses, fruits, leaves, twigs, bark, roots

**No. of young:** 1

**Lifespan:** About 70 years

**Size:** 3–4 m (10–13 ft)

## SAVANNA TRAIL
African bush elephants live on the savanna, an area of grassland dotted with trees. Using the same paths year after year, they wander across the savanna looking for food and water. The adults teach their young where to find the paths. During the wet season, elephants feed on freshly sprouted grass, and they eat tree branches and twigs in the dry season.

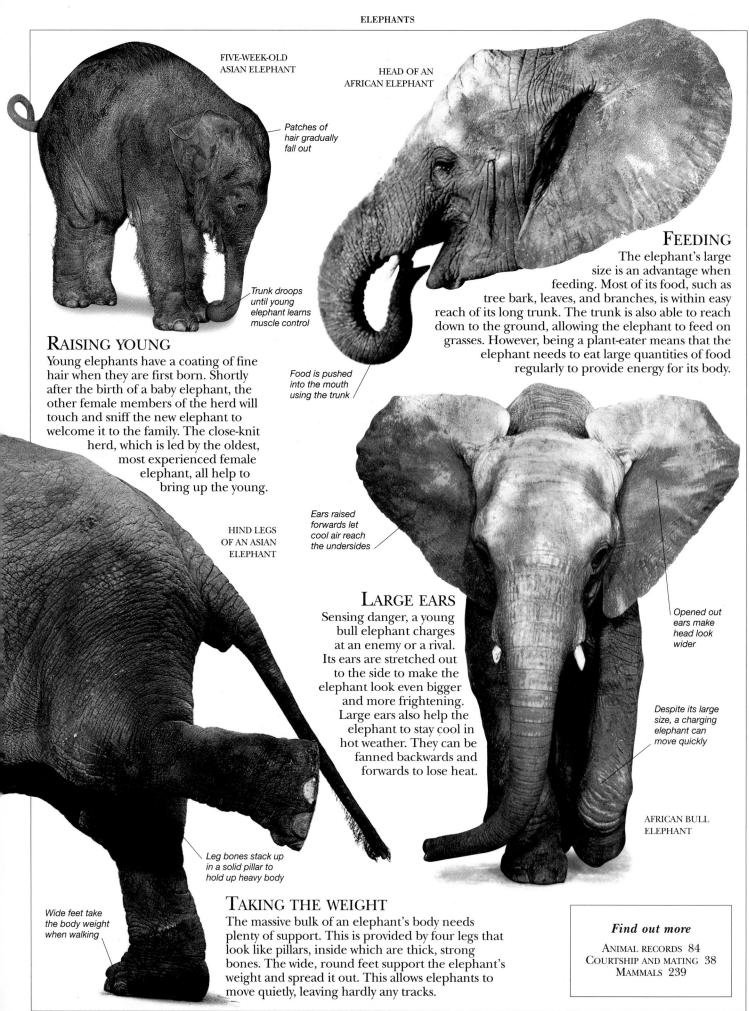

FIVE-WEEK-OLD
ASIAN ELEPHANT

HEAD OF AN
AFRICAN ELEPHANT

*Patches of
hair gradually
fall out*

*Trunk droops
until young
elephant learns
muscle control*

## RAISING YOUNG

Young elephants have a coating of fine
hair when they are first born. Shortly
after the birth of a baby elephant, the
other female members of the herd will
touch and sniff the new elephant to
welcome it to the family. The close-knit
herd, which is led by the oldest,
most experienced female
elephant, all help to
bring up the young.

## FEEDING

The elephant's large
size is an advantage when
feeding. Most of its food, such as
tree bark, leaves, and branches, is within easy
reach of its long trunk. The trunk is also able to reach
down to the ground, allowing the elephant to feed on
grasses. However, being a plant-eater means that the
elephant needs to eat large quantities of food
regularly to provide energy for its body.

*Food is pushed
into the mouth
using the trunk*

HIND LEGS
OF AN ASIAN
ELEPHANT

*Ears raised
forwards let
cool air reach
the undersides*

## LARGE EARS

Sensing danger, a young
bull elephant charges
at an enemy or a rival.
Its ears are stretched out
to the side to make the
elephant look even bigger
and more frightening.
Large ears also help the
elephant to stay cool in
hot weather. They can be
fanned backwards and
forwards to lose heat.

*Opened out
ears make
head look
wider*

*Despite its large
size, a charging
elephant can
move quickly*

AFRICAN BULL
ELEPHANT

*Leg bones stack up
in a solid pillar to
hold up heavy body*

*Wide feet take
the body weight
when walking*

## TAKING THE WEIGHT

The massive bulk of an elephant's body needs
plenty of support. This is provided by four legs that
look like pillars, inside which are thick, strong
bones. The wide, round feet support the elephant's
weight and spread it out. This allows elephants to
move quietly, leaving hardly any tracks.

*Find out more*

ANIMAL RECORDS 84
COURTSHIP AND MATING 38
MAMMALS 239

# ERMINES, POLECATS, AND MINK

THESE SMALL, FAST-MOVING, skilful killers belong to the same group of meat-eating mammals as tigers and wolves. Ermines, polecats, and mink have long, supple bodies, short legs, and small ears. Their body shape allows them to chase prey into its burrow. They hunt mainly at night, tracking down prey using sight and hearing, and their excellent sense of smell. First, they pounce, deliver a killing bite, and then tear the prey apart with their small but very sharp teeth. Ermines, polecats, and mink usually hunt alone. Each has its own territory that it marks with a scent to warn its neighbours to stay away. Mink hunt on land and in water.

Summer coat is a brown colour with a white chin, chest, and belly

ERMINE OR STOAT

Mouth has stabbing teeth used to kill prey

## ERMINE

Like their relatives, ermines stand on their hind legs to look around and sniff for prey. In colder, northern places, their coats turn white in winter to blend in with the snowy landscape. This hides them from prey and enemies such as owls.

## MINK

Mink live close to rivers and streams under cover of dense vegetation. They are excellent swimmers and divers that catch fish, frogs, and crayfish in water. On land they hunt rodents and other small animals. Mink make a den in a burrow or between tree roots on the riverbank where they shelter and store food.

AMERICAN MINK

Long fur keeps mink warm

Tail has black tip

SCALE

## FACT BOX

**Family:** Mustelidae

**No. of species:** 65

**Habitat:** Forests, woodland, mountains, grasslands, farmland

**Distribution:** Europe, Asia, North and South America

**Food:** Rodents, rabbits, birds, insects, lizards, fish, frogs

**Gestation period:** 35–45 days

**No. of young:** 3–10

**Lifespan:** 1–6 years

**Size:** 15–56 cm (6–22 in)

EUROPEAN POLECAT

## POLECAT

The polecat is easily identified by its white face mask and long, bushy tail. Polecats eat any animals they can find from insects to prey larger than themselves, such as rabbits. Tame polecats, called ferrets, are used by people to hunt and catch rabbits.

White mask on face

### Find out more

# FISH

THERE ARE 25,000 DIFFERENT TYPES of fish worldwide. In fact, there are more types of fish than there are types of amphibians, reptiles, birds, and mammals put together. Fish have spread throughout the world's oceans, from the ice-cold polar oceans to warm tropical seas. They also live in fresh waters, from huge rivers and great lakes to small pools, and even pitch-dark underground streams. Fish need oxygen to survive but rather than coming to the surface for air, they are able to take in oxygen underwater. They feed on plants and other sea creatures, moving through water using their powerful tails and body fins.

*Pouch carries and protects eggs*

*Dorsal fin helps fish to balance*

## FATHERHOOD

Like pipefish, male seahorses have special egg-carrying pouches in their bellies. In the breeding season, the female lays her eggs in the pouch for safety. Several other groups of fish, called mouthbrooders, carry their eggs and newly hatched young in their mouths until they are ready to fend for themselves.

YOUNG FRENCH ANGELFISH

CARIBBEAN SEAHORSE

*Tail can grip onto plants and rocks*

*Tail fin propels fish forward*

*Water taken in contains dissolved oxygen*

*Gills enable fish to extract oxygen from water*

*Slimy coating helps fish to glide through water*

*Pectoral and pelvic fins help the fish to steer up or down, and left or right*

## PARTS OF A FISH

Fish come in all shapes and sizes. Some, such as angelfish, have slender, crescent-shaped bodies while others, such as pipefish, have long, thin bodies. All fish have a backbone and an internal skeleton. They breathe through a pair of gills that take out oxygen from the water. Fish swim or move around by using fins. The pelvic and pectoral pairs on either side of the body are used for steering, while the dorsal fin on its back helps the fish to balance.

### FACT BOX

**Classes:** Cartilaginous fish: Chondrichthyes;
**Bony fish:** Osteichthyes; Jawless fish: Agnatha

**Habitat:** Saltwater seas and oceans; freshwater ponds, lakes, and rivers

**Distribution:** Worldwide

**Food:** Algae, seaweed, coral, invertebrates, other fish

SPINY SCALES OF PORCUPINE FISH

## SCALES

Most bony fish are covered with a layer of thin, flexible scales. Some have spiny scales that overlap one another, like tiles on a roof. Sharks and rays have very different kinds of scales called denticles. These are small toothlike structures sunk deep in the skin.

SHARK DENTICLE

## OCEAN LIFE
Fish are able to live in a range of water habitats and adopt different lifestyles. Many of them are cold-blooded and cannot alter their body temperature to adjust to changes in their environment. Some are docile grazers that feed on seaweed in warm tropical oceans, while others are fearsome predators that lurk in the cold weed fringes of northern lakes and rivers.

ZEBRA
PIPEFISH

*Dark, upright
stripes blend in
with dark, upright
stems and stalks*

*Red tail is used as
a warning flag to
scare enemies*

## STANDING IN LINE

The zebra pipefish has a series of dark stripes along its very long, slim body. These make the fish almost invisible as it lines the stripes up with the vertical stems of water plants. Many fish have colours or patterns that camouflage them against their surroundings. This helps them to escape being noticed and eaten by predators or prey.

*Gravel thrown up by
burrowing fish falls
back down on the fish
and helps to hide it*

*Bony, razor-sharp
blade is kept
hidden in a groove*

## GOING UNDERGROUND

Wrasses escape trouble by burrowing into the sand or mud of the seabed where they live. As soon as they sense an approaching predator, they dive head downwards into a patch of gravel and burrow by flexing their bodies into an S-shape. Safely hidden from the sight of predators, the fish will go to sleep in their burrow.

SURGEONFISH

## KNIFE CARRIER

Surgeonfish have a secret weapon to defend themselves against predators. When threatened, they can suddenly flick out a bony, knife-like structure, as sharp as a surgeon's scalpel, from a groove near their tail. Many other fish have special defences, such as poisonous flesh, spiny suits of armour, or the ability to swell their bodies up like balloons.

*Body bends into
an S-shape to help
fish burrow quickly*

## WINGED FISH

Rays are often described as flying rather than swimming through water. This is because of the way in which they use their wide fins, called wings, to move. A ripple starts from the head of the fish and travels down through the body, making the wings flap up and down.

*Wings flap up and
down to move ray
through water*

STINGRAY

TWINSPOT
WRASSE

*Long, poisonous
spine lies at base of
the tail*

***Find out more***

FRESH WATER 70
MOVEMENT 28
OCEANS 74
VERTEBRATES 345

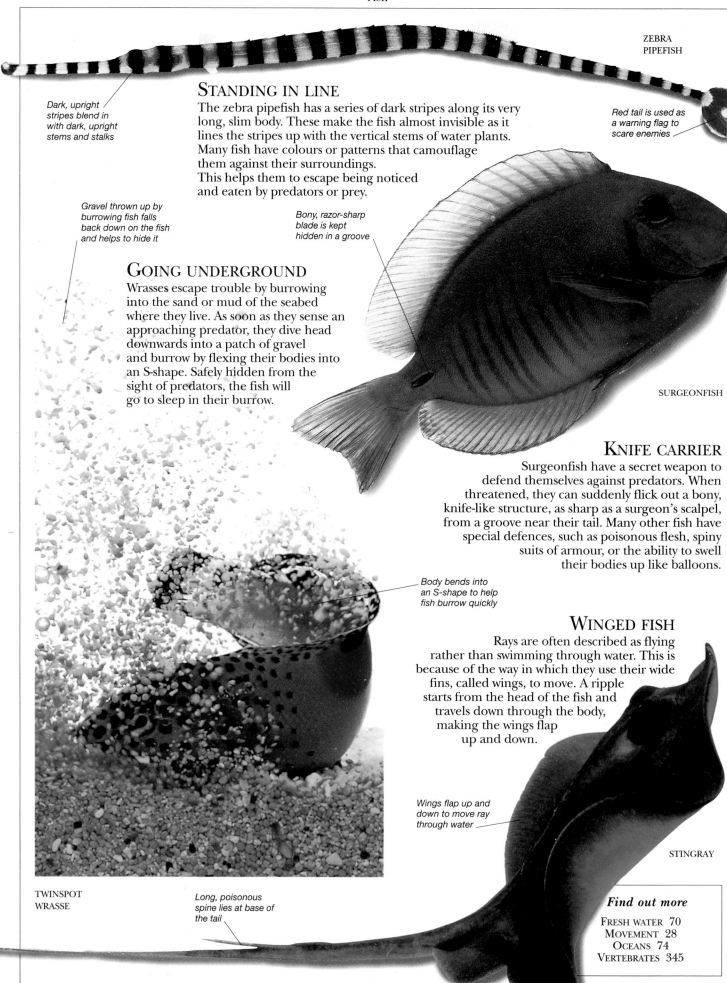

# FLEAS

*Crown of bristles help flea to lodge in host's fur*

**COMMON CAT FLEA**

*Energy is stored in hind legs*

FLEAS ARE TINY, FLIGHTLESS insects. They live as parasites, feeding on the blood of other animals, including cats, birds, dogs, rats, rabbits, – and humans. They suck up the blood of their hosts (victims) using their tube-like mouthparts. Fleas can carry and pass on germs that cause dangerous diseases as they move from victim to victim.

*Strong legs attach at the insect's thorax (middle section)*

**LEAPING CAT FLEA**

*Bristles point backwards to stop flea falling off the host*

*Powerful back legs kick down as the insect leaps upwards*

## SHAPE OF A PARASITE

Fleas have small heads and flattened, wingless bodies that allow them to slip easily through the hair or feathers of their hosts. The tiny bristles that cover their bodies help fleas to keep a firm hold on their victim even when the animal scratches itself to rake them off.

## HIGH-JUMP CHAMPION

Being wingless, fleas cannot fly, but they can jump very well. They are able to leap up to 130 times their own height, which allows them to hop aboard much larger animals. As the flea gets ready to leap, the muscles attached to its thorax relax. The thorax then clicks outwards, flinging the flea high in the air.

**SCALE**

*Strong hooked claws are ready to grip onto victim when the flea pounces*

*Thorax muscles relax*

*Body becomes darker in colour when it is full of blood*

*Antennae are sensitive to sounds and movements*

## FEEDING

Fleas detect the presence of possible victims with the help of their antennae. As the host animal approaches, sensitive hairs all over the flea's body pick up tiny air currents caused by movements and sounds. As the animal passes, the flea leaps on board. Its mouthparts pierce the host's skin and form a tiny tube to suck the animal's blood.

*Sucking mouthparts*

---

### FACT BOX

**Family:** Siphonaptera

**Habitat:** Lives on bird and mammal hosts

**Distribution:** On land

**Food:** Animal blood

**No. of eggs:** Infinite

**Lifespan:** 25 to 30 years

**Size:** 30–60 mm (up to one-quarter of an inch)

---

### *Find out more*

EGGS AND NESTS 42
INSECTS 212
MOVEMENT 28

# FLIES

TACHINID FLY

BEETLE MIMIC

ROBBER FLY

FLIES ARE ONE OF THE LARGEST groups of insects, with more than 90,000 different types. They are found worldwide – in deserts, forests, swamps, and mountains, and even on the the icy continent of Antarctica where very few creatures can survive. They feed mainly on plants, animals, and rotting food. The fly family includes mosquitoes, gnats, midges, hoverflies, and bluebottles, but dragonflies and butterflies are not true flies. Most insects have four wings, but flies have just one pair. In place of their hind wings there are tiny organs called halteres. These help them to balance and fly backwards, forwards, and even upside-down at great speed.

BLUEBOTTLE MAGGOTS

*Feet can grip awkward surfaces*

*Long, spindly legs*

*Compound eyes can see in colour*

*Antenna senses smells and movements*

ADULT HOUSEFLY

## LIFE CYCLE

Bluebottle larvae (maggots) become adult flies after about three weeks. The legless maggots start out as eggs which hatch out in fresh or salt water, soil, dung, rotting meat, or inside the bodies of other animals, where they feed and grow.

## FEEDING

Houseflies have hooks and sticky pads on the bottoms of their feet. These help the flies to climb up walls, cling to smooth surfaces, and even to walk upside-down in search of food. Flies do not eat solid food as they have no jaws. Instead, their mouthparts work like sponges, sucking or licking up liquid foods such as plant sap and flower nectar.

*Halteres help the fly steer and balance*

*Thorax contains muscles that power flight*

### FACT BOX

**Family:** Diptera

**No. of species:** 90,000

**Habitat:** Widespread in forests, deserts, swamps, icy wastes, fresh and also salt water

**Distribution:** Worldwide

**Food:** Plants, live animals, rotting meat, dung, rubbish

**Size:** Up to 50 mm (2 in)

*Cranefly's wings look flimsy but are powerful*

*Sensitive hairs all over the fly's body detect currents in the air*

ADULT CRANEFLY

SCALE

## BODY PARTS

Craneflies are slim and delicate, with long, spindly legs. They are one of the most basic types of fly and look quite different from the more advanced flies such as bluebottles. These are more chunky and sturdy, and can fly faster. The thorax (middle section) of the fly's body is packed with powerful muscles that help it to flap its wings and to walk. Behind the wings are halteres which look like tiny drumsticks. These help the insect to balance when flying.

*Long mouthpart pierces flesh and sucks out blood*

*Abdomen swells up to store blood*

TSETSE FLY

## BLOOD SUCKER

Tsetse flies can drink up to three times their own weight in blood. They feed mostly on humans and cattle. The blood is stored in their abdomens (rear end of body) which swell up, almost lifting the flies off their feet.

### Find out more

BEES 111
BUTTERFLIES AND MOTHS 121
INSECTS 212
MOVEMENT 28

# FOXES

RED FOX

FOXES BELONG TO THE SAME FAMILY of meat-eaters as dogs and wolves. They can be easily told apart from their relatives by their narrow, pointed faces, large ears, and bushy tails. The 21 kinds of fox are found in all types of habitat, ranging from hot deserts or forests, to the cold of the Arctic. One kind, the red fox, even lives in cities, feeding at night on the household rubbish left by humans. When searching for food, foxes can travel for long distances without tiring. They are foragers, eating anything that they come across, including fruit, insects, and small animals. Some foxes live in small family groups, but most of them hunt for food on their own.

Long bushy tail helps fox to balance when pouncing on prey

SCALE

## RED FOX

Foxes have strong, slim bodies with long legs. Their thick fur helps to keep them warm, and its colour helps them to blend in against woodland so that they are not seen by enemies or prey. Foxes have very good senses of sight, hearing, and smell, as shown by their large eyes, ears, and nose.

Long legs enable fox to move quickly over long distances

## FROM CUB TO ADULT

The newborn cub is blind and helpless, protected and fed by its mother. As the cub grows, it changes shape – its ears, snout, and legs get longer.

Alert and curious, the cub is starting to look grown up

NEWBORN CUB     TWO WEEKS     FOUR WEEKS     SIX WEEKS     EIGHT WEEKS     TEN WEEKS

Long fur forms a parting along the backbone

## LARGE EARS

The bat-eared fox lives in hot climates, such as savannahs or deserts. It has large, pointed ears which are able to pick up the tiniest sounds made by its prey. Unlike other foxes, bat-eared foxes eat mainly insects. They have sharp, teeth which can be used to crush the outer cases of the insects' bodies.

Heat lost through the ears helps foxes to stay cool

BAT-EARED FOX

### FACT BOX

**Family:** Canidae

**Habitat:** Woodlands, grasslands, and deserts

**Distribution:** Europe, Africa, Asia, North and South America

**Food:** Small mammals and birds, insects, fruits, carrion

**No. of young:** 1–8 cubs

**Lifespan:** 6 years

**Size:** 90–150 cm (35–59 in)

## MAKING A KILL

The fox can leap up to 1 m (3 ft) into the air, to pounce on its victim and take it by surprise. Red foxes have a special way of hunting and killing rodents, such as mice. If a fox thinks a small animal is nearby, it stands very still and listens for any rustles or squeaks. It uses its large ears and keen hearing to pinpoint the exact position of the prey and then makes a precise pounce to kill.

RED FOX

*Strong, muscular body*

*Front paws will be stretched out ready to land on the prey and squash it*

*Small ears prevent heat loss*

## CHANGING COLOUR

In summer, the Arctic fox has a thin coat of grey-brown fur, which helps it to blend in with the dull brown rocky landscape. In the icy winter, when the surroundings are covered in snow, the fox's thick fur turns white. This hides the fox from prey, such as birds and rodents, and enemies like polar bears.

*Strong hind legs propel fox into the air*

*Thick fur enables fox to survive in temperatures as low as −50°C (−58°F)*

ARCTIC FOX IN SUMMER COAT

*Fox is always alert, looking out for prey and danger*

## INTELLIGENT HUNTER

Foxes use stealth and intelligence to find prey and to avoid enemies, such as dogs and humans. They catch earthworms at night by listening for the worm's bristly body scratching across the ground, and can dart after rabbits at high speed. When threatened by enemies, the fox may disappear into its burrow, hide in thick undergrowth, or run away rapidly.

*Fur-covered paws stop feet getting cold when it walks on ice and snow*

RED FOX

*Hair between the claws blurs pawprint*

### Find out more

# FROGS AND TOADS

THERE ARE MORE THAN 4,300 different types of frog and toad. They are the largest group of amphibians (animals that can live on both land and water). They live in a surprising range of habitats, not just in lakes, marshes, and other wet places, but also in grasslands, mountains, and even deserts. The main differences between them are that most frogs have smooth skin, and live in or near water. Toads have skin covered with warts, and live mainly on land.

Jelly surrounding eggs protects them from fish and other predators

1. FROGSPAWN

AMERICAN BULLFROG

Ear detects the approach of predators

Tadpoles begin to swim and feed

2. 10-DAY-OLD TADPOLE

3. 9-WEEK-OLD TADPOLE

First hind leg appears

## FROGSPAWN

Most frogs and toads return to the water to mate. The females each lay masses of eggs (frogspawn) in the water, then the male fertilizes them. Some species lay their eggs in clumps, others in long strings, like necklaces. The eggs hatch into small, legless tadpoles, which slowly develop into tiny versions of adult frogs.

## HEARING

Many frogs and toads have keen hearing. This helps them to detect enemies before they are caught. They also listen out for the distinctive calls of possible mating partners. Most frogs and toads have large circular ears that are visible just behind each eye.

Front legs develop

Tail has gone completely

4. 12-WEEK-OLD TADPOLE

## BODY PARTS

Frogs and toads with short legs move about by crawling on all fours or by making brief hops. Many species have long, powerful hind legs that enable them to make huge leaps. Frogs with long slender bodies and large webbed feet are able to swim very well.

High-set protruding eyes allow frog to see above water while rest of body is submerged

5. YOUNG COMMON FROG AT 16 WEEKS

SCALE

SOUTH AFRICAN BULLFROG

FOOT OF
TREE FROG

Pads filled with
sticky mucus help
tree frogs to keep
their grip on tree
trunks and branches

These frogs are named
after their tomato
shape and colour

## STRONG HOLD

Tree frogs are able to keep
a hold on the smoothest
of surfaces. The secret
to this skill lies in the
special sticky pads
on the ends of
their fingers.

ASIAN TREE
TOAD

Unusually
smooth skin

MADAGASCAN
TOMATO FROGS

## COLOURFUL SKINS

Many frogs and toads carry distinctive skin
markings and colours. Male frogs looking
for a mate use their bright colours to warn
rival males to keep away from their territory.
Their bold markings also act as a warning to
would-be predators that the frog or toad
being hunted is highly poisonous to eat.

### FACT BOX

**Family:** Anura

**No. of species:** 4,350

**Habitat:** Ponds, marshes, lakes,
forests, grasslands, deserts

**Distribution:** All continents,
except Antarctica

**Food:** Adults are meat-eaters;
tadpoles eat water plants

**Eggs:** Up to 20,000

**Size:** 3–40 cm (1–16 in)

## TOAD TYPES

Although it is a member of the common
toad family, the Asian tree toad has some
slightly different features. Its skin is smooth
rather than dry and warty, and it has discs
on its fingers for gripping on to trees.

## SWIMMING

Frogs learn to swim as soon as they
are born. While they are still
tadpoles, they move around in water
by making a series of S-shaped waves
with the body. Once their limbs
develop, they use their strong hind
legs to propel them through the
water, drawing the legs up and then
sharply pushing them outwards.

Front legs
stretch forward

Back legs
kick out

Knees drawn up
towards body

ORIENTAL
FIRE-BELLIED TOAD

Arms held flat
against body

### Find out more

AMPHIBIANS 92
RAINFORESTS 62
SALAMANDERS AND NEWTS 305
SWAMPS 72

# GAZELLES

TIMID AND GRACEFUL, GAZELLES are mammals that live on the open plains or deserts of Africa and Asia. These small antelopes are relatives of even-toed animals such as antelope and cattle. They graze together in large herds, so that they can keep a lookout for each other's safety. Gazelles can run at speed to escape predators such as cheetahs, jackals, and hyenas and, when alarmed, they bounce high into the air, with all four legs stretched down stiffly. This is called stotting or pronking, and warns other gazelles of danger. It also helps to confuse their enemies.

## GAZELLE FEATURES

As they graze, goitered gazelles clear spaces for new grass shoots to sprout. Like most gazelles, they have long necks and legs. Their slender bodies are pale fawn above and white underneath. The horns have ring-like ridges along them.

Knees are protected with hairy tufts

GOITERED GAZELLE

### FACT BOX

**Family:** Bovidae

**Habitat:** Grassland, scrub, desert

**Distribution:** Africa, Middle East, India, China

**Food:** Grass, herbs, and woody plants

**No. of young:** 1

**Lifespan:** Up to 12 years

**Size:** 38–172 cm (16–72 in)

MALE INDIAN BLACKBUCK HORN

SCALE

Horn is twisted into a spiral and has a ridged surface

GERENUK OR WALLER'S GAZELLE

## PERMANENT HORNS

Both male and female gazelles usually have horns that curve forwards and then backwards in an S-shape. Females use their horns to defend their food resources, especially in the dry season or in winter. Males use theirs to compete with rivals during the mating season. Horns stay on a gazelle's head all the time and are not shed each year, like a deer's antlers.

## GREEN IS BEST

Gerenuks are able to feed while standing on their back legs. This gives them enough height so that by stretching their long slender necks they are able to reach the juicy green leaves of acacia trees. Gazelles are plant-eaters that graze on grass, small green plants, and the leaves and shoots of woody plants. Usually, they eat whatever plants are greenest.

## FIGHTING MALES

During the breeding season, male gazelles claim the territories where they will mate with females. The winner is usually decided by a fight or by the two males locking horns and pushing each other. Whichever one proves to be the weaker male usually runs away to find a new territory.

MALE THOMSON'S GAZELLES

Rivals try to push each other away with their horns

### Find out more

# GEESE

GOOSE
FOOT

THE WATERFOWL FAMILY INCLUDES GEESE, which spend more time on land than their close relatives, ducks and swans. However, their boat-shaped bodies and webbed feet enable them to swim well when they need to. Geese live in large flocks, which travel together over long distances in search of warm weather and food. Their loud, honking cries and fierce hissing has earned them the reputation of being good guards. Domestic breeds are often used to protect properties, as well as being valued for their eggs.

*Large area of webbing between front three toes*

## WEBBED FEET
The long toes of a goose are joined together by tough webbing (skin). Together, their strong legs and broadly webbed toes power the goose through the water.

*Hard "nail" used to rip out tough plants*

CANADA GEESE

*Long, broad wings help geese to fly high over long distances*

*Outstretched neck keeps body streamlined in flight*

## GOSLING
Baby geese are called goslings. Within a few hours of hatching from their eggs, they are able to walk, swim, and find their own food.

*Thick layer of soft down keeps gosling warm until adult feathers grow*

BABY GOOSE OR GOSLING

## MIGRATION
In spring, some geese migrate (fly to their summer home) from Europe, Asia, and North America. They head towards the Arctic, where the long daylight hours and large supplies of food provide ideal conditions for the geese to breed.

*Bristly tongue sticks to food*

*Long neck makes it possible to reach food on the ground*

SCALE

GREYLAG GOOSE
(WHITE FORM)

*Broad, boat-shaped body keeps goose afloat when swimming*

## FACT BOX
**Family:** Anatidae
**Habitat:** Arctic tundra, scrub, open woodland, estuaries, marshes, and farmland
**Distribution:** Across the northern hemisphere
**Food:** Grass, marsh plants, grain, and potatoes
**No. of eggs:** 1–11
**Size:** 0.5–1 m (2–3 ft)

## LOUD WARNING
Geese are always on the look-out for danger. If they suspect that a predator is approaching their territory, they raise the alarm by making a loud, honking call. They spend most of their day grazing on grass. Their broad bills grip and tear at the grass, and a hard "nail" on the side of their beaks is useful for dealing with tough stalks.

*Small hind toe*

***Find out more***
BIRDS 115
DUCKS 166
MIGRATION 78
PLANT-EATERS 30
SWANS 334

# GIBBONS

SOMETIMES REFERRED TO AS lesser apes, gibbons are the smallest members of the ape family. All gibbons spend their whole lives in the treetops of Southeast Asian rainforests. They swing rapidly from branch to branch searching for fruit and leaves to eat. They are the only apes to live in pairs and stay with the same partner for life. Gibbons usually live in small family groups, made up of a mother, a father, and two or three young.

Extra long arms swing hand-over-hand

Long fingers hook tightly onto branches

## FOREST ACROBATS

A gibbon uses its extra-long arms to swing at top speed through treetops. In the same way that humans move their left and then their right legs to walk, so a gibbon uses its left hand and then its right to reach out for the next branch. In fact, gibbons cannot walk on all fours because their arms are longer than their legs.

SEQUENCE OF A GIBBON SWINGING

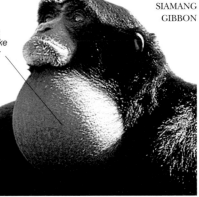

SIAMANG GIBBON

Throat pouch expands like a balloon to make the call louder

ADULT GIBBON

Gibbons sleep sitting upright

SCALE

Wrists can be rotated without losing grip

## SINGING GIBBONS

Gibbons are known for their hooting and whooping calls, which can be heard at dawn and dusk. The loudest noise is made by Siamang gibbons, who inflate their special throat sacs to create a booming effect. Each family of gibbons has a territory of its own, which it guards by singing out warnings to rival gibbons.

Baby clings to mother for warmth and protection

## CUSHIONED SEAT

Gibbons do not sleep in nests at night, but sit up in the forks of tree branches. The tough pads of hard skin on their bottoms serve as hard-wearing cushions for sitting on. All gibbons are tail-less, have long arms, and wrists that can be rotated when swinging from tree to tree.

MOTHER AND BABY LAR GIBBON

## BABY CARE

A female gibbon usually has a baby every two to three years. When it is born, the baby gibbon is naked except for a cap of fur on its head. It nestles up to its mother for warmth and feeds on her milk for the first year. The young stay with their parents until they are between six and eight years old.

### FACT BOX

**Family:** Hylobatidae

**Habitat:** Tropical rainforest, monsoon forest

**Distribution:** Southeast Asia

**Food:** Fruit, leaves, insects

**Gestation period:** 7–8 months

**Lifespan:** Up to 30 years

**Size:** 45–90 cm (18–35 in)

### *Find out more*

APES 97
BABOONS 100
CHIMPANZEES 139
COMMUNICATION 26
GORILLAS 192

## FOREST CANOPY

Resting on a high branch in the forests of Southeast Asia, this gibbon is well out of reach of any would-be predators. Gibbons spend their lives almost entirely in the trees. They use their long arms to swing from tree to tree and can even run upright along large branches. They also live close to their favourite foods of fruit, flowers, leaves, insects, young birds, and eggs.

# GIRAFFES

RELATIVES OF CATTLE AND ANTELOPE, giraffes are hoofed mammals that usually live in small herds. They are also the tallest animals living on land. Their height allows them to feed on leaves and twigs from the tops of trees, food that cannot be reached by any of their plant-eating neighbours. Despite their size, giraffes move gracefully, moving both legs on one side at the same time. They can gallop at up to 48 kmh (30 mph).

Bristle-covered horns

Large eyes provide good vision

ADULT GIRAFFE

A bony growth resembling a third "horn" sometimes grows on the forehead

## HEAD HIGH

When grazing on exposed grassland, giraffes are constantly on the lookout for predators. Thanks to their long necks, they have a clear all-round view of their surroundings. Male and female giraffes carry pairs of horns covered by hairy skin. Males use these horns for fighting each other when competing for females.

## STANDING TALL

Young giraffes are born with the distinctive body shape and pattern of an adult giraffe. They have a very long neck, supported by a short body with a sloping back, and long legs. The giraffe will kick out with its plate-sized hooves to defend itself, and its young, against lions and other predators.

ADULT GIRAFFE AND YOUNG

Neck is supported by just seven long bones

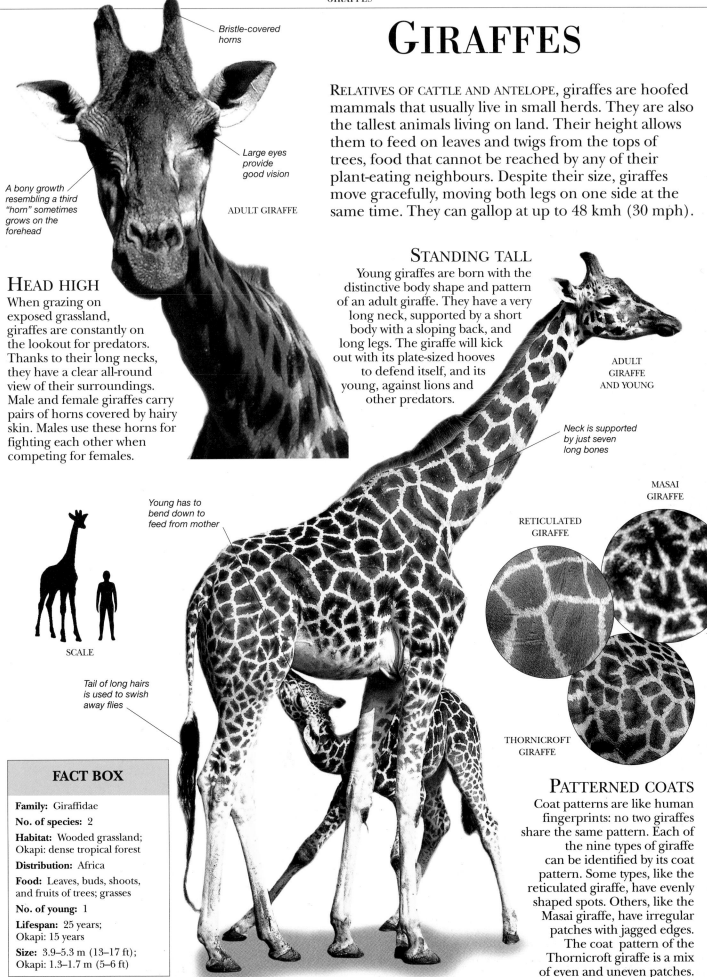

Young has to bend down to feed from mother

SCALE

Tail of long hairs is used to swish away flies

MASAI GIRAFFE

RETICULATED GIRAFFE

THORNICROFT GIRAFFE

## PATTERNED COATS

Coat patterns are like human fingerprints: no two giraffes share the same pattern. Each of the nine types of giraffe can be identified by its coat pattern. Some types, like the reticulated giraffe, have evenly shaped spots. Others, like the Masai giraffe, have irregular patches with jagged edges. The coat pattern of the Thornicroft giraffe is a mix of even and uneven patches.

### FACT BOX

**Family:** Giraffidae

**No. of species:** 2

**Habitat:** Wooded grassland; Okapi: dense tropical forest

**Distribution:** Africa

**Food:** Leaves, buds, shoots, and fruits of trees; grasses

**No. of young:** 1

**Lifespan:** 25 years; Okapi: 15 years

**Size:** 3.9–5.3 m (13–17 ft); Okapi: 1.3–1.7 m (5–6 ft)

## SAVANNA GRAZERS

Giraffes make their home in the African grasslands, or savanna. The savanna is always hot, but has dry and rainy seasons. Many grazing animals feed on savanna grasses, but are forced to move elsewhere for food in the dry season. Only giraffes and elephants have a year-round supply of food. They can reach the shoots and leaves growing on the trees of the savanna.

## FOREST RELATIVE

The okapi is the only other member of the giraffe family. It lacks the giraffe's long neck, has black and white stripes on its rear end, and lives a solitary life in dense, tropical forest. Like the giraffe, it uses its long, black tongue to browse on bushes and trees.

With poor eyesight, the okapi uses large ears and good hearing to detect danger

OKAPI

ADULT GIRAFFE

With eyes so high above the ground, the giraffe can see over long distances

Thick, rubbery lips protect giraffe from sharp thorns

## BROWSING

Giraffes browse on the leaves and twigs of acacia and other thorny shrubs and trees. They use their flexible tongue – up to 46 cm (18 in) long – to grip hold of the plant, and grooved teeth to strip leaves. Male giraffes stretch their necks to reach the topmost leaves, while females feed on lower branches. In this way they avoid competing with each other.

Markings get darker with age

Herd members recognize each other's coat patterns

Front legs are longer than back legs

GIRAFFE HERD

## HERD LIFE

Female giraffes and their young live in small herds of up to 12 members. These herds provide protection for the young from predators. Young males also live in small groups, but become more solitary as they get older.

***Find out more***

# GLIDING MARSUPIALS

SQUIRREL
GLIDER

Stretched folds
of skin form
parachute

VARIOUS DIFFERENT GROUPS OF ANIMALS, including flying fish, flying frogs, lizards and snakes, and flying squirrels, are expert gliders. They hold out their fins, flaps of skin, or other body parts, so that they glide gracefully through the air. Gliding marsupials live in woodlands and forests in Australia, New Guinea, and nearby islands. They climb among the trees and launch themselves into the air to glide down to the trunk of another tree.

## MOVEMENT

The squirrel glider is not a true squirrel. It leaps from high branches and then glides by spreading the folds of skin between its limbs and the sides of its body into a broad "parachute". It steers its way among tree branches, using its tail as a rudder.

RINGTAIL
POSSUM

Small, ball-
shaped nest
of dry leaves in
a tree hollow

PYGMY GLIDING
POSSUM IN DEN

## DAYTIME SHELTER

Gliders, such as this pygmy gliding possum, are active at night. By day, they rest in a tree hollow, lined with a layer of dried leaves. They often stay in family groups, huddling together for warmth during the cold weather.

Strong fingers
form a powerful
grip, helping the
possum to
grasp branches

### FACT BOX

**Family:** Squirrel glider and other lesser gliders: Petauridae; Feathertail glider: Acrobatidae; Greater glider: Pseudocheiridae

**Habitat:** Woodlands and forests

**Distribution:** Australia, New Guinea and nearby islands

**Food:** Sap, gum, flowers and nectar of plants, insects, spiders, and small vertebrates

## EVOLUTION

Most marsupial gliders are related to ringtail possums. This group of marsupials have strong tails that they can use as fifth limbs when climbing and leaping through the trees. Over millions of years, some ringtails developed large skin folds that enabled them to glide rather than just leap.

# GOATS

NUBIAN GOAT
AND KIDS

LIKE SHEEP, THEIR CLOSE RELATIVES, wild and domesticated (working) goats belong to the cattle family. In the wild, goats live in small groups mainly in cold, mountainous places. Male goats are called billies or rams, and the female goats are called nannies or does. Their young are called kids. They are all hooved, plant-eating mammals, but many of the domesticated goats have been bred for special features such as long, woolly coats, or impressive, ornamental horns.

MALE ANGORA
GOAT

## CARING MOTHER

Kids are able to stand up on their feet very soon after birth. They follow their mother everywhere for protection and to feed on her milk.

Kid feeds on its
mother's milk

Long, backward-
pointing horns

SAANEN
GOAT

Typical
beard
of hair

## WORKING GOATS

This Saanen goat is a working animal, kept for its ability to produce about 3,000 litres (5,000 pints) of milk a year. Goats provide people with milk, meat, and sometimes wool.

Sharp horns used
for fighting rivals

Long, curly
hair is clipped
twice a year

Two toes tipped
with hooves

## MOUNTAIN HIGH

As well as having a beard of hair under its chin, the wild mountain goat also has a mane of long hair on its throat and chest. It can climb easily over rugged, rocky ground, thanks to its split hooves which give the goat a better grip on uneven surfaces.

## WOOLLY COAT

Angora goats have thick coats of long, silky hair known as mohair. They are a domestic breed, raised purely for their hair which is woven into fabric or yarn.

Thick shaggy
coat keeps
goat warm

SCALE

MOUNTAIN
GOAT

### FACT BOX

**Family:** Bovidae

**Habitat:** Mountains, alpine meadows, woodland, dry grasslands

**Distribution:** Worldwide, apart from Antarctic

**Food:** Grasses, shrubs, and other plants

**No. of young:** 1–2

**Lifespan:** 8 years

**Size:** 65–109 cm (25–43 in)

*Find out more*
DEER AND ANTELOPE 154
MAMMALS 239
MOUNTAIN LIFE 58
SHEEP 318

# GORILLAS

MOUNTAIN
GORILLA

SOMETIMES CALLED "KING OF THE APES", gorillas are members of the great ape family, which also includes chimpanzees, orang-utans, and bonobos. They are peaceful vegetarians that spend most of their time resting and eating in their forest habitat. Gorillas live in groups of females and their young, led by a large male, known as a silverback. The male leader, who is twice the size of a female gorilla, decides where the group will feed and when it should stop to settle for the night. When danger threatens, the silverback displays his full size and strength to defend his family.

MALE WESTERN
LOWLAND
GORILLA

## NEST MAKERS

Gorillas make not one but two nests in which to sleep or rest. Every gorilla over the age of four makes itself a fresh nest of dried grasses and leaves in which to sleep at night. During the daytime, it will make a smaller day-nest where it will rest after feeding, or shelter from rain.

*Adult male gorilla has a large patch of silver fur*

*Ground nest of dried grass*

## WARM FUR

Mountain gorillas live in colder places than their lowland cousins, so have longer, thicker fur for extra warmth. Although their fur protects them from the cold, it is not waterproof.

## TAIL END

Until they are about three years old, infant gorillas have white tail tufts. These show up well against their dark fur and help their mothers to keep track of them as they play in the forest.

*Tuft of white fur*

YOUNG GORILLA

*Young gorillas ride on their mother's wide rump*

## GETTING AROUND

Gorillas spend most of their time on the ground, moving around on all fours. They keep their feet flat on the ground, but curl up their fingers so that their bony knuckles take the weight of their bodies. When they are showing off or carrying something with their hands, gorillas are able to cross short distances by walking on just two legs.

*Pot belly shows a full store of food*

*Lower jaw sticks forwards*

*Skin is thicker on the backs of the knuckles*

FEMALE
WESTERN
LOWLAND
GORILLA

SCALE

### FACT BOX

**Family**: Pongidae

**Habitat**: Lowland rainforest, mountain forests

**Distribution**: Central Africa

**Food**: Plant leaves, shoots, roots, bark and berries; fungus

**No. of young**: 1

**Lifespan**: Up to 35 years

**Size**: Up to 1.8 m (6 ft)

## TROPICAL FORESTS

Gorillas live only in the lush, wet forests of West and Central Africa. These areas provide many different plants for gorillas to eat all year round, as well as places for them to sleep. The forests where lowland gorillas live are warm and tropical, but mountain gorillas live in much colder forests. At night, the temperature in the mountains can even drop below freezing point.

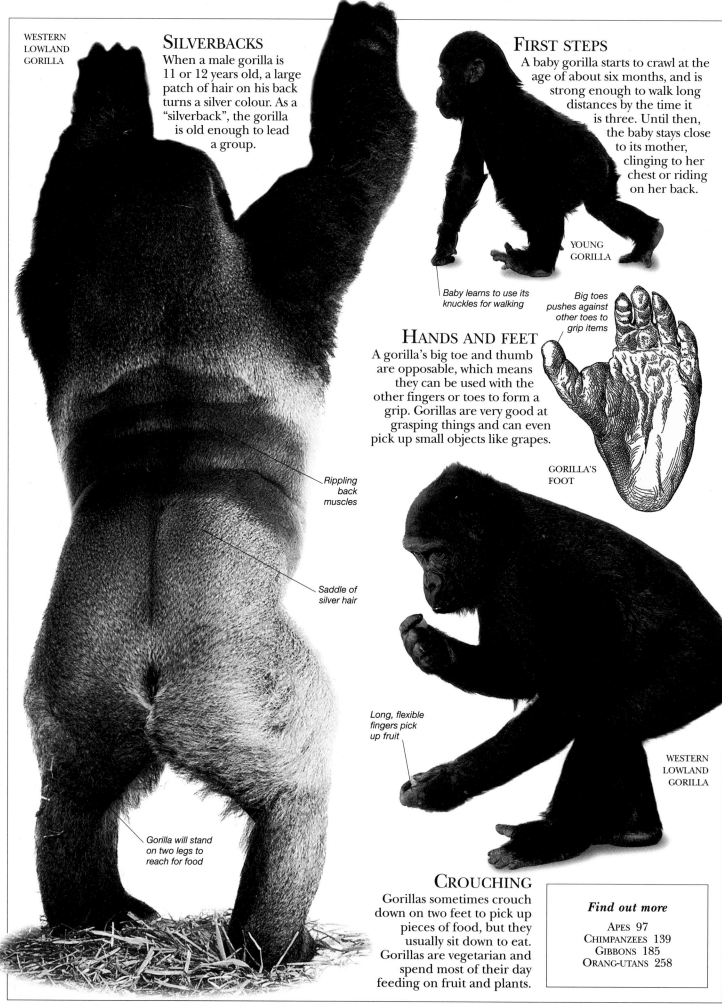

## SILVERBACKS

When a male gorilla is 11 or 12 years old, a large patch of hair on his back turns a silver colour. As a "silverback", the gorilla is old enough to lead a group.

WESTERN LOWLAND GORILLA

## FIRST STEPS

A baby gorilla starts to crawl at the age of about six months, and is strong enough to walk long distances by the time it is three. Until then, the baby stays close to its mother, clinging to her chest or riding on her back.

YOUNG GORILLA

Baby learns to use its knuckles for walking

Big toes pushes against other toes to grip items

## HANDS AND FEET

A gorilla's big toe and thumb are opposable, which means they can be used with the other fingers or toes to form a grip. Gorillas are very good at grasping things and can even pick up small objects like grapes.

GORILLA'S FOOT

Rippling back muscles

Saddle of silver hair

Long, flexible fingers pick up fruit

WESTERN LOWLAND GORILLA

Gorilla will stand on two legs to reach for food

## CROUCHING

Gorillas sometimes crouch down on two feet to pick up pieces of food, but they usually sit down to eat. Gorillas are vegetarian and spend most of their day feeding on fruit and plants.

**Find out more**

APES 97
CHIMPANZEES 139
GIBBONS 185
ORANG-UTANS 258

# GRASSHOPPERS AND CRICKETS

MORE OFTEN HEARD THAN SEEN, grasshoppers and crickets are among the world's noisiest insects. Their loud chirping sounds heard in summer are made to attract a mate. They belong to a large family of about 20,000 species, which includes locusts. Grasshoppers and crickets are found all over the world except in very cold, snowy places. They live in deserts, grasslands, forests, and even high on mountains. Some live underground. These insects are mainly plant-eaters, but some crickets also eat dead animals, and a few species hunt live prey. They have powerful back legs, which they use to leap in the air to escape from enemies.

## SINGING

Male grasshoppers and crickets sing loud chirping "songs" in the breeding season to warn away other males and to attract females. They produce the sounds by rubbing rough patches on their wings together, or by rubbing their hind legs against their wings. Different species have different songs so the females listen to the songs carefully to track down the right mate.

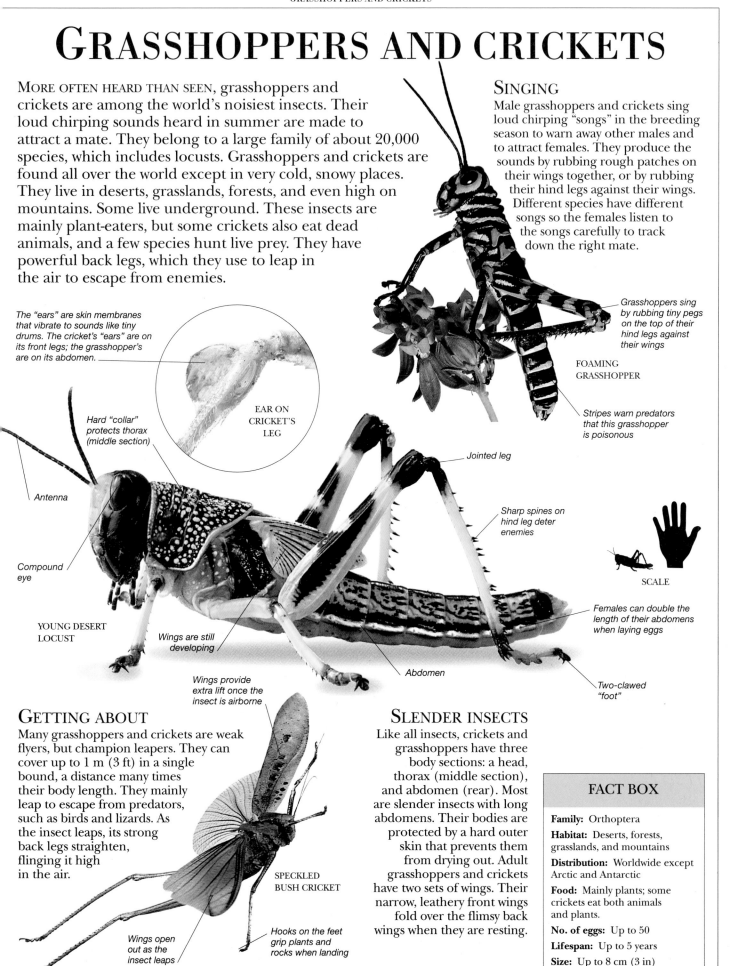

The "ears" are skin membranes that vibrate to sounds like tiny drums. The cricket's "ears" are on its front legs; the grasshopper's are on its abdomen.

EAR ON CRICKET'S LEG

Grasshoppers sing by rubbing tiny pegs on the top of their hind legs against their wings

FOAMING GRASSHOPPER

Stripes warn predators that this grasshopper is poisonous

Hard "collar" protects thorax (middle section)

Jointed leg

Sharp spines on hind leg deter enemies

Antenna

Compound eye

SCALE

YOUNG DESERT LOCUST

Wings are still developing

Females can double the length of their abdomens when laying eggs

Abdomen

Two-clawed "foot"

## GETTING ABOUT

Many grasshoppers and crickets are weak flyers, but champion leapers. They can cover up to 1 m (3 ft) in a single bound, a distance many times their body length. They mainly leap to escape from predators, such as birds and lizards. As the insect leaps, its strong back legs straighten, flinging it high in the air.

Wings provide extra lift once the insect is airborne

SPECKLED BUSH CRICKET

Wings open out as the insect leaps

Hooks on the feet grip plants and rocks when landing

## SLENDER INSECTS

Like all insects, crickets and grasshoppers have three body sections: a head, thorax (middle section), and abdomen (rear). Most are slender insects with long abdomens. Their bodies are protected by a hard outer skin that prevents them from drying out. Adult grasshoppers and crickets have two sets of wings. Their narrow, leathery front wings fold over the flimsy back wings when they are resting.

### FACT BOX

**Family:** Orthoptera

**Habitat:** Deserts, forests, grasslands, and mountains

**Distribution:** Worldwide except Arctic and Antarctic

**Food:** Mainly plants; some crickets eat both animals and plants.

**No. of eggs:** Up to 50

**Lifespan:** Up to 5 years

**Size:** Up to 8 cm (3 in)

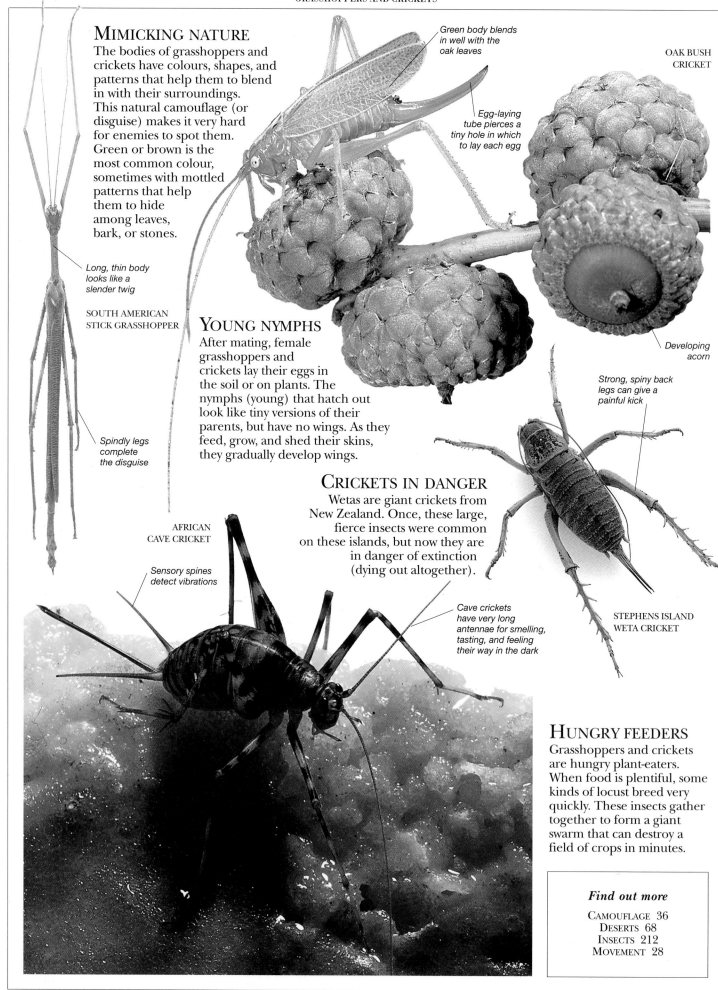

## MIMICKING NATURE

The bodies of grasshoppers and crickets have colours, shapes, and patterns that help them to blend in with their surroundings. This natural camouflage (or disguise) makes it very hard for enemies to spot them. Green or brown is the most common colour, sometimes with mottled patterns that help them to hide among leaves, bark, or stones.

Green body blends in well with the oak leaves

OAK BUSH CRICKET

Egg-laying tube pierces a tiny hole in which to lay each egg

Long, thin body looks like a slender twig

SOUTH AMERICAN STICK GRASSHOPPER

Developing acorn

Strong, spiny back legs can give a painful kick

Spindly legs complete the disguise

## YOUNG NYMPHS

After mating, female grasshoppers and crickets lay their eggs in the soil or on plants. The nymphs (young) that hatch out look like tiny versions of their parents, but have no wings. As they feed, grow, and shed their skins, they gradually develop wings.

## CRICKETS IN DANGER

Wetas are giant crickets from New Zealand. Once, these large, fierce insects were common on these islands, but now they are in danger of extinction (dying out altogether).

AFRICAN CAVE CRICKET

Sensory spines detect vibrations

Cave crickets have very long antennae for smelling, tasting, and feeling their way in the dark

STEPHENS ISLAND WETA CRICKET

## HUNGRY FEEDERS

Grasshoppers and crickets are hungry plant-eaters. When food is plentiful, some kinds of locust breed very quickly. These insects gather together to form a giant swarm that can destroy a field of crops in minutes.

*Find out more*

CAMOUFLAGE 36
DESERTS 68
INSECTS 212
MOVEMENT 28

# GUINEA PIGS

COARSE-HAIRED
GUINEA PIG

Coat can be
a mixture of
different
colours

THE GUINEA PIG IS A DOMESTICATED mammal that belongs to the rodents, the large group that includes mice and squirrels. Guinea pigs are kept as pets worldwide. Their relatives in the wild are called cavies. They live in the treeless grasslands of South America. Groups of up to 40 cavies will often use the abandoned burrows dug out by other small mammals, to hide from predators or to shelter during the cold winter.

MOTHER AND BABY
GUINEA PIG

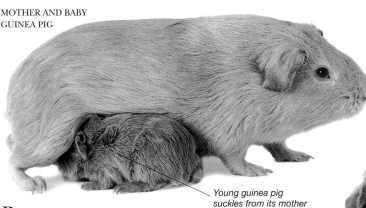

Young guinea pig
suckles from its mother

## COLOURFUL COATS

While cavies (wild guinea pigs) have brown or grey fur, domestic guinea pigs have been bred in many different colours. Their fur can be short or long, as well as smooth or coarse.

Large, alert eyes

ADULT
GUINEA PIG

## RAISING YOUNG

When guinea pigs are born they are covered in fur. They feed on their mother's milk for 21 days, but can eat solid food within the first week of life.

SCALE

## BODY SHAPE

Guinea pigs and their wild relatives, cavies, have stout bodies with short legs and no tail. The large head has small, furless ears. The strong front feet have four toes with sharp claws that are used for burrowing.

### FACT BOX

**Family:** Caviidae

**Habitat:** In the wild: grasslands, forests, and rocky areas

**Distribution:** South America

**Food:** Grasses and small plants

**Gestation period:** 58–72 days

**No. of young:** 1–13

**Lifespan:** Guinea pig: up to 8 years; cavy (in wild): 3–4 years

**Size:** 25 cm (10 in)

In the wild, cavies live
together in small groups

Sharp claws used for
digging and scrabbling

FAMILY OF
CAVIES

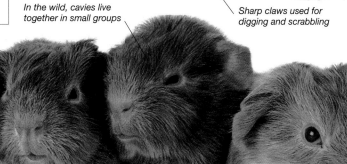

## SOCIAL LIFE

Guinea pigs are social animals. Their wild relatives, cavies, live in small family groups of up to 10 members. They communicate with each other using chirps, squeaks, or burbles to show excitement or to warn of danger.

### Find out more

ANIMAL HOMES 46
RODENTS 303

# GULLS

KELP
GULLS

GULLS ARE THE MOST FAMILIAR of all seabirds. Although they are commonly known as seagulls, some gulls spend little time by the sea. They often prefer to move far inland, especially in winter, where they scavenge for food on rubbish tips and roost on lakes and reservoirs. Gulls breed in large colonies (groups) and lay their eggs in sturdy, cup-shaped nests made from twigs, leaves, and grass. Once their young have matured some migrate to warmer areas for the winter.

Gull glides down to pick up the next gust of wind

GLIDING
GULL

Upward gust of air lifts gull higher

## FLIGHT PATTERN

Gulls are often seen gliding and soaring in large, looping arcs. They are experts at using the wind and air currents above the sea waves to keep them up in the air. They also make use of updraughts of air along sea cliffs. This technique saves them valuable energy as the gulls do not need to flap their wings when they are being carried by air.

Grooves in bill carry salt down to tip where it drips off

SKELETON OF
A HERRING
GULL'S HEAD

Hooked beak for tearing flesh

Black spot behind eye

ADULT BLACK-
HEADED GULL
IN WINTER

## SPECIAL FEATURES

Like other birds, gulls do not have teeth to tear up and grind their food. They rely on their long, hooked beaks for catching prey and breaking up food into smaller pieces. Gulls also have large salt glands in their heads, to control their intake of this essential mineral. Too much salt would harm gulls, so the glands release any excess amounts, which flow away down grooves in the bill.

White underparts blend in with the pale sky

Black tipped tail and wings

## FACT BOX

**Family:** Laridae

**Habitat:** Sea coasts, open ocean, inland on fresh waters, open country, urban areas

**Distribution:** Worldwide

**Food:** Fish, crabs, shellfish, and other sea creatures, small mammals, adult and young birds, bird eggs, food scraps

**No. of eggs:** Usually 1–3

**Lifespan:** Up to 32 years

**Size:** 26–75 cm (10–30 in)

## BLENDING IN

The black-headed gull has a white head in winter, but in the breeding season it grows a hood of chocolate-brown feathers. The darker feathers of the head stand out against the white feathers of the body. This means that the gull's head movements can be seen clearly as it performs its courtship display. It also helps others of its kind to spot it at a distance when food has been found.

Webbed feet for swimming

SCALE

*Find out more*

BIRDS 115
GLIDERS 190
MOVEMENT 28

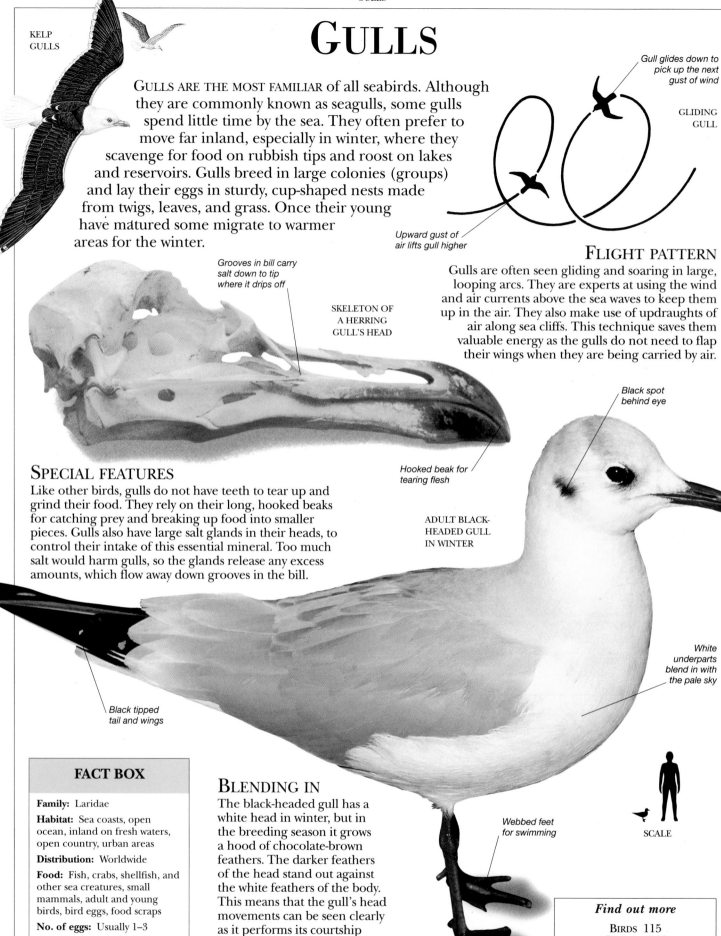

# HAMSTERS AND GERBILS

FAMILIAR AS PETS, THE GOLDEN HAMSTER and the Mongolian gerbil are just two of the many types of hamster and gerbil found worldwide. These closely related animals are rodents, a group of mammals that also includes rats and mice. Hamsters and gerbils dig burrows in which they build nests, and both are most active at night. They feed on seeds and other plant food which they gather and take back to their burrows. There they can eat the food in safety or add it to their stores.

Tail

GERBIL

Large ears

Golden coat colour helps gerbil blend in with its sandy surroundings

## IN THE WILD

Hamsters have rounded bodies with short, stumpy tails. Loose folds of skin – called cheek pouches – run along the side of their jaws. They fill these pouches with food to carry back to their burrow.

Front paws are used like hands to hold food when eating

## AGILITY

Like hamsters, gerbils have large ears and eyes, but they also have a long tail, and long hind legs and feet for leaping. Gerbils can survive in dry places because they do not need to drink very much, and dig burrows in the sand to avoid the Sun's heat.

## BUILDING NESTS

A wild gerbil shelters from heat, cold, or danger in a nest inside its burrow. Gerbils – whether in the wild or as pets – collect vegetation and shred it to make a nest.

DWARF HAMSTER

SCALE

GERBIL

Thick coat keeps the gerbil warm during cold spells

## FACT BOX

**Family:** Muridae

**No. of species:** Hamster: 18; gerbil: 87

**Habitat:** Dry grasslands, deserts, and mountain slopes

**Distribution:** Europe, Middle East, Africa, and Asia

**Food:** Seeds, shoots, leaves

**No. of young:** Hamster: 2–16; gerbil: 1–12

**Gestation period:** Hamster: 16 days; gerbil: 30 days

**Lifespan:** About 3 years

**Size:** 10–18 cm (4–8 in)

## FUR-FREE BABIES

At two days old, hamster babies are blind, helpless, and have no fur. Their mother may place them inside her cheek pouches if danger threatens.

MOTHER AND YOUNG

*Find out more*

EGGS AND NESTS 42
MAMMALS 239
MICE 246
RATS 291
RODENTS 303

# HEDGEHOGS

HEDGEHOGS BELONG to a group of mammals called insectivores (insect-eaters), that also includes shrews and moles. They are small, solitary animals that feed at night. A hedgehog's back and the top of its head are covered with a dense layer of spines. Its young are born blind and naked, with pale pink skin. By the time the babies leave the nest, three to four weeks after being born, their bodies are protected with a coat of about 3,000 spines.

HEDGEHOG IN A BALL

## SELF DEFENCE

When threatened by a predator, the hedgehog makes its needle-sharp spines stand on end, and rolls itself up tightly into a prickly ball. This makes it impossible for any predator to open up the ball, because it would be stabbed by the vicious spines.

### FACT BOX

**Family:** Erinaceidae

**Habitat:** Grasslands, savanna, deserts, farmland, woodland

**Distribution:** Europe, Asia, and Africa

**Food:** Beetles, earthworms, slugs, bird eggs, small mammals

**No. of young:** 4–5

**Lifespan:** Up to 7 years

**Size:** 15–35 cm (6–14 in)

#### Find out more

LONG-EARED DESERT HEDGEHOG

Long ears help the hedgehog keep cool

## DESERT BURROWER

The desert hedgehog avoids the hot daytime sun by resting in the cool of a burrow. Its long ears help it to radiate heat, cooling it down in the hot desert air. At night, it hunts for food. Like all other types of hedgehog, the desert hedgehog has poor eyesight, and relies on good senses of smell and hearing to find food in the dark.

SCALE

Hedgehogs gather dry plant materials for nest-building

## WINTER REST

When autumn sets in, the European hedgehog prepares to hibernate (sleep through winter). It makes itself a warm nest from grasses, twigs, and leaves, and eats as much as possible to build up a fat store. This helps its body to survive the long period of inactivity.

EUROPEAN HEDGEHOG

# HIPPOPOTAMUSES

AS WELL AS THE WATER-LOVING common hippopotamus, there is a second type, the pygmy hippopotamus, which prefers to live in forests. Common hippopotamuses are large, bulky plant-eaters. They spend up to 18 hours a day immersed in lakes and rivers where they can rest, save energy, and avoid the heat of the African sun. Their nearly hairless skin produces a pink, oily liquid that acts as a sunscreen and helps prevent any wounds from becoming infected by dirty water. Feeding takes place at night, when a herd emerges from the water and follows a well-established trail that leads to a favourite feeding site.

ADULT
HIPPOPOTAMUS

## LYING LOW

A hippo's eyes, ears, and nostrils are positioned high on its head. This means that it can still keep a lookout for danger – and breathe – while the rest of its body stays cool under water and avoids being dried out by the hot midday sun.

## UNDER WATER

In deep water, hippopotamuses can walk or run along the river bed. Once under water, their ears and nostrils close to keep the water out, enabling them to stay submerged for up to five minutes. Hippopotamuses are excellent divers and swimmers. Their smooth bodies move easily through water as they paddle with their webbed toes.

HIPPOPOTAMUS
UNDERWATER

### FACT BOX

**Family:** Hippopotamidae

**Habitat:** Rivers and lakes in grassland; Pygmy hippopotamus: tropical forests, swamps

**Distribution:** Africa

**Food:** Grasses; Pygmy hippopotamus: leaves, shoots, fruit, roots

**Lifespan:** 45 years; Pygmy hippopotamus: Up to 35 years

**Size:** 3–5 m (10–17 ft); Pygmy hippopotamus: 1.5–1.75 m (5–6 ft)

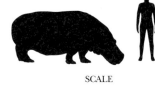

SCALE

Skin scarred from fights with other hippopotamuses

## SHEER BULK

Hippopotamuses have bulky, barrel-shaped bodies, large heads, and short legs. They have large canine teeth called tusks that are used for fighting. They also have large cheek teeth that grind up grasses.

ADULT
HIPPOPOTAMUS

Webbed toes act like paddles for swimming underwater

Thick lips crop grasses

201

## AT THE WATER'S EDGE

Hippopotamuses live by lakes or rivers in the grasslands of Africa. They are never to be found far from water. By day they rest at the waterside or, if it gets hot or danger threatens, in the water itself. When temperatures fall at night, the herd follows well-worn paths to hippopotamus "meadows". After feeding on grasses until sunrise, they return to rest by the water.

MALE
HIPPOPOTAMUSES

*Mouths held
open wide to
display tusks*

MOTHER AND YOUNG
PYGMY HIPPOPOTAMUSES

## SWAMP LIFE

Pygmy hippopotamuses live
alone or in small groups in swampy,
forest areas. They feed at night on
grasses, leaves, and fruits. Unlike
their larger relatives, they spend
little time in water. However,
if threatened, they escape
along tunnel-like paths
through the dense
undergrowth and hide
in streams or rivers.

## RIVALRY

Rival male hippopotamuses
threaten each other by
opening their mouths very
wide to show off their large
tusks. If threats do not deter
the rivals, then they fight
each other with their tusks.
Male hippopotamuses are
aggressive and defend
their territories and
females fiercely.

*Sharp tusks used for
threat and fighting*

ADULT
HIPPOPOTAMUS

## DEFENCE

Despite its weight and size,
a hippopotamus can move quickly on
land to defend itself and its young.
Although it stays in water during the day,
the hippopotamus moves onto the land at
night in order to graze on grassland.

*Short
sturdy legs*

*Herd stays close
together to deter
predators*

## SAFETY IN NUMBERS

Hippopotamuses usually live in
herds of about 10–20 animals, or
sometimes in much larger
groups. They communicate with
each other by using snorts and
bellows. The herd consists
mainly of females and their
young, who climb on their
mother's back for safety. Being
close together gives added
protection against predators
such as crocodiles.

HIPPOPOTAMUS
HERD

*Find out more*

COURTSHIP AND MATING 38
GRASSLAND 64
MAMMALS 239

# HORSES

ALL MEMBERS OF THE HORSE FAMILY have just one toe (a hoof) on each foot. For this reason they are called "odd-toed animals". Horses and ponies are strong, intelligent animals that live together in herds. Wild horses live in open country, where they feed on grasses and plants, often travelling great distances to find new grazing land. The stallions (or males) defend their territory and their mares (female horses) by lashing out with their front feet. Any rivals that get too close to a stallion receive a hard bite.

Broad shoulders and body provides pulling power

DAPPLE-GREY PERCHERON

DARTMOOR PONY

Thick, sturdy neck and long mane

## HEAVY HORSES

Within the horse family is a group known as "heavy horses", which includes the Percheron, the Brabant, the Shire, and the Suffolk Punch. The sheer strength of these large-framed horses has been used for many centuries as the engine for farm equipment. In fact, modern engines are still rated in terms of their horsepower.

## FELL PONIES

Ponies are small, stocky members of the horse family. In the wild, they live in harsh, bleak areas such as moors and fells, where they are able to survive with little food. They are noted for their surefootedness, which enables them to travel across rugged, uneven ground.

Hoof is made of strong horn

SCALE

## BACK TO THE WILD

Domestic horses that have been set free and now run wild are called feral horses, mustangs, or brumbies. They travel together in large herds, grazing on open grassland.

Herd members "nuzzle" or groom each other's manes

HERD OF FERAL CARMARGUE HORSES

Dark stripe
on back

## PATCHWORK COATS

Many wild horses have patterned coats that help to camouflage them, especially when they run at speed. The Pinto pony has a skewbald pattern of large, white patches on a chestnut coat. A pattern of large black-and-white patches is called piebald.

Large white
patches break up
the pony's profile

PINTO PONY

## ASSES

Asiatic wild asses, such as the kulan, onager, and kiang, are often known as the "half-ass" species. They are relatives of the African wild (or "true") ass. Wild asses are similar in size to ponies but have a striped back and short manes. In winter, onagers grow a thick coat to protect them from icy cold winds.

ASIATIC
WILD
KULAN ASSES

Each species
has its own
pattern of stripes

COMMON
ZEBRAS

Ears can be
turned towards
a sound

## FACT BOX

**Family:** Equidae

**Habitat:** Grassland, semi-deserts, mountain plateaus, moorland. Domestic breeds: Enclosed fields

**Distribution:** Worldwide, except Antarctica. Zebra: Africa

**Food:** Mainly coarse grasses, thornbushes, shrubs. Domestic breeds: Grass, hay, and grains

## HORSES' HOOVES

A horse's tough hoof protects the foot bones. It is made of a horny protein, that is found in fingernails. When it is nervous or frightened, a horse will paw or rub its hoof against the ground.

## STAND FIRM

Zebras are the only striped members of the horse family. They live on the African grasslands in large, social herds that graze together. If they or their young are threatened by lions or hyenas, zebras stand together and fight back – they never hide.

*Elegant head*

SHAGYA
ARAB HORSE

*Tail held high is a typical Arab trait*

*Eyes set high on head*

## ARAB BLOOD

The origins of most domestic horses can be traced back to the breeds raised in North Africa and Arabia. Known as Arab horses, these breeds are valued for their speed, courage, and gentle nature, as well as great stamina (staying power).

*Large, open nostrils for taking in air*

*Slender legs are capable of great speed*

## HEAD FEATURES

The horse has good, all-round vision thanks to the high position of the eyes on either side of its long, slender head. Its ears are usually pricked forwards but when held backwards they signal anger or fear. The horse's large, open nostrils are important for taking in plenty of air when running fast.

WELSH
COB HORSE

## WELSH COB

Light draught horses, such as the tough, hardy Welsh Cob, have been bred for pulling waggons, carts, and carriages. They are valued for their ability to withstand travelling long distances and for their courage.

*Tail docked for safety when working*

*Long mane and fringe (forelock)*

SHIRE HORSE

*Sturdy, arched neck*

## BIG AND SMALL

There are more than 150 domestic breeds of horse and pony. A giant shire horse standing next to a tiny Shetland pony shows the great range of sizes among domestic horses. They are both valued for their strength – in fact, the only animal stronger than a shire horse is an elephant.

SHETLAND
PONY

*Strong, muscular legs*

### Find out more

DONKEYS AND ASSES  163
GRASSLANDS  64
PLANT-EATERS  30
TAPIRS  336
ZEBRAS  361

# HUMANS

THE MOST INTELLIGENT ANIMALS ON EARTH, humans belong to the primates, a group of mammals that includes monkeys and apes. Like those of other primates, human hands and feet have five fingers or toes tipped by nails. Their eyes face forward to allow them to judge distances accurately. Like their closest relatives, the apes, humans have no tail, but unlike apes, they lack long body hair. Instead, they wear clothes to stay warm, which enables them to live in most places on Earth. Young humans remain with their parents for between 14 and 18 years. During this time they learn the many skills they will need to survive in human society.

## BRAIN POWER

For their size, humans have brains that are much bigger and more complex than other mammals. In particular, they have a very large cerebrum – the part of the brain involved in thinking, creating, remembering, and learning. It is responsible for individual personalities and emotions, as well as the ability to see, hear, taste, smell, and feel. Although it makes up just two per cent of the body's weight, the brain uses up to 20 per cent of its energy.

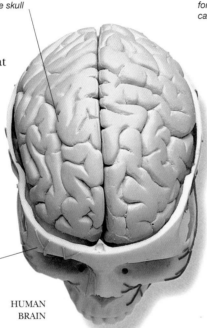

Large cerebrum folds to fit inside skull

Bony skull protects brain

HUMAN BRAIN

Arms are used for holding and carrying objects

ADULT MALE HUMAN

## FACT BOX

**Family:** Hominidae

**Habitat:** Most land habitats, living in houses and other shelters

**Distribution:** Worldwide

**Food:** Animals, plants, and their products

**No. of young:** 1–2

**Lifespan:** Up to 100 years

**Size:** 1.5–2 m (5–6.5 ft)

## HUMAN BODY

Humans stand upright, and their bodies are supported by long, strong legs, and large feet. Their heads have flattened faces and eyes that face forward. The arms and hands are used to lift, carry, and hold objects. Most of the human body is covered with short, fine hairs. Only the head and, in men, the face and chest, have a covering of longer coarse hair.

## COMMUNICATION

Humans are social animals, who communicate with each other in many ways. For example, facial expressions are used to show feelings such as happiness, anxiety, or anger. Humans are the only animals to use spoken and written language as a form of communication. Speech and writing enables humans to pass on knowledge and to develop cultures.

Smile shows happiness

Face muscles pull on the skin to produce a scowl

Feet support body and push it off the ground during walking and running

YOUNG FEMALE SMILING

YOUNG FEMALE SCOWLING

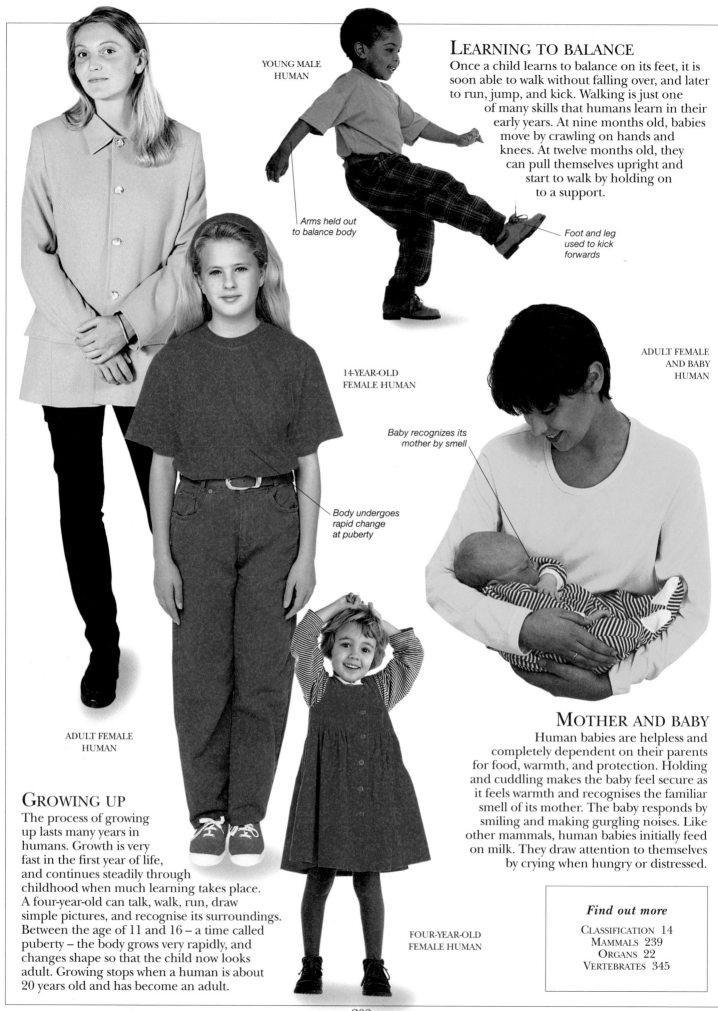

## LEARNING TO BALANCE

Once a child learns to balance on its feet, it is soon able to walk without falling over, and later to run, jump, and kick. Walking is just one of many skills that humans learn in their early years. At nine months old, babies move by crawling on hands and knees. At twelve months old, they can pull themselves upright and start to walk by holding on to a support.

YOUNG MALE HUMAN

*Arms held out to balance body*

*Foot and leg used to kick forwards*

ADULT FEMALE AND BABY HUMAN

14-YEAR-OLD FEMALE HUMAN

*Baby recognizes its mother by smell*

*Body undergoes rapid change at puberty*

ADULT FEMALE HUMAN

## MOTHER AND BABY

Human babies are helpless and completely dependent on their parents for food, warmth, and protection. Holding and cuddling makes the baby feel secure as it feels warmth and recognises the familiar smell of its mother. The baby responds by smiling and making gurgling noises. Like other mammals, human babies initially feed on milk. They draw attention to themselves by crying when hungry or distressed.

## GROWING UP

The process of growing up lasts many years in humans. Growth is very fast in the first year of life, and continues steadily through childhood when much learning takes place. A four-year-old can talk, walk, run, draw simple pictures, and recognise its surroundings. Between the age of 11 and 16 – a time called puberty – the body grows very rapidly, and changes shape so that the child now looks adult. Growing stops when a human is about 20 years old and has become an adult.

FOUR-YEAR-OLD FEMALE HUMAN

### Find out more

CLASSIFICATION 14
MAMMALS 239
ORGANS 22
VERTEBRATES 345

# HUMMINGBIRDS

FOUND ONLY IN THE AMERICAS, hummingbirds include the world's smallest and most brightly coloured birds. There are about 330 different kinds, ranging from the tiny bee hummingbird to the giant hummingbird. All take their name from the humming sound made by the fast beating of their wings. They feed on nectar and insects, using their long slender bills. During winter, some North American species migrate to Mexico for the warm weather and new food supplies.

Long, slender bill can also catch small insects

Nostril flaps keep pollen clear of airway

RUFOUS HUMMINGBIRD

SCALE

## FLIGHT
Fast-beating wings enable the hummingbird to hover in one place, move forwards and sideways, or fly backwards. Small hummingbirds beat their wings at a rate of between 70 and 80 beats per second. Their wings move even faster – up to 200 beats per second – during courtship displays or when chasing rivals.

## NECTAR-SIPPER
Hummingbirds feed on the sugary nectar produced inside flowers. As they hover in front of a flower, the birds insert their long, slender bills which sip up the nectar. This food provides their bodies with the energy needed to power their rapid wing beats.

Powerful, highly flexible wings enable bird to hover in one place

HUMMINGBIRD HOVERING IN MID-AIR

Glossy feathers appear to change colour in different lights

Feathers close together to push against the air

Pair of pea-sized eggs

## NESTS
The small, rounded eggs of the hummingbird are protected in cup-shaped nests, made from moss, bark, and leaves. The nest materials, which are bound together with the silk of spiders' webs, blend in with the surroundings. This helps to keep the eggs safe from predators.

HUMMINGBIRD NEST AND EGGS

## FACT BOX

**Family:** Trochilidae

**Habitat:** Mountains, woodlands, rainforests, grasslands

**Distribution:** North, Central and South America, the Caribbean

**Food:** Mainly nectar; also some pollen, insects, and spiders

**No. of eggs:** 2

**Size:** 5–35 cm (2–14 in)

### Find out more

# HYENAS

THERE ARE THREE DIFFERENT KINDS OF HYENA – spotted, which is the largest of the three, striped, and brown. All hyenas are meat-eaters and are mainly active at night, either hunting or feeding on carrion (the remains of dead animals). In the day, they rest in burrows or caves. Hyenas share the same common features – strong front legs and shoulders, large heads, and hairy manes that run along their sloping backs.

HYENA SKULL

Large, back teeth crush and grind bones

Short jaws produce a strong grip

## STRONG JAWS

Hyenas have short, powerful jaws and strong teeth. These allow them to crush and swallow large bones and to cut through the tough parts of carcasses left behind by other meat-eaters. Any pieces that they cannot digest, such as horns, hooves, and hair are brought up in pellets.

## KEEPING IN TOUCH

Spotted hyenas communicate with each other over long distances by leaving scent marks across their territories. They are also known for exchanging loud, whooping calls, which sound like laughter.

SPOTTED HYENA

Dark mane can be raised to make hyena look larger

Large, bushy tail

Distinctive sloping shoulders

STRIPED HYENA

Good sense of smell

Hind legs are shorter than the front legs

## SCAVENGERS

Striped and brown hyenas are not as noisy or aggressive as spotted hyenas. They tend to eat carrion, but also feed on live insects and small mammals, as well as eggs and fruit. Their young are suckled for up to 12 months, with adult members of the pack bringing back food for them.

Four-toed, clawed feet

SCALE

### FACT BOX

**Family:** Hyaenidae

**Habitat:** Dry, open grasslands, scrub, and stony desert

**Distribution:** India, Turkey, Middle East, and some parts of Africa and Russia

**Food:** Large mammals, carrion

**Gestation period:** 3–4 months

**Lifespan:** 25–30 years

**Size:** 70–90 cm (27–35 in)

### Find out more

## GRASSLAND ARENA

Hyenas live on dry, open savanna grasslands where there are plenty of grazing animals for them to eat. They usually sleep in burrows or among tall grasses or rocks during the day and emerge at dusk. Hyenas specialize in feeding on carrion but they are also predators, especially spotted hyenas. By hunting together, they can overcome large grazing animals such as zebras.

# INSECTS

THERE ARE MORE INSECTS within each 3 sq km (1 sq mile) of land than there are humans on Earth. They live in every type of habitat and are found worldwide. Butterflies, bees, beetles, ants, flies, and grasshoppers are all familiar insects. Fleas, lice, earwigs, cockroaches, and termites are also insects, but scorpions, spiders, and centipedes are not. You can tell insects from other minibeasts by counting their legs – all adult insects have six legs. Most insects also have wings and can fly.

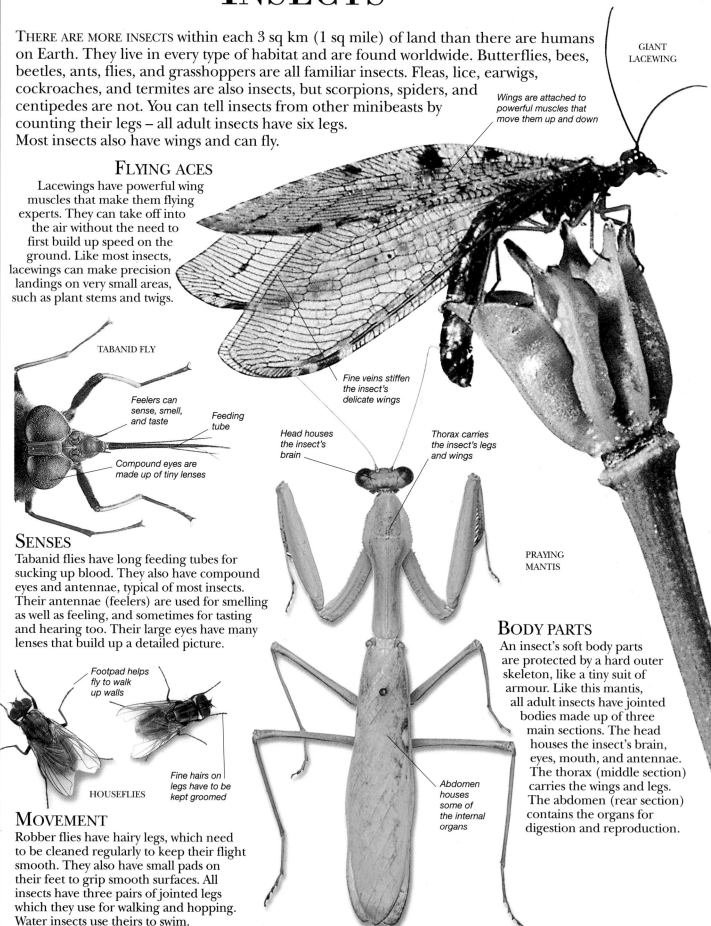

GIANT LACEWING

Wings are attached to powerful muscles that move them up and down

## FLYING ACES

Lacewings have powerful wing muscles that make them flying experts. They can take off into the air without the need to first build up speed on the ground. Like most insects, lacewings can make precision landings on very small areas, such as plant stems and twigs.

TABANID FLY

Feelers can sense, smell, and taste

Feeding tube

Compound eyes are made up of tiny lenses

Fine veins stiffen the insect's delicate wings

Head houses the insect's brain

Thorax carries the insect's legs and wings

PRAYING MANTIS

## SENSES

Tabanid flies have long feeding tubes for sucking up blood. They also have compound eyes and antennae, typical of most insects. Their antennae (feelers) are used for smelling as well as feeling, and sometimes for tasting and hearing too. Their large eyes have many lenses that build up a detailed picture.

Footpad helps fly to walk up walls

Fine hairs on legs have to be kept groomed

HOUSEFLIES

## MOVEMENT

Robber flies have hairy legs, which need to be cleaned regularly to keep their flight smooth. They also have small pads on their feet to grip smooth surfaces. All insects have three pairs of jointed legs which they use for walking and hopping. Water insects use theirs to swim.

Abdomen houses some of the internal organs

## BODY PARTS

An insect's soft body parts are protected by a hard outer skeleton, like a tiny suit of armour. Like this mantis, all adult insects have jointed bodies made up of three main sections. The head houses the insect's brain, eyes, mouth, and antennae. The thorax (middle section) carries the wings and legs. The abdomen (rear section) contains the organs for digestion and reproduction.

MATING PAIR OF
MEXICAN BEAN
BEETLES

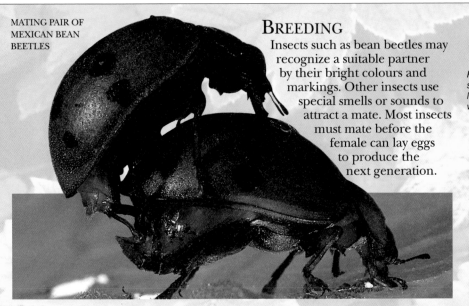

## BREEDING

Insects such as bean beetles may recognize a suitable partner by their bright colours and markings. Other insects use special smells or sounds to attract a mate. Most insects must mate before the female can lay eggs to produce the next generation.

HOVERFLY

*Hoverfly's striped body looks just like a wasp's markings*

## LOOKALIKES

Hoverflies copy the stripes and colours of wasps so closely that enemies leave them alone. Insects such as wasps, bees, and ladybirds all have brightly coloured bodies and black stripes or spots. These bold patterns warn predators that they are poisonous or taste nasty, or are armed with a painful sting.

### FACT BOX

**Order:** Insecta

**No. of species:** More than 1 million

**Habitat:** Widespread on land and in fresh water; a few species live in salt water.

**Distribution:** All continents and seas

**Food:** Wide variety of foods, including plants, live or dead animals, blood, dung, and glue

*Wasp's sting pierces the victim's body and paralyzes it*

*Weevil will provide fresh meat for the wasp's young when it hatches out*

## USEFUL STING

Wasps are armed with stings which they use to defend themselves against predators. They also use their stings to kill or paralyze their prey, such as spiders, weevils, or even young wasps. Rather than feeding on their prey, some female wasps drag their victims to a sheltered place and then inject or lay their eggs on the body. This ensures that when the eggs hatch there will be a supply of food ready for the larvae (young).

WEEVIL HUNTING A WASP
ATTACKING A WEEVIL ON
A FLOWER BUD

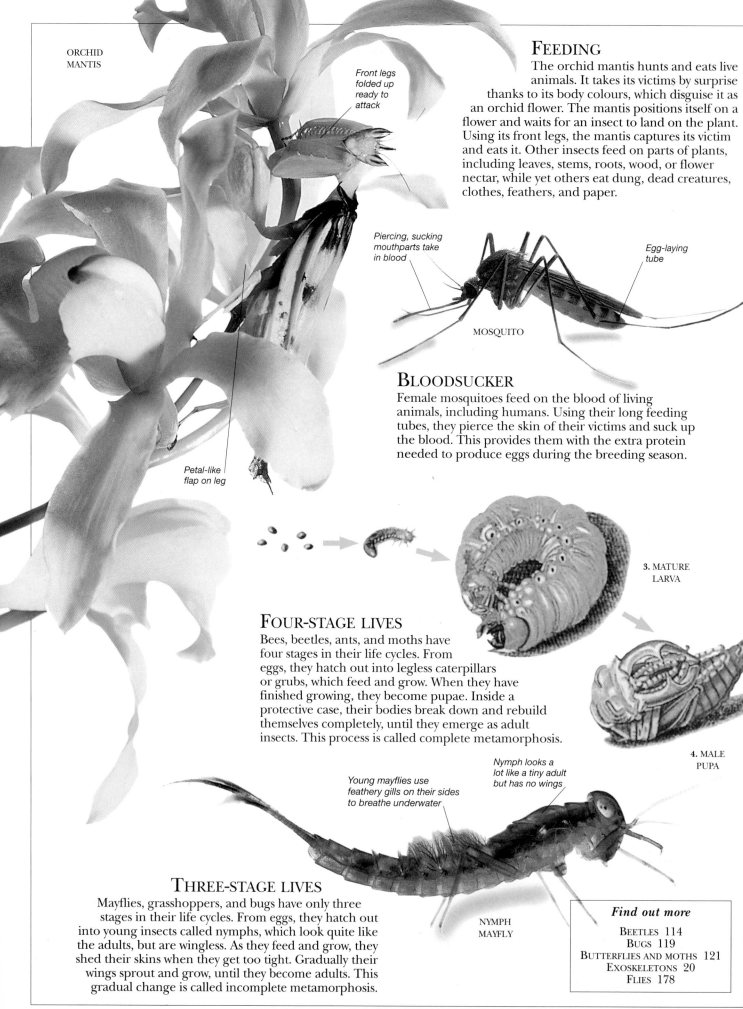

ORCHID
MANTIS

Front legs
folded up
ready to
attack

Petal-like
flap on leg

# FEEDING

The orchid mantis hunts and eats live
animals. It takes its victims by surprise
thanks to its body colours, which disguise it as
an orchid flower. The mantis positions itself on a
flower and waits for an insect to land on the plant.
Using its front legs, the mantis captures its victim
and eats it. Other insects feed on parts of plants,
including leaves, stems, roots, wood, or flower
nectar, while yet others eat dung, dead creatures,
clothes, feathers, and paper.

Piercing, sucking
mouthparts take
in blood

Egg-laying
tube

MOSQUITO

# BLOODSUCKER

Female mosquitoes feed on the blood of living
animals, including humans. Using their long feeding
tubes, they pierce the skin of their victims and suck up
the blood. This provides them with the extra protein
needed to produce eggs during the breeding season.

3. MATURE
LARVA

# FOUR-STAGE LIVES

Bees, beetles, ants, and moths have
four stages in their life cycles. From
eggs, they hatch out into legless caterpillars
or grubs, which feed and grow. When they have
finished growing, they become pupae. Inside a
protective case, their bodies break down and rebuild
themselves completely, until they emerge as adult
insects. This process is called complete metamorphosis.

4. MALE
PUPA

Nymph looks a
lot like a tiny adult
but has no wings

Young mayflies use
feathery gills on their sides
to breathe underwater

# THREE-STAGE LIVES

Mayflies, grasshoppers, and bugs have only three
stages in their life cycles. From eggs, they hatch out
into young insects called nymphs, which look quite like
the adults, but are wingless. As they feed and grow, they
shed their skins when they get too tight. Gradually their
wings sprout and grow, until they become adults. This
gradual change is called incomplete metamorphosis.

NYMPH
MAYFLY

# INVERTEBRATES

THE ANIMAL KINGDOM IS DIVIDED into two main types – those with backbones, called vertebrates, and those without backbones, known as invertebrates. About 90 per cent of all animals have no backbone. Of the 33 or so different animal groups that belong to this category, insects are by far the largest group. Invertebrates are only distantly related to one another and each type is very different from the others. Many invertebrates are found only in the sea, but others live on land and are extremely common worldwide.

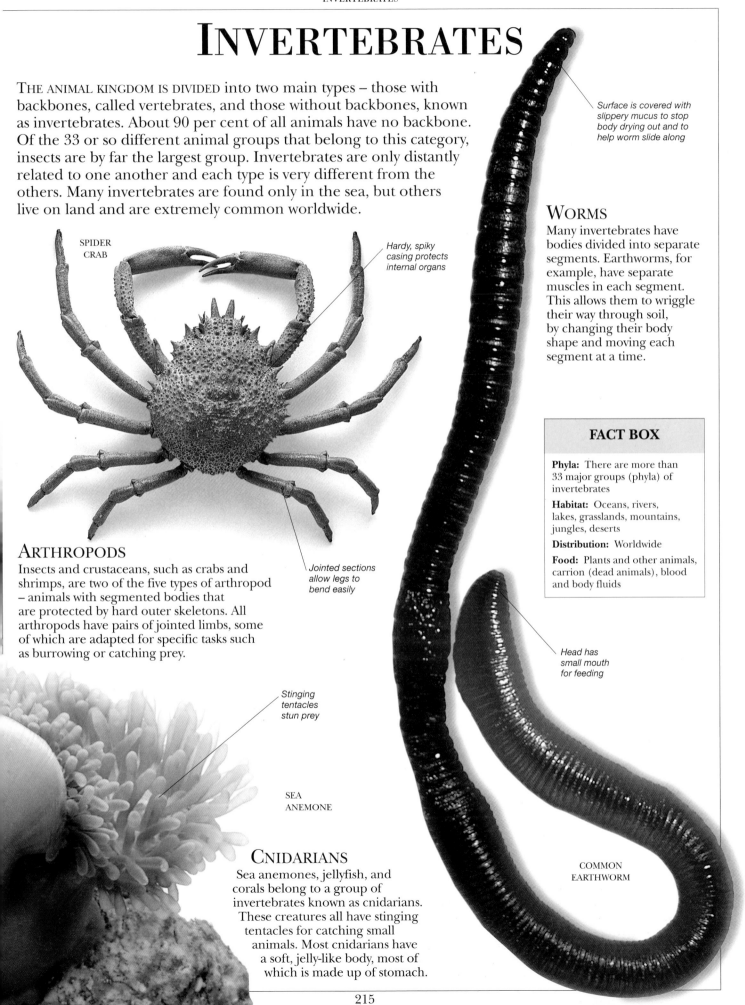

SPIDER CRAB

*Hardy, spiky casing protects internal organs*

*Surface is covered with slippery mucus to stop body drying out and to help worm slide along*

## WORMS
Many invertebrates have bodies divided into separate segments. Earthworms, for example, have separate muscles in each segment. This allows them to wriggle their way through soil, by changing their body shape and moving each segment at a time.

## ARTHROPODS
Insects and crustaceans, such as crabs and shrimps, are two of the five types of arthropod – animals with segmented bodies that are protected by hard outer skeletons. All arthropods have pairs of jointed limbs, some of which are adapted for specific tasks such as burrowing or catching prey.

*Jointed sections allow legs to bend easily*

### FACT BOX

**Phyla:** There are more than 33 major groups (phyla) of invertebrates

**Habitat:** Oceans, rivers, lakes, grasslands, mountains, jungles, deserts

**Distribution:** Worldwide

**Food:** Plants and other animals, carrion (dead animals), blood and body fluids

*Head has small mouth for feeding*

*Stinging tentacles stun prey*

SEA ANEMONE

## CNIDARIANS
Sea anemones, jellyfish, and corals belong to a group of invertebrates known as cnidarians. These creatures all have stinging tentacles for catching small animals. Most cnidarians have a soft, jelly-like body, most of which is made up of stomach.

COMMON EARTHWORM

SPINY
STARFISH

Skin is stretched
over a spiny
skeleton

Body is evenly
balanced when
divided through
the middle

Long, cylindrical
body with very
stretchy walls

Eyes at tips of longer
pair of tentacles

UNDERSIDE OF
COMMON SNAIL

Two pairs of soft,
sensitive tentacles
are used to detect
movement or
find food

ROUNDWORM

Smooth foot
glides over
surfaces

Soft body can
retreat into shell

Body has no
symmetry

SPONGE

## BODY SYMMETRY

Almost all invertebrates have symmetrical bodies. Echinoderms (spiny-skinned animals), such as starfish, are radially symmetrical. This means that their bodies can be divided across the middle in any direction to make two equal halves. Worms, insects, and snails, in contrast, are bilaterally symmetrical. They have different front and rear ends, so they can be divided lengthways to make two equal halves.

## ROUNDWORMS

Nematodes (thread animals), such as roundworms, can be found in every habitat, from the deepest seabeds to the tops of mountains. Many of them live as parasites, taking nourishment from inside other animals or plants.

## SNAILS

Although snails are protected by rigid shells, they have soft bodies. They belong to the mollusc group of invertebrates that also includes slugs, sea-slugs, octopuses, and squids. Unlike insects, molluscs do not have limbs with joints. Snails and most other molluscs move about by gliding on a large, flat pad, called the foot.

## SPONGES

Unlike most other invertebrates, sponges do not have symmetrical bodies. They look more like strange plants than animals. They grow fixed in one place, and have no eyes, ears, brain, nerves, heart, or blood. They feed by pumping a current of water through their bodies, by the beating of tiny hairs, and by sieving out minute food particles. Almost all sponges live in the sea.

### Find out more

CLASSIFICATION 14
CRUSTACEANS 153
INSECTS 212
JELLYFISH AND ANEMONES 219
MOLLUSCS 249
VERTEBRATES 345

# JAGUARS

THE JAGUAR IS THE LARGEST CAT in South America and
the only big cat found in the Americas. It is a similar
creature to the leopard, but has a heavier body and
is not as graceful or as agile. Jaguars are active
mainly at night. Hunting alone in the Amazon
forests, they stalk or ambush prey such as
tapirs, agoutis, and deer. They are also skilled
at catching fish, turtles, and frogs. Adult
jaguars only meet up for mating. Once the
young have reached two years of age, they
leave their mother and fend for themselves.

*Coat carries jaguar's scent*

## SPOTTED COAT

The jaguar's spotted coat is made up of two
layers. The undercoat is formed with a layer of
fine, soft wool. This is covered by an outer coat
of coarse, long hairs, which carries the pattern
of spots. As well as keeping the jaguar warm,
the coat keeps the jaguar well hidden against a
backdrop of forest or grassland as it hunts its prey.

*Spots become smaller around the face*

JAGUAR

## SENSES AND SKILLS

Jaguars rely on their good eyesight
and hearing when hunting at night.
In the dim light, their pupils open
wide to let in as much light as
possible. During the day, when
jaguars rest, the pupils become
narrow to keep out bright
sunlight. An ability to swim also
broadens the jaguar's hunting
ground – these big cats have even
been known to kill crocodiles.

FOREST JAGUAR

### FACT BOX

**Family:** Felidae

**Habitat:** Tropical forests, swamps, grasslands

**Distribution:** From Belize to northern Argentina

**Food:** Large and small mammals, birds, turtles, fish

**Gestation period:** 3-4 months

**Lifespan:** Up to 20 years

**Size:** Up to 1.8 m (6 ft)

SCALE

*Small spots in centre of rosettes*

*Strong neck holds head low during an ambush*

ADULT JAGUAR

## LONE HUNTER

Unlike most big cats, jaguars
have short, sturdy legs – and so
prefer to ambush rather than
outrun their prey. Good climbers,
jaguars also hunt in trees, where
they prey on monkeys.

*Short, powerful legs*

### Find out more

## SPOTTED KILLERS

Jaguars live in dense forests and swamps in Central and South America. Although they can swim and climb well, they cannot run fast for long. This means they have to get close to their prey to make a successful kill. They usually stalk their prey on the ground, but sometimes lie in wait from a low branch above a track. Having eaten their fill, these jaguars are taking a leisurely rest.

# JELLYFISH AND ANEMONES

ALTHOUGH THEY LOOK DIFFERENT, jellyfish and anemones belong to the same family, which also includes corals. They are both sea creatures with soft, boneless bodies and stinging tentacles. Jellyfish are shaped like bells or umbrellas, with long, frilly arms and slender tentacles. They are free-swimming creatures, known as medusas. Anemones have tube-like bodies with waving tentacles, and live on the surfaces of shells and rocks.

SNAKELOCK ANEMONE

Base attaches itself to rocks

## CATCHING PREY

Jellyfish and anemones are meat-eaters. They capture small sea creatures with their tentacles, which are armed with stinging cells. The cells release a poison that stuns the victim, then the tentacles push it into the creature's mouth. Some jellyfish produce a deadly poison, but anemone stings do not harm humans.

Stinging cells on the tentacles release poison when touched

Mouth is hidden by clusters of tentacles

Outer skin

## BODY SHAPES

The jellyfish's body is made up of two layers of cells that form an inner and outer skin. The layers are separated by a jelly-like material. The mouth opening is on the bottom of the bell. Anemones and their relatives, corals, are stout, tube-shaped creatures known as polyps. One end of the tube is the base, which sticks onto rocks. The mouth is at the other end, surrounded by a ring of tentacles.

Mouth is underneath bell-shaped body

Inner skin

COMMON JELLYFISH

Tiny prey are captured by the jellyfish's tentacles

### FACT BOX

**Class:** Jellyfish: Scyphozoa Anemone: Anthozoa

**No. of species:** 9,000

**Habitat:** Jellyfish: Salt or fresh water. Anemone: Salt water

**Distribution:** Jellyfish: Seas, oceans, inland lakes. Anemone: Rocky seabeds and rockpools

**Food:** Small aquatic creatures

**Reproduction:** Jellyfish: Eggs develop into polyps, which bud jellyfish. Anemone: Lay eggs, bud, or divide in half.

**Lifespan:** About 5 years

**Size:** Jellyfish: Up to 2.4 m (8 ft) Anemone: Up to 90 cm (36 in)

## GETTING ABOUT

Jellyfish move using a form of jet propulsion. The rounded bell contracts and forces out any water under the bell. This pushes the jellyfish forwards. As the muscles of the bell relax, the bell once again fills with water. Some jellyfish simply float on the sea surface and drift with the tides. Anemones have a slimy dish on the base of their bodies that helps them to slide over rocks.

the bell

Lion's mane jellyfish has the largest span – up to 2.4 m (8 ft) across

LION'S MANE JELLYFISH

Tentacles trail behind the jellyfish's body as it swims along

SCALE

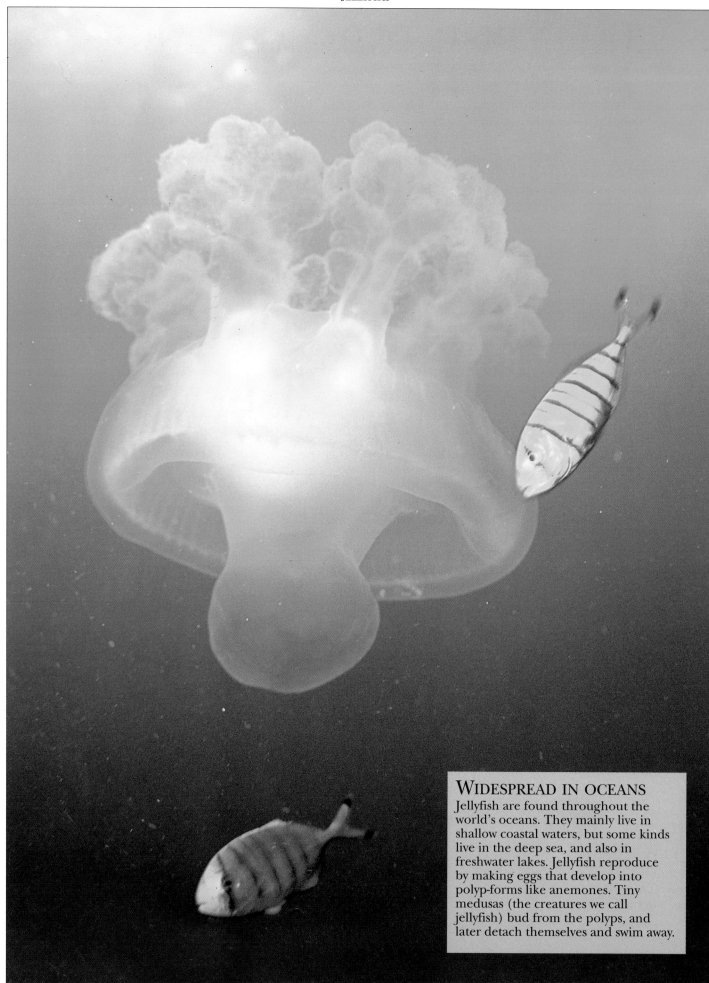

## WIDESPREAD IN OCEANS
Jellyfish are found throughout the world's oceans. They mainly live in shallow coastal waters, but some kinds live in the deep sea, and also in freshwater lakes. Jellyfish reproduce by making eggs that develop into polyp-forms like anemones. Tiny medusas (the creatures we call jellyfish) bud from the polyps, and later detach themselves and swim away.

# KANGAROOS AND WALLABIES

## BODY SHAPE

Kangaroos and wallabies have upright, furry bodies, with long, powerful hind legs, long feet, and short front legs. Their long, thick tails are used as a "fifth leg" to help support the body.

RED KANGAROO

LIKE MANY MAMMALS LIVING IN AUSTRALIA, kangaroos and wallabies are marsupials, or mammals with pouches. The young grow and develop inside a pouch of skin on the front of their mother. Most kangaroos and wallabies live in dry areas, resting in the heat of the day, and coming out at night to feed on grasses. Kangaroos are the largest species in this marsupial family.

Tail is used for balance

Legs swing forward for "landing"

HOPPING SEQUENCE

Kangaroo rests on its short front legs when feeding

Long feet are used to propel kangaroo forward during hopping

## HOPPING

Kangaroos and wallabies move about using their powerful hind legs. When hopping, their long feet push away from the ground together, giving enough lift to send the body forward. Hopping makes it possible for these animals to travel long distances when searching for food. At full speed, large kangaroos can reach up to 48 kmh (30 mph).

SCALE

RED-NECKED WALLABY AND JOEY

## RAISING YOUNG

When a baby wallaby is born, it is tiny and furless. After a few months' rapid growth inside its mother's pouch, the young "joey" leaves for short periods. It returns to feed and sleep, or if danger threatens. After nine months the joey is too big to fit into the pouch, but still sticks its head inside to feed.

Four-month-old joey returns to mother's pouch to suckle

### FACT BOX

**Family:** Macropodidae

**No. of species:** 46

**Habitat:** Dry grassland. Tree kangaroo: Tropical rainforests

**Distribution:** Australia, New Guinea, Tasmania

**Food:** Mainly grasses. Tree kangaroo: Leaves and fruit

**Gestation period:** 30 days

**No. of young:** 1

**Lifespan:** Up to 20 years

**Height:** 61–183 cm (2–6ft). Rufous rat kangaroo: 41–51 cm (16–20 in)

Pouch for holding young

## OUT ON THE PLAINS

The large Eastern Grey kangaroos live on the dry plains and in the woodlands of Australia. During the heat of the day, kangaroos seek the shade provided by large rocks and trees. They emerge in the evening to search for, and graze on, grasses and other small plants. Water is scarce in these areas, but kangaroos have the ability to survive without drinking for long periods.

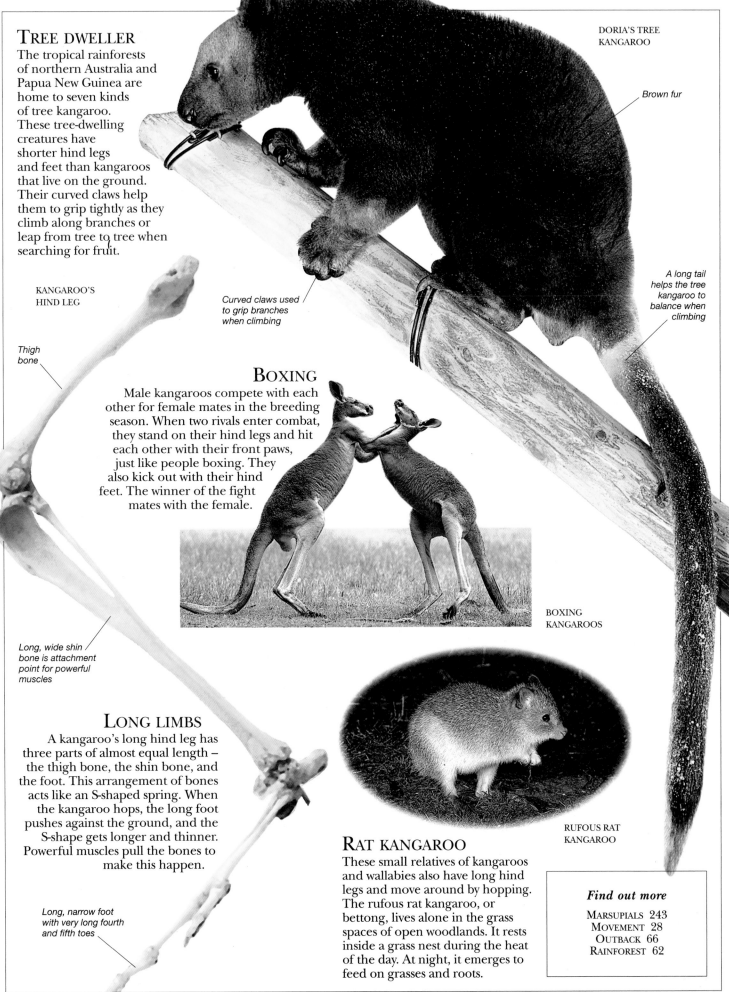

## TREE DWELLER

The tropical rainforests of northern Australia and Papua New Guinea are home to seven kinds of tree kangaroo. These tree-dwelling creatures have shorter hind legs and feet than kangaroos that live on the ground. Their curved claws help them to grip tightly as they climb along branches or leap from tree to tree when searching for fruit.

DORIA'S TREE KANGAROO

Brown fur

A long tail helps the tree kangaroo to balance when climbing

KANGAROO'S HIND LEG

Curved claws used to grip branches when climbing

Thigh bone

## BOXING

Male kangaroos compete with each other for female mates in the breeding season. When two rivals enter combat, they stand on their hind legs and hit each other with their front paws, just like people boxing. They also kick out with their hind feet. The winner of the fight mates with the female.

BOXING KANGAROOS

Long, wide shin bone is attachment point for powerful muscles

## LONG LIMBS

A kangaroo's long hind leg has three parts of almost equal length – the thigh bone, the shin bone, and the foot. This arrangement of bones acts like an S-shaped spring. When the kangaroo hops, the long foot pushes against the ground, and the S-shape gets longer and thinner. Powerful muscles pull the bones to make this happen.

Long, narrow foot with very long fourth and fifth toes

RUFOUS RAT KANGAROO

## RAT KANGAROO

These small relatives of kangaroos and wallabies also have long hind legs and move around by hopping. The rufous rat kangaroo, or bettong, lives alone in the grass spaces of open woodlands. It rests inside a grass nest during the heat of the day. At night, it emerges to feed on grasses and roots.

*Find out more*

MARSUPIALS 243
MOVEMENT 28
OUTBACK 66
RAINFOREST 62

# KESTRELS

THE KESTRELS ARE A GROUP of small birds of prey that belong to the falcon family. They live in open country, feeding mainly on small mammals and insects. Kestrels living in urban areas eat more small birds, such as sparrows. Rather than build a nest of their own, they lay their clutch of eggs in a tree hollow, on the ledge of a cliff, or in the abandoned nest of a larger bird.

COMMON KESTREL

## HUNTING

A hovering kestrel appears to hang in mid-air. Suspended by its fast-beating wings, the kestrel watches for its prey before swooping.

Small, rapid wing beats help kestrel to hover in mid-air

## MARKINGS

Unlike most birds of prey, many male and female kestrels have different plumages. Male common kestrels are bright red-brown, with a blue-grey head and tail. The females, which are larger than the males, are dull brown, with barred tail feathers.

TAIL FEATHERS OF FEMALE KESTREL

Large eyes with colour vision

Fanned out tail provides balance

Hooked bill

SCALE

### FACT BOX

**Family:** Falconidae

**Habitat:** Open country, urban areas, forests

**Distribution:** Worldwide, except Antarctic

**Food:** Small mammals, birds, reptiles, insects

**No. of eggs:** 1–7

**Lifespan:** Up to 16 years

**Size:** 15–39 cm (6–15 in)

## KEY FEATURES

Kestrels have extremely keen eyesight for spotting their prey. They have narrow, pointed wings for fast flight, and long tails for accurate steering. These birds use their strong, needle-sharp talons (claws) for seizing prey and carrying it back to a perch, where they tear the meat apart with their strong, hooked bills.

COMMON KESTREL

### Find out more

# KINGFISHERS

THERE ARE MORE THAN 80 types of kingfishers around the world. They range in size from the tiny rufous-backed kingfisher to the giant kingfisher of Africa and the laughing kookaburra of Australia. Although some kingfishers catch and eat fish, many of them live far from water and feed on other prey. They have stocky bodies, and most have large, long, sharp-tipped bills and short tails. Kingfishers are often heard before they are seen, because of their loud, rattling, whistling, or piping calls. Laughing kookaburras are well-known for their long, loud, cackling laughs.

*Non-stop beating wings allow bird to hover in mid-air*

WHITE-THROATED KINGFISHER

*Large bill for holding prey*

BELTED KINGFISHER

## PERCHING

Most kingfishers watch for prey from a perch, such as a bare branch overhanging a river or in a forest. When the bird spots a fish in the water or an insect or lizard on the ground, it dives down to seize the creature with its bill. The birds' feet are adapted for perching, with three toes pointing forwards and one backwards to provide a strong grip.

SCALE

## DIVING

Some kingfishers, such as the large belted kingfisher, do not need a perch to hunt from. Instead, they hover over open water, changing position until they have spotted a fish. Then they plunge beneath the surface and seize their prey.

KINGFISHER WING

## PLUMAGE

Many kingfishers have bright, jewel-like plumage (feathers), often in patterns of metallic blue, green, chestnut, and white. Many of the feathers are iridescent – they look glossy and very colourful in bright sunlight.

*Feathers look bright and glossy in sunlight*

*Fast, even wing beat*

## FLIGHT PATTERN

Kingfishers fly in a straight line, rather than soaring high in the sky. Their fast-beating wings make a whirring sound as the birds dart from perch to perch in search of food.

### FACT BOX

**Family:** Green and giant kingfishers: Cerylidae; small blue-and-rufous kingfishers: Alcedinidae; kookaburras and relatives: Dacelonidae

**Habitat:** Alongside water or in woodland and dry scrubland

**Distribution:** Most of world

**Food:** Fish, insects, reptiles

**No. of eggs:** 2–7

**Size:** 10–45 cm (4–18 in)

*Find out more*
BIRDS 115
FRESH WATER 70
WOODLANDS 60

# KOALAS

LIKE THE KANGAROO AND MOST other Australian mammals, koalas are marsupials. This means that their young are roughly the size of bees when they are born, and grow inside a pouch on their mother's belly. Koalas are good climbers that feed, sleep, and breed in the branches of eucalyptus (gum) trees – they only climb down when moving to a new tree. Although they eat up to 1 kg (2 lbs) of eucalyptus leaves every night, koalas have to spend most of the day resting because the leaves do not give them much energy.

HEAD OF
KOALA

Large head with
cheek pouches

KOALA

SCALE

## CHEEK POUCHES

The koala has cheek pouches for storing eucalyptus leaves. Once its pouches are full, the koala grinds up the leaves with its flat cheek teeth.

KOALA'S
FOREARM

### FACT BOX

**Family:** Phascolarctidae
**Habitat:** Eucalyptus forest
**Distribution:** Eastern Australia
**Food:** Leaves and shoots of eucalyptus trees
**No. of young:** 1
**Lifespan:** 13–18 years
**Size:** 60–85 cm (24–34 in)

Hands pull leaves
and shoots towards
koala's mouth

Front arms
grip tightly
as koala
climbs
tree

## GOOD GRIP

Koalas use their strong arms, large hands, and big claws to hold on tightly to branches when they are climbing or feeding.

Hind legs
move up the
tree by jumping

Sharp clawed
fingers grip well
on tree bark

## TREE CLIMBER

Koalas climb trees with a series of jumps. They grip the tree with their hands, then bring their hind feet up together in a jump. They then move their hands up the trunk, and repeat the jump so that they move upwards.

### Find out more

# LEMURS

THE MONKEY-LIKE LEMURS are found only on
the large island of Madagascar, east of Africa.
In Madagascar's forests, they live the same sort of life
as their relatives the monkeys in Africa and Asia.
Lemurs have grasping fingers and toes, and eyes that face
forward to help them judge distance when climbing and
jumping in the trees. They differ from monkeys by having
a dog-like snout and an excellent sense of smell. This
enables them to detect the scents left as "messages"
by other lemurs. Smaller lemurs are usually
active at night, and the larger ones during
the day.

SIFAKA
HOPPING

## LEAPING LEMURS

Sifakas use their long hind legs to leap
from tree to tree. By day, small groups
spend their time high up in the forest
branches feeding, sunbathing, and
resting. On rare visits to the ground,
sifakas hop forward on their strong
hind legs with their arms held above
their head to help them balance.

*Long striped tail
acts as a "smelly
flag" to put off
rival lemurs*

## WARNING SIGNALS

Ring-tailed lemurs live in groups of up
to 30, and spend much more time on the
ground than other lemurs. They use their
long, striped tails to communicate with
others in the group. Held upright, their tails
help them see each other as they forage for
food in open country. In addition, male
lemurs wipe their tails with smelly scent
from their arms. They then wave their tails
at rival groups in "stink battles" as a warning
to stay away from their territory.

*Dog-like snout with
forward-facing eyes
helps identify lemur*

## SUNBATHING

Ring-tailed lemurs often start
their day by sunbathing to warm
themselves up after a cool night.
To do this, they sit on the
ground, or on a low branch,
facing the rising sun with
arms outstretched. At
midday, however,
if it is very hot,
lemurs seek
shade under a
tree or up in
the branches.

RING-TAILED
LEMUR

RING-TAILED LEMUR

*Sunbathing
pose with arms
outstretched*

SCALE

*Grasping toes
on feet*

### FACT BOX

**Family:** Lemuridae (lemurs)
and Indridae (sifakas)

**Habitat:** Forest and rocky areas
with trees

**Distribution:** Madagascar

**Food:** Fruit, leaves, flowers,
bark; some eat insects and eggs

**Size:** Head and body length
30–55 cm (12–21.5 in); tail
length 25–65 cm (10–25.5 in)

*Find out more*

ISLANDS 76
MAMMALS 239
MONKEYS 252
RAINFORESTS 62

# LEOPARDS

LEOPARDS ARE ELEGANT AND POWERFUL cats that live on their own. They use scent marks and rough, rasping calls to claim their own living and hunting areas. In fact their roar sounds like someone sawing a rough piece of wood. Their spotted coat gives them good camouflage as they stalk their prey. In forests, the coat is darker with more spots to help them hide in the shadows. Leopards often relax under shady rocks or on branches high in the trees – exactly the place where monkeys will go and be caught by these agile cats. Leopards also hunt guineafowl, hares, warthogs, and small antelopes.

CLOUDED LEOPARD

Larger cloud-like patches against light body colour

Broad paw on short leg

## BLACK PANTHER

Some leopards are born with black coats, and they are called black panthers. From close up, faint spots show up on the dark coat. Black panthers will have brothers and sisters that have normal golden coats with clear spots.

BLACK PANTHER

## TREE CATS

Clouded leopards spend most of their life in the trees. They hunt at night, lying on tree branches waiting to pounce on rabbits or young buffalo below. Their very long tails – up to 65 cm (25 in) provide balance.

Long tail for balance

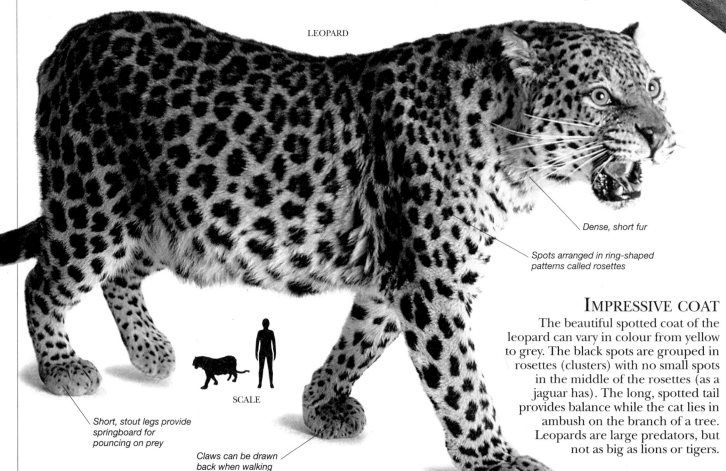

LEOPARD

Dense, short fur

Spots arranged in ring-shaped patterns called rosettes

SCALE

Short, stout legs provide springboard for pouncing on prey

Claws can be drawn back when walking to keep sharp

## IMPRESSIVE COAT

The beautiful spotted coat of the leopard can vary in colour from yellow to grey. The black spots are grouped in rosettes (clusters) with no small spots in the middle of the rosettes (as a jaguar has). The long, spotted tail provides balance while the cat lies in ambush on the branch of a tree. Leopards are large predators, but not as big as lions or tigers.

Lurking among the snowy alpine meadows and forests of the Himalayan mountains, the snow leopard is a top predator in a hostile environment. It makes huge leaps over ravines and climbs bare rock faces to chase wild sheep, goats, ibex, markhor, and other prey. In winter, the snow leopard follows its prey down the mountains to the shelter of the forests.

## FACT BOX

**Family:** Felidae, includes jaguars

**Habitat:** Forest, grassland, mountain, urban areas

**Distribution:** Africa, Middle East, central and southern Asia

**Food:** Small mammals, birds; snow leopards eat sheep, goats, and deer as well

**Gestation period:** 3 months

**Lifespan:** 12 years (up to 20 years in captivity)

**Size:** 60–190 cm (24–75 in)

Dozes in trees for safety and shade

LEOPARD

LEOPARD CUB

Cubs have dark woolly fur with fuzzy spots

## TREE CLIMBER

Leopards are brilliant at climbing trees. They pull themselves up with their powerful legs and sharp claws. Often they spend the day sleeping up on a tree branch, and they also store food there so it will not be stolen by other animals. A leopard is so strong it can climb a tree holding the carcass of a large dead animal.

## CUB CARE

Female leopards usually have three cubs at a time. The cubs are blind at first. They stay hidden until they can follow their mother around at about six to eight weeks old. The mother feeds and cares for the cubs on her own until they are 18 months to two years old. The cubs then leave to find their own hunting areas.

SNOW LEOPARD

Long, sensitive whiskers to feel its way in the dark

## SPOTTED KILLER

Leopards are more silent and cunning hunters than lions. They hunt at night, and may ambush their prey from trees. Leopards kill either with a bite to the throat, or by twisting an animal's neck to break the backbone. They may take several days to eat a large animal.

## SNOW-BOUND LIFE

The snow leopard's fur becomes extremely thick and heavy in winter, and this enables it to keep warm in the cold Himalayan mountains where it lives. It also has wide, furry paws that stop it sinking into the snow. In summer, when the weather is less severe, the coat becomes thinner. The cat will then move higher in the mountains up to 3,600 m (12,000 ft).

### Find out more

CAMOUFLAGE 36
CATS 128
CHEETAHS 136
JAGUARS 217
WOODLANDS 60

# LIONS

UNLIKE THE OTHER BIG CATS, lions hunt together, share their prey, and help to rear each other's cubs. They live in groups called prides, made up of three to 15 females with their cubs, together with two or three males. The females, called lionesses, are all related and can be grandmothers, mothers, daughters, sisters, cousins, or aunts. The lionesses catch food for the pride while the males protect the pride from rival lions and hyenas. By banding together, these cats help one another to defend their homes and food supply, and to hunt for very large prey such as buffalo and wildebeest. A lion on its own cannot compete for food with a gang of hyenas.

Lioness bites prey

## MOTHER'S LOVE

Lionesses give birth every two years to about five cubs. At birth, the cubs are very small and weigh a fraction of the weight of their mother. The mother and other lionesses in the pride will suckle the cubs for up to six months, although they also start eating meat when they are three months old.

MALE LION

Mane makes male lion look bigger and more frightening to enemies

Mane protects male's neck and back from teeth and claws during a fight

SCALE

Large size ensures male can push in at a kill and steal food from females

## DEADLY FEMALES

The lionesses do most of the hunting. They hunt together in groups so they can kill animals such as zebras and wildebeest, which are much larger than they are. Hunting lionesses suffocate their prey with a bite to the throat or by holding its muzzle (nose and jaw) with their teeth so the animal cannot breathe.

## MAGNIFICENT MALES

Male lions look different from females because they have a magnificent hairy mane. In all the other cats, males and females look the same. Male lions keep other lions out of the area in which their pride lives by pacing around it, roaring, and marking trees and rocks with urine. They are slower than females and can be easily spotted by their prey. So they leave the hunting to the females and just turn up for the feast afterwards. The females let the male lions feed first.

### FACT BOX

**Family:** Felidae

**Habitat:** Grasslands, deserts

**Distribution:** Africa, south of the Sahara; northwest India

**Food:** Antelopes, zebras, giraffe, crocodiles, birds

**Gestation period:** 3.5–4.25 months

**Lifespan:** About 15 years

**Size:** Body: 1.4–2 m (54–78 in); tail: 67–100 cm (26.3–40 in)

## A PRIDE OF PREDATORS

The lions' tawny gold coats blend in well with the grasses on the African savanna, allowing them to stalk their prey unseen. Lions follow herds of grazing animals around the savanna, preying on gazelle, antelope, and zebra. By hunting together, lions can kill much larger animals, such as buffalo and giraffe. They are also much more likely to kill healthy adult prey than the other savanna carnivores.

LION'S SKULL

*Strong jaw-closing muscles join on to skull*

## POWERFUL SKULL

A lion's skull is highly adapted to help the lion kill and eat animals. The jaws are short and powerful, with sharp, pointed canine teeth and strong, cutting cheek teeth. There are large eye sockets and ear cavities because a lion has very keen senses of sight and hearing to help it hunt its prey.

*Canine teeth to seize and tear prey*

## YOUNG OF THE PRIDE

While the adults in the pride go off to hunt, lion cubs face many dangers, both from other meat-eaters, such as hyenas, and other lions. Four out of five cubs die before their second birthday. If a male lion takes over a pride, he will kill the cubs. He will only look after his own cubs, not those belonging to another lion. Cubs are also not very good at competing for food at kills and may die of starvation.

## CUB CARRIER

Just like a domestic cat, a mother lion can carry a young cub by the scruff of the neck. This does not hurt the cub at all, and it just hangs limply without struggling. By carrying her cubs in her mouth, a mother lion can carry them quickly and easily to a place of safety – although she can only carry one cub at a time.

*Cub perfectly safe in mother's jaws*

*Young cubs are spotted for camouflage*

### Find out more

CATS 128
CHEETAHS 136
JAGUARS 217
LEOPARDS 227
TIGERS 339

# LIZARDS

ANOLE
LIZARD

FROM GIANT KOMODO DRAGONS TO tiny geckos, lizards are the largest and most widespread group of reptiles today. There are nearly 4,000 different kinds of these tough, scaly-skinned creatures. Most have slim bodies and large heads, four legs that are the same length, and a long tail. Lizards are usually found in tropical places where they spend a lot of their time basking in the sunshine to keep warm. They are mainly predators, eating insects and other small animals, which they crush with their pointed teeth. Baby lizards usually hatch out of eggs, but some are born fully-formed without an egg stage.

## RED SIGNAL

Male anole lizards will flick down their bright red throat suddenly to warn off rival males or to attract females. Two lizards of the same size may have a red throat "battle" for hours at a time. But a smaller lizard will give up immediately if a larger lizard flashes its red throat.

Geckos have no moveable eyelids

New brightly coloured skin underneath

GECKO

Old skin peeling off

## A NEW SKIN

Lizards shed their outer skin from time to time. This is called sloughing. It allows the lizard to replace worn-out skin and to grow bigger. The old skin comes off in large flakes, often taking a few days to fall off completely. Some lizards peel their old skin off with their mouths and then swallow it.

Opening mouth wide makes neck frill stand out

Frill is large flap of loose skin that is normally folded flat

Frill is often four times the width of the body

SCALE

FRILLED LIZARD

## FEARSOME FRILLS

When it is threatened by a predator, the Australian frilled lizard spreads out its large neck frill and hisses to appear bigger and more dangerous than it really is. Other lizards puff up their bodies with air to make themselves look too large to swallow. But most lizards are well camouflaged and hide from their predators.

## FACT BOX

**Family:** 16 families including Chamaeleontidae (chameleons); Iguanidae (iguanas); Gekkonidae (geckos); Varanidae (monitor lizards)

**Habitat:** Rainforests to deserts, mostly tropical and subtropical; some in caves or burrows

**Distribution:** Worldwide except northern Canada, northern Eurasia and Antarctica; a few survive in northern Norway

**Food:** mostly insects, mammals, birds and other reptiles; about 2 per cent eat plants

**Size:** 1.5–152 cm (0.6–60 in)

## SCALY SKIN

All lizards have a tough, scaly skin. This forms a waterproof covering that stops the animal from drying out. The scales overlap to form a single protective sheet, like the chain-mail armour worn by knights. Burrowing lizards have smooth scales to help them slide through the soil.

BEARDED DRAGON

Powerful legs and feet are good for digging

Skin can change colour for camouflage and to absorb more of the Sun's heat

## SPINY LIZARD

To frighten predators away, the Australian bearded dragon can expand the "beard" under its chin to make itself look more scary. This lizard also has some sharp spines. These help to protect it from predators.

Shinglebacks live in dry places and use the tail to store fat

SHINGLEBACK

## FANTASTIC FEET

Most lizards are swift and agile, and many have special feet and toes to help them move. Climbing lizards have long, sharp claws for extra grip. Geckos have special toe pads that allow them to walk upside-down gripping to the ceilings. Monitor lizards and plated lizards have powerful feet for digging.

COMMON LIZARD

## TELLING THE TAIL

Lizards' tails have many different uses. Australian shinglebacks and gila monsters have stubby tails to store fat and water for energy. Tree-living chameleons have long, curly, gripping tails to hold onto twigs as they move about. Some lizards can even lose their tails on purpose when they are attacked by a predator to confuse the attacker and allow escape. It can soon re-grow a new tail.

Head and tail are the same shape to confuse enemies and draw attention away from the lizard's real head

### Find out more

DEFENCE 34
DESERTS 68
RAINFORESTS 62
REPTILES 297

# LLAMAS AND GUANACOS

LLAMA

LLAMAS, GUANACOS, ALPACAS, AND VICUNAS live high up in the harsh foothills of the Andes Mountains of South America. They are well suited to this wild land with thick fur to keep them warm. They can also climb steep mountain paths without difficulty as their hooves give good grip. All four species belong to the same family as camels. Llamas and alpacas are tamed to carry loads, and domesticated like cows and sheep to provide wool, milk, meat, and other products. Vicunas and guanacos are wild and live in small family groups.

*Male guanacos fighting for territory*

## MIGHTY LLAMAS

Llamas have been used by people of the Andes to carry heavy loads, such as bales of maize, for thousands of years. They were a vital means of transport in the ancient Inca Empire, and still help people survive today in harsh mountainous areas.

## UNTAMED GUANACOS

Wild relatives of the llama, guanacos need little water, and roam the mountains up to heights of 4,250 m (13,900 ft). A strong male will lead his family group to graze on dry grass and shrubs. If danger threatens, he warns his group with a bleating noise. The young are driven out to fend for themselves when they are about one year old.

### FACT BOX

**Family:** Camelidae

**Habitat:** Mountain grassland, shrubland; alpacas also live in marshes; and guanacos in forests

**Distribution:** Andes Mountains

**Food:** Grasses and leaves

**Gestation period:** 11–12 months

**Lifespan:** 15–24 years

**Size:** Across four species ranges from 91–114 cm (36–45 in)

## DEFENDING LAND

Male guanacos and vicunas often fight each other with their teeth and hooves, and spit at each other to defend their territories (the areas that they live in with their families). Each territory has two parts – one for feeding in the day, and a smaller one for sleeping on higher ground.

### Find out more

CAMELS 124
CATTLE 131
DEER AND ANTELOPE 154
MOUNTAIN LIFE 58

GUANACOS

SCALE

*Shaggy, thick fur keeps guanacos warm in mountains*

# LOBSTERS

COMMON LOBSTER

LOBSTERS LOOK LIKE CRABS WITH stretched-out claws and tails. Like crabs, they have a powerful pair of pincers at the front. In many species one pincer is bigger and used for crushing, while the smaller one is used as a cutting tool.

These creatures usually spend the daytime hiding in crevices, among rocks or in mud burrows, with only their claws and antennae showing. They emerge at night to hunt for food. Lobsters are themselves caught in fishermen's lobster-pots, attracted by bait such as rotting fish. They are fished because many people like to eat them. This has led to lobsters becoming scarce in many places.

SCALE

CRAWFISH

## WALK THE SEA BED

Lobsters stroll slowly across the sea bed using their four pairs of walking legs. But if they are frightened by a hungry seal or shark, they can shoot backwards at lightning speed by flapping their rear body and tail.

## FACT BOX

**Families:** Lobsters belong to the group of animals called crustaceans which includes crabs

**Habitat:** Mostly sea beds, wrecks of ships; some species, known as crayfish, are found in fresh water

**Distribution:** Worldwide

**Food:** Left-over scraps or stolen from other sea-creatures; live prey include shellfish and worms

**Nest:** None, eggs are attached to female's rear legs

**Size:** 10–106 cm (3.9–42 in)

SQUAT LOBSTER

## CRAWFISH

Another name for the crawfish is the spiny lobster. This refers to the sharp spines that dot the animal's stout armour-plated body and larger limbs, providing a formidable defence against predators. These lobsters travel over the seabed in lines of up to 50.

### Find out more

The claws, legs, and edges of a squat lobster's body are covered with sharp spines

Antennae (feelers) help lobsters find their way

## UNDER ATTACK

Lobsters use their impressive claws both to attack and cut up prey, and to defend themselves against enemies – including humans. They can give a person a very painful nip. Most lobsters walk over the sea bed using their claws to pick up pieces of food or smash open the shells of other animals.

# LORISES AND BUSHBABIES

SMALL, HAIRY-FACED LORISES AND bushbabies are active at night, and they have very large eyes to see in dim light. These tree-dwellers also have a snout that gives a good sense of smell to seek out prey, or predators. Like their bigger mammal relatives – monkeys, apes, and humans – lorises and bushbabies have very flexible fingers and toes, with nails rather than claws. Lorises dwell in dense forest cover and move slowly through the branches. Bushbabies live in both forest and bush country and, by contrast with the lorises, are agile, fast-movers.

## SLOW BUT STEALTHY LORIS

Grasping a branch with its hands and feet, a loris moves very slowly through the leaves and twigs. At nightfall, it becomes active, and moves with great stealth in search of food. If a loris sees or smells prey, it creeps up slowly and strikes. Unlike its bushbaby relative, the loris has no tail, and rarely jumps. By day, it sleeps rolled up in a ball. It can stay hidden by leaves for many hours.

SLENDER LORIS

Large eyes for seeing in dim light of nightfall

SCALE

Toes grip branch for support

## FACT BOX

**Family:** Lorisidae (lorises) and Galagonidae (bushbabies)

**No. of species:** Lorises: 5; bushbabies: 9

**Habitat:** Forest and grassland with trees

**Distribution:** Africa, south and Southeast Asia

**Food:** Insects, small animals, fruit, leaves, shoots, tree gums

**Gestation period:** 110–193 days

**Lifespan:** 10–15 years

**Size:** 10–46 cm (4–18 in); tail 18–52 cm (7–20 in)

## HANDS AND FEET

Lorises and bushbabies use their grasping hands and feet to hang on to branches as they move through trees and shrubs. These animals also use their hands to pluck fruit and leaves and put them into their mouths, and to grab prey such as insects and small lizards.

BUSHBABY

## TAILED JUMPER

Bushbabies are expert leapers. They use their powerful back legs to jump from branch to branch, or tree to tree. Their long tail provides balance when they jump, and their large, forward-facing eyes help them judge distances when leaping in the dark. Bushbabies pounce on prey and grab it with their hands. They also use their large ears to detect flying insects which are then snatched from the air.

Long tail helps bushbaby keep its balance when jumping

### Find out more

APES 98
CHIMPANZEES 139
GORILLAS 192
RAINFORESTS 62

# MAMMALS

CHIMPANZEE GROUP

ANIMALS AS DIFFERENT AS AARDVARKS, bats, whales, lions, and humans have one vital thing in common. They are all are mammals, members of a group of more than 4,000 species that are found right across the world – swimming, walking, flying, living underground or high up in the trees. Mammals are "warm-blooded" creatures, with a layer of hair or fur on the skin helping to keep heat in. Female mammals are the only animals to produce milk – a rich liquid food which helps newborn mammals grow rapidly. Mammals look after their offspring during the early stages of their life, when they are at risk from attackers, and help them learn how to survive.

Sensitive snout sniffs out food

SHORT-BEAKED ECHIDNA

## LIVING IN FAMILIES

Some mammals, such as chimpanzees, live in family groups. With so many pairs of eyes and ears looking out for danger, the group provides extra protection against attack by predators. Its members can share looking after young and finding food. Chimpanzees are intelligent mammals, and show their feelings using sounds, facial expressions, and body movements.

## EGG LAYER

The echidna is one of only three types of mammals that lays eggs. A female echidna lays a single, soft-shelled egg in a skin pouch. It hatches after ten days, and the tiny newborn feeds on milk that seeps through its mother's skin. These spiky animals sniff out ants and termites with their long snouts.

## MILK SUPPLY

Newborn kittens clamber onto their mother to feed on her milk. Unable to see, each kitten feels its way to a teat. It sucks the teat to release milk made by special glands in the skin. These milk-making glands are called mammary glands and this gives us the name mammals. The milk is rich in all the foodstuffs needed by a young mammal to grow, and it also contains chemicals that help protect the young from disease.

DOMESTIC CAT AND KITTENS

Teats run along mother cat's belly

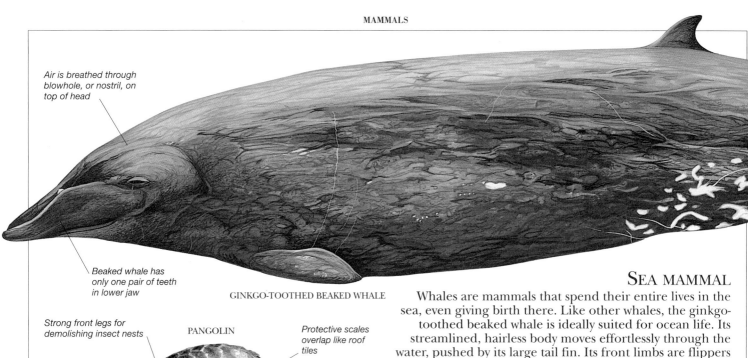

Air is breathed through blowhole, or nostril, on top of head

Beaked whale has only one pair of teeth in lower jaw

GINKGO-TOOTHED BEAKED WHALE

## SEA MAMMAL

Whales are mammals that spend their entire lives in the sea, even giving birth there. Like other whales, the ginkgo-toothed beaked whale is ideally suited for ocean life. Its streamlined, hairless body moves effortlessly through the water, pushed by its large tail fin. Its front limbs are flippers that are used for steering. The ginko-toothed beaked whale can stay under water for long periods hunting for squid and fish, before returning to the surface to breathe.

Strong front legs for demolishing insect nests

PANGOLIN

Protective scales overlap like roof tiles

## SCALY COVERING

Pangolins are armour-plated mammals that live in Africa and Asia. Their skin is covered by overlapping scales with sharp edges that form a shield to protect them from predators. If threatened, these tank-like creatures curl up tightly into a ball to conceal their head and feet. Pangolins eat ants and termites. They catch them with their long tongue, which is coated with sticky saliva.

### FACT BOX

**Family:** Class called Mammalia with more than 4,000 species

**Habitat:** All types

**Distribution:** Worldwide

**Food:** Herbivores (plant-eaters); carnivores (meat-eaters); insectivores (insect-eaters); and omnivores (eat plants and animals)

**Size:** From 33 mm (1.3 in) (Kitti's hog-nosed bat) to 24 m (79 ft) (blue whale)

**Lifespan:** 1 year (pygmy shrew) to 100 years (humans)

## FASTEST MAMMAL

The cheetah can reach speeds of 100 kmh (62 mph) over short distances as it chases fast-running prey such as gazelle. It can achieve this speed because of its muscular body and its long legs and stride length. The cheetah's claws act like the spikes on running shoes to give extra grip.

Tail helps balance when turning sharply

Very flexible back makes long strides possible

CHEETAH

Same size as large
bumblebee

KITTI'S
HOG-NOSED
BAT

Ivory tusks used for
defence and to dig
for food and water

The trunk is an
extension of the nose
and upper lip

AFRICAN
ELEPHANT

Wide rounded foot
spreads animal's
weight

# TINIEST MAMMAL

Discovered in Thailand in 1973,
Kitti's hog-nosed bat is both the
smallest bat and smallest mammal.
During the day it rests in caves, its
body temperature falling to save
energy. At night it flies through
bamboo forests in search of insects.

# SENSITIVE SNOUTS

The 15 species of elephant
shrews are not related to
elephants or shrews.
These African
mammals live on the
ground in a wide
variety of habitats
from deserts to
rainforests. They
push their sensitive
snouts into dead
leaves and rotting logs
to find beetles,
termites, spiders, and
other small animals. If
threatened by predators, such
as eagles or snakes, they run
rapidly to find cover.

FOREST ELEPHANT SHREW

Probes and
sniffs with
long snout to
find food

# TRUNK-NOSED MAMMAL

Pillar-like legs support the bulk of the
African elephant, the largest land
mammal. Up to 3.7 m (12 ft) tall,
and weighing more than 5,500 kg
(13,000 lb), this elephant lives on the
African savanna (grasslands). The
smaller Asian elephant is found in
India and Southeast Asia. In both
types, the trunk is used like a hand to
grasp leaves and grasses, to greet
other members of the herd, and to
shower water over the head and back.

Heavy horns meet
at base

MUSK OX

# SHAGGY-COATED MAMMAL

A close relative of sheep and goats,
musk oxen have the longest fur of
any mammal. Musk oxen live in
herds in the cold north of
Canada and Greenland. A
thick layer of dense underfur
keeps out cold and wet. The
outer layer of coarse guard
hairs protects the musk ox
from snow and rain.

Guard hairs
almost reach to
the ground

***Find out more***

ANIMAL RECORDS  84
APES  97
CATS  128
ELEPHANTS  170
HUMANS  207
MEAT-EATERS  32
PLANT-EATERS  30
SKELETONS  18
WHALES  353

# MANATEES AND DUGONGS

SLOW-MOVING MAMMALS OF SEAS and rivers, manatees and dugongs spend all their lives in water. They are the only mammals that graze on plants in the sea, just like cows do on land. Because of this, both groups are sometimes called sea cows. They look like overgrown seals. Manatees have a rounded tail, while the dugong's tail is divided into two distinct flukes (parts), like that of a whale.

*Calf feeding on mother's milk*

WEST INDIAN MANATEE

## FACT BOX

**Family:** 3 species of manatee (Trichechidae); 1 species of dugong (Dugongidae)

**Habitat:** Dugong: sea; manatees: rivers, estuaries, coastal waters; Amazon manatee: only in rivers

**Distribution:** Dugong: Indian and Pacific oceans; manatees: Florida, Caribbean, South America, West Africa

**Food:** Dugong: sea grasses; manatees: various water plants

**Size:** 3–4 m (10–13 ft)

WEST INDIAN MANATEE

## MOTHER'S MILK

A mother manatee or dugong is a devoted parent. She feeds milk to her single offspring, called a calf, for up to two years. At birth, the baby is large, about 100 cm (36 in) long. A young calf rarely ventures far from its mother, and she frequently protects it by clasping it beneath one of her flippers or lets it ride on her back.

## WATER PLANT-EATERS

These mammals munch their way through large areas of water plants with strong cheek teeth. They use their large flippers to walk on the river or sea floor, and to scratch for food. Manatees can feed on plants at the surface and those growing on the seabed, but dugongs only feed on sea-grasses growing on the bottom.

WEST INDIAN MANATEE

*Scar from being hit by propeller blade*

*Flippers used for walking, scratching, and pushing food into mouth*

## SCARED BUT PROTECTED

In Florida, many manatees are injured and bear scars from the propellers of boats passing too close. The scars actually help naturalists to identify individual animals they are studying. While it is difficult to prevent boating accidents, these harmless mammals are protected by laws against hunting.

### Find out more

CATTLE 131
DOLPHINS AND PORPOISES 160
FRESH WATER 70
OCEANS 74
WHALES 353

SCALE

# MARSUPIALS

KANGAROOS, KOALAS, AND THEIR RELATIVES are all marsupials, or pouched mammals. Marsupials differ from other mammals in the way the tiny marsupial babies grow and develop. At birth, the tiny, undeveloped baby wriggles out and moves to the inside of a furry pouch on the mother's belly. Once inside, the baby suckles on a teat to drink the mother's milk. The pouch gives the blind and hairless baby a safe place to grow and develop. Most marsupials live in Australia and New Guinea, including koalas, kangaroos, cuscuses, wombats, Tasmanian devils, dunnarts, and wallabies. A few species, such as the opossums, are found in America.

TASMANIAN DEVIL

TREE KANGAROO

## BONE CRUNCHER

With powerful jaws and sharp teeth, the Tasmanian devil is a meat-eating marsupial that devours every part of its prey – including skin and bones. A slow mover, the Tasmanian devil hunts at night, and uses smell to hunt prey, such as snakes and lizards, and to locate dead sheep and wallabies. By day, it rests in a burrow, bush, or hollow log. The size of a small dog, this animal is probably called a "devil" because of the strange, whining noises that it makes.

## TREE LIFE

Tree kangaroos are found in the tropical forests of northern Australia and New Guinea. Unlike their ground-living relatives, these kangaroos have longer front legs, and shorter hind feet and legs. They move quickly through the trees, jumping from branch to branch, gripping the bark with curved claws and rough foot pads.

Large ears pick up sounds of possible danger

RED KANGAROO

Long tail provides balance when jumping

## FAST HOPPER

Kangaroos are the biggest marsupials – they can stand up to 2 m (78 in) tall. They move not by walking but by hopping. Their long, powerful back legs and feet work like springs. In a short burst of speed, a kangaroo can reach speeds of up to 56 kmh (25 mph). Their long, thick tail helps them balance when hopping.

Reddish-brown fur

Long feet push off the ground during jumping

Tail acts as "fifth" leg while kangaroo is at rest

Tail can be 100 cm (40 in) long

# KANGAROOS' SMALLER COUSINS

Wallabies look like kangaroos but are smaller. These marsupials often live in groups, called mobs. They dwell in open woodland and graze at night on grasses but, unlike kangaroos, will also eat leaves and other plants. When feeding, wallabies balance on their tail and short front legs, and move slowly by swinging their long back legs forward. Female wallabies and kangaroos have a well-developed pouch on their belly that opens forwards. The young wallaby, or joey, develops inside this pouch.

RED-NECKED WALLABY

Young possum feeds on milk

SUCKLING POSSUM

Female has pouch on belly

Powerful hind legs used for hopping not walking

Leaves form part of wallaby's diet

# TINY YOUNG

At one month old, baby marsupials, such as the possum, are tiny, blind, and hairless. Their legs are hardly more than buds. They attach themselves to the mother's teat inside the pouch to feed on the nourishing milk. The babies will stay in the mother's pouch for about four months, until they have grown and developed enough to go into the outside world.

# AMERICAN MARSUPIALS

This cat-sized Virginia opossum is the only North American marsupial. Opossums are found in most habitats, where they forage alone on the ground and in trees for fruit, eggs, insects, and other small animals. Virginia opossums also live near humans and feed on their rubbish. This flexibility, and the fact that they can have litters of ten offspring up to three times a year, explains why their numbers are growing.

VIRGINIA OPOSSUM

Gripping tail helps opossum to climb trees

Round face with small ears and large eyes

SPOTTED CUSCUS

# SLOW CLIMB

A spotted cuscus grips tightly with its feet as it climbs slowly through the branches. Its prehensile (gripping) tail wraps around branches to help this marsupial hang on. Cuscuses live in trees in the tropical forests of North Australia and New Guinea.

## BURROWER

Looking and walking rather like small bears, wombats live in forests and scrubland. During the day, they shelter in deep, long burrows that they dig using their powerful front legs and strong claws. At night, wombats follow well-worn paths through the forest, and graze on grasses.

COMMON WOMBAT

### FACT BOX

**Order:** Marsupialia

**Habitat:** Deserts to forests

**Distribution:** Australasia, North and South America

**Food:** Group includes plant-eaters, meat-eaters, insect-eaters, and omnivores (plant- and animal-eaters)

**No. of young:** 1 (kangaroo) to 20 (opossum)

**Size:** Pilbara ningauis 5 cm (2 in); red kangaroo 2 m (78 in)

*Tail is more than twice the length of the head and body*

*Tail held in a stiff curve when moving*

## MICE-LIKE MARSUPIAL

Dunnarts are sometimes called marsupial "mice" because they have a body with a pointed face, large ears, and slender legs – just like a mouse. Long-tailed dunnarts live on the ground in dry parts of western Australia. They feed at night mainly on grasshoppers and spiders, but they will also catch lizards and mice. Dunnarts shelter in burrows or in nests built in hollow logs or under rocks.

LONG-TAILED DUNNART

*Large head with tufted ears*

*Body covered with dense, woolly hair*

*Grasping hands with sharp claws grip tree bark*

*Large eyes help dunnart see in the dark*

## GUM LEAF DIET

Koalas spend most of their lives sitting and resting in the fork in the branches of eucalyptus trees. These marsupials only go down to the ground to move to another tree. Their single source of food and water are the leathery gum leaves of the eucalyptus, which they feed on at night-time. Eucalyptus leaves are not very nutritious – this is why koalas need to save energy by resting for up to 18 hours a day.

# MICE

MICE HAVE SHORT GREY or brown fur, a long scaly tail, and five toes on each foot. They also have sharp front teeth for cutting food. Most mice are active at night, although the harvest mouse is also active during the day. Their senses of sight, hearing, and smell are very good, and mice are equipped with highly sensitive whiskers for finding their way in the dark. Like their close but bigger relatives, the rats, some mice, such as the house mouse, are regarded as pests. This is because they spoil food, cause damage to homes (they can eat through books and wires), and spread diseases.

## FACT BOX

**Family:** Muridae
**Habitat:** Forest, woodland, grasslands, mountains
**Distribution:** Worldwide, except for Antarctic
**Food:** Seeds, berries, shoots; insects in some species
**No. of young:** 2–12
**Size:** Head and body length 5.7–9.5 cm (2.25–3.75 in); tail length 5–10.5 cm (2–4.2 in)

## HELPLESS YOUNG

Baby mice are born naked, blind, and without ears in a cosy nest. They are totally dependent on their mother for milk and protection. At six days old they have fur and can move and squeak. Two weeks later, they have left the nest. A female mouse can produce up to 10 litters each year, with up to 12 babies in each litter.

Scaly tail is about same length as the body

HOUSE MOUSE

Large sensitive ears

Body covered by short grey to brown fur

SCALE

## LIFE ON THE STALKS

The tiny harvest mouse is one of the smallest of all mice. It lives in fields and hedges. In spring and summer it can be found climbing nimbly up and down the stalks of reeds and grasses in search of seeds and shoots. Harvest mice live alone for most of the year, except when they meet to breed. Young are born in a tennis ball-sized nest built between stalks above the ground.

## IN EVERY PLACE

The house mouse gets its name because it has been associated with humans and their houses for thousands of years. As people have explored the world, they have taken house mice with them – often without knowing. House mice are found almost everywhere because they will eat anything, can live in any place, and they breed very quickly.

Explores thistle head in search of food

EUROPEAN HARVEST MOUSE

Gripping tail acts as a fifth leg to help mouse climb

### Find out more

## SWAYING IN THE STEMS
The harvest mouse lives on tall, thin plants such as wheat or reeds. It eats their seeds and leaves. This tiny mouse uses its gripping hands and grasping tail to scamper up, down, and between stems. In summer, it builds nests between swaying stalks high above the ground. In winter, when plants die back, it lives in a burrow or a barn.

# MOLES

MOLES ARE EXPERT TUNNELLERS – THEIR short front legs and broad, clawed, spade-like feet form a perfect tunnel-digging machine. They spend most of their life underground where they eat, sleep, breed, and patrol their tunnels to look for worms and insects. They also spend much of their time keeping their connecting tunnels and nests in good repair. Moles lead a solitary life except when males and females meet up to mate.

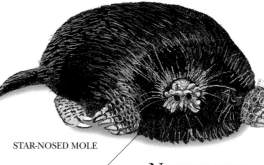
STAR-NOSED MOLE

Fleshy tentacles very sensitive to touch

## NOSEY MOLE
The star-nosed mole from North America gets its name from the sensitive, fleshy tentacles at the end of its snout. It hunts for food on the ground surface and is also an excellent swimmer, catching both fish and insects in water.

## FACT BOX

**Family:** Talpidae
**No. of species:** 29
**Habitat:** Burrows in soft soil
**Distribution:** Europe, North Asia, North America
**Lifespan:** 3–5 years
**No. of young:** 2–7
**Size:** Head and body length 95–180 mm (3.7–7.1 in); tail length 15–34 mm (0.6–1.3 in)

EUROPEAN MOLE

SCALE

## NATURAL DIGGER
Moles are perfectly shaped for an underground life. Their bodies are like cylinders, and they have short legs and no ears sticking out. This means they can squeeze easily along tunnels. Powerful muscles move the shovel-like front feet to dig new tunnels. Although eyesight is poor, both the mole's snout and stumpy tail are very sensitive to touch. This helps the animal to feel its way, and find food, whether moving forwards or backwards.

Bristly snout picks up the tiniest vibrations

Nest is lined with grass and leaves

### Find out more
ANIMAL HOMES 46
MAMMALS 239
MOVEMENT 28
SENSES 24

Molehill is a mound of earth above main nest

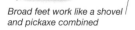
Broad feet work like a shovel and pickaxe combined

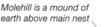
Mole stores worms in its larder

## LIFE UNDERGROUND
Moles dig tunnels that are linked and extend outwards from a central nest. Large molehills above ground are formed where a vertical tunnel reaches the surface. Moles eat earthworms, or insects that have fallen into the tunnel, or store them in a special "larder".

# MOLLUSCS

MOLLUSCS ARE A LARGE GROUP of animals with soft bodies. They include snails, clams, squid, octopuses, and scallops. Most molluscs have a hard shell to protect their bodies, but octopuses and many slugs have no shell. Molluscs make their homes in a wide variety of places, from the depths of the oceans to rocky seashores, and from freshwater ponds and rivers to dry land. This diversity of homes has helped molluscs form one of the largest groups of creatures. There are over 100,000 different species.

GREAT POND SNAIL

*Shell coils in a spiral*

QUEEN SCALLOP

*Shell made of two halves called valves*

COMMON STRIPED SNAIL

## IN FRESH WATER

The great pond snail spends its life in ponds, lakes, or slow-flowing streams. But it breathes air to survive. It has a single lung under the widest part of its shell and breathes through a small hole that it can open or close. It scrapes off algae from water plants.

## HOMES WITH HINGES

All bivalves (members of the mollusc group) have two matching shells held together by a toothed hinge. The word "bivalve" means two-shells. The group includes scallops, mussels, clams, and oysters. Most bivalves spend their life lying still in sandy burrows or attached to rocks. Scallops, however, are able to swim well. They clap their shells together to take in and squirt out water to propel themselves out of harm's way.

BLUE GIANT CLAM

*Markings on shell spiral in a clockwise direction*

## CLOCKWISE COIL

Snail shells are coiled into a clockwise spiral over the right side of the snail's body. Coiling makes the shell compact and portable. However, the snail's body has to fit this lop-sided arrangement and twist around to fit inside.

*Algae give off vivid colours*

## SAFE HAVEN

The blue giant clam of the Indian and Pacific Oceans gets its amazing colours from the millions of microscopic algae that find a safe haven on the clam's mantle (tough outer skin). As with other bivalves, the two halves of the clam's shell are open for feeding, but they close shut if the creature is threatened.

## CHAMBERS GALORE

The chambered nautilus is a sea-dwelling mollusc that has a shell with many chambers. As it grows, it adds a new chamber to its shell. Each chamber is separated by a curved plate. The nautilus lives only in the largest, newest chamber, on the outside.

CHAMBERED NAUTILUS

Curved plate seals off each chamber

## FACT BOX

**Family:** Molluscs

**Habitat:** Land, fresh water, salt water

**Distribution:** Oceans: all continents except Antarctica

**Food:** Animals, plants, fungi, algae

**No. of species:** Over 100,000

**Size:** From size of a pinhead to 15 m (50 ft) wide

## ARMOUR-PLATED

Chitons are an unusual group of molluscs found in oceans. They have flat, rounded bodies. The upper body is protected by an armour of eight shelly plates, which are held together by a tough, leathery belt. When threatened, a chiton rolls into a tight ball.

Eight interlocking plates

Leathery belt

CHITON

## QUICK MOVER

Cuttlefish belong to the most active group of molluscs, called cephalopods, which includes octopuses and squids. Their bodies are not protected by an outer shell, but they can dart backwards rapidly to avoid danger. They do this by squirting out jets of water from a siphon (internal tube).

Siphon (muscular tube) ejects water to give rapid bursts of speed

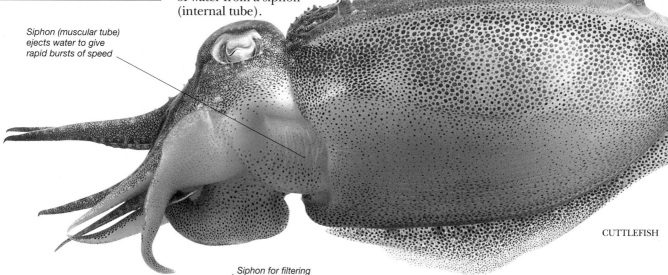

CUTTLEFISH

DOG WHELK IN ROCK POOL

Protective shell

Siphon for filtering water and food

Tiny yellow eggs of dog whelk

## SNAIL SHELLS ON THE SEASHORE

All molluscs begin life as tiny eggs that hatch out into larvae (young). Sea snails such as whelks that are found in rock pools, develop a shell early, but many molluscs develop a shell only later, as they grow. The shell is made of calcium carbonate, a kind of lime. Mollusc shells have three layers for added strength: a hard outer layer, a chalky middle layer, and a smooth, shiny inner layer.

### Find out more

OCTOPUSES AND SQUID  255
SLUGS AND SNAILS  323

# MONGOOSES

*Looks out to protect young from danger*

FAST-MOVING AND VERY AGILE, mongooses are experts at catching small prey such as insects and lizards. Most live on the ground, often sheltering in burrows, but a few climb trees. They have long bodies, dense fur, short legs with clawed feet, and bushy tails. Excellent senses of sight, hearing, and smell help mongooses to track down a scorpion or snake, and provide early warning of danger especially from swooping eagles or owls. Most mongooses are solitary or live in pairs. A few species – including dwarf and yellow mongooses, and meerkats – live in large groups.

MEERKAT

SCALE

## FACT BOX

**Family:** Viverridae

**Habitat:** Tropical forests, woodlands, grasslands, deserts

**Distribution:** Asia, Africa, Madagascar

**Food:** Insects, scorpions, snakes, lizards, frogs, birds, fruit, eggs

**No. of species:** 36

**Size:** Head and body length: 18–65 cm (7–25.5 in); tail length: 12–51 cm (5–20 in)

*Bites back of cobra's neck*

INDIAN GREY MONGOOSE

## SNAKE KILLER

Although mongooses mainly feed on small vertebrates, some larger mongooses kill and eat snakes. These snakes may be large, but the snake's venom (poison) does not seem to affect the mongoose. It avoids being bitten by moving swiftly around the snake. When the snake tires, it is killed by a powerful bite to the neck.

*Yellow fur gives this mongoose its name*

YELLOW MONGOOSE

## MEERKATS

Like other mongooses, meerkats often stand on their hind legs to check their surroundings. Meerkats live in groups. Each group has a territory with feeding sites and burrows. Every meerkat takes turns to play different roles. While some look for food, others "baby-sit" the young. Some will stand guard on the look out for enemies. At the first sign of danger, the guards bark out a warning and the entire group disappears down their burrows.

## EXTENDED FAMILY

Yellow mongooses live in open country with loose soil, where they dig burrows. The burrows are shared by pairs of mongooses to make an extended family of up to 50. By day, they look for food in pairs, foraging under rocks for insects.

### Find out more
CATS 128
CIVETS AND GENETS 142
HYENAS 210
MEAT-EATERS 32

# MONKEYS

COLOBUS
MONKEY

CLOSE RELATIVES OF APES AND humans, monkeys are
playful, clever animals. There are two main
groups of monkeys. The "New World"
monkeys of Central and South America
live in the trees. They are good climbers
and leapers, and some have special
prehensile (gripping) tails. The "Old
World" monkeys of Africa and Asia live
in all sorts of places, such as forests,
grasslands, and swamps. These
monkeys do not have prehensile
tails, but they all have tough
sitting pads on their bottoms.
They go to sleep sitting up.

SULAWESI
CRESTED MACAQUE

## SKY DIVER

Colobus monkeys glide from
tree to tree by spreading out
their limbs and the spectacular
cape of white hair on their
backs. They feed on leaves in
the trees and have a big
stomach with lots of bacteria to
help them digest their tough
diet. The long tail does not
grip branches but helps the
monkey to steer when flying
between trees.

*Long, bushy tail
acts as rudder in
mid-flight*

### FACT BOX

**Family:** Callitrichidae
(marmosets and tamarins);
Cebidae (capuchin-like
monkeys); Cercopithecidae
(Old World monkeys)

**Habitat:** Mainly forests, some
species in grasslands

**Distribution:** Tropical and
temperate areas of Central and
South America, Africa, and Asia

**Food:** Fruit, leaves, seeds, nuts,
insects, birds' eggs

## SUPER TROOPERS

The macaques of Asia live in troops
ruled over by an older male who
protects the troop and leads it to
new feeding sites. They are very
successful because they eat almost
anything and quickly learn new
feeding habits. Large cheek pouches
help them to carry food to
a safe place for eating.

SCALE

*Chestnut-coloured
tiara (crown)
on head*

*Thick tail hangs
down when walking*

## OLD AND NEW

The De Brazza's monkey
has strong arms and legs
for bounding across the
swampy forests of Central
Africa. Like other Old
World monkeys, its nostrils
are narrow, close together,
and point downwards.
New World monkeys
have nostrils that are
wide open, far apart,
and face outwards.

*Long, strong limbs
make running and
bounding easy*

DE BRAZZA'S
MONKEY

## SEEKING SAFETY

Vervet monkeys are the most common monkeys in open areas of the African grasslands. They sleep and hide in the scattered clumps of trees and bushes for safety. They differ from most other monkeys, which spend more time feeding and moving through dense forests. Vervets usually live in small groups of between 6 and 20 individuals, though large groups of up to 100 have been known.

## MONKS OF THE FOREST

The capuchins of the South American forests are good at running along branches high up in the trees. They grip the branches tightly with their long fingers and toes and use their curly tail as an anchor. Their cap of dark fur looks like a monk's hood or "capuche", which is where the monkey's name comes from.

Cap of dark fur looks like a monk's hood

CAPUCHIN

BALD UAKARI

Long fingers grip branch while running

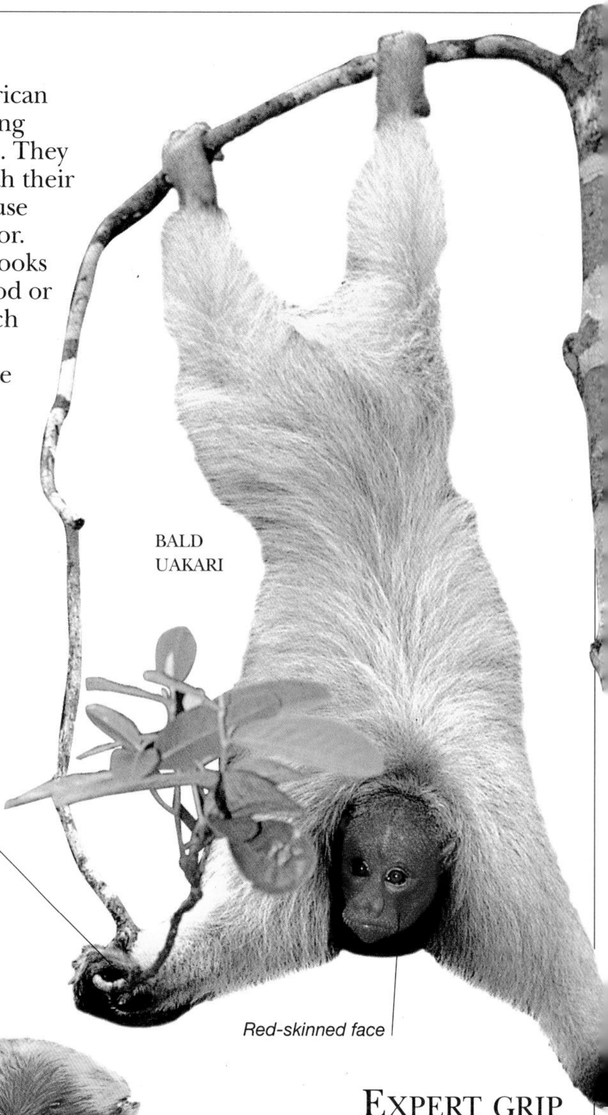

Hands and feet give excellent grip in trees

## LONG FLESHY NOSE

The male proboscis monkey of Borneo has a strange, floppy nose, which gets in the way when he eats. Scientists are not sure why the male has such an odd-shaped nose, but females may find the longer noses more attractive. Proboscis monkeys are very agile, leaping through the mangrove swamps using their long tails as a counter-balance. They sometimes dive into water from heights of up to 15 m (50 ft).

Red-skinned face

Large nose can measure up to 7.6 cm (3 in)

## EXPERT GRIP

The uakaris of the Amazon rainforests are expert tree-climbers and terrific leapers, even though they do not have a long tail for balancing or gripping. They often swing from branches or hang by their feet to feed on fruit. Uakaris are shy monkeys, despite their bright red faces.

Big stomach holds large amounts of tough mangrove leaves while they are slowly digested

### Find out more

APES 97
BABOONS 100
CHIMPANZEES 139
GIBBONS 185
GORILLAS 192
ORANG-UTANS 258

PROBOSCIS MONKEYS

# OCTOPUSES AND SQUID

IN PAST CENTURIES, SAILORS TOLD stories of giant, many-armed monsters that dragged ships down to the ocean depths. These stories were probably inspired by octopuses and squid. These clever, keen-eyed creatures are found throughout the oceans. Octopuses, squid, and their relatives, cuttlefish, are members of the mollusc family. This large group of animals includes shelled creatures such as snails and oysters. Unlike snails, octopuses have no protective shells, while squid and cuttlefish have thin shells inside their bodies.

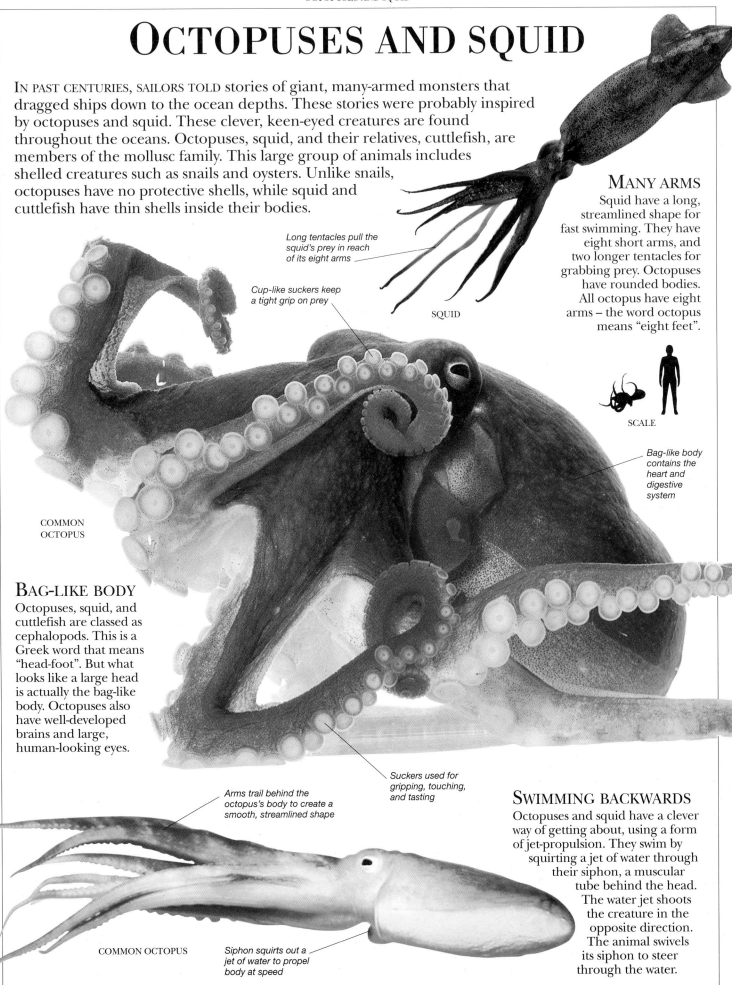

*Long tentacles pull the squid's prey in reach of its eight arms*

*Cup-like suckers keep a tight grip on prey*

SQUID

## MANY ARMS
Squid have a long, streamlined shape for fast swimming. They have eight short arms, and two longer tentacles for grabbing prey. Octopuses have rounded bodies. All octopus have eight arms – the word octopus means "eight feet".

SCALE

*Bag-like body contains the heart and digestive system*

COMMON OCTOPUS

## BAG-LIKE BODY
Octopuses, squid, and cuttlefish are classed as cephalopods. This is a Greek word that means "head-foot". But what looks like a large head is actually the bag-like body. Octopuses also have well-developed brains and large, human-looking eyes.

*Arms trail behind the octopus's body to create a smooth, streamlined shape*

*Suckers used for gripping, touching, and tasting*

## SWIMMING BACKWARDS
Octopuses and squid have a clever way of getting about, using a form of jet-propulsion. They swim by squirting a jet of water through their siphon, a muscular tube behind the head. The water jet shoots the creature in the opposite direction. The animal swivels its siphon to steer through the water.

COMMON OCTOPUS

*Siphon squirts out a jet of water to propel body at speed*

# EIGHT-ARMED OCEAN SWIMMER
Octopuses and squid have been swimming in the world's oceans for over 100 million years. Some types of octopus keep to shallow coastal waters; others live in the depths. Most squid live in the open oceans. Mysterious giant squid swim in the deep sea. Huge specimens over 21 m (69 ft) long have been washed ashore, and even bigger squid probably lurk in the depths.

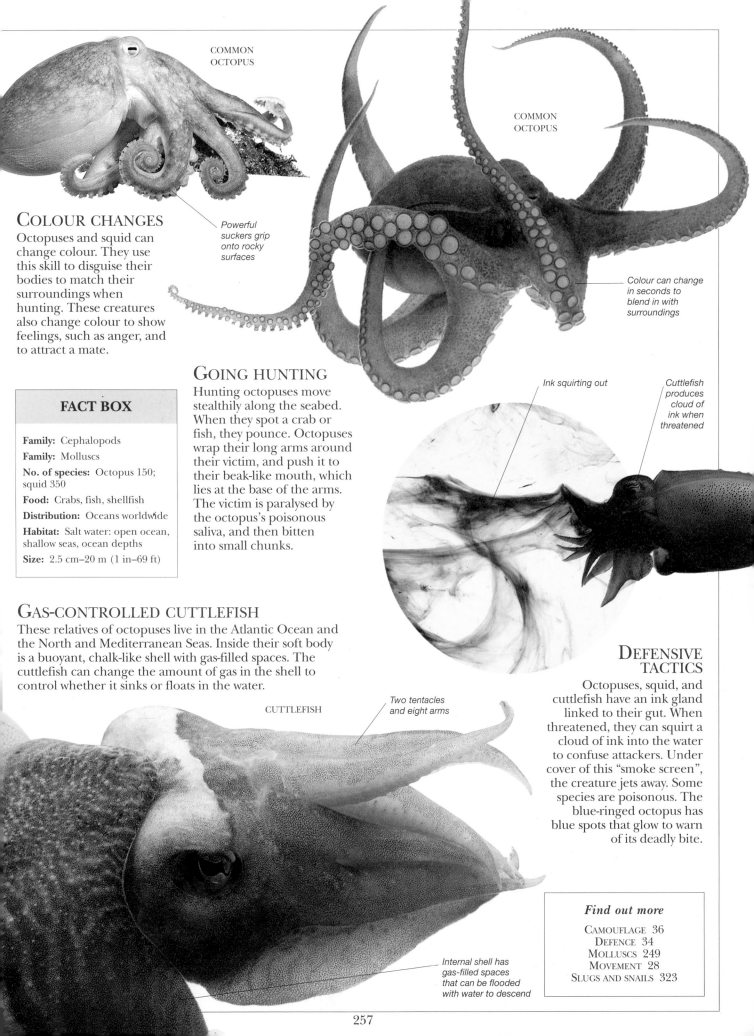

COMMON
OCTOPUS

COMMON
OCTOPUS

*Powerful
suckers grip
onto rocky
surfaces*

## COLOUR CHANGES

Octopuses and squid can
change colour. They use
this skill to disguise their
bodies to match their
surroundings when
hunting. These creatures
also change colour to show
feelings, such as anger, and
to attract a mate.

*Colour can change
in seconds to
blend in with
surroundings*

### FACT BOX

**Family:** Cephalopods

**Family:** Molluscs

**No. of species:** Octopus 150;
squid 350

**Food:** Crabs, fish, shellfish

**Distribution:** Oceans worldwide

**Habitat:** Salt water: open ocean,
shallow seas, ocean depths

**Size:** 2.5 cm–20 m (1 in–69 ft)

## GOING HUNTING

Hunting octopuses move
stealthily along the seabed.
When they spot a crab or
fish, they pounce. Octopuses
wrap their long arms around
their victim, and push it to
their beak-like mouth, which
lies at the base of the arms.
The victim is paralysed by
the octopus's poisonous
saliva, and then bitten
into small chunks.

*Ink squirting out*

*Cuttlefish
produces
cloud of
ink when
threatened*

## GAS-CONTROLLED CUTTLEFISH

These relatives of octopuses live in the Atlantic Ocean and
the North and Mediterranean Seas. Inside their soft body
is a buoyant, chalk-like shell with gas-filled spaces. The
cuttlefish can change the amount of gas in the shell to
control whether it sinks or floats in the water.

## DEFENSIVE
TACTICS

Octopuses, squid, and
cuttlefish have an ink gland
linked to their gut. When
threatened, they can squirt a
cloud of ink into the water
to confuse attackers. Under
cover of this "smoke screen",
the creature jets away. Some
species are poisonous. The
blue-ringed octopus has
blue spots that glow to warn
of its deadly bite.

*Two tentacles
and eight arms*

CUTTLEFISH

*Internal shell has
gas-filled spaces
that can be flooded
with water to descend*

### Find out more

CAMOUFLAGE 36
DEFENCE 34
MOLLUSCS 249
MOVEMENT 28
SLUGS AND SNAILS 323

# ORANG-UTANS

RED-HAIRED APES, ORANG-UTANS ARE the largest tree-living animals in the world. They climb and swing through the rainforest trees that grow on the Asian islands of Borneo and Sumatra. Orang-utan means "man of the woods" in the Malay language, because these apes look rather like people and live in the forest. They are related to chimpanzees, gorillas, gibbons, and humans. Unlike the other apes, orang-utans live on their own, although mothers and babies stay together for about eight years. A baby orang-utan clings to its mother's fur as she moves through the trees and sleeps in a nest of leaves that she makes at night.

Sparse reddish fur with coarse grey skin showing through in places

Strong arm can take all its weight

## TEACHING SKILLS

A young orang-utan will stay with its mother for at least three years. During that time, it will learn how to find and eat fruit among the trees and on the jungle floor. On the ground, it walks on all fours, and moves very clumsily.

## FEET LIKE HANDS

An orang-utan's feet look like its hands – and are used as such. When it climbs trees, an orang-utan can grasp branches with both its hands and feet. Even swinging from branch to branch, it may hold on with one hand and one foot rather than two hands.

Move slowly through trees in search of fruit

Clasping tree with feet as well as hand

Keen eyesight to spot ripe fruit

## FRUIT FEAST

Orang-utans mostly eat tropical fruit, such as mangoes, durians, and lychees. In the rainforest, trees bear fruit at different times of the year. So orang-utans have to make a "mental map" of where the fruit trees are and when their fruit ripens.

SCALE

## SOLITARY SWINGER

In the hot and humid forests of Borneo and Sumatra, orang-utans move slowly through the trees in search of tasty fruits to eat. Each orang-utan, or a mother and her baby, live in their own area of forest, which has just enough food for their needs. If they lived in groups, or even in pairs, there would not be enough food to go round.

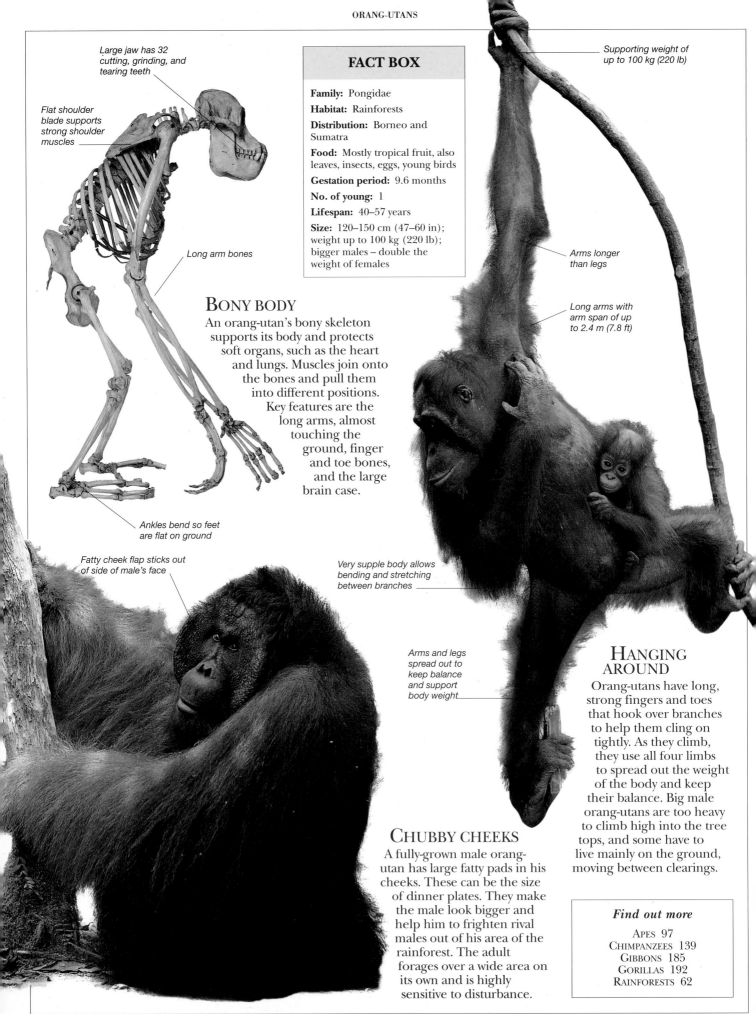

Large jaw has 32 cutting, grinding, and tearing teeth

Flat shoulder blade supports strong shoulder muscles

Long arm bones

Supporting weight of up to 100 kg (220 lb)

Arms longer than legs

Long arms with arm span of up to 2.4 m (7.8 ft)

**FACT BOX**

**Family:** Pongidae

**Habitat:** Rainforests

**Distribution:** Borneo and Sumatra

**Food:** Mostly tropical fruit, also leaves, insects, eggs, young birds

**Gestation period:** 9.6 months

**No. of young:** 1

**Lifespan:** 40–57 years

**Size:** 120–150 cm (47–60 in); weight up to 100 kg (220 lb); bigger males – double the weight of females

## BONY BODY

An orang-utan's bony skeleton supports its body and protects soft organs, such as the heart and lungs. Muscles join onto the bones and pull them into different positions. Key features are the long arms, almost touching the ground, finger and toe bones, and the large brain case.

Ankles bend so feet are flat on ground

Fatty cheek flap sticks out of side of male's face

Very supple body allows bending and stretching between branches

Arms and legs spread out to keep balance and support body weight

## HANGING AROUND

Orang-utans have long, strong fingers and toes that hook over branches to help them cling on tightly. As they climb, they use all four limbs to spread out the weight of the body and keep their balance. Big male orang-utans are too heavy to climb high into the tree tops, and some have to live mainly on the ground, moving between clearings.

## CHUBBY CHEEKS

A fully-grown male orang-utan has large fatty pads in his cheeks. These can be the size of dinner plates. They make the male look bigger and help him to frighten rival males out of his area of the rainforest. The adult forages over a wide area on its own and is highly sensitive to disturbance.

### Find out more

APES 97
CHIMPANZEES 139
GIBBONS 185
GORILLAS 192
RAINFORESTS 62

# OSTRICHES AND EMUS

THE WORLD'S LARGEST BIRD IS the ostrich of Africa. It is taller than most human beings. The ostrich is also flightless, along with its relatives in other parts of the world – the emu, cassowaries, rheas, and kiwis. Instead of flying, these birds can run very fast to escape predators. Many millions of years ago, they were able to fly, but they lost the power of flight, chiefly because they lived on islands safe from any enemies. Most of these birds spend much of their time feeding on many different kinds of plant leaves, roots, flowers, and seeds. They also snap up insects and even small lizards and tortoises in their strong bills.

Powerful leg muscles

OSTRICH

Each stride covers about 3.5 m (11. 5 ft)

SCALE

Long neck and keen eyesight help spot attackers at great range

OSTRICH

## RUNNING STYLE

An ostrich can run faster than a thoroughbred racing horse. In fact its feet are like a horse's hoof, helping the ostrich to sprint at speeds of up to 50 kmh (32 mph) across the flat grasslands and deserts to escape predators. Its legs are also longer and larger than those of any other bird.

An ostrich egg has a similar volume to 24 hens' eggs

OSTRICH EGGS

## BIGGEST EGGS

An ostrich egg is the largest of any bird. It is so strong that an adult human could stand on one without breaking it. Each egg is 15–20 cm (6–8 in) long and weighs 1–1.8 kg (2.2–4 lb). The female sits on her eggs in the dusty, scratched-out hollow nest during the day. The male guards at night against hyenas, jackals, and lions.

## KILLING KICK

As they cannot fly off when under attack, all ostriches and their relatives have several other defences apart from running off at high speed. Their massive legs with their huge, clawed feet can rip into any unwary intruder, even a big cat. When threatened, ostriches (and emus and rheas) often lie flat on the ground, with their necks stretched out in front. This gives rise to the saying about the foolish ostrich "with its head in the sand". In fact, this position helps to conceal the bird as its hump-backed body looks just like a boulder or clump of earth.

Larger toe has flat nail for fast running, and lunging at would-be attacker

# WANDERING FLIGHTLESS

Ostriches are able to thrive in the harsh conditions of Africa's dry open country where food is scarce. Their powerful, long legs and hoof-like feet allow them to travel hundreds of kilometres in search of the plants on which they depend. Ostriches roam in small flocks and often graze with other animals, such as zebras and gnus, searching for seeds and insects.

## NOCTURNAL KIWI

Unlike other flightless birds, the plump, duck-sized kiwis of New Zealand hide away in burrows by day, and feed at night. Kiwis have a keen sense of smell, with nostrils near the tip of the long bill. They stick their bills deep into damp soil, dead leaves, or rotting wood, and sniff around to find earthworms or other tasty morsels, then snap them up.

BROWN KIWI

SOUTHERN CASSOWARY

## CARING FATHERS

Male cassowaries, rheas, emus, and some kiwis do all the work of rearing the family. The male mates with several females. He then makes a nest hollow in the ground. The females lay their eggs in the hollow over a period of a few weeks. The male then guards and incubates the eggs, and cares for the young. Rhea males defend their offspring fiercely, even attacking people on horseback.

*The male cares for the eggs and chicks for nine months*

## FACT BOX

**Family:** Ostriches and relatives are grouped together as ratites

**Habitat:** Grassland, deserts; cassowaries and kiwis in forests

**Distribution:** Widely scattered

**Food:** Most eat plant food, also some small animals

**Nest:** Hollow scraped in ground, except for kiwis, which nest in burrows

**Eggs:** 5–50

**Size:** 0.35–2.75 m (0.14–9 ft)

*Coarse, shaggy plumage more like mammal's hair than feathers*

GREATER RHEA

## IN SECOND PLACE

The emu is the second largest bird, after the ostrich. It is common in the open woodlands, grasslands, and dry scrublands of Australia. As well as running fast, emus are good swimmers. Over land and water they cover great distances as they wander in search of fruits, berries, insects, and water.

EMU

## SHAGGY RHEAS

Not as big as ostriches, rheas are still an impressive size, and have very shaggy feathers. They are the only flightless birds to be found in South America. They live in the southern half of the continent, in grasslands and scrublands. Rheas will gather together in small flocks when they are not breeding. They eat a wide range of plants, including prickly thistles, but will also feed on insects, small lizards and snakes, and small or young birds.

*Up to 1.4 m (5 ft) in height*

*Grows to almost 2 m (6 ft) tall*

### Find out more

BIRDS 115
EGGS AND NESTS 42
GROWING UP 44
ISLANDS 76
RAINFORESTS 62

# OTTERS

SUPERB SWIMMERS AND DIVERS, OTTERS spend much of their lives in water. They move their powerful webbed hind feet and tapering tail – flattened from top to bottom – to travel through the river or sea. Otters can close their small ears and nostrils when underwater to prevent water entering them. Their flattened heads, streamlined bodies, and luxurious coats of waterproofed hair allow quick movement through the water. Beneath the long-haired outer coat there is a thick layer of underfur, which traps tiny air bubbles. These also keep otters warm in cold water.

EURASIAN RIVER OTTER

Sharp teeth for seizing and tearing up fish

Long, waterproof hair

EURASIAN RIVER OTTER

SCALE

## NATURAL FISHERMEN

Eels, frogs, crayfish, snakes, and a variety of fish are chased by otters. They eat them on the river or lake bank after catching them. Many otters chase their prey underwater and seize it in their jaws. Their stiff whiskers sense prey and help them avoid obstacles in the dark or in muddy rivers or lakes.

YOUNG EURASIAN RIVER OTTERS

Young cubs play with one another

## FOREPAW AND TAIL POWER

An otter is very agile with its forepaws. It uses its small webbed hands to hold and move food about when eating. Some species also use their outstretched forepaws to catch fish underwater. The stout, powerfully-muscled tail provides support as the otter stands upright. The tail is thick at base and tapers towards the tip.

## FUN SEEKERS

Like human children, otters are playful creatures. They are fond of sliding, which they do down the slippery, muddy banks of rivers or on snow-covered slopes. They tuck their legs back for maximum speed and make a headlong belly flop down a steep bank. Otter are also known to play tag and have mock fights.

# IN AND OUT OF WATER

Otters spend much of their lives in water. Most species are found in fresh water, some in coastal waters, and others in both. This allows them to specialize in hunting fish and other water-dwelling prey so that they are not competing with other flesh-eating mammals in their environment. As well as supplying them with food, the water environment provides the otters with safe breeding sites in the banks.

## FACT BOX

**Family:** Mustelidae, which also includes badgers, skunks, and weasels

**No. of species:** 13

**Habitat:** Mostly fresh water (rivers, lakes, canals, marshes), but sometimes on seashores; the sea otter spends all its life in the sea, in coastal waters

**Distribution:** Worldwide, except for Australia, Antarctica and some islands

**Food:** Fish, crabs, frogs, molluscs, sea urchins

**Size:** 66–240 cm (26–94 in)

EURASIAN OTTER

Long, slim muscular body

Rolling motion when running makes otter appear hunch-backed

Forepaws shorter than short hind feet

## RUNNING STYLE

When on land, most otters are fast runners and leapers. They use a mixture of running, bounding, and sliding when travelling over snow or ice. Otters can make leaps of 50 cm (20 in) or more. They also sometimes travel many kilometres overland to reach new rivers to settle in.

## CRACKING SHELLS

The sea otter's big, rounded teeth are not strong enough to crack the hard shells of the sea urchins, shellfish, and crabs it likes to eat. To solve this problem it carries a large, flattish stone from the seabed to the surface in a special pocket of skin in its armpit. As it floats on its back with the stone on its chest, the otter bashes the prey until the shell breaks open. It then uses its chest as a dining table.

SEA OTTER

Big, seal-like head

Crab shell cracked open by otter's stone tool

## GIANT-SIZED

The world's largest otter is the size of a large dog and is called the giant river otter. It lives in shallow slow-moving rivers in the marshes, swamps, and forests of South America, especially those in the Amazon region. Here, it uses its large feet, with very well-developed webbing between the toes, to swim in the rivers. These otters will also dive together in groups to chase fish.

*Can grow to 240 cm (94 in)*

### Find out more

BADGERS 102
FRESH WATER 70
MAMMALS 239
OCEANS 74

GIANT RIVER OTTER

# OWLS

THERE ARE OVER 200 DIFFERENT kinds of owls in the world. Most of them sleep during the day. As darkness falls, owls come out to hunt. They also search for prey before dawn, when there is a little light. Some owls, such as barn owls, can even hunt in pitch darkness, in the middle of a moonless night, aided by amazingly keen hearing. Only a few owls, including the snowy owl in the Arctic, hunt in broad daylight. As with other birds of prey, owls have hooked beaks and sharp claws, but they also have silent flight, for swooping down and surprising prey at night.

Huge eyes fill over half an owl's skull

OWL SKULL

Fanned-out feathers control speed of descent

## ACUTE HEARING

The shape of an owl's head ensures that a sound will be heard on one side a fraction of a second before being detected by the other ear. This helps the owl to pinpoint the prey precisely in total darkness by even the tiniest sounds.

SCALE

Broad wing helps owl fly and glide slowly in search of prey

## SILENT KILLER

Striking silently from above, an owl swings its feet forwards as it approaches its prey. The owl spreads its toes as wide as possible to trap its victim and prevent it from escaping its grasp. The talons pierce its prey, often killing it outright, or else the owl finishes it off with a nip to the neck.

BARN OWL

Forward-looking eyes help owl to judge distance

Powerful legs cushion impact of hunting and landing

Ear tuft partly raised for courtship display

INDIAN EAGLE OWL

Tail feathers help to stabilize the bird as it swoops down on its prey

## EAR TUFTS

Many owls, including very big eagle owls, and the small scops owls, have prominent ear tufts on their head. Despite their name, these have nothing to do with hearing – they are simply movable tufts of long feathers that may help camouflage the owl as it sleeps during the day.

Curved talons spread out to dig in and hook prey so it cannot escape

## SILENT SWOOPERS

Most owls, like this barn owl, spend the day roosting in trees, barns, or other sites. They fly out only in the dying evening light to patrol the countryside for prey at night. Many owls live in woods or forests, but some hunt in open country such as farmland. You are most likely to see a barn owl hunting in summer, when the days are long and the owls have hungry chicks to feed.

# PELLETS

Owls swallow their prey whole. Later, they regurgitate (bring up) the indigestible parts of their prey from their stomachs. They eject pellets of the undigested bits of prey through their open beak. These pellets, containing such remains as mouse skulls and beetle wing-cases, show naturalists what the owl was eating.

OWL PELLET

*Complete pellet with undigested fur and bones*

BARN OWL

*Fringed edges to wing flaps deaden sound of flapping*

# FLIGHT FEATHERS

Owls fly silently. This is because their flight feathers are soft and velvety. In some owls, the feathers near the tips of the wings have comb-like fringes through which air can pass. This allows them to hear the smallest sound made by prey and to surprise it in the stillness of the night.

*Tail sticks out after a mouse is swallowed whole*

EAGLE OWL CHICK

*Head can turn 180 degrees to look over shoulder*

*Huge, human-like eyes*

# HEAD SPINNING

Owls have huge eyes for keen night vision. The owl is unable to move them in their sockets. Instead, 14 vertebrae (bones) in the neck (humans have only seven) allow the owl to turn its head three-quarters of the way around. This means an owl can see behind as well as in front of it to detect the slightest movement.

*White feathers for winter camouflage*

# HUNGRY YOUNG

Baby owls are called chicks. They grow a thick layer of soft down to keep them warm. Owl chicks need a steady supply of food, such as mice, so they make loud begging calls to let their parents know they are hungry. Owls breed when they are likely to catch most prey.

SNOWY OWL

*Use claws to keep firm grip on branches or ground*

### Find out more
BIRDS 115
EGGS AND NESTS 42
SENSES 24
WOODLANDS 60

*Daytime hunter blends in well with Arctic tundra*

## FACT BOX

**Family:** Tytonidae (barn and bay owls), Strigidae (other owls)

**Habitat:** Mainly woods, forests, but also Arctic tundra, grasslands, and deserts

**Distribution:** Worldwide except Antarctica

**Food:** Mammals, birds, frogs, small reptiles, fish, insects

**Nest:** Mostly holes in trees

**Eggs:** 1–16, white

**Size:** 13–75 cm (5–30 in)

# PANDAS

ONE OF THE RAREST OF MAMMALS, the giant panda spends most of its life chewing away on bamboo stems. Indeed it can easily munch its way through 600 bamboo stems each day. The giant panda has thick fur to keep out the cold, and a thumb-like growth on the front paw to help grip bamboo while eating. Both the giant panda and the red panda live in the cold, misty mountain forests of Asia. Despite their similar lifestyles, the two are not related. The giant panda belongs to the bear family, while the red panda is part of the raccoon family whose other members live in North and South America.

HAND BONES

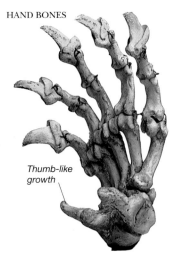

*Thumb-like growth*

GIANT PANDA

*Rounded ears*

*Bear-like face with black markings around eyes*

*Long snout with big nose gives good sense of smell*

SCALE

*Thick waterproof fur keeps panda dry*

## EXTRA THUMB

There is a growth on one of the panda's wrist bones that forms an extra 'thumb'. This can touch the real thumb and first finger, and is used to grip bamboo stems as the panda strips off leaves. Red pandas also have this growth, but it is smaller.

*Mother cuddles young in den*

## CARING CUDDLES

Female pandas look after their young for about 18 months. Newborn pandas are tiny, blind, pink, and helpless, and are cuddled by their mothers in a special den. By three months the young take their first steps, but cannot walk well until they are a year old.

## BLACK AND WHITE BEAR

Giant pandas have a striking black and creamy white coat with stripes and blobs. While the body is mainly creamy-white, the arms, legs, and ears are black. Each eye also has a black zone around it. The fur is waterproofed and keeps the bulky body warm and dry. Like other bears, pandas have a big head, short tail, and good sense of smell.

## REMOTE CHINESE FORESTS

Giant pandas live alone in the mountain forests of central China where there are plenty of bamboo plants. A panda spends most of its day among the bamboo, stripping leaves and shoots from the narrow stems. In winter, the forests are cold and snowy. Thick fur helps to keep the panda warm, and it can take shelter in a hollow tree, cave, or rock crevice.

GIANT PANDA

# A ROUGH DIET

Bamboo is difficult to digest. For this reason the panda must eat a lot of bamboo each day. In fact it spends between 12 and 16 hours each day feeding. During that time it will consume 15–30 kg (22–66 lb) of bamboo leaves, stems, and shoots. A panda's throat also has a tough lining to protect against sharp bamboo splinters.

## FACT BOX

**Family:** Giant panda: Ursidae; Red panda: Procyonidae

**Habitat:** Bamboo forest

**Distribution:** Giant panda: Central China; red panda: Himalayas to southwest China

**Food:** Bamboo leaves, shoots, roots, grass, fruits, small animals; red panda also eats birds' eggs

**No. of young:** Giant panda: 1–2; red panda 1–4

**Lifespan:** Giant panda: up to 30 years; red panda: up to 13 years

**Size:** Giant panda 122–152 cm (48–60 in); red panda 51–64 cm (20–25 in)

Black-and-white stripes on face

LESSER
RED PANDA

# TREE CLIMBER

A good climber, the cat-sized red panda moves quickly through tree branches of the mountain bamboo forests. Its sharp claws help it climb up trees by gripping the branches. By day this panda spends most of the time up in the branches of trees asleep, curled up with its long, red-and-brown striped bushy tail wrapped around its head. At night, the panda goes down to the ground and forages for food – bamboo shoots, roots, fruits, birds' eggs, and small animals. The long whiskers on its snout help the panda to navigate at night.

Whiskers act as sensors when moving in dark

# JAWS AND TEETH

A giant panda strips bamboo with its teeth. Inside its massive head are large jaws and very strong jaw muscles, which pull the jaws together. When this happens, the tough bamboo shoots and leaves are crushed between the panda's large, flat cheek teeth. This releases any goodness from the plants. However, most of the tough bamboo fibres pass straight through the animal's digestive system.

Teeth for stripping bamboo

### Find out more

BEARS 106
CONSERVATION 82
RACCOONS 290

# PARROTS, MACAWS, AND COCKATOOS

SOME OF THE MOST BEAUTIFULLY and brightly coloured of all birds are parrots. Most of them live in tropical parts of the world, especially Central and South America and South-east Asia and Australia. The 350 species in the parrot family include not just those called parrots, but also cockatoos, lories, lorikeets, parakeets, macaws, the budgerigar, and lovebirds. All parrots have strong necks and big heads with large, sharply hooked bills. Most parrots live among trees, and are skilled climbers.

BLUE-AND-YELLOW MACAW

PARROT CHICK

Fluffy grey down feathers begin to grow on blind chick after one week

## FURRY CHICK

A baby parrot hatches from the egg blind, naked, and helpless. After about a week, it grows a thin covering of feathers. At about a month old, it starts to acquire its first proper plumage. Most are not fully adult or ready to start breeding until two to four years old.

Two claws face forward, two face backward on each foot, giving good grasp on perches

## WORLD'S LARGEST

Macaws are some of the world's largest parrots, and can be 1 m (3 ft) in length. They live in the rainforests of Mexico, and Central and South America. With their huge, immensely powerful bills, they can crack open large seeds and nuts with ease – even extremely hard brazil nuts. A macaw's bite could sever a human finger.

Vivid blue and yellow feathers help identify this macaw

Bright yellow crest raised in alarm

SULPHUR-CRESTED COCKATOO

## CRESTED BIRDS

Cockatoos are a group of 20 species of parrots from Australia, New Guinea, the Solomon Islands, and some Indonesian islands. Most cockatoos are mainly white or mainly black, and they all have a distinctive crest of feathers on the head. They can raise or lower this, to signal alarm or aggression.

SCALE

Fleshy toes fold around object delivering it to powerful bill

LOVEBIRDS

## FEEDING STYLES

Parrots are the only birds that hold food up to their bills with their feet when eating. They collect food with their bill, but often hold nuts in one foot while they crack open the hard shell. Most parrots eat the seeds, fruit and nuts of a wide variety of trees and shrubs. Lories and lorikeets feed mainly on the nectar of flowers.

### FACT BOX

**Family:** Psittacidae

**Habitat:** Most in forests and woodlands, some in grassland and other open country

**Distribution:** In warmer areas worldwide

**Food:** Seeds, nuts, fruit; some drink nectar from flowers; others eat insects

**Nest:** Most lay eggs inside tree

**Eggs:** 1–8, white

**Size:** 8–100 cm (3–39 in)

FEMALE ECLECTUS PARROT

## LITTLE LOVEBIRDS

Lovebirds are small, sparrow-sized parrots that live in Africa. Pairs spend much of their time perched together, preening each other tenderly with their bills. They pair for life and breed in noisy colonies.

## NUT CRACKER

Both halves of a parrot's beak are hinged onto the skull. This means that a parrot can open its bill very wide to pluck and eat large fruit and nuts. Strong jaw muscles give the parrot an amazingly powerful bite, so that it can crack hard shells and split husks. Its large, leathery tongue is like a finger, and helps hold the food.

PARROT'S SKULL

Lower half used like chisel to split seed coats

Sharp cutting edges

MALE ECLECTUS PARROT

### Find out more

BIRDS 115
EGGS AND NESTS 42
GROWING UP 44
MOVEMENT 28
RAINFORESTS 62

Male is almost all-green, so different from the female that he was once thought to be a separate species

## TELLING THE DIFFERENCE

Male and female parrots of most species have the same colours, but in a few species the sexes look very different. The eclectus parrot is one example – the male is a uniform green, but the female is a remarkable red and blue. Males and females live in pairs or flocks, and feed, fly, and sleep close together. Often, when they are feeding, one or more "sentries" will keep watch for predators. They will screech loudly if danger threatens.

Female has vibrant colours quite different from male

# PEACOCKS

PEACOCKS ARE MEMBERS OF THE pheasant family, a group of birds in which the males have beautiful and elaborate feathers, used to attract mates. Wild peacocks live in the hilly forests and farmlands of India, Pakistan, and Sri Lanka. People have also taken them to live in parks and gardens all over the world. For most of the year, peacocks live in small groups or family parties. In the breeding season, however, males defend their own special areas, called territories, and battle with other males. Peacocks show off their colourful feathers in a special dance to attract the female peahens for mating. They also make very loud, cat-like calls during the breeding season.

## FALSE EYES

The shining feather "eyes" change colour as the feathers move. This is because of the special shape of the feathers, and the way the coloured pigment inside each strand splits up light into different colours. The male sheds his spectacular feathers after the breeding season.

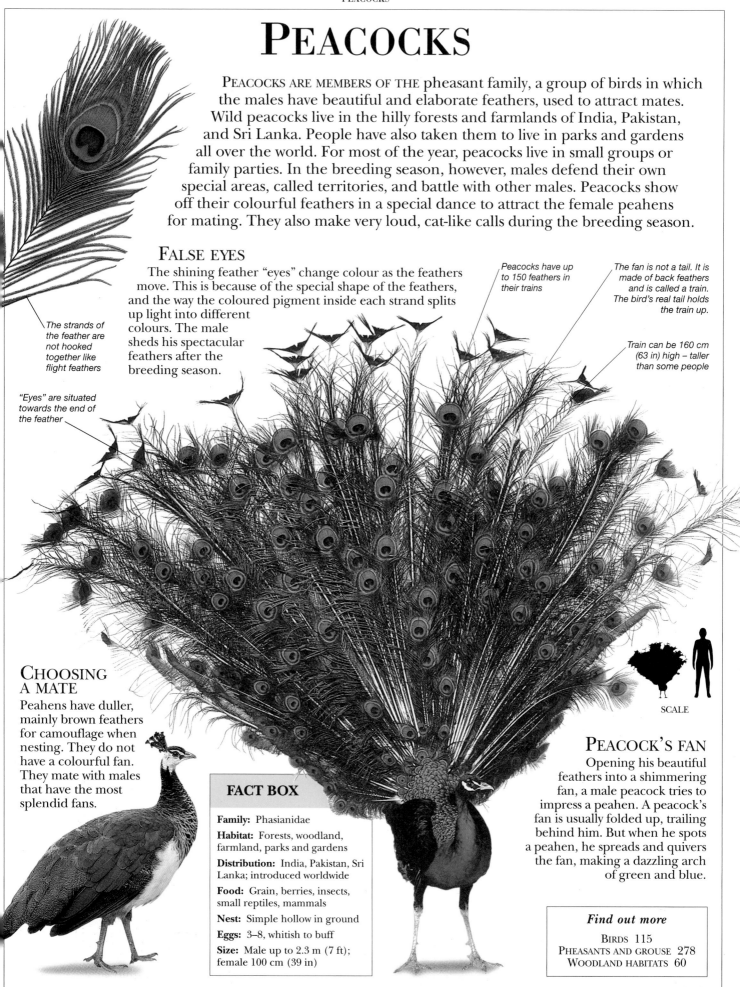

The strands of the feather are not hooked together like flight feathers

"Eyes" are situated towards the end of the feather

Peacocks have up to 150 feathers in their trains

The fan is not a tail. It is made of back feathers and is called a train. The bird's real tail holds the train up.

Train can be 160 cm (63 in) high – taller than some people

SCALE

## CHOOSING A MATE

Peahens have duller, mainly brown feathers for camouflage when nesting. They do not have a colourful fan. They mate with males that have the most splendid fans.

## FACT BOX

**Family:** Phasianidae

**Habitat:** Forests, woodland, farmland, parks and gardens

**Distribution:** India, Pakistan, Sri Lanka; introduced worldwide

**Food:** Grain, berries, insects, small reptiles, mammals

**Nest:** Simple hollow in ground

**Eggs:** 3–8, whitish to buff

**Size:** Male up to 2.3 m (7 ft); female 100 cm (39 in)

## PEACOCK'S FAN

Opening his beautiful feathers into a shimmering fan, a male peacock tries to impress a peahen. A peacock's fan is usually folded up, trailing behind him. But when he spots a peahen, he spreads and quivers the fan, making a dazzling arch of green and blue.

### Find out more
BIRDS 115
PHEASANTS AND GROUSE 278
WOODLAND HABITATS 60

# PENGUINS

GLIDING THROUGH THE OCEANS LIKE TORPEDOES, penguins are brilliant swimmers. They use their stiff, strong wings as flippers to "fly" underwater, and have spiky tongues to help them grip slippery fish. Many penguins live in the cold waters around Antarctica. They have dense, oily feathers and a thick blanket of fat under the skin to keep them warm. Penguins have to come out of the water to lay eggs and raise their chicks. Then they gather together in large groups called rookeries, which may be some distance from the sea. As penguins cannot fly, on land they waddle clumsily or slide on their stomach like black-and-white toboggans.

Narrow wings are like oars for pushing the penguin along

Big, webbed feet used for steering

## SWIMMING AND DIVING

When penguins swim fast, they jump above the surface of the water like porpoises or dolphins. This is called porpoising, and it helps the penguins to breathe without slowing down. It is also easier to move through air than water.

Golden-orange patches on their ears, bill and upper breast.

SCALE

KING PENGUIN

### FACT BOX

**Family:** Spheniscidae

**Habitat:** Seawater, ice, rocky islands, coasts

**Distribution:** Oceans of the southern hemisphere

**Food:** Crustaceans, fish, squid

**Nest:** Stones, grass, mud, caves, or burrows

**Eggs:** 1–2

**Size:** 40–115 cm (16–45 in)

## PENGUIN COLOURS

The best way to tell one kind of penguin from another is to look at the colours, markings, or crests that they have on their heads. These show up when the birds swim on the surface of the water and help the penguins to recognize each other. The markings are also used during courtship displays, to help the penguins attract a mate.

Penguins' wings cannot be folded up like the wings of most birds

Penguin chick hatching from its egg

Penguins have three layers of tiny overlapping waterproof feathers

## NESTS AND EGGS

Most penguins lay two eggs at a time. Both parents usually take turns to keep the eggs warm until they hatch, after about one to two months. When they are two to three weeks old, the chicks of most species huddle together in groups while their parents go to sea for food. The chicks cannot join their parents in the water until they have grown waterproof adult feathers.

Legs situated at end of body so penguin stands upright

# HUDDLING HERD

Emperors are the biggest penguins. They huddle together for warmth to breed in the most hostile habitat on Earth – the pack ice of Antarctica. Their closeness to one another helps them survive freezing temperatures and winds of more than 160 kmh (100 mph).

EMPEROR PENGUINS

In the densest part of the huddle there may be ten adults to 1 sq metre (10.76 sq ft)

Penguins on the outside of the huddle will get a turn in the middle where it is warmer

So much heat is trapped in the centre of the huddle that steam may rise

Emperors often turn their back to the constantly shifting wind

Chicks are carried on the parents' feet, kept warm by a fold of skin on the adult's belly

# CHINSTRAP PENGUIN

Chinstrap (also called bearded) penguins are named for the narrow band of black feathers running from ear to ear. They are the most numerous of all penguins. They nest in huge colonies of hundreds of thousands on Antarctic islands and on the continent itself, on the Antarctic peninsula. They are among the most aggressive of all penguins, and drive off larger penguins if they try to nest near them.

CHINSTRAP PENGUIN

# ROCKHOPPER PENGUIN

The rockhopper gets its name from its skill and speed at climbing steep rocks to reach its clifftop nesting colonies. Instead of waddling like other penguins, it hops from boulder to boulder, its head thrust forward, flippers back, and feet together. It is the smallest of the penguins that breed in the islands around the Antarctic.

ROCKHOPPER PENGUIN

Parent bird gently preens one of its two recently hatched chicks

# PHEASANTS AND GROUSE

RATHER THAN FLY, PHEASANTS AND grouse prefer to run. These large sturdy birds live on the ground, but when they are threatened, they will rocket explosively up into the air. They can then fly short distances with rapid, whirring beats of their stubby, rounded wings. Both junglefowl (which were bred to create the domestic hen) and peacocks are members of the pheasant family. In all of these birds, the males are larger and more brightly coloured than the females.

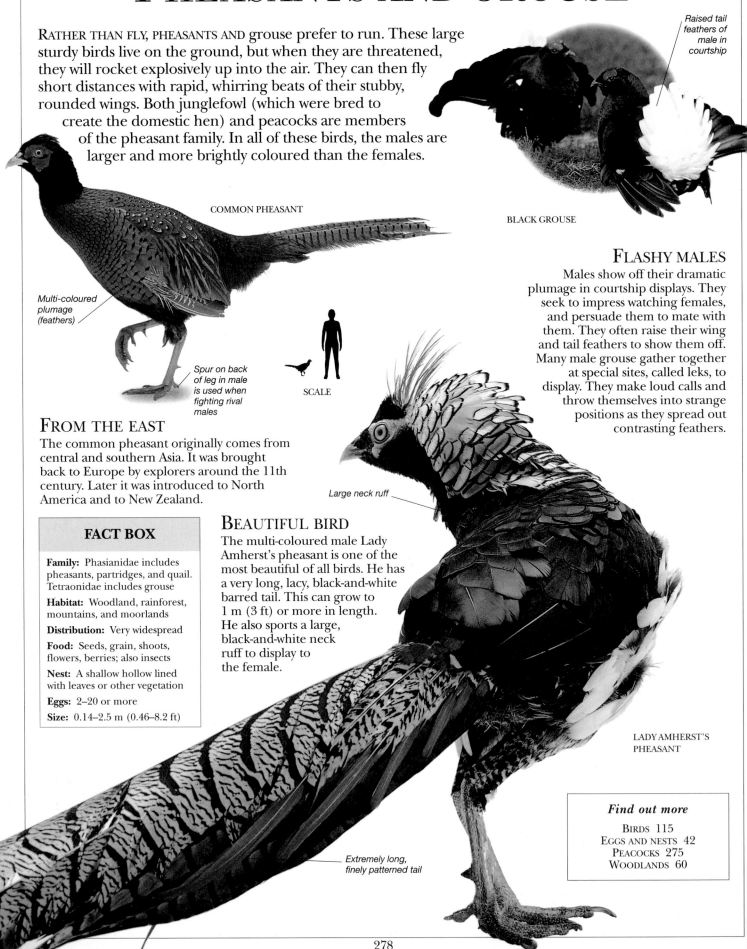

Raised tail feathers of male in courtship

BLACK GROUSE

COMMON PHEASANT

Multi-coloured plumage (feathers)

Spur on back of leg in male is used when fighting rival males

SCALE

## FLASHY MALES

Males show off their dramatic plumage in courtship displays. They seek to impress watching females, and persuade them to mate with them. They often raise their wing and tail feathers to show them off. Many male grouse gather together at special sites, called leks, to display. They make loud calls and throw themselves into strange positions as they spread out contrasting feathers.

## FROM THE EAST

The common pheasant originally comes from central and southern Asia. It was brought back to Europe by explorers around the 11th century. Later it was introduced to North America and to New Zealand.

Large neck ruff

## BEAUTIFUL BIRD

The multi-coloured male Lady Amherst's pheasant is one of the most beautiful of all birds. He has a very long, lacy, black-and-white barred tail. This can grow to 1 m (3 ft) or more in length. He also sports a large, black-and-white neck ruff to display to the female.

### FACT BOX

**Family:** Phasianidae includes pheasants, partridges, and quail. Tetraonidae includes grouse

**Habitat:** Woodland, rainforest, mountains, and moorlands

**Distribution:** Very widespread

**Food:** Seeds, grain, shoots, flowers, berries; also insects

**Nest:** A shallow hollow lined with leaves or other vegetation

**Eggs:** 2–20 or more

**Size:** 0.14–2.5 m (0.46–8.2 ft)

LADY AMHERST'S PHEASANT

Extremely long, finely patterned tail

### Find out more

BIRDS 115
EGGS AND NESTS 42
PEACOCKS 275
WOODLANDS 60

# PIGEONS AND DOVES

OFTEN SEEN IN GARDENS and on public buildings, pigeons have thrived in cities and towns. Together with doves, they have small heads, rather plump bodies, and thick plumage (feathers). Pigeons and doves are unusual among birds because they feed their young for their first few days on a sort of milk similar to that of mammals. It is rich in protein and appears as a chalky substance. Their method of drinking is also unusual in birds – they dip their bill and suck without raising their heads. Most other birds have to lift their head to swallow water.

VICTORIA CROWNED PIGEON

Cere (area of skin at base of bill) contains nostrils

WOOD PIGEON

Ring of white feathers on neck help to identify this pigeon

SCALE

## CROWNED PIGEONS

There are three types of crowned pigeon, which live only in New Guinea in the Pacific Ocean. They are the largest of the pigeons – about the size of a large chicken – and are identified by their showy crests of lacy feathers on top of the head. Their heavy bodies can weigh as much as 2.4 kg (5.3 lb).

### FACT BOX

**Family:** Columbidae

**Habitat:** From rainforests to deserts, gardens, and cities

**Distribution:** Worldwide, except the Antarctic and remote islands

**Food:** Seeds, fruit, buds, plant food, including farm crops

**Nest:** Flimsy platform of sticks or dead stems of plants

**Eggs:** 1–2, white

**Size:** 15–79 cm (6–31 in)

Plumage (feathers) mainly bluish-grey

Yellow throat patch

Plumage of soft green

## IN TOWN AND COUNTRY

Wood pigeons are a familiar sight in town gardens and parks, and on farmers' fields. Their soft cooing song is also one of the most beautiful sounds of the countryside. They can be identified by their plumage, which is mainly bluish-grey, and a ring of white feathers on their necks. They grow up to 40 cm (16 in).

## FRUIT DOVES

As you would expect from their name, fruit doves feed mainly on fruits and berries. Some, however, do eat insects too. This group of over 50 species spend most of their lives in trees. They have beautiful plumage, mainly in soft greens and yellows. This acts as a camouflage in a background of leaves.

BLACK-NAPED FRUIT DOVE

### Find out more

BIRDS 115
CONSERVATION 82
GRASSLANDS 64
RAINFORESTS 62
WOODLANDS 60

# PIGS

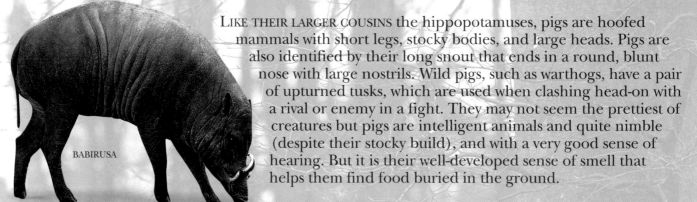

LIKE THEIR LARGER COUSINS the hippopotamuses, pigs are hoofed mammals with short legs, stocky bodies, and large heads. Pigs are also identified by their long snout that ends in a round, blunt nose with large nostrils. Wild pigs, such as warthogs, have a pair of upturned tusks, which are used when clashing head-on with a rival or enemy in a fight. They may not seem the prettiest of creatures but pigs are intelligent animals and quite nimble (despite their stocky build), and with a very good sense of hearing. But it is their well-developed sense of smell that helps them find food buried in the ground.

BABIRUSA

## CURLY TEETH

Four of the babirusa's teeth stick out of its face and curl sharply backwards. These special teeth are called tusks. The top tusks grow upwards through the pig's muzzle (nose and jaws), curving back towards the eyes. The babirusa's tusks may be attractive to females, or help to frighten off competing males. This strange-looking pig is found in the forests of Sulawesi, Indonesia.

### FACT BOX

**Family:** Suidae, includes 16 species native to Europe, Africa, and Asia

**Habitat:** Forests, woodlands, grasslands, farms

**Distribution:** Worldwide

**Food:** Vegetation, fruits, fungi, insects, worms, mice, and scraps

**Gestation period:** Domestic and wild pigs about 16 weeks

**Size:** Body 87–180 cm (32–70 in); tail 15–50 cm (6–20 in)

SADDLEBACK PIG

White saddle on back gives this pig its name

## DOMESTIC PIGS

Domesticated pigs, such as this saddleback breed, are related to the wild boar. There are many domestic breeds of pigs including Vietnamese pot-bellied pigs, Gloucester Old Spots, and Tamworths. Domestic pigs are bred by farmers to provide pork, bacon, and ham. They are also popular as pets.

WILD BOAR

## WILD BOARS

The wild boar is the largest wild pig. Young boars have stripey coats, which help to camouflage them in their woodland home. The baby pigs are born in a grass nest, but start to follow their mother around when they are 10 days old. They stay close to their mother until she has her next piglets.

Stripes on coat of young boar

DOMESTIC PIG
AND PIGLETS

## PIG LITTER

Domestic pigs give birth to a litter of about ten piglets. Each sow can have about 22 piglets in a year. Like all mammals, the piglets suck their mother's milk. They feed for about three weeks or so before they are taken away from their mother.

*Sow lays down so piglets can feed*

*Hungry piglets struggle to find a teat*

SCALE

*White, bristly mane on back*

## FORAGING FOR FOOD

Most pigs have a varied diet. They use their snouts, which are flattened and sensitive at the tip, to turn over soil in search of roots, insect larvae, and other food. Pigs usually forage in small family groups. In France, people use pigs to sniff out an underground fungus called a truffle, which is invisible from the surface. Female pigs are used for this because the truffles give off a scent like a male pig, which the females find attractive.

*Long, sensitive snout*

BUSH PIG

DOMESTIC PIGS
FORAGING

## BRISTLY BEAST

The African bush pig, also called the red river hog, has a white mane along its bristly coated back. The mane stands up when the pig is excited or alarmed. This pig also snorts and grunts when it is frightened or as it feeds. A bush pig eats almost anything, from plants to small mammals, birds, and dead animals.

*Pigs forage for food in groups*

### Find out more
CAMELS 124
DEER AND ANTELOPE 154
GIRAFFES 187
HIPPOPOTAMUSES 201
MAMMALS 239

# PLATYPUSES

IT IS DIFFICULT TO MISTAKE A PLATYPUS. It has a long snout that is shaped like a duck's bill, but which is soft and bendy. It also has webbed feet (ideal for swimming), short fur, and a long, flat tail used to store fat. Its strange-looking body is well suited to a life in, or next to, streams and lakes. Platypuses shelter in burrows during the day, and hunt by night. They are one of just three kinds of mammals, known as monotromes, that lay eggs. In spring, females dig special burrows where they lay their eggs. When the eggs hatch, the young feed on their mother's milk, just like other mammals.

Broad, flat tail is used to store fat

Hind feet used for steering

DUCK-BILLED PLATYPUS

## POISONED SPUR

The male platypus has a poison spur (claw) on the ankle of each hind foot. Platypuses use their poison spurs during the breeding season to drive away rival males. The hollow spur is jabbed into the rival, delivering a dose of painful poison. The platypus may also use this weapon against enemies – including humans – but never to catch prey.

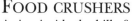

Webbed front feet for swimming

SCALE

## FACT BOX

**Family:** Ornithorhynchidae

**Habitat:** Streams, rivers, lakes

**Distribution:** Australia

**Food:** Crayfish, shrimps, insect larvae, worms, tadpoles, fish

**No. of eggs:** 1–3

**Lifespan:** More than 10 years

**Size:** Head and body length 30–45 cm (12–17.8 in); tail length 10–15 cm (4–6 in)

## FOOD CRUSHERS

A view inside the bill of an adult platypus shows that it has no teeth. Instead, it has rows of tough, horny ridges. Those near the front are sharp and used for cutting food. Those near the back are flatter. These crush food, including crunchy snails, crayfish, and insects.

## UNDERWATER HUNTER

The platypus's streamlined body is covered with dense, waterproof fur. It dives to the bottom of the lake or stream using its webbed front feet to paddle, and back feet to steer. Under water its eyes and ears close. The platypus probes the muddy bottom with its bill, using an electrical sense to detect prey. During hunting under water, food is stored in cheek pouches. Back at the surface, food is chewed and crushed in the bill.

### *Find out more*

COURTSHIP AND MATING 38
MAMMALS 239

# POLAR BEARS

THE BIGGEST OF THE BEARS, polar bears are also the largest meat-eating animals that live on land. They are found in the freezing, icy wastes of the Arctic where few other animals can survive. Polar bears spend most of the year on ice floes, large chunks of ice that float on the sea. They roam over long distances each day in search of prey, particularly seals. Polar bears usually live alone, except during the breeding season in spring. Pregnant female bears spend winter in dens under the snow where they give birth. Their young stay with their mothers for up to two years.

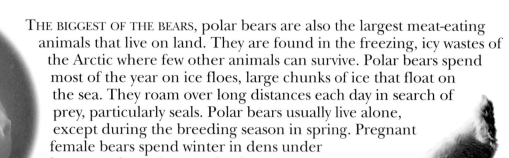

YOUNG POLAR BEARS

Wrestling with open mouths

SCALE

## ICY SWIMMERS
Polar bears paddle extremely well using their big front paws. Thick fur keeps them warm and they can swim for many hours in the freezing water. These bears swim both under the ice and in the open sea. They can swim up to 40 km (25 miles) between ice floes in search of food.

Thick white fur warms in the sun and black skin beneath absorbs heat

Long neck keeps small head above water when swimming

## PLAY FIGHTING
Polar bear cubs often play fight. The young bears wrestle on the ice and chase each other. They "fight" with open mouths to show off their teeth, and bite each other, but without hurting. By play fighting, they learn how to fight for real, which they will need to do to survive own their own.

POLAR BEAR

### FACT BOX

**Family:** Ursidae

**Habitat:** Ice floes, coastal areas

**Distribution:** Arctic region around North Pole

**Food:** Mainly seals, but also seabirds, fish, small mammals, and carrion

**Gestation period:** 8–9 months

**Lifespan:** 25–30 years

**Size:** 2–2.5 m (6.6–8.5 ft)

## WHITE WATERPROOFS
Polar bears are protected from the Arctic cold by a thick layer of fat, called blubber, under the skin – and by a dense, waterproof coat of long, creamy-white fur. The hairs that make up the fur are hollow and trap heat like little "greenhouses". The fur also provides camouflage to hide the bear from its prey. Only the nose and the pads on the paws lack hair. The foot pads have dimples that, with the claws, help the bear grip the ice.

### Find out more
ARCTIC 54
BEARS 106
CAMOUFLAGE 36

## ON OPEN ICE

Polar bears live in the Arctic. Aside from the Arctic fox, they are the only land mammals able to survive in this location. They are found mainly on floating ice packs, but may move onto land when the ice melts during the short Arctic summer. Normally, polar bears are solitary, but they will collect together if there is plenty of food nearby.

# PORCUPINES

A PORCUPINE'S BODY BRISTLES WITH big, hard, sharp-tipped hair called spines, or quills. The largest spines on a porcupine's back can be up to 35 cm (14 in) long, and there may be as many as 30,000 spines covering some species. The quills protect the porcupine against predators, such as leopards, hyenas, or bobcats. Porcupines are rodents, like rats, mice, and squirrels. They are among the largest of all the group – some are as big as a sheep.

SPINES

## SPINE RATTLING

Most porcupines can rattle their spines to threaten an enemy. Those spines at the tip of the tail are thick, hollow, and thin-walled, and make a hissing rattle. Porcupines wave their tails to warn away predators .

SCALE

## IN THE TREES

Many porcupines spend their lives in trees. They are slow climbers, and most have long tails that they can curl around a branch to secure a hold as they go up. Porcupines are mainly night-time eaters. Many spend the daytime resting in rough nests of leaves that they build in the trees.

Long spines raised in defensive crest

Quills break off easily into attacker

Strong, sturdy legs for walking, jumping and swimming

Coarse, stiff, bristly hairs

AFRICAN CRESTED PORCUPINE

## FACT BOX

**Family:** Erethizontidae (the Americas); Hystricidae (Europe, Africa, Asia)

**Habitat:** Mostly in forests, but some in plantations, savannas, rocky areas, and deserts

**Distribution:** Southern Europe, Africa, and from Arabia to China and Indonesia; also Canada to north-east Argentina

**Food:** Twigs, buds, fruits; also gnaw bones to obtain calcium and to sharpen their teeth

**Size:** 38–131 cm (15—52 in)

## BACKWARD ATTACK

When threatened by an enemy, porcupines may charge backwards, sticking up the big spines at the rear. They drive these into the attacker's face or body, where they work their way deep into the predator's flesh.

### Find out more

# PUFFINS

WITH THEIR CLOWN-LIKE FACES and huge, triangular, multi-coloured bills, puffins are very easy to recognize. These seabirds have neat black-and-white plumage and big, rounded heads. They spend much of their time standing upright or bustling about at their noisy breeding colonies. The four different species breed on the grassy tops of sea-cliffs and islands, and then spend winter out at sea. Puffins swim and dive with great skill. Underwater, they propel themselves by using powerful strokes of their big, webbed feet, aided by the oar-like movements of their wings.

## HIDEAWAY

Puffins dig out burrows in the soil for nesting in. They use their bills as pickaxes, and their sharp-clawed feet to dig and kick away the waste soil. Puffins also move into abandoned rabbit burrows. Hiding their nests away helps them keep their eggs and chicks hidden from gulls and other predators. It also protects the parents and egg from the harshest weather.

Black and white plumage (feathers)

ATLANTIC PUFFIN

SCALE

## EXPERT DIVERS

Atlantic puffins can dive down to depths of 60 m (196 ft) to catch fish. The birds then usually stay underwater for about 20 seconds, though some dives last as long as two minutes. Puffins can carry anything from four to 30 small fish, such as sand eels, in their bills when returning to feed their chicks. One birdwatcher, however, recorded a puffin carrying 61 fish.

Egg is usually white, but may be spotted with brownish or purplish blotches

## PROTECTED EGG

Puffins almost always lay just a single egg each season, which is protected in a burrow. The parents share the job of sitting on the egg to keep it warm until it hatches, in about six weeks.

Feet change from dull yellow to bright orange in breeding season

### FACT BOX

**Family:** Alcidae (auks, which also include guillemots, razorbills, auklets, and murrelets)

**Habitat:** Breed on sea cliffs and islands; other times at sea

**Distribution:** North Atlantic and North Pacific

**Food:** Small fish, especially sand eels; also shrimps

**Nest:** Hollow with dry grass

**Eggs:** 1, white

**Size:** 30–38 cm (12–15 in)

Almost twice as many feathers as gulls to help stay warm in cold northern seas

# RABBITS AND HARES

BROWN HARE

WITH THEIR LONG EARS AND short fluffy tails, rabbits and hares are a familiar sight worldwide. When these mammals emerge as darkness falls to feed on grasses and soft shoots, they are constantly alert and use their big eyes and ears, and twitching nose to provide early warning of danger. If threatened by a fox or other predator, they bound away at high speed on their hind legs and feet to find cover. Rabbits dig burrows to provide protection during the day and shelter in cold weather. Hares are larger than rabbits and can run faster. They do not dig burrows but rest in a dip in the grass called a form.

## HARING AROUND

Hares depend on speed to escape their enemies. Using their powerful hind legs and feet, they can reach speeds of up to 80 kmh (50mph) over short distances. They often follow a zig-zag route, or leap into the air, to confuse the predator so it loses them.

Grey-brown fur helps hiding from enemies

Long, narrow ears pick up faintest sounds

## SPEEDY BREEDERS

Female rabbits have from one to nine young in each litter, and can produce up to 30 kittens (young) each year. When born, rabbit kittens are hairless, blind, and helpless. They are not ready to leave their underground nest for three weeks. If they survive, rabbits can live for ten years or even longer.

### FACT BOX

**Family** Leporidae

**Habitat** Grasslands, scrublands, forests, deserts, and tundra

**Distribution** Americas, Asia, Africa, Europe; European rabbit introduced into Australia and New Zealand

**Food** Grasses, leaves, buds, berries, bark, twigs

**Size** Head and body length 25–76 cm (10–30 in)

SCALE

FEMALE EUROPEAN RABBIT AND THREE-WEEK-OLD YOUNG

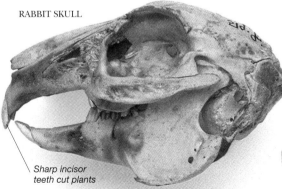

RABBIT SKULL

Sharp incisor teeth cut plants

## CUT AND CRUSH

At the front of each jaw a rabbit has large incisor teeth that gnaw and cut grasses and other plants. Despite daily use, the incisors never wear down because they grow constantly throughout life. The flattened cheek teeth at the back crush and grind up plant food so that it is easier to digest.

## SOFT-SOIL SHELTER
Rabbits prefer grassy areas with shrubs and trees, which have soft soil in which to burrow. By day, rabbits shelter in their burrows but come out at dusk to feed through the night. European rabbits live in large groups in a system of burrows called a warren. Each warren will have many entrances and may go as deep as 3 m (10 ft).

BLACK-TAILED
JACKRABBIT

Small rounded
ears

NORTH AMERICAN PIKA

Long ears help
detect enemies

Calls out to warn
others to stay out
of its territory

## RABBIT RELATIVE

Pikas are small rabbit relatives found in rocky, mountainous areas of Asia and North America. They usually live alone, each defending its own small territory. If danger threatens, they rapidly disappear to hide in rock crevices. Pikas have short legs and no tail, and small rounded ears. They feed during the day on grasses and other plants to see them through the winter.

Short legs

## BIG EARS

The jackrabbit is a North American hare that lives in hot, dry places. Its big ears work like radiators to give off heat and keep the jackrabbit cool when daytime temperatures are high. The ears also provide super-hearing to detect approaching enemies. Like most desert-dwelling animals, jackrabbits shelter from the intense daytime heat and are active at night.

White fur
provides
camouflage
in winter

## WINTER WHITE

The Arctic hare lives in the cold, northern regions. As winter approaches, its grey-brown coat turns white. This helps the hare blend in with its snowy surroundings so it cannot be seen by predators such as the arctic fox or snowy owl. The fur also becomes thicker to provide extra warmth in freezing conditions. When the snow melts in the spring, the coat changes colour back to grey-brown. This fare feeds on juicy green plants and grass in the summer months, and twigs and shoots during the winter.

ARCTIC HARE

### Find out more

ARCTIC 54
CAMOUFLAGE 36
GRASSLANDS 64
PLANT-EATERS 30

Fur under paws
keeps feet warm
and provides grip
on snow

# RACCOONS AND COATIS

RACCOONS HAVE BOLDLY-MASKED FACES that make them look like bandits. In fact they are often called "bandits" because they raid rubbish bins, food stores, and farmers' crops, leaving a trail of litter and debris behind them. Raccoons and their relatives, which include coatis, ringtails, and the lesser panda, have long bodies and tails ringed with light and dark bands. They are good climbers and spend much of their lives in trees.

RING-TAILED COATI

## FACT BOX

**Family:** Procyonidae which includes raccoons, coatis, ringtails, kinkajous, lesser panda

**Habitat:** Woods and forests; also city parks and gardens

**Distribution:** The Americas; lesser panda in Asia

**Food:** Fish, frogs, lizards, birds, eggs, fruit, nuts, seeds, scraps

**Size:** 51–136 cm (20–54 in)

## LONG SNOUTS FOR ROOTING

The tree-dwelling coatis of South America stick their long, flexible snouts into crevices and holes, searching out insects and worms. They also dig into the soil or leaves to find plant roots to eat. Their long tails help them balance when they are climbing in trees.

RACCOON

Black "bandit mask" markings

## FORWARD MOTION

Ringtails have very flexible hind feet. This allows them to run very fast up or down tree branches or over rocks head-first. They also have fox-like faces with large eyes and ears, and large, ringed tails – which gives them their name.

AMERICAN RINGTAIL

Long, black-ringed tail

Fox-like face

Long, pointed muzzle

## RAIDING SUCCESS

Raccoons are successful animals because they eat almost anything and live anywhere. They have adapted well to living alongside humans, and can be seen at night in American towns raiding rubbish bins for waste food. They use their forepaws – which have long, sensitive fingers – almost as skilfully as monkeys do, examining food and placing it into their mouths. In wilder surroundings, they use their forepaws to clutch crayfish, crabs, and frogs from swampy pools.

SCALE

### Find out more

MAMMALS 239
PANDAS 270
WOODLANDS 60

# RATS

RATS ARE HIGHLY SUCCESSFUL ANIMALS. This is because they eat anything, including rubbish thrown out by humans, and also because females can have up to twelve young every five to six weeks throughout the year. Two species in particular – brown and black rats – have lived closely with humans for centuries. These rats dwell in or near houses and other buildings, and raid human food stores. They also spread diseases, such as bubonic plague, rabies, and salmonella that infect humans. Rats are rodents like mice, their close but smaller relatives. Like other rodents, rats have long, narrow incisor (front) teeth that they use to gnaw and cut up food.

NEWBORN BROWN RAT

## FAST-GROWING BABY

A newborn brown rat lies in a nest of straw and fur. The young rat is hairless, helpless, and blind. It is kept warm, protected, and fed by its mother. But within 15 days it will be covered with fur and able to see. At 22 days old, it will leave the nest, and when it is two or three months old, the rat will be able to breed.

*Chisel-like incisor teeth inside jaw*

BROWN RAT

## CITY DWELLER

People in cities are never far from brown rats. In fact, these rats are also called house rats. They live not only in buildings but, as good swimmers, can survive underground in sewers as well. Brown rats breed rapidly, and a female can have 12 litters each year. They cause considerable damage by spoiling food, and chewing through electric cables and water pipes.

*Body covered by grey-black fur*

BLACK RAT

SCALE

## BALANCING TAIL

The black rat looks much like all other rats. It has a long body with an equally lengthy hairless tail to help it balance when climbing, something it does very well. The head has a long snout with long whiskers, and large eyes and ears. The senses of hearing, sight, smell, and touch are all very good.

*Tail with protective scales helps rat balance*

### FACT BOX

**Family:** Muridae

**Habitat:** Fields, farms, towns

**Distribution:** Worldwide

**Food:** Seeds, nuts, vegetables, fruits, insects, small animals, human food scraps and waste

**Gestation period:** 21 days

**No. of young:** Up to 12

**Lifespan:** Up to 3 years

**Size:** Body: 20–30 cm (8–12 in); tail: 20–32 cm (8–12.5 in) long

***Find out more***

MICE 246
RODENTS 303
SKELETONS 18

# RATTLESNAKES

RATTLESNAKES ARE ONE OF THE easiest types of snakes to identify because of the dry, bare scales at the end of their tail, which they rattle as a warning. There are more than 25 species, and most are found in the USA. They range in size from the 50-cm (20-in) long pygmy rattlesnake to the huge eastern diamondback rattlesnake, which can reach lengths of 2.4 m (8 ft) and is the largest poisonous snake in North America. Most rattlesnakes live in dry, desert areas and all rattlesnakes give birth to their young instead of laying eggs.

Special sensors help snake to "see" nearby animal's body heat

Coiled up ready to strike at its prey or an enemy

RATTLESNAKE

## HEAT HOLES

Two special holes on a rattlesnake's head pick up the heat given off by its prey. This helps the snake to work out exactly where its prey is, even in the dark. Because of these holes, called pits, rattlesnakes are known as a type of pit viper.

### FACT BOX

**Family:** Viperidae

**Habitat:** Desert; scrub, prairies, grassland, forests, rainforests

**Distribution:** America – from Canada to Argentina

**Food:** Lizards, birds, small mammals, such as rabbits

**Young:** Give birth to variable number of young, depending on species and size

**Size:** 30–200 cm (12–78 in)

SCALE

## TAIL RATTLE

To warn intruders to keep away, rattlesnakes shake the end of their tail. This gives a buzzing, rattling alarm sound. The rattle is made up of a loosely-linked hollow scales. These scales are the remains of the tail left behind every time a rattlesnake sheds its skin, which is about three or four times a year.

Tail vibrates up to 50 times a minute

Rattlesnakes cannot hear the sound of their own rattle

## POISON BAGS

Rattlesnakes are very poisonous snakes. They have large, broad heads because the bags of poison on either side of the head take up a lot of space. Rattlesnakes inject poison, called venom, into their prey with their sharp fangs. Muscles around the venom bags squeeze venom down the fangs. When the fangs are not being used, they are folded back against the roof of the rattlesnake's mouth.

RATTLESNAKE

***Find out more***

SNAKES 325
REPTILES 297

# RAYS

RAYS ARE FISH THAT LOOK like they have been flattened from top to bottom. Their eyes lie on top of their heads and their mouths and gills are on the underside. Unlike most fish, which have bony bodies, rays (like sharks) have skeletons made of gristly body tissue called cartilage. The family of rays includes the diamond-shaped rays and skates that live on the sea floor, and the stingrays with vicious spines whose poison can kill humans. Other rays include giant mantas that glide the surface waters, spreading 6 m (20 ft) from wing-tip to wing-tip as they flap their fins like wings in the water. The weird-looking sawfish, with jaws like saw blades, is also a ray.

THORNBACK RAY

ATLANTIC RAY

## THORNY THREAT

Thornback rays get their name from the rows of big spines, like thorns, running down their back. These help defend them against sharks and other hunters. Thornbacks bury themselves in the sand or mud, with only their thorns sticking out.

SCALE

Large row of spines run from tip of tail to head

## ELECTRIC RAYS

Like many rays, electric rays usually stay out of sight beneath the sand or mud. Only their eyes and breathing holes show above the seabed. If a diver or fisherman were to touch one by accident, they would get a powerful shock. Mostly, the ray uses this power to stun or kill prey such as crabs, other fish, or clams.

SPOTTED RAY

## SPOTTED RAY

With its pattern of spots blending in perfectly with the dappled sea floor, the spotted ray is hard to see as it lies half-buried in the sand or mud. The ray waits for food, such as shellfish, which it crunches with its strong, flattened teeth. Sometimes, a ray will dart up to seize a fish. It will then use its body to curl the prey towards its mouth, which is on the underside of the body.

Small opening on each side of head for breathing

### FACT BOX

**Family:** Includes skates and rays (Rajidae), sting-rays (Dasyatidae) and 11 other families

**Habitat:** On or near seabeds; some in upper layers of oceans

**Distribution:** Worldwide; most in warmer saltwaters

**Food:** Clams, crabs, worms, and fish; manta rays filter tiny drifting plankton (sea animals)

**No. of young:** Rays: 1–60; skates lay eggs: up to 100 in a season

**Size:** 0.1–6.7 m (0.3–22 ft) wide

Markings blend in well with seabed as ray hides in sand

## OCEAN GLIDERS
Cownose rays swim almost continously, rarely ever resting on the bottom of the seabed. They gather in "schools", numbering more than 1,000. Unlike many rays which dwell and feed on the seabed, Cownose rays prefer to swim near the surface and are creatures of the open waters.

# REINDEER

REINDEER ARE THE ONLY TYPE of deer in which the females have antlers as well as the males. This may help the females to compete with the males for plant food in the winter. Reindeer live in the snowy Arctic Circle (they are called caribou in North America) where food is scarce. To find enough to eat all year round, reindeer spend their lives on the move. They travel thousands of miles south in the winter to the largest areas of forest in the world, and back again north for the summer to the Arctic tundra (barren wastes).

*Two bull reindeer lock antlers together in a fight to decide who will mate with the females*

*Sharp hooves to grip slippery ice and dig through snow*

## LOCKED HORNS

In autumn, the rutting (mating) season, male reindeer have furious and noisy battles to decide who is the strongest. They run straight at each other, smashing their antlers together and neck wrestling with antlers interlocked.

## SNOWSHOE HOOVES

Reindeer have dew claws, which hang above and behind the hooves. They give extra grip if the reindeer begins to sink in squelchy mud or soft snow. They also help to scrape away snow to feed on lichens.

## MALE REINDEER

The bulls (adult male reindeer) often live on their own, except when they join the females at breeding time. Their antlers can be more than 152 cm (60 in) long – bigger than those of the females. Male reindeer shed their antlers at the end of each mating season. Females shed them in the spring.

### FACT BOX

**Family:** Cervidae

**Habitat:** Arctic tundra and conifer forest

**Distribution:** Northern North America, Scandinavia, northern Asia

**Food:** Lichens, mosses, leaves, shoots, berries, fungi

**Gestation period:** 8 months

**Size:** Body length up to 2.2 m (7.2 ft); tail length 21 cm (8 in)

*Antler made of solid bone*

*The lower branch points forward and has several points at the tip*

SCALE

*Thick, hollow body hairs trap warm air*

### Find out more

ARCTIC 54
DEER AND ANTELOPE 154
GAZELLES 183
MIGRATION 78

*Furry muzzle prevents frostbite*

## MIGRATING HERDS

Reindeer, also known as caribou, make the longest overland migration of any animal on Earth. Some herds journey 9,000 km (5,600 miles) every year. In spring, they trek northwards to reach the Arctic tundra lands of North America and Siberia, where they feed on leaves, berries, and fungi. In the autumn, as the snow begins to fall, the herds travel south again to the shelter of the forests, where they spend the winter feeding mainly on lichens. These North American reindeer are migrating over the snow and ice of Alaska.

# REPTILES

REPTILES ARE ANIMALS WITH A dry, scaly skin and a bony skeleton. There are about 6,000 different species of reptile, which are divided into three main groups: turtles and tortoises, snakes and lizards, and crocodiles and alligators. Most of them live in warm places because they depend on the Sun and warm surfaces to keep warm. They bask in the Sun to store energy for hunting and feeding. Many of them live on land, but sea and freshwater turtles, sea and water snakes, crocodiles, and alligators live in the water. Most reptiles lay eggs with waterproof shells but some give birth to live young. The young usually hatch or are born on land and look like tiny copies of their parents.

HINGEBACK TORTOISE

## SHELLED REPTILES

Tortoises and turtles are reptiles with shells, rather like a box with legs. Their shells protect them from enemies and bad weather, but make them slow movers.

SCALE

## LIZARDS ON THE MOVE

There are over 3,000 species of lizard – more than any other kind of reptile. Many spend their days moving among tree branches, grasses, or rocks, hunting for insects and spiders. Lizards are agile movers and some can even fly up to 15 m (50 ft) between trees. Others can walk upside down across ceilings.

Scaly skin protects body from drying out and damage

PRICKLENAPE LIZARD

Most lizards have legs of equal length that end in long toes

Sharp claws for extra grip on trees

## CROCODILES AND ALLIGATORS

Looking like old logs with huge teeth, crocodiles and alligators lurk beneath the water in wait of buffalo, fish, and sometimes humans. These reptiles have survived on Earth since the days of the dinosaurs because they are well suited to their environment. Most live in tropical fresh water, but some live in the sea.

Short, broad snout and sharp teeth for eating frogs, snails, and insects

Lizards usually have long tails to help them to balance

Crocodiles can always grow new teeth to replace those that fall out

SPECTACLED CAIMAN

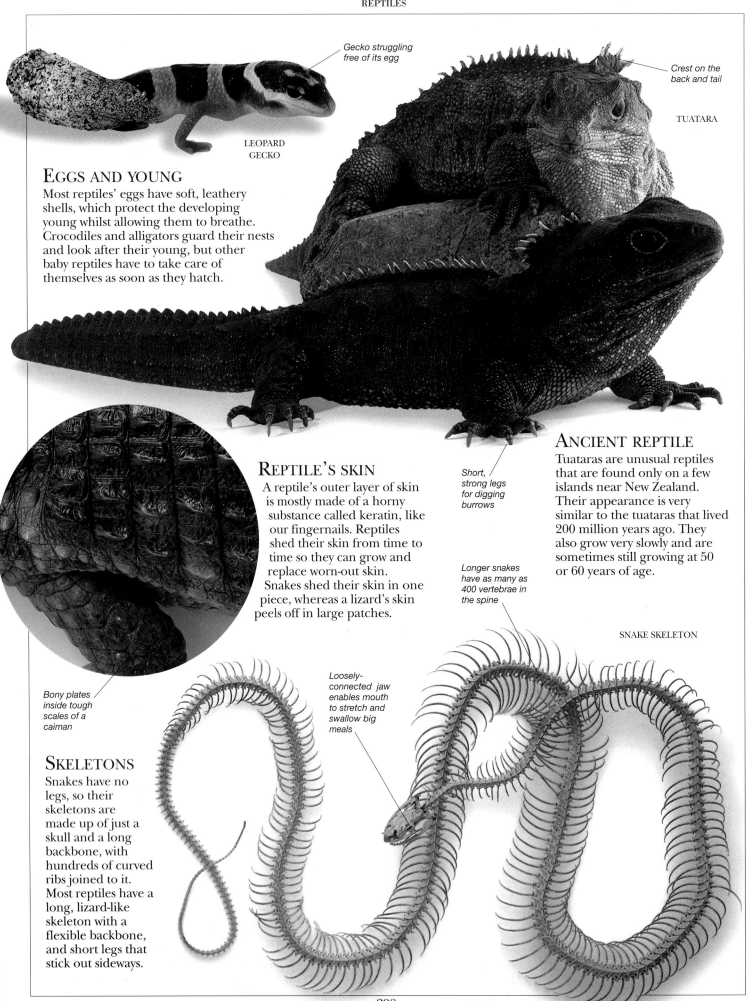

Gecko struggling
free of its egg

Crest on the
back and tail

TUATARA

LEOPARD
GECKO

## EGGS AND YOUNG

Most reptiles' eggs have soft, leathery
shells, which protect the developing
young whilst allowing them to breathe.
Crocodiles and alligators guard their nests
and look after their young, but other
baby reptiles have to take care of
themselves as soon as they hatch.

## REPTILE'S SKIN

A reptile's outer layer of skin
is mostly made of a horny
substance called keratin, like
our fingernails. Reptiles
shed their skin from time to
time so they can grow and
replace worn-out skin.
Snakes shed their skin in one
piece, whereas a lizard's skin
peels off in large patches.

Short,
strong legs
for digging
burrows

## ANCIENT REPTILE

Tuataras are unusual reptiles
that are found only on a few
islands near New Zealand.
Their appearance is very
similar to the tuataras that lived
200 million years ago. They
also grow very slowly and are
sometimes still growing at 50
or 60 years of age.

Longer snakes
have as many as
400 vertebrae in
the spine

SNAKE SKELETON

Bony plates
inside tough
scales of a
caiman

Loosely-
connected jaw
enables mouth
to stretch and
swallow big
meals

## SKELETONS

Snakes have no
legs, so their
skeletons are
made up of just a
skull and a long
backbone, with
hundreds of curved
ribs joined to it.
Most reptiles have a
long, lizard-like
skeleton with a
flexible backbone,
and short legs that
stick out sideways.

ALLIGATOR

## SCALY SWIMMERS

Crocodiles and alligators are graceful, powerful swimmers. They sweep their strong tail from side to side to propel themselves through the water. Sea and freshwater turtles swim more slowly, using their front legs to "fly" underwater. Snakes wriggle their long bodies from side to side to swim along.

## CAMOUFLAGE

With colours and patterns that look like dead leaves, the Gaboon viper is almost invisible on the forest floor. Its markings also break up the outline of its body so the snake's shape is hard to pick out. A camouflaged body helps reptiles to hide from predators or sneak up on their prey without being seen.

Internal organs shaped to fit very long, slender, and flexible body

AMERICAN CORN SNAKE

Transparent eye shield instead of eye lid

### Find out more

CROCODILES 150
INVERTEBRATES 215
LIZARDS 234
RATTLESNAKES 292
SNAKES 325
TURTLES AND TORTOISES 342

## POISONS

A lot of people think that all snakes are poisonous, but this is not so. The corn snake is a non-poisonous species, and less than a quarter of all snakes are poisonous. Only about 300 types are able to kill people. Apart from snakes, the only poisonous reptiles are two lizards, the gila monster and the Mexican beaded lizard.

Streamlined face for fast swimming

## REPTILE SENSES

The eyes and nostrils of crocodiles are located high on their heads allowing them to see and breathe as they lie in the water. Their face and body is shaped for fast swimming. Crocodiles and other reptiles have senses quite similar to human senses. Most of these animals see well, and they have a highly developed sense of smell, which they use to track down prey. The hearing of some reptiles, such as snakes, is not so good, but they can taste and smell the air with their tongues.

CROCODILE

# RHINOCEROSES

THESE BIG PLANT-EATERS are the largest mammals on land, apart from elephants. The word rhinoceros means "horned nose". They use their big horns, thick skin, and large size to protect themselves from predators. Their barrel-shaped bodies are supported by short, stocky legs, and covered by thick, hairless skin that hangs in folds around the body and acts like armour. Rhinos (their shortened name) have one or two horns made of keratin, the same material found in our hair and nails. They use their horns to threaten rivals, and to drive enemies away from themselves and their young.

INDIAN RHINO CALF

*Grey skin colour for black (and white) rhino*

*Large ears swivel to pick up sounds*

## RHINO CALF

Young rhino calves eat grass but will continue drinking their mothers' milk until they are one year old. Young rhinos are up on their feet within hours of being born and start to eat vegetation at a few weeks old. A calf remains with its mother for two or three years, but is chased away when the next calf is born.

*Thick skin protects against sharp thorns and enemies' bites*

*Horn can reach up to 120 cm (47 in) in length*

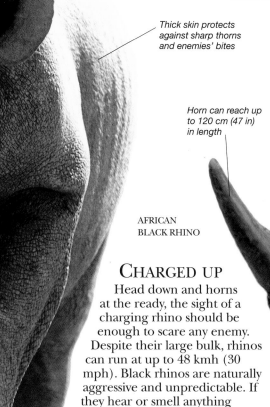

AFRICAN BLACK RHINO

## CHARGED UP

Head down and horns at the ready, the sight of a charging rhino should be enough to scare any enemy. Despite their large bulk, rhinos can run at up to 48 kmh (30 mph). Black rhinos are naturally aggressive and unpredictable. If they hear or smell anything suspicious, they will charge. They mark the borders of their territories with dung piles and urine sprays, and soon drive out any intruders.

AFRICAN WHITE RHINO

SCALE

## WIDE MOUTH

The white, or square-lipped, rhino lives in open grasslands. The biggest of the rhinos, it uses its wide mouth to graze on grasses, just like cattle do. White rhinos are less aggressive and more sociable than black rhinos, with females forming small groups.

## WELL-WORN TREADER

The black rhinoceros is found in Africa, mainly in the national parks of Kenya and Tanzania. It lives in dry grasslands, near to woodland or thorny bushes, where it feeds on twigs and newly-growing shoots. Rhinos follow well-worn paths to lakes or waterholes where they drink. They also wallow in mud to keep themselves cool in the heat of the day, and to give themselves a protective covering against annoying insects.

## FACT BOX

**Family:** Rhinocerotidae

**No. of species:** 5

**Habitat:** Grassland, scrubland, forest

**Distribution:** Africa, south and southeast Asia

**Food:** Leaves, shoots, twigs, fruits, grasses

**Gestation period:** 14–18 months

**Lifespan:** 30–35 years

**Size:** Head and body length 2–4.2 m (6.6–13.9 ft); shoulder height 100–200 cm (36–78 in)

Indian rhinos have deep folds in their skin, making them look as though they are wearing armour

INDIAN RHINO

AFRICAN BLACK RHINO

Upper lip helps to grip, pull, and break branches

## HOOKED LIP

A black rhino feeds on twigs and leaves using its hook-shaped upper lip. The lip is also able to curl round and grip tough vegetation, and then pull it into the rhino's mouth.

## WATER-SEEKERS

With so little hair, all rhinos can easily become overheated in the tropical sun. They need to cool off by lying in water or wallowing in mud. As the mud dries, it forms a sunblock. These animals also depend on watery areas for food. Indian rhinos live in swampy places, grazing on long grasses and water plants, and picking at fruit and twigs. A rhino will charge at any animal that comes between it and its waterhole.

## HORN REMOVAL

This black rhino has had his horns removed – but for a good reason. The people that protect black rhinos cut off their horns so that they will not be killed by poachers. Removing the horns from a rhino is painless – just like having a haircut. Poachers sell rhino horns to make ancient medicines and handles for daggers. Those who protect the rhinos travel to their remote habitats. Here they set up special patrol watches that guard against poaching.

AFRICAN BLACK RHINO

Horn removed

# RODENTS

RODENTS MAKE UP THE LARGEST GROUP of mammals on the planet. All of them have two pairs of sharp incisor (front) teeth that they use to gnaw seeds and other tough food. These teeth develop throughout their lives and never wear down. It is these constantly growing, chisel-like teeth that identify rodents from other groups of mammals. There are three main types of rodents: mouse-like rodents include mice, rats, and jerboas; squirrel-like rodents include squirrels, woodchucks, and beavers; and rodents which include guinea pigs and capybaras.

*Bushy tail helps squirrel to balance while jumping*

PREVOST SQUIRREL

BROWN RAT

*Snout has long sensitive whiskers*

## TREE CLIMBER

Tree squirrels, like the Prevost squirrel from the forests of Southeast Asia, are brilliant climbers and jumpers. They use their strong hind legs to leap from branch to branch. During the day, they forage for seeds, nuts, and insects. At night, they rest in tree hollows, or dreys (nests) made of leaves and twigs.

*Tail covered in protective scales*

*Uses soles of feet to walk*

WOODCHUCK

## LIVING CLOSE-BY TO HUMANS

The brown rat walks on the soles of its feet and, when climbing, uses its toes to grip and long tail to help it balance. Like other mouse-like rodents it has a pointed snout, large eyes and ears, sensitive whiskers, and short legs. Quick to learn, able to eat anything, a rapid breeder, and unafraid of humans, the brown rat has spread all over the world.

## BURROWING SQUIRREL

The woodchuck, or groundhog, is a relative of tree-living squirrels. This stocky, short-legged rodent lives in open woodland in North America where it digs burrows and eats grasses, berries, and fruit. In winter, when snow falls and food is scarce, woodchucks go into their burrows to start a long hibernation (winter sleep). They are kept alive by stores of body fat built up by eating extra food during the summer.

*Strong feet and claws used for digging burrows*

### FACT BOX

**Order:** Rodents belong to the order Rodentia; in this order there are about 29 families

**No. of species:** About 1,800

**Habitat:** All types

**Distribution:** Worldwide except Antarctica

**Food:** Mainly nuts, seeds, fruits, leaves, roots

**No. of young:** 1–20

**Lifespan:** 6 months–10 years

AMERICAN
BEAVER

*Sleek, streamlined
body suited to
swimming*

*Thick waterproof fur
keeps beaver warm*

*Flat tail used
for swimming
and steering*

## WOOD-CHOPPING TEETH

Beavers have huge, gnawing teeth that
can cut down trees up to 100 cm (39 in)
wide. They use the branches, along with
mud and stones, to create dams. In the pool
that forms behind the dam, they construct
a lodge (nest) with an underwater
entrance. This safe, secure home
provides the beaver family with
shelter from predators and
cold winter weather.

## DESERT DWELLER

Jerboas, and some other rodents, are able
to survive in hot, dry deserts. During the
heat of the day, they rest in cool burrows
that they dig using their front feet. They do
not need to drink, as they get all the water
they need from their food. Jerboas are
active at night, when it is cooler. They use
their long, powerful hind legs and feet to
hop across the sand in search of seeds. If a
snake or other hungry enemy
attacks, the jerboa leaps
high into the air to
make its escape.

DESERT JERBOA

*Large eyes
aid night
vision*

*Long back
legs and feet*

*Long tail helps
jerboa to balance
when hopping*

*Front paws used for
holding food and for
digging burrows*

## WATER LOVERS

Looking like giant guinea pigs, capybaras are the
largest of the rodents. They are excellent swimmers
and divers in the lakes and swamps of South
America. When they swim only the eyes, ears, and
nostrils can be seen. Capybaras graze in small
groups on grasses and water plants.

CAPYBARA

*Close to top of head,
the eyes, ears, and
nostrils remain above
water when swimming*

### Find out more

BEAVERS 109
GUINEA PIGS 197
MAMMALS 239
MICE 246
RATS 291
SQUIRRELS AND CHIPMUNKS 330

# SALAMANDERS AND NEWTS

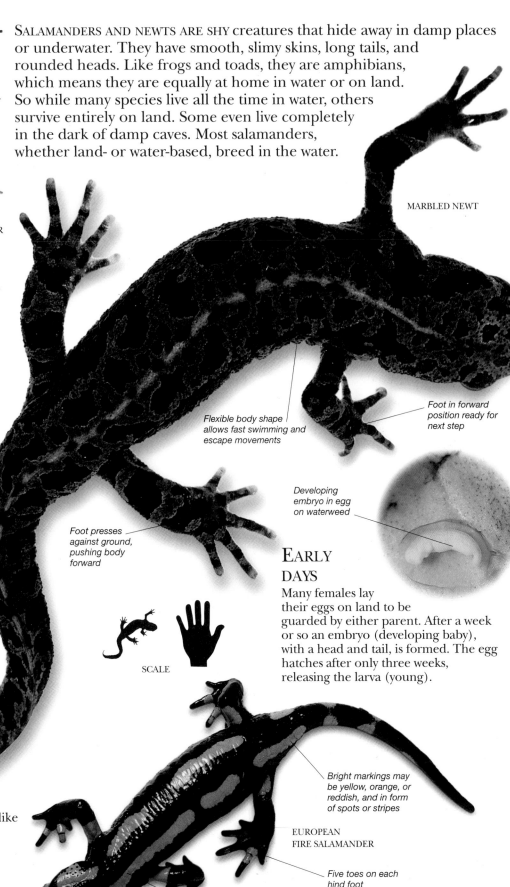

SALAMANDERS AND NEWTS ARE SHY creatures that hide away in damp places or underwater. They have smooth, slimy skins, long tails, and rounded heads. Like frogs and toads, they are amphibians, which means they are equally at home in water or on land. So while many species live all the time in water, others survive entirely on land. Some even live completely in the dark of damp caves. Most salamanders, whether land- or water-based, breed in the water.

*Gills in young for breathing underwater*

TIGER SALAMANDER

MARBLED NEWT

## YOUNG TIGERS

Tiger salamander larvae (young) become young adults in 12 weeks. As larvae they have gills for breathing, but lose these when they become adult. As adults they breathe through lungs and their skin, and are the world's largest land-living salamander. They can grow to as long as 33 cm (13 in).

*Flexible body shape allows fast swimming and escape movements*

*Foot in forward position ready for next step*

*Developing embryo in egg on waterweed*

## ON ALL FOURS

Most newts and salamanders walk or crawl quite slowly on land, underground, or in the trees. Some even walk over the muddy bottoms of ponds using just the tips of their fingers and toes. Some can swim and burrow using their hands, feet, and tails. For quick bursts of speed they lash their tails from side to side.

*Foot presses against ground, pushing body forward*

SCALE

## EARLY DAYS

Many females lay their eggs on land to be guarded by either parent. After a week or so an embryo (developing baby), with a head and tail, is formed. The egg hatches after only three weeks, releasing the larva (young).

*Bright markings may be yellow, orange, or reddish, and in form of spots or stripes*

EUROPEAN FIRE SALAMANDER

## WHAT'S IN A NAME?

With its striking pattern of flame-like markings, the European fire salamander is well named. "Salamander" comes from the ancient Greek word for a mythical, lizard-like monster that was thought to live in fire, which it could put out with its cold body.

*Five toes on each hind foot*

*This large salamander lives mainly in mountain forests*

## IN A DAMP HOME
The blue ridge two-lined salamander lives in the mountain forests of south-eastern USA where there is plenty of rain. It rarely ventures far from ponds, although the blue ridge is one of a group of salamanders that does not breed in water. Other types dwell all the time in water, and there are even some species that spend their lives deep inside cave systems, in underground lakes and streams.

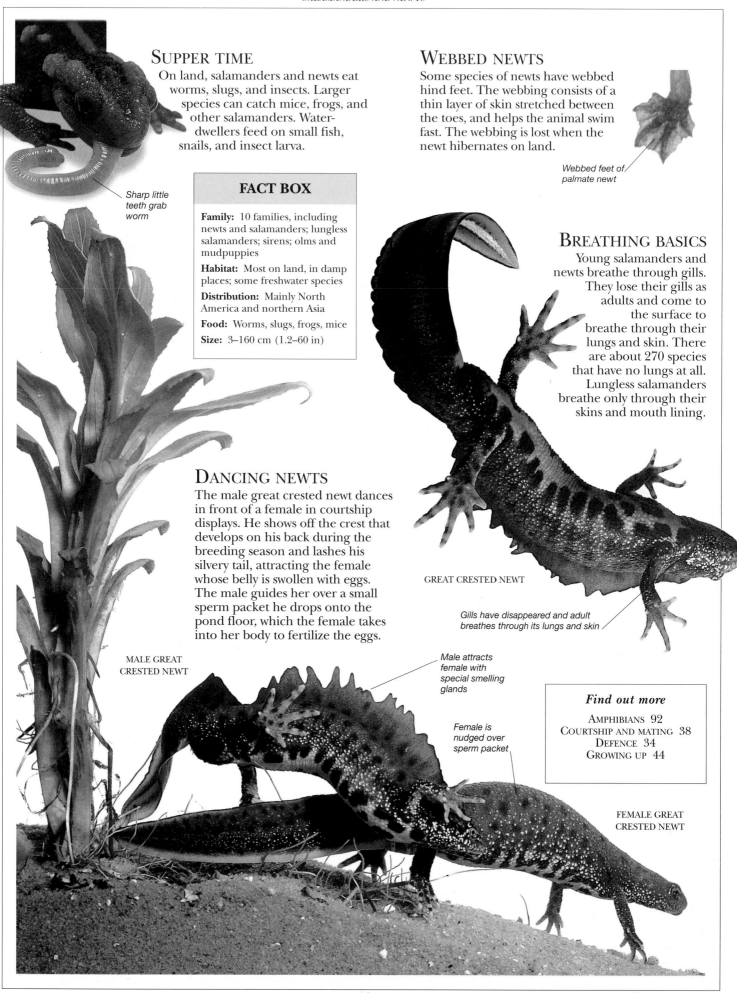

## SUPPER TIME

On land, salamanders and newts eat worms, slugs, and insects. Larger species can catch mice, frogs, and other salamanders. Water-dwellers feed on small fish, snails, and insect larva.

*Sharp little teeth grab worm*

## WEBBED NEWTS

Some species of newts have webbed hind feet. The webbing consists of a thin layer of skin stretched between the toes, and helps the animal swim fast. The webbing is lost when the newt hibernates on land.

*Webbed feet of palmate newt*

### FACT BOX

**Family:** 10 families, including newts and salamanders; lungless salamanders; sirens; olms and mudpuppies

**Habitat:** Most on land, in damp places; some freshwater species

**Distribution:** Mainly North America and northern Asia

**Food:** Worms, slugs, frogs, mice

**Size:** 3–160 cm (1.2–60 in)

## BREATHING BASICS

Young salamanders and newts breathe through gills. They lose their gills as adults and come to the surface to breathe through their lungs and skin. There are about 270 species that have no lungs at all. Lungless salamanders breathe only through their skins and mouth lining.

GREAT CRESTED NEWT

*Gills have disappeared and adult breathes through its lungs and skin*

## DANCING NEWTS

The male great crested newt dances in front of a female in courtship displays. He shows off the crest that develops on his back during the breeding season and lashes his silvery tail, attracting the female whose belly is swollen with eggs. The male guides her over a small sperm packet he drops onto the pond floor, which the female takes into her body to fertilize the eggs.

MALE GREAT CRESTED NEWT

*Male attracts female with special smelling glands*

*Female is nudged over sperm packet*

### Find out more

AMPHIBIANS 92
COURTSHIP AND MATING 38
DEFENCE 34
GROWING UP 44

FEMALE GREAT CRESTED NEWT

# SALMON, TROUT, AND PIKE

SALMON, TROUT, AND THEIR RELATIVES pike are streamlined, powerful fish with slim, tapering bodies and forked tails. Salmon and trout mostly breed in streams and rivers, and migrate to sea. They are famous for making epic journeys in which they can overcome huge obstacles such as waterfalls and rapids. Pike are found only in freshwaters. Salmon and trout can be identified by the small fin (called the adipose fin), between the fin on the back and the tail – this fin lacks the bony supporting struts (called rays) found in the other fins.

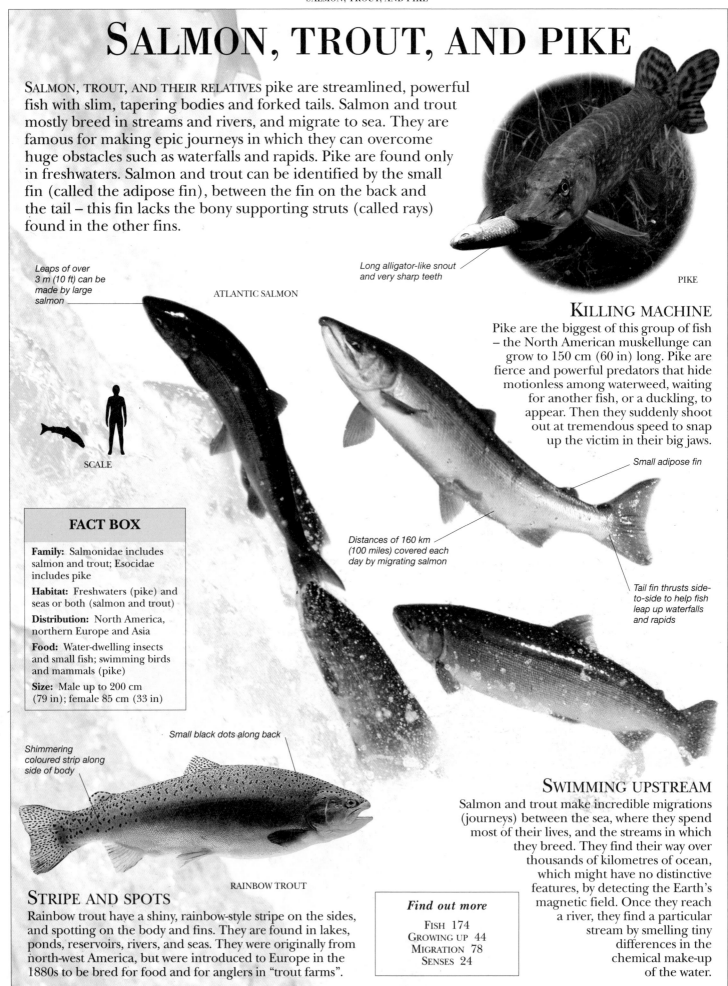

PIKE

Long alligator-like snout and very sharp teeth

Leaps of over 3 m (10 ft) can be made by large salmon

ATLANTIC SALMON

SCALE

## KILLING MACHINE

Pike are the biggest of this group of fish – the North American muskellunge can grow to 150 cm (60 in) long. Pike are fierce and powerful predators that hide motionless among waterweed, waiting for another fish, or a duckling, to appear. Then they suddenly shoot out at tremendous speed to snap up the victim in their big jaws.

Small adipose fin

Distances of 160 km (100 miles) covered each day by migrating salmon

Tail fin thrusts side-to-side to help fish leap up waterfalls and rapids

### FACT BOX

**Family:** Salmonidae includes salmon and trout; Esocidae includes pike

**Habitat:** Freshwaters (pike) and seas or both (salmon and trout)

**Distribution:** North America, northern Europe and Asia

**Food:** Water-dwelling insects and small fish; swimming birds and mammals (pike)

**Size:** Male up to 200 cm (79 in); female 85 cm (33 in)

Small black dots along back

Shimmering coloured strip along side of body

RAINBOW TROUT

## SWIMMING UPSTREAM

Salmon and trout make incredible migrations (journeys) between the sea, where they spend most of their lives, and the streams in which they breed. They find their way over thousands of kilometres of ocean, which might have no distinctive features, by detecting the Earth's magnetic field. Once they reach a river, they find a particular stream by smelling tiny differences in the chemical make-up of the water.

## STRIPE AND SPOTS

Rainbow trout have a shiny, rainbow-style stripe on the sides, and spotting on the body and fins. They are found in lakes, ponds, reservoirs, rivers, and seas. They were originally from north-west America, but were introduced to Europe in the 1880s to be bred for food and for anglers in "trout farms".

*Find out more*

FISH 174
GROWING UP 44
MIGRATION 78
SENSES 24

# SCORPIONS

Scorpions are small, armoured creatures related to spiders. Like spiders, they have eight legs, but most scorpions are recognized by a pair of large front pincers that end in powerful claws. Many people fear scorpions for their stings, but in fact, most scorpion stings are usually no more deadly than those of wasps. The sting is used for self-defence and to kill prey, which they hold firm in their pincers. Scorpions live mainly in warm places, including deserts. By day, they hide under stones or in cool burrows. At night, they come out to hunt.

*Sharp stinging spine*

## PAINFUL STING

A scorpion's sting is a sharp spine at the tip of its long, curving tail. It is fed by two poison glands at the tail base. Scorpions use their stings in self-defence when they feel threatened. The Sahara scorpion is one of the few species armed with poison strong enough to kill a person. Most scorpions' stings are painful, but not dangerous to humans.

## POWERFUL PINCERS

Scorpions kill their prey chiefly using their pincers. They only sting their victims if they put up a fierce fight. They can kill quite large animals such as lizards, but they only have small mouths. The scorpion's pincers tear its victim into small pieces and crush it into a mush that can be sucked into its mouth.

SCORPION

*Tail made up of six segments to allow it to bend*

*Body protected by hard outer skin like a suit of armour*

*Eyes*

SCALE

*Pincers grab prey firmly and hold it still*

***Find out more***

INSECTS 212
INVERTEBRATES 215
SPIDERS 327

## GOING HUNTING

Scorpions have six to twelve eyes, but their eyesight is poor. They rely on a keen sense of touch to track down prey in the dark. Scorpions have a pair of comblike sensory organs on their undersides which detect the vibrations of their prey.

*Young scorpions look like tiny versions of their parents*

## FACT BOX

**Order:** Scorpiones

**No of species:** More than 1,200

**Habitat:** Warm places from rainforests to deserts

**Distribution:** Worldwide except Arctic and Antarctic

**Food:** Insects, spiders, scorpions, lizards, mice

**Nest:** Under rocks or in underground burrow

**Size:** 6–20 cm (2–8 in)

## RIDING HIGH

Male and female scorpions clasp pincers and do a jerky dance before mating. Once fertilized, the eggs develop inside the female. They hatch out from the eggs inside their mother and are born alive. The babies ride around on their mother's back for two to three weeks, until they are strong enough to look after themselves.

IMPERIAL SCORPION

# SEAHORSES

THE MOST UN-FISHLIKE OF FISHES, seahorses look like underwater knights from a chessboard as they swim along in an upright position. They are entirely encased in armour plating, made up of bony rings. The rings make their armour very hard but also flexible. Seahorses have their eyes mounted on turrets. Each turret can swivel in different directions, so that while one eye searches ahead for prey, the other eye can look up on its own to check for any approaching predator. Seahorses feed by sucking up tiny plankton (drifting sea creatures) into their long, tube-shaped mouths.

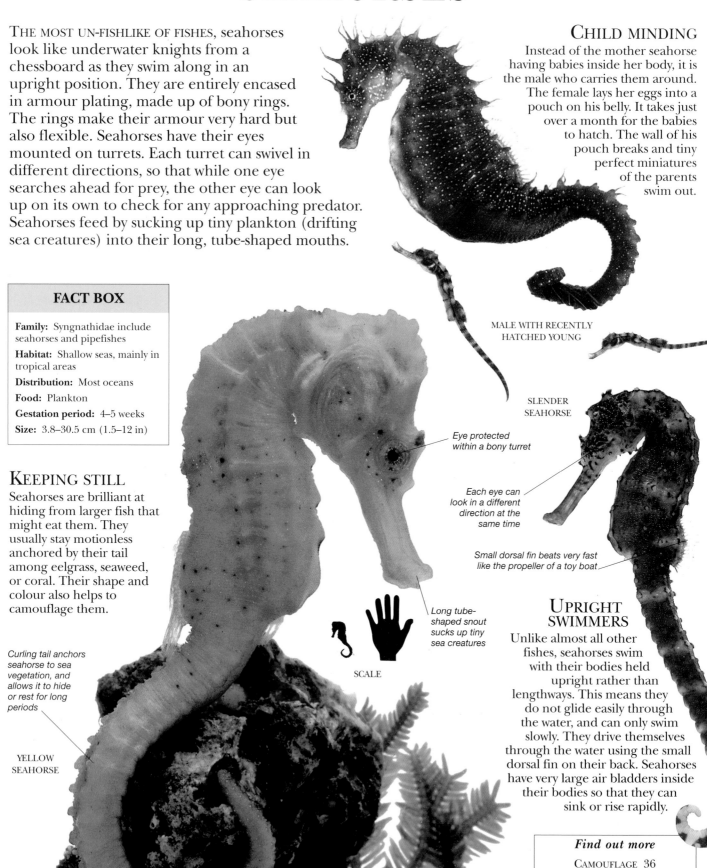

## CHILD MINDING
Instead of the mother seahorse having babies inside her body, it is the male who carries them around. The female lays her eggs into a pouch on his belly. It takes just over a month for the babies to hatch. The wall of his pouch breaks and tiny perfect miniatures of the parents swim out.

MALE WITH RECENTLY HATCHED YOUNG

SLENDER SEAHORSE

## FACT BOX

**Family:** Syngnathidae include seahorses and pipefishes

**Habitat:** Shallow seas, mainly in tropical areas

**Distribution:** Most oceans

**Food:** Plankton

**Gestation period:** 4–5 weeks

**Size:** 3.8–30.5 cm (1.5–12 in)

## KEEPING STILL
Seahorses are brilliant at hiding from larger fish that might eat them. They usually stay motionless anchored by their tail among eelgrass, seaweed, or coral. Their shape and colour also helps to camouflage them.

Eye protected within a bony turret

Each eye can look in a different direction at the same time

Small dorsal fin beats very fast like the propeller of a toy boat

Curling tail anchors seahorse to sea vegetation, and allows it to hide or rest for long periods

YELLOW SEAHORSE

Long tube-shaped snout sucks up tiny sea creatures

SCALE

## UPRIGHT SWIMMERS
Unlike almost all other fishes, seahorses swim with their bodies held upright rather than lengthways. This means they do not glide easily through the water, and can only swim slowly. They drive themselves through the water using the small dorsal fin on their back. Seahorses have very large air bladders inside their bodies so that they can sink or rise rapidly.

### Find out more
CAMOUFLAGE 36
COURTSHIP AND MATING 38
FISHES 174
OCEANS 74

## SHALLOW MARINE WATERS
Seahorses mostly live in shallow seawater worldwide. They do not rely on a streamlined shape or speed to chase after food and escape enemies like most fish. Instead they have developed a protective armour-plating and the ability to hide among seaweed and coral, anchored by their remarkable tail.

# SEALS AND SEA LIONS

*Males fight to mate with females*

WITH THEIR SMOOTH, STREAMLINED BODIES, seals and sea lions are mammals that are superb swimmers. Instead of feet they have flippers, and a thick layer of blubber (fat) under their skin helps keep them warm – even in the coldest polar waters. The skin is covered with waterproof hair, which also protects them from rough rocks or sand when ashore. Seals need to come up for air and they also have their pups (young) on land. They are related to cats, dogs, and other meat-eating mammals, and they hunt mainly for fish and squid.

MALE SOUTHERN
ELEPHANT SEALS

## FACT BOX

**Family:** Three families in the Order Otariidae: Odobenidae: Phocidae: includes the 19 species of true seals; Otobenidae: the eared seals and sea lions; and the walrus

**Habitat:** Mostly in the sea; a few in fresh water

**Distribution:** Worldwide, but most live in cooler seas

**Food:** Mainly fish and squid

**Size:** 1.2–6.5 m (4–21 ft)

## RAGING BULLS

Bull (male) elephant seals compete against one another to mate with cows (females). The top bull on a stretch of breeding beach is known as the beachmaster. Much of the fighting is simply a show of strength, but serious injuries and some deaths occur from damage by their sharp teeth.

## EARED SEALS

Fur seals and sea lions are called eared seals because they have small outer ears. Eared seals swim by rowing through the water with powerful strokes of their front flippers. They are much less clumsy on land than true seals, because they can move their hind flippers forwards to walk on all fours.

*Small ears visible on the outside*

GALAPAGOS
SEA LION

*Sensitive whiskers to help find way in murky waters*

*Totally streamlined with no trace of outer ears*

HARP SEAL
MOTHER
WITH CUB

*Mother lets cub suckle her rich milk for just two weeks*

## HIGH-FAT DIET

Seal pups grow rapidly, thanks to their mother's extremely rich milk, which contains about 50 per cent fat. Because it is so rich in energy, the pup suckles for only a short time before being weaned on to fish and other prey. Much of the fat goes to form the thick layer of blubber beneath the skin. This keeps the seal warm and helps it remain buoyant in the water.

*Hind flippers brought forward for walking*

*Large muscular flippers help seal to shuffle about on land*

SCALE

## ON LAND AND SEA
A sea lion shuffles its way towards a breeding colony on one of the Galapagos Islands off the South American coast of Ecuador. Though they breed and rest on land, seals and sea lions are most at home in the sea. They favour cool water, brought in by cold currents – perfect conditions for large populations of fish, their main prey.

*Mother looks on with
her pup trapped in ice*

## FAMILY GROUP

Seals gather together to
breed in colonies called
rookeries, which may be
packed with more than a
million individuals. Other
colonies may contain just
a few animals. Seals
choose isolated beaches
or islands, or floating ice,
for breeding sites,
because these are
difficult for predators to
reach. Male sea lions
may mate with 50 or
more females on land.

HARBOUR SEAL
PUP AND
MOTHER

FEMALE SOUTH
AMERICAN SEA LION

*Female sea lion may
weigh only half as
much as a big male*

SOUTH AMERICAN SEA LION PUP

## DANGER IN THE ICE

Seals often have to swim under thick ice.
As they need to come up for air
regularly, they enlarge natural cracks in
the ice sheet with the claws on their front
flippers. The cracks serve as breathing
holes. Sometimes, however, pups may
become trapped in the ice cracks.

## SUBMARINE ACROBATICS

Extremely graceful and speedy swimmers, seals
can dart in different directions very quickly.
This helps them find and chase fast-moving
fish, and to escape predators, such as sharks,
killer whales, and polar bears. Seals are also
expert divers, holding their breath and
slowing down their heartbeat to save
oxygen. Some can stay underwater
for more than 70 minutes, and
elephant seals have been known
to reach depths of up to 1 km
(0.6 mile) or more.

*Flattened head with
short face helps seal
slip speedily through
water*

### Find out more

ARCTIC 54
MAMMALS 239
OCEAN 74
WALRUSES 350

# SHARKS

JAWS OF A GREAT
WHITE SHARK

THE TINY, SPINED PYGMY SHARK is only the size of a cigar, while the gigantic, but harmless, whale shark is the world's largest fish. In between there are over 400 different species of sharks of amazingly different shapes and sizes. Most of the world's sharks are not the fearsome, huge man-eaters of popular imagination – people are more likely to be killed by lightning, or a bee sting, than to be attacked by a shark. But that does not make them less fearsome – after all they have been the number-one predator fishes for 500 million years.

GREAT WHITE
SHARK

Triangular
dorsal (back)
fin controls
steering,
diving, and
balance

## GREAT WHITE JAWS

The great white shark's awesomely strong jaws can rip into the body of prey with a force of many tonnes. They contain a terrifying battery of very sharp, triangular, teeth with saw-edges, like steak knives. Each tooth can be over 6 cm (2.4 in) long and can easily cut a massive chunk of flesh from a victim in a single bite.

Tail fin designed for
high speed dashes

Pectoral (side)
fins held out like
fixed wings stop
shark from sinking

Very tough skin covered
in minute teeth called
"denticles"

## LONE HUNTER

The most fearsome of all sharks is the great white shark, which may grow to over 6 m (20 ft) long. It usually hunts alone and can kill animals as large as sea lions and porpoises, as well as other sharks. The great white is responsible for a good proportion of attacks on humans, mistaking people swimming or surfing at the surface for seals.

Lateral line
sensors pick
up vibrations
in water

SCALE

PORT JACKSON
SHARK

Pupil closes
to a slit in
bright light

ANGEL SHARK

## NO GREAT LOOKER

Most sharks rely less on eyesight and more on other senses to detect prey. They only use their eyes for the final rush attack on the prey. Many sharks are used to living on the dark seabed or in murky waters, and if they come across bright light, they can shut their pupils to just a slit to avoid being blinded.

## SHARP-SMELLING

Sharks have a fantastic sense of smell. A shark can sniff out just 10 drops of tuna juice in a swimming pool. It can also smell blood in the water nearly 0.5 km (0.3 mile) away. A shark can also pick up vibrations of passing prey from its "lateral line" – a row of sensors along its side.

## KILLERS IN THE CORAL
Medium-sized reef-dwelling sharks, such as this grey reef shark, are kings of the food chain in the coral reefs. They prowl along the Great Barrier Reef, off Australia's east coast, as well as in other Indian and Pacific Ocean reefs. While some sharks inhabit tropical lagoons, other species dwell in the cold Arctic.

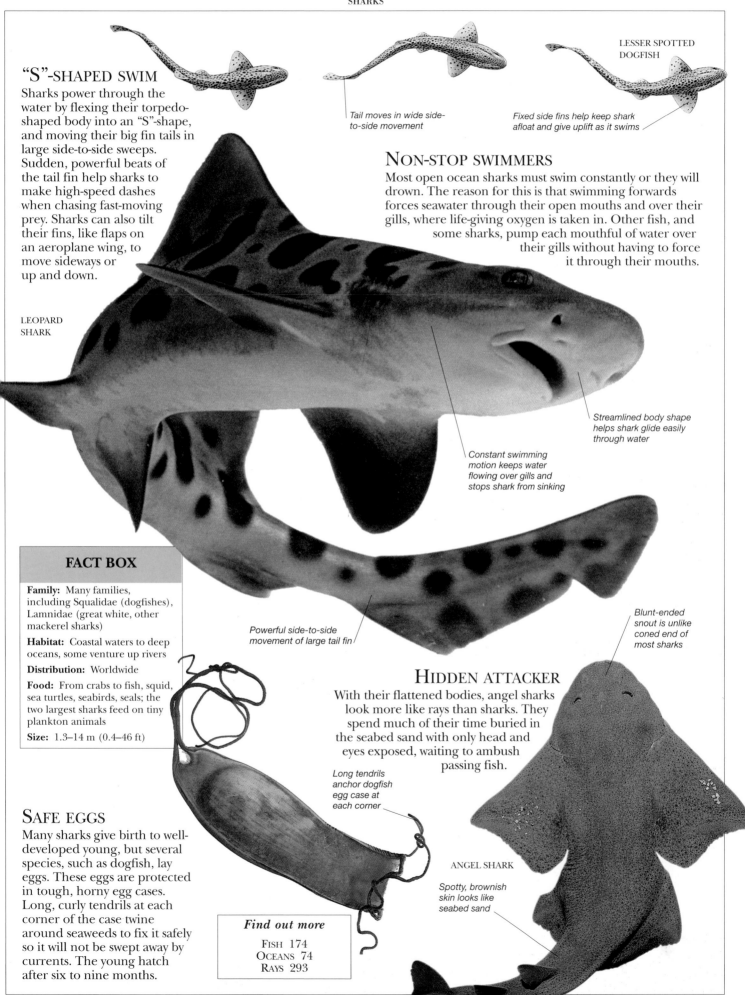

LESSER SPOTTED
DOGFISH

*Tail moves in wide side-to-side movement*

*Fixed side fins help keep shark afloat and give uplift as it swims*

## "S"-SHAPED SWIM

Sharks power through the water by flexing their torpedo-shaped body into an "S"-shape, and moving their big fin tails in large side-to-side sweeps. Sudden, powerful beats of the tail fin help sharks to make high-speed dashes when chasing fast-moving prey. Sharks can also tilt their fins, like flaps on an aeroplane wing, to move sideways or up and down.

## NON-STOP SWIMMERS

Most open ocean sharks must swim constantly or they will drown. The reason for this is that swimming forwards forces seawater through their open mouths and over their gills, where life-giving oxygen is taken in. Other fish, and some sharks, pump each mouthful of water over their gills without having to force it through their mouths.

LEOPARD
SHARK

*Streamlined body shape helps shark glide easily through water*

*Constant swimming motion keeps water flowing over gills and stops shark from sinking*

### FACT BOX

**Family:** Many families, including Squalidae (dogfishes), Lamnidae (great white, other mackerel sharks)

**Habitat:** Coastal waters to deep oceans, some venture up rivers

**Distribution:** Worldwide

**Food:** From crabs to fish, squid, sea turtles, seabirds, seals; the two largest sharks feed on tiny plankton animals

**Size:** 1.3–14 m (0.4–46 ft)

*Powerful side-to-side movement of large tail fin*

*Blunt-ended snout is unlike coned end of most sharks*

## HIDDEN ATTACKER

With their flattened bodies, angel sharks look more like rays than sharks. They spend much of their time buried in the seabed sand with only head and eyes exposed, waiting to ambush passing fish.

*Long tendrils anchor dogfish egg case at each corner*

ANGEL SHARK

*Spotty, brownish skin looks like seabed sand*

## SAFE EGGS

Many sharks give birth to well-developed young, but several species, such as dogfish, lay eggs. These eggs are protected in tough, horny egg cases. Long, curly tendrils at each corner of the case twine around seaweeds to fix it safely so it will not be swept away by currents. The young hatch after six to nine months.

*Find out more*

FISH 174
OCEANS 74
RAYS 293

# SHEEP

WILD SHEEP LIVE IN MOUNTAINOUS places, and can survive the harsh, cold conditions there. Their woolly coats keep them warm, and their split hooves allow them to move easily over rocky ground. Sheep spend summers grazing on grasses high up in alpine meadows, but move down to the foothills in winter when the weather gets colder. Both rams (males) and ewes (females) have horns, but those of the ram are much bigger. Domestic (farmed) sheep have a much thicker coat – called a fleece – than wild sheep.

*Newborn lamb*

## SPRING LAMBS

Ewes give birth in the spring. Most have just one lamb, but sometimes they have twins. Soon after it is born, the young lamb struggles to its feet and follows its mother for protection and food. Lambs form groups of their own and play together. They return to their mothers from time to time to suckle.

## DOMESTIC SHEEP

Sheep were first domesticated (used by people) about 10,000 years ago. Today there are over 200 different types of domestic sheep, providing wool, meat, and milk. They do not shed their winter coat naturally in the spring as wild sheep do, so they have to be sheared (have their wool cut).

DOMESTIC SHEEP

## FACT BOX

**Family:** Bovidae

**Habitat:** Mountain, cliffs, dry grasslands, desert; domestic sheep: grasslands and pasture

**Distribution:** North America, Asia, Europe; domestic sheep: worldwide

**Food:** Grass and small plants

**No of species:** 7

**Size:** Head to tail length: 110–200 cm (43–79 in)

**Lifespan:** 10–15 years

SCALE

Large horns of ram grow backwards then curl forwards

Coat has coarse hairs on top and woolly fur underneath

Downward curving forehead

Flattened cheek teeth inside mouth grind grasses

## WILD SHEEP

All wild sheep look similar to the American bighorn sheep, which lives in the Rocky Mountains. For most of the year, males and females lead separate lives. In the breeding season rams compete for females to breed with. They rear up and clash their horns head on, making a loud noise as their skulls bang together. The winner of the battle mates with the females.

AMERICAN BIGHORN SHEEP

Split hooves help sheep scramble over rocks without slipping

# SHREWS

ONE OF THE SMALLEST OF ALL LAND mammals is a shrew, and these animals are all small and very active. They belong to the group of insect-eaters that also includes the moles and hedgehogs. Despite their lack of size, shrews eat very large amounts of food. They need to feed every two to three hours and live in places where there is plenty of food. They eat not only insects and earthworms, but whatever else they can find, including fruit and dead animals. A few species hunt in water. Shrews are secretive animals that live on their own. They defend their feeding areas fiercely – any intruders are driven away with a chorus of screams and twitterings.

Long, pointed snout

Short legs

EUROPEAN COMMON SHREW

Dense, velvety fur covers body

EURASIAN WATER SHREW

Tail acts as rudder to help steer under water

## SHARED FEATURES

All shrews share the same features – they have long pointed snouts used to probe for insects and worms in soil and leaf litter. Their hearing and sense of smell, used to detect food, is very good; but their eyes are small and vision poor. They can also run very quickly although their legs are short.

## FACT BOX

**Family:** Soricidae

**Habitat:** Forest, woodland, grassland, scrub, desert

**Distribution:** Europe, Asia, Africa, North America, northern South America

**Food:** Mainly insects and worms

**No of species:** 280

**Lifespan:** 12–18 months

**Size:** Head/body 3.5–18 cm (0.6–7 in); tail 0.9–12 cm (0.6 – 4.75 in)

## UNDERWATER HUNTER

Water shrews live near streams and hunt for food underwater. Each dive lasts for between five to 20 seconds. The large back feet act like flippers to push the shrew through the water as it searches for fish, frogs, snails, and insects. Once prey is found, the shrew bites and paralyzes it with its poisonous saliva.

SCALE

## ALWAYS HUNGRY

Shrews are on the look out for food, such as this tasty earthworm, day and night. They only take short breaks to rest or sleep. The reason for their big appetite is that shrews are small and lose body heat very quickly. Once eaten, food is digested rapidly to generate extra warmth. Small shrews eat more than their body weight in food each day.

Long, pointed snout with sensitive whiskers

**Find out more**

HEDGEHOGS 200
MOLES 248

# SKUNKS

*Tail fluffed up to make it bigger and more bushy*

VIVID BLACK-AND-WHITE MARKINGS help to identify skunks easily. These warn predators to keep their distance. If this message is ignored, the skunk squirts a spray of stinking liquid into its enemy's face. The liquid comes from two glands – like tiny water pistols – in the skunk's rear end. It burns the attacker's skin, stings its eyes, and can make a would-be predator blind and breathless for a short time. People sprayed by skunks often throw away their clothes because the smell is so bad.

STRIPED SKUNK

*Bold black-and-white marking warns off enemies*

SPOTTED SKUNK

## FACT BOX

**Family:** Mustelidae, which includes the meat-eating otters and polecats

**Habitat:** Woods, grassland, open rocky land, deserts; urban areas

**Distribution:** North America

**Food:** Insects, small mammals, lizards, snakes, birds' eggs, fruit

**No. of species:** 13

**Lifespan:** Up to 6 years

**Size:** Head and body 28–49 cm (11–19.3 in); tail 16–43 cm (6.3–17 in)

## SPOTTED SKUNK

The coat of spotted skunks is patterned with small white stripes and spots. If spotted skunks are threatened they do a handstand by raising the rear part of their body. If the attacker ignores this warning, it gets sprayed. Spotted skunk forage alone for food at night like other skunks.

SCALE

MOTHER WITH YOUNG

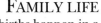

*Skunk stamps feet as a warning*

*Young skunks stay close to mother who feeds and protects them*

## STAY AWAY OR ELSE

This is what an angry striped skunk would look like to an attacker. When threatened, the skunk stamps its front feet and walks with stiff legs. It fluffs up its tail and long black-and-white coat to make itself look bigger. If this warning fails, the skunk turns its back on the enemy and squirts smelly, stinging fluid into its face. Skunks hit their target even if it is over 2 m (6.5 ft) away.

## FAMILY LIFE

Skunk births happen in a den or burrow in April and May. At first, the young which may number up to nine, are blind and helpless. At one month old, they have black-and-white fur, and can see. Two weeks later they are able to spray just like their mother. At two months old, they stop drinking their mother's milk and eat solid food. By autumn they are on their own.

*Find out more*

DEFENCE 34
MEAT-EATERS 32
OTTERS 264

# SLOTHS

SLOTHS EAT, SLEEP, AND EVEN give birth hanging upside-down from tree branches. They grip the branches using long, hooked claws on the toes of their front and hind feet. There are two families of sloths – two-toed sloths have two toes on each front foot, while three-toed sloths have three toes. Both families have three toes on their hind feet. Sloths generally feed at night, moving slowly along branches high above the ground. They find leaves and other food by smell and touch. By day sloths usually hang, without moving, to avoid attracting enemies such as jaguars or eagles. Sloths live on their own and only meet to breed.

THREE-TOED SLOTH

## COLOUR CHANGE
Sloths often look green. This is because in hot, wet forest conditions, green algae (simple plants) grow in the sloth's fur. Their green colour helps to hide sloths from enemies.

## BRANCHING OUT
A three-toed sloth hangs from a branch with her single youngster. The young sloth grips its mother's belly fur with its tiny claws as she climbs, rests, or feeds. It will be carried by her until it is about six months old.

Three claws on hind foot grip branch firmly

TWO-TOED SLOTH

Long fur grows downwards

## FACT BOX

**Family:** Two-toed sloths: Megalonychidae; three-toed sloths: Bradypodidae

**Habitat:** Tropical rainforests

**Distribution:** Central and South America

**Food:** Leaves, twigs, buds, fruit

**Gestation period:** 180–350 days

**Lifespan:** 12 years

**Size:** 40–75 cm (15.7–29.5 in)

## TREE LIFE
Sloths are extremely well equipped to hang from branches. Their strong, curved claws lock so tightly onto branches that they will not fall off even if they fall asleep. Sloths rarely leave the trees, but do go down to the ground about once a week to expel waste. They move with difficulty on the forest floor, and soon return to their branches.

Two claws on front foot

Round, flattened face with small ears

### Find out more
MAMMALS 239
RAINFORESTS 62

Head can be turned to see all round while hanging upside-down

SCALE

## RAINFOREST TREES
Hot, humid, and wet all year round, the tropical forests of South America provide an ideal habitat for sloths. The vegetation is lush, and there are always plenty of leaves for the sloths to eat. Sloths hang from the branches of forest trees by their claws when resting or feeding. Remaining still most of the time means that sloths are not so easily spotted by their predators.

# SLUGS AND SNAILS

SLUGS AND SNAILS ARE SLOW-MOVING creatures with soft, slimy bodies. Snails have a hard shell to draw into if threatened. Most slugs have no shell and hide in damp places in the soil or among debris. Both types of animal belong to a large group called molluscs. The family also includes octopuses, clams, whelks, and limpets. Slugs and snails are found in damp places on land, and in freshwater ponds, lakes, and rivers, as well as in the oceans. Many sea slugs are very brightly coloured.

GARDEN SLUG

Slimy skin

## SLIDING ALONG

Slugs and snails get about with the help of their broad foot. Muscles in the foot move like waves to push the animal forward. Snails lay a trail of slime to help them glide along.

SCALE

Hard shell helps protect snail from birds and other enemies

## MOBILE HOME

Snails carry their "homes" on their backs. Their shells are hollow, coiling cones made mainly of chalk. In dry weather, snails hide in their shells and rest. When the snail is active, the head and muscular foot stick out of the shell. Most snails have two pairs of tentacles on their heads. Their eyes lie at the tips of the longer tentacles. The mouth contains a tongue called a radula, with tiny rows of teeth for rasping at food.

Snail's eyes are found at tips of rear tentacles

Tentacle

Short tentacle

COMMON SNAIL

### Find out more

MOLLUSCS 249
OCTOPUSES AND SQUID 255
PLANT EATERS 30

Snail's broad foot is used to help it crawl along

## FACT BOX

**Family:** Gastropods, part of the mollusc family

**No of species :** Over 72,000

**Habitat:** Land (from deserts to rainforests); fresh and salt water

**Distribution:** Worldwide except Arctic and Antarctic

**Food:** Plants, animals, fungus, algae

**Size:** Microscopic to 70 cm (27 in)

## A SNAIL'S PACE

Most land slugs and snails come out to feed at night or in wet weather. They spend the day hiding in dark, damp places to keep moist and avoid predators. In the winter land snails hibernate, hidden under stones or leaves.

## GARDEN FEEDER
Slugs are common in gardens where they feed on fungus, decaying matter, and plants (which is why gardeners consider them a pest). Slugs and snails need to live in damp places to keep their bodies moist. In fact, of the 72,000 species in the world, most are found in the seas and oceans.

# SNAKES

ALL SNAKES ARE LONG, THIN ANIMALS with no legs, scaly skins, and forked tongues for tasting and smelling the air. They are reptiles and are related to lizards, crocodiles, and turtles. There are 2,700 different kinds of snake, and they live all over the world, except in very cold places. This is because they need warmth to survive, so snakes are most common in deserts and rainforests. There are snakes small enough to fit into the palm of a hand, and snakes so big they can kill and eat crocodiles. They all eat meat and swallow their prey whole because their teeth cannot break up their food into small pieces. Despite people's fear of snakes, most of these creatures are not poisonous and pose no threat.

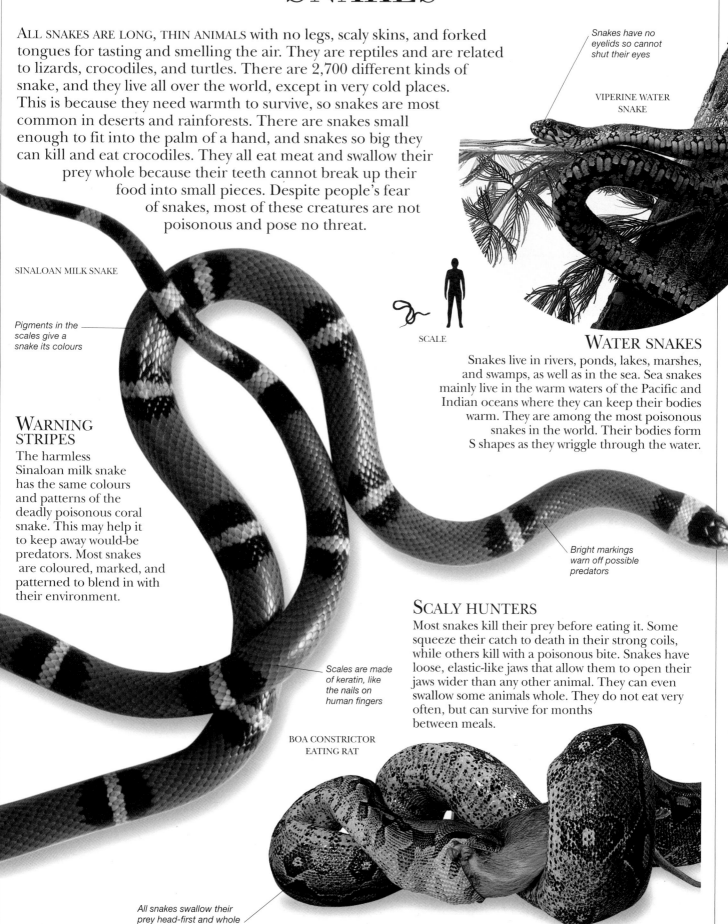

Snakes have no eyelids so cannot shut their eyes

VIPERINE WATER SNAKE

SINALOAN MILK SNAKE

Pigments in the scales give a snake its colours

SCALE

## WATER SNAKES

Snakes live in rivers, ponds, lakes, marshes, and swamps, as well as in the sea. Sea snakes mainly live in the warm waters of the Pacific and Indian oceans where they can keep their bodies warm. They are among the most poisonous snakes in the world. Their bodies form S shapes as they wriggle through the water.

## WARNING STRIPES

The harmless Sinaloan milk snake has the same colours and patterns of the deadly poisonous coral snake. This may help it to keep away would-be predators. Most snakes are coloured, marked, and patterned to blend in with their environment.

Bright markings warn off possible predators

## SCALY HUNTERS

Most snakes kill their prey before eating it. Some squeeze their catch to death in their strong coils, while others kill with a poisonous bite. Snakes have loose, elastic-like jaws that allow them to open their jaws wider than any other animal. They can even swallow some animals whole. They do not eat very often, but can survive for months between meals.

Scales are made of keratin, like the nails on human fingers

BOA CONSTRICTOR EATING RAT

All snakes swallow their prey head-first and whole

Egg is quite different to bird's egg – it is tough and leathery

Sharp egg tooth on snout helps baby break out

## TREE SLIDERS

Tree snakes have long, thin, flat bodies and pointed heads to help them slide through tree branches. Many of them also have long, thin tails that grip tightly around branches. A few tree snakes can even glide from tree to tree. They spread out their long ribs and curve the underside of their body to turn themselves into a sort of living parachute.

## HATCHING OUT

Most snakes lay eggs, usually in a safe, warm, moist place such as in the soil, under a rock or a log, or among rotting plants. Most do not look after their eggs or their young.

Green or brown camouflage colours keep tree snake well hidden among leaves and branches

### FACT BOX

**Family:** There are ten main families including Elapidae (cobras, mambas, coral snakes); Viperidae (rattlesnakes, adders, asps, and vipers); Boidae (boas and pythons)

**Habitat:** Very varied including deserts and rainforests; fresh water, swamps, marshes, oceans, mountains, and urban

**Distribution:** All continents except Antarctica; tropical seas

**Food:** Mammals, birds, eggs, fish, and many other animals

GREEN CAT SNAKE

## FAMILY LIFE

Male and female snakes do not live together, but do come together to mate. Male snakes find females by following their scent trails. Some male snakes will wrestle to see which is the strongest in order to mate with the female.

KING SNAKE

Mating snakes: females are usually larger than males

Short, thick body with short, thin tail

## DESERT MOVEMENT

The sidewinder rattlesnake has developed an unusual sideways, looping movement across loose sand. Many desert snakes travel in this way. It is called sidewinding and helps to stop the snake sinking down into the loose sand. Only a small part of the body touches the hot sand at any one time.

Body wriggles in a diagonal fashion, one section at a time

### Find out more

SIDEWINDER RATTLESNAKE

# SPIDERS

ALL SPIDERS ARE HUNTERS. These eight-legged mini-beasts paralyze or kill their victims by stabbing them with their poisoned jaws. The black widow spider's bite can even kill a person. Many spiders also build webs to catch their prey. The webs, woven with fine silk threads, are amazing structures. Spiders are sometimes confused with insects, but you can tell the difference by counting their legs. All insects have six legs, but spiders have eight. Spiders belong to a group of creatures called arachnids. This family also includes scorpions, ticks, and mites.

## WEIGHTY WEB

The beautiful round web some spiders weave is called an orb web. It looks delicate, but can hold 4,000 times the spider's own weight. Other spiders weave webs shaped like baskets, nets, or funnels. Many orb-web spiders weave a new web every night.

*Leg-like extensions called pedipalps help the spider to capture its prey*

RED-KNEED
TARANTULA

SCALE

*Spider's eggs are laid inside a silk cocoon*

BLACK
WIDOW

## WRAPPED UP

The black widow spins a protective silk cocoon to lay her eggs in. The cocoon is glued to a plant stem, where the female waits for the eggs to hatch. The baby spiders have nothing to eat except each other, until they are big enough to break out of the cocoon and build their own webs. So out of 100 babies, only 25 may survive.

*Hairs pick up vibrations caused by prey passing by*

*Body and limbs have no bones*

*Strong legs used to dig burrows*

## HAIRY SPIDERS

Spiders vary in size and shape. Some are small and slender. Others, such as tarantulas, are large, fat, and hairy. Tarantulas are the world's biggest spiders, and are found in North and South America. They hunt for mice, lizards, and small birds at night. Like other spiders they have pedipalps (limb-like organs) to cut up and crush their food. Unlike most other spiders, tarantulas do not spin webs, but instead live in burrows in dry soils mainly in deserts.

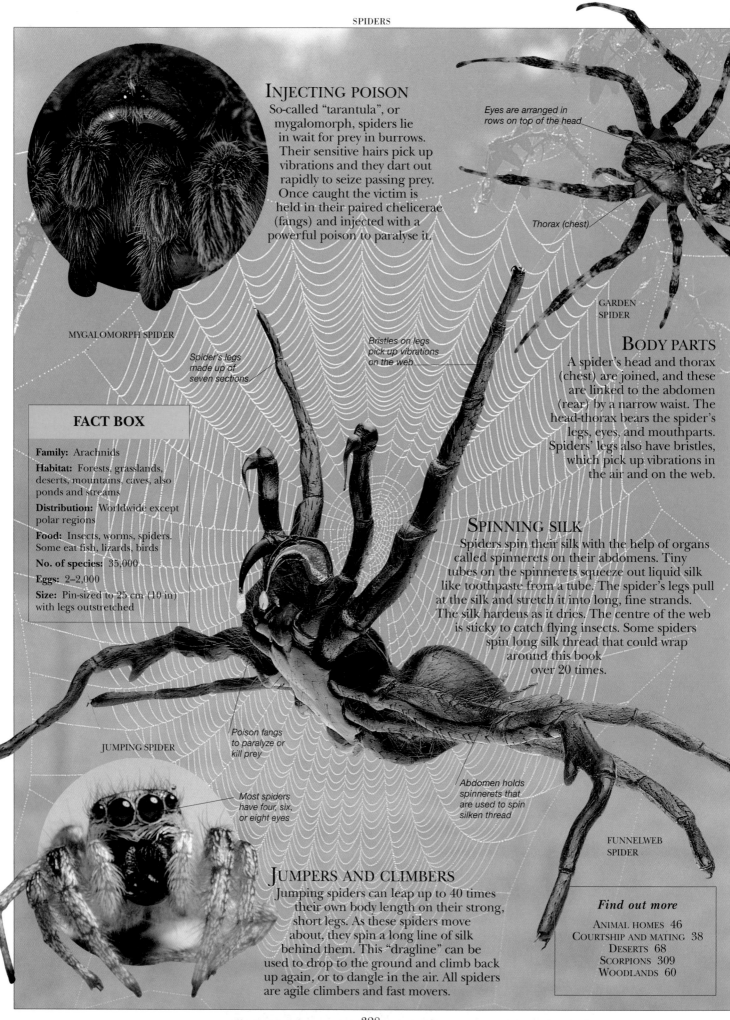

## INJECTING POISON

So-called "tarantula", or mygalomorph, spiders lie in wait for prey in burrows. Their sensitive hairs pick up vibrations and they dart out rapidly to seize passing prey. Once caught the victim is held in their paired chelicerae (fangs) and injected with a powerful poison to paralyse it.

*Eyes are arranged in rows on top of the head*

*Thorax (chest)*

GARDEN SPIDER

MYGALOMORPH SPIDER

*Spider's legs made up of seven sections*

*Bristles on legs pick up vibrations on the web*

## BODY PARTS

A spider's head and thorax (chest) are joined, and these are linked to the abdomen (rear) by a narrow waist. The head-thorax bears the spider's legs, eyes, and mouthparts. Spiders' legs also have bristles, which pick up vibrations in the air and on the web.

### FACT BOX

**Family:** Arachnids

**Habitat:** Forests, grasslands, deserts, mountains, caves, also ponds and streams

**Distribution:** Worldwide except polar regions

**Food:** Insects, worms, spiders. Some eat fish, lizards, birds

**No. of species:** 35,000

**Eggs:** 2–2,000

**Size:** Pin-sized to 25 cm (10 in) with legs outstretched

## SPINNING SILK

Spiders spin their silk with the help of organs called spinnerets on their abdomens. Tiny tubes on the spinnerets squeeze out liquid silk like toothpaste from a tube. The spider's legs pull at the silk and stretch it into long, fine strands. The silk hardens as it dries. The centre of the web is sticky to catch flying insects. Some spiders spin long silk thread that could wrap around this book over 20 times.

JUMPING SPIDER

*Poison fangs to paralyze or kill prey*

*Most spiders have four, six, or eight eyes*

*Abdomen holds spinnerets that are used to spin silken thread*

FUNNELWEB SPIDER

## JUMPERS AND CLIMBERS

Jumping spiders can leap up to 40 times their own body length on their strong, short legs. As these spiders move about, they spin a long line of silk behind them. This "dragline" can be used to drop to the ground and climb back up again, or to dangle in the air. All spiders are agile climbers and fast movers.

### Find out more

# SPONGES

THEY LOOK A LOT LIKE plants, but sponges are actually animals. In fact, they are the simplest many-celled animals on Earth. These creatures lived in ancient oceans 500 million years ago, and were among the first creatures to evolve on Earth. Many sponges have no obvious body parts – all parts of a sponge's body appear to be the same, and there is no "right way up". They spend their lives attached to rocks, posts, and other objects underwater. Some have vibrant colours ranging from red, pink, orange, and yellow, to green and white.

## HONEYCOMB STRUCTURE

The surface of a sponge is like a honeycomb with a network of fine pores (holes) called ostia. A larger opening called the osculum is found at the top of the sponge. Sponges feed by drawing in water, which contains their food of tiny plants and animals, through the fine holes. The food is filtered and absorbed, then waste and water passes out of the osculum.

*Fine pores*

SCALE

## SPONGY SHAPES

Sponges are found in all the world's oceans, even the icy Antarctic. Others live in freshwater lakes and rivers. They also come in many different shapes and sizes. Some are round, others are shaped like chimneys, or vases. Some sponges are tiny, but others grow so big a human diver could fit inside.

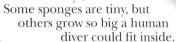

BROWN SPONGE

BARREL SPONGE

### FACT BOX

**Family:** Poriferae

**Habitat:** Salt and fresh water

**Distribution:** Oceans worldwide; inland lakes, rivers

**No. of species:** 5,000

**Food:** Tiny animals and plants (plankton)

**Lifespan:** Over 100 years (large species)

**Size:** 1–100 cm (0.4–39 in)

## SPONGE SKELETONS

The bodies of some sponges are stiffened by skeletons made up of tiny rod-like grains called spicules. Sponges are classified according to what the grains are made of – either calcite (limestone), glassy silica, a tough fibre called spongin, or a mix of all three.

*Small creatures can live inside holey structures*

*Sponge attached to rock on seabed*

### Find out more

INVERTEBRATES 215
OCEANS 74
ORGANS 22

# SQUIRRELS AND CHIPMUNKS

BRIGHT-EYED AND BUSHY-TAILED, squirrels are lively, fast-moving mammals. Like their rodent relatives, mice and hamsters, squirrels have sharp front teeth that they use to nibble nuts and seeds. There are two main groups of squirrels. Tree squirrels, such as the grey squirrel, are expert climbers and leap with ease from branch to branch. Ground squirrels, like the chipmunk, live in burrows. All squirrels have large eyes with good vision and sensitive whiskers.

CHIPMUNK

Coat marked with black stripes

CUTAWAY OF GREY SQUIRREL NEST

## FACT BOX

**Family:** Sciuridae

**Habitat:** Forest, woodland, grassland, scrub; also city parks

**Distribution:** Widespread; not in Australia, New Zealand, Madagascar, or southern South America

**Food:** Nuts, seeds, fruit, roots, flowers, buds, seeds, insects

**Lifespan:** 5–10 years

**Size:** Head and body 5–60 cm (2–24 in); tail 5–35 cm (2–13.8 in)

## LIFE ON THE GROUND

Chipmunks live on the ground, nesting in burrows under logs and rocks, and are often seen at picnic sites in North America. In autumn they store nuts and seeds in their burrow. This keeps them alive during the winter months when it is too cold to go out.

## INSIDE THE NEST

A squirrel's nest, called a drey, is made with twigs on the outside, and a cosy lining of grasses and leaves inside. The squirrel builds its football-sized drey in a fork in tree branches or inside a hollow in the tree's trunk. In winter, the squirrel sleeps in the drey at night and when the weather is very cold.

Bushy tail is twitched to send signals to other squirrels

Large ears help squirrel pick up the quietest sounds

GREY SQUIRREL

Sensitive whiskers on snout

SCALE

Food held between front paws

Long tail aids balance when squirrel jumps and climbs

## LOOKING OUT FOR FOOD

In the trees, squirrels run and jump skilfully, gripping the branches with their sharp claws. On the ground they move with small leaps, always on the lookout for food or danger. When they find some food, they sit down, hold it in their front paws, and gnaw it with their front teeth. At night, they wrap their bushy tail around them to keep themselves warm.

# STARFISH AND SEA URCHINS

ALL STARFISH AND THEIR RELATIVES (brittle stars, sea urchins, sea cucumbers, sea lilies, and feather stars) live in the sea, mostly on the seabed and in coral reefs. Some burrow into sand or mud, and some sea urchins can even bore into rocks to hide from predators. All are built like a bicycle wheel, with equal spokes radiating from a central disc. This is very different from most animals, which have a distinct head and tail at either end of their body. Starfish have huge numbers of tiny, very mobile tube feet, tipped with suckers, for feeding and walking.

STARFISH

SAND DOLLAR SKELETON

## SHAPED LIKE A STAR

Most starfish have five arms, which spread out like a drawing of a star, giving these creatures their name. Not all starfish have just five arms – some North American species have as many as 50. Starfish have neither a head nor brain, nor do they have a "back" or "front".

SCARLET SERPENT BRITTLE STAR

Flexible arms move like a snake

SCALE

Central disk contains mouth and jaw

## SAND BURROWERS

Sand dollars burrow down into sand, helped by their tiny spines. Their skeletons are made up of tiny mineral particles fused together to form a tough, rigid shell.

### FACT BOX

**Phylum:** Echinodermata, which includes sea cucumbers, brittle stars, sand dollars, and sea lilies

**Habitat:** Seabeds, seashores, coral reefs

**Distribution:** Worldwide, but mostly tropical seas

**Food:** Seaweeds, worms, shellfish, other starfish, tiny food particles filtered out of water

**Size:** 4 mm (0.16 in) long (sea cucumber) to 138 cm (54 in) across (starfish)

Very fragile jointed arms used for moving and catching food

## BRITTLE STARS

Brittle stars have very long, slender, and bendy arms. This helps them escape from predators. However, as their name suggests, their arms are also brittle and can break off easily. The central disc is small compared to the length of the arms, and flatter than the bigger discs of starfish.

Wave arms to move fast

Spines used for food gathering and movement

## LIVE SEA URCHIN

Many sea urchins move slowly across rocks on their tube-feet. They graze on tiny seaweeds or animals that live on the rock's surface. Other sea urchins burrow through sand or mud, feeding on small particles of plant and animal matter. Tiny spines covering the sea urchin's surface are used for defence.

Arms can be shed on purpose to avoid being seized in an attack

### Find out more

CORALS 145
INVERTEBRATES 215
OCEANS 74
SKELETONS 18

SEA URCHIN

# STICK INSECTS

STICK INSECTS ARE EXPERT AT CAMOUFLAGE (natural disguise). The colours, shapes, and patterns on their bodies allow them to blend in so well with their background that predators cannot see them. Stick insects can slowly change their body colour to match their surroundings exactly. Even their eggs are disguised to look like seeds. Some stick insects have warts and spines that look like the buds and prickles on twigs. Others resemble leaves and bark. By day, they hide motionless among the vegetation. At night, they move about to feed on leaves.

Thin brown body looks like a small twig

STICK INSECT

## LIVING STICKS

Stick insects are usually brown or green, with long, slender bodies, very thin, jointed legs, and long antennae. The males of many species have wings, but the females are often wingless.

Brown spots mimic a nibbled leaf

## LICHEN-LIKE

Some stick insects can mimic the look of lichen – which is not a plant but a combination of a fungus and algae. Should such a disguise not fool a predator, young stick insects, known as nymphs, have another safety feature – they can regrow an arm or a leg if it is bitten off.

Flattened body looks like dry leaf

SCALE

LEAF INSECT

## FACT BOX

**Family:** Phyllidae

**Habitat:** Woodlands and forests in warm countries

**Distribution:** Worldwide except Antarctic

**No. of species:** Over 2,000

**Food:** Leaves

**Eggs:** Often disguised as seeds

**Size:** 2.5–48 cm (1–19 in)

## MASTERS OF DISGUISE

Leaf insects have flattened bodies and look just like leaves. These insects complete their disguise by walking with a swaying motion, like a leaf caught in the breeze. There are other species that resemble fierce ants or scorpions.

Flap on insect's leg adds to leafy disguise

### Find out more

CAMOUFLAGE 36
INSECTS 212

# SWALLOWS

SLIM, STREAMLINED SWALLOWS ARE SMALL birds that spend most of their lives in the air. They have long, pointed wings and forked tails, which help them to fly with superb skill, twisting and turning to snap up fast-flying insects in mid-air. They catch their prey in their bills. Although very short and flattened from top to bottom, their bills have a wide gape to trap the insects. Some swallows build nests in trees, while others occupy old barns, garden sheds, or even the top of a garden tool. Many species make long migrations – the swallows of northern Europe fly over 11,000 km (6,000 miles) to their African wintering grounds.

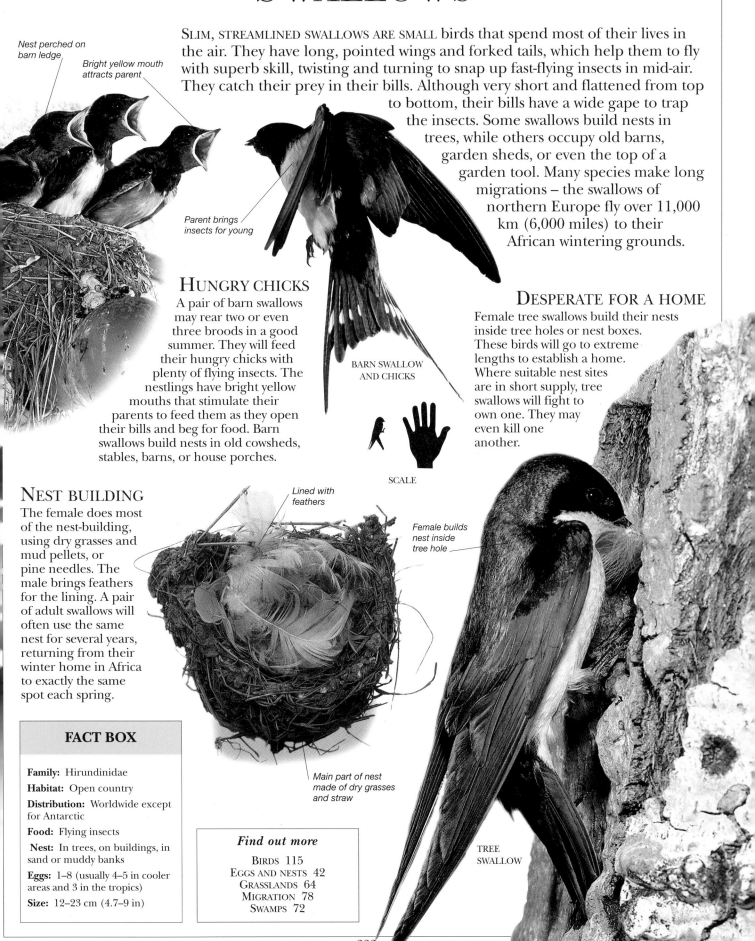

*Nest perched on barn ledge*

*Bright yellow mouth attracts parent*

*Parent brings insects for young*

BARN SWALLOW AND CHICKS

SCALE

## HUNGRY CHICKS

A pair of barn swallows may rear two or even three broods in a good summer. They will feed their hungry chicks with plenty of flying insects. The nestlings have bright yellow mouths that stimulate their parents to feed them as they open their bills and beg for food. Barn swallows build nests in old cowsheds, stables, barns, or house porches.

## DESPERATE FOR A HOME

Female tree swallows build their nests inside tree holes or nest boxes. These birds will go to extreme lengths to establish a home. Where suitable nest sites are in short supply, tree swallows will fight to own one. They may even kill one another.

## NEST BUILDING

The female does most of the nest-building, using dry grasses and mud pellets, or pine needles. The male brings feathers for the lining. A pair of adult swallows will often use the same nest for several years, returning from their winter home in Africa to exactly the same spot each spring.

*Lined with feathers*

*Female builds nest inside tree hole*

*Main part of nest made of dry grasses and straw*

TREE SWALLOW

### FACT BOX

**Family:** Hirundinidae

**Habitat:** Open country

**Distribution:** Worldwide except for Antarctic

**Food:** Flying insects

**Nest:** In trees, on buildings, in sand or muddy banks

**Eggs:** 1–8 (usually 4–5 in cooler areas and 3 in the tropics)

**Size:** 12–23 cm (4.7–9 in)

### *Find out more*

BIRDS 115
EGGS AND NESTS 42
GRASSLANDS 64
MIGRATION 78
SWAMPS 72

# SWANS

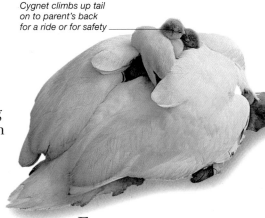

*Cygnet climbs up tail on to parent's back for a ride or for safety*

IDENTIFIED BY THEIR VERY LONG, graceful necks, swans are elegant birds in water and in flight. The largest of all waterfowl (a family that includes geese and ducks), they are also among the heaviest of all flying birds. Mute swans, for instance, can weigh up to 18 kg (40 lb) and to take off, they must patter along the surface of open water, or land, for a long distance, flapping their wings, to get their heavy bodies airborne. Swans in the northern hemisphere have all-white plumage, while the two South American species are white with small amounts of black. The Australian black swan is entirely black.

CYGNET

*Soft, greyish down feathers damp at first from liquid inside egg*

## FREE RIDE FOR YOUNG

Parent swans sometimes let their cygnets (young swans) climb onto their backs and enjoy a ride or fall asleep. The cygnets are nestled safely, warm and dry, among the adult's feathers. Swans pair for life and make devoted parents. They guard their nests, eggs, and young fiercely against foxes, pike, and other predators.

## EGG AND YOUNG

Swans' eggs are among the largest laid by any birds. The baby swans, which hatch from the eggs after about a month, are known as cygnets. They are duller than their parents – those of the white swans are brownish-grey.

SCALE

*Mobile, muscular neck has more bones than any other animal*

### FACT BOX

**Family:** Anatidae, which includes swans, geese, and ducks

**Habitat:** Lakes, reservoirs, rivers

**Distribution:** Fresh waters, mainly in northern hemisphere

**Food:** Mainly leaves, stems, and roots of submerged plants

**Nest:** Huge, often floating pile of sedges or rushes

**Eggs:** 1–14, usually 4–7, white, pale or cream

**Size:** 90–180 cm (35–72 in)

*Hard area for tearing off tough water plants and grubbing up roots*

MUTE SWAN

## MUTE BY NAME

Many swans make loud, trumpeting calls, but mute swans are well-named because they are mostly silent. However, they will hiss or grunt if threatened, and when in flight, their powerful wings make a loud throbbing sound. As with other swans, their long necks help them to reach down to the bottom of lakes and rivers to pull up plant food. Swans will often "up-end", submerging their head, neck, and most of their body to get at food.

*Sturdy, webbed feet allow swan to paddle very well*

### Find out more

## GRACEFUL WATER DWELLER

Swans live and feed mainly in fresh waters. Their long necks allow them to reach deep below the surface. Under water they can bite off stems or roots of water plants anchored on the lake or river bed. Swans are waterfowl, as are ducks and geese, and these aquatic birds can also graze on grass and other plants on land. However, on land they tend to be more clumsy.

# TAPIRS

TAPIRS ARE PLANT-EATING MAMMALS that live in forests near rivers and swamps. These shy, solitary creatures only come out at night to sniff their way through the forest and pull plants into their mouth. Tapirs are related to rhinoceroses and, like their bulkier relatives, they are good swimmers and divers, and spend a lot of time in the water. They can even stay underwater for several minutes if they need to hide from danger. Tapirs are not so bashful when seeking a mate, as they meet up every so often for a noisy courtship display.

*75 571 2*

Strong pulling
front teeth

*♀ 75 571*

Sharp grinding
back teeth

## TAPIR TEETH

Tapirs have long jaws with rows of well-developed molar teeth at the back. These teeth have sharp cutting ridges along the top to help the tapir grind and crush its tough plant food. At the front of the jaw are long incisor and canine teeth for pulling plants and fruit.

### FACT BOX

**Family:** Tapiridae

**Habitat:** Forests

**Distribution:** South and Central America, Southeast Asia

**Food:** Grasses, water plants, leaves, buds, soft twigs, and fruit

**Gestation period:** 14 months

**Lifespan:** 30 years

**Size:** 1.8–2.5 m (6–8 ft) long

## FUR COATS

The Andean tapir lives in the Andes mountains of South America. It has a thick fur coat to protect it from the cold. Other tapirs live in warmer places and have much thinner coats. The fur on all baby tapirs is spotted and striped for the first six months.

SCALE

MALAYAN TAPIR

### Find out more

Hoof has
three toes

Compact body for
pushing through
dense undergrowth

## BLACK AND WHITE

The Malayan tapir lives in the dense rainforest of Southeast Asia – the only tapir species not in South America. It looks as if it is wearing a white saddle. In fact the black-and-white patches help to break up the outline of its body, so enemies cannot see it very easily in the forest at night.

# TERMITES

MOST INSECTS LEAD SOLITARY LIVES, but termites are different. Along with wasps, bees, and ants, termites are one of the few kinds of insects that live together in groups. Termites are also expert builders. Their colonies (nests) are often large mounds with chimneys that tower high above the ground. Inside the colony, the different castes (kinds) of termites are well organised and have various jobs to do. Each nest contains a queen and king and their young, who are soldiers and workers.

QUEEN WITH WORKERS

SCALE

SOLDIER TERMITE

## QUEEN OF THE NEST

The queen is the only female in the nest who can lay eggs. She does so every few seconds for much of her life (up to 15 years). The queen's abdomen swells with eggs until she looks like a small sausage. She remains in a special chamber in the nest, joined by the king, who fertilises all the eggs. The queen is fed continuously by the many workers of her nest.

TERMITE NEST

Termite mound up to 6 m (15 ft) tall

Chimney allows warm air to escape to keep the nest cool

Network of passages lead between chambers

Ground level

"Fungus garden"

Nursery containing eggs

Royal chamber, the largest cell, holds the king and queen

## TERMITE MOUND

Inside a termite mound, a maze of tunnels lead to different chambers that hold the queen, eggs, and larvae (young termites). Some termites feed on fungus growing on piles of shredded leaves brought back to the nest. This food supply is kept in separate chambers called "fungus gardens".

Armoured head

Strong jaws

### FACT BOX

**Family:** Isoptera

**Habitat:** Tropical and temperate areas

**Distribution:** Worldwide except Antarctic

**Food:** Wood, plants, fungus

**Eggs:** Queen lays up to 30,000 eggs per day

**Size:** Workers: up to 5 mm (0.2 in); queen: up to 15 cm (6 in)

## GUARDS

Larger, fierce termites, called soldiers, guard the covered trails along which food is carried by the workers, into the nest. Soldier termites have armoured heads and strong jaws, and some squirt poisonous chemicals at their enemies through their long snouts. Both soldiers and workers feed only on plant material.

## TERMITE TOWERS
Termites build spectacular homes for themselves. Some make round nests in trees, but many nest underground. In hot countries, termites build tall chimneys over their nests that tower up to 5 m (16 ft) into the air. These shafts allow air to circulate inside the nest, to keep the temperature even, and are made of earth mixed with saliva.

# TIGERS

TIGER
WITH DEAD
ANTELOPE

THE BIGGEST AND STRONGEST CATS in the world are tigers. The largest is the Siberian tiger, which can be over 3 m (10 ft) in length, and weigh as much as three people. A tiger's size and strength help it to catch large prey, such as deer and cattle. One tiger was observed by naturalists dragging a wild ox some distance, which 13 men could not move at all. The stripes on the tiger's coat provide brilliant camouflage against dappled light and shade. So a tiger can creep really close to its prey before seizing it with its sharp claws and teeth.

BENGAL TIGER

TIGER CUB

## TOP HUNTER

Silence and stealth when ambushing prey are the tiger's main hunting skills. It will kill its prey either by biting the back of the victim's neck to cut through the spine, or biting the throat to suffocate the animal. If a kill is made in the open, a tiger usually drags its prey into thick cover to feed.

*Superb night-time vision*

*Whiskers act like sensors to help tiger feel its way in the dark*

## CARING FOR THE CUBS

The cubs feed on their mother's milk until they are about six months old. They do not open their eyes until they are one or two weeks old. If in danger, their mother carries them in her mouth to a safe place.

SCALE

## SHARP SENSES

Tigers rely on sight and hearing to hunt. They do this at night and can see about six times better than humans in dim light. Their eyes glow in the dark because they reflect any light that shines on them. Touch-sensitive whiskers also help them find their way in the dark.

*Sharp pointed teeth*

## DEADLY TEETH

Huge, pointed canine teeth seize the tiger's prey and deliver the killing bite. The sharp cheek teeth help to slice up its food. The rough tongue enables a tiger to lick nearly all the meat until only skin and bones remain.

## FOREST STALKER

Tigers live in hot grasslands, forests, swamps, and jungles mainly in India and Indonesia. In these habitats the black stripes on a tiger's coat break up the outline of its body, making it camouflaged as it hunts for prey. Tigers also survive in Siberia where they dwell in cold, snowy places.

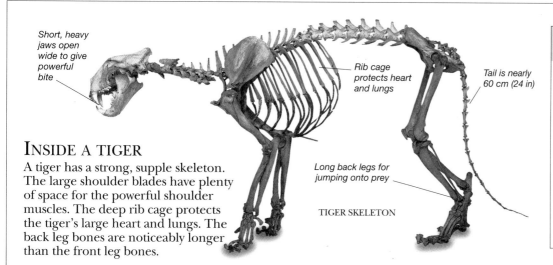

*Short, heavy jaws open wide to give powerful bite*

*Rib cage protects heart and lungs*

*Tail is nearly 60 cm (24 in)*

*Long back legs for jumping onto prey*

TIGER SKELETON

## INSIDE A TIGER

A tiger has a strong, supple skeleton. The large shoulder blades have plenty of space for the powerful shoulder muscles. The deep rib cage protects the tiger's large heart and lungs. The back leg bones are noticeably longer than the front leg bones.

### FACT BOX

**Family** Felidae

**Habitat:** Most types of forest, grasslands, mangrove swamps

**Distribution:** India, Siberia, Manchuria, China, Sumatra, Java, Malaysia. Numbers limited to 6,000 in the wild

**Food:** Deer, pigs, cattle, antelope; some smaller mammals and birds

**Lifespan:** 15–25 years

**Size:** 1.4–3.5 m (4.5–11.5 ft)

## WHITER FUR

There are eight subspecies of tiger, and they have a variety of markings and shadings, depending on their local habitat. The stripes, sometimes pale, are always there. A rare cat, found now almost only in zoos, is the white tiger of north India. It is named after the chalky white coat, which has stripes that are darker than usual.

*Chalk-coloured fur*

*Very dark stripes*

WHITE TIGER

## SPECIAL SNIFF

Male tigers sometimes lift their top lip and pull a strange face. This is called the flehmen reaction. It may help them to sniff a female's scent up into a special structure next to the nose, which tells them if the female is ready to mate.

MALE TIGER

*Scent organ next to nose*

### Find out more

CAMOUFLAGE 36
CATS 128
CHEETAHS 136
JAGUARS 217
LEOPARDS 227

BENGAL TIGERS

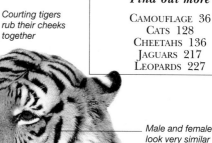

*Courting tigers rub their cheeks together*

*Male and female look very similar*

## COURTSHIP

Male tigers find females by the roars and scent marks they make. Two male tigers may sometimes fight a fierce battle over a female tiger, called a tigress. The male that wins the fight rubs his body against hers before mating. A pair of tigers may mate as many as a hundred times over a period of two days.

# TORTOISES AND TURTLES

THE ONLY REPTILES WITH TOUGH BONY shells as part of their skeletons are tortoises, turtles, and terrapins. There are over 250 different kinds. Tortoises usually live on land, while turtles live in the sea, and terrapins live in fresh water. Many tortoises and turtles can pull their heads and legs inside their shells, making it difficult for predators to eat them. Most pull their heads straight back, but side-necked turtles bend their necks sideways. Tortoises and turtles use their sharp jaws to tear up their food because they do not have teeth.

RED-EARED
TERRAPIN

### TERRAPINS

Like turtles, terrapins have a flat shell to give them a streamlined shape. This makes swimming through water easier. Terrapins live in fresh water ponds, lakes, rivers, and swamps and spend some time on land.

### FRESH WATER TURTLES

Most turtles living in fresh, not salty, water have webbed feet and light, flat shells to make swimming easier. They can stay underwater for a long time – some hibernate underwater for weeks. Turtles can breathe through the skin, the lining of the throat, and an opening at the back of the body, as well as through their lungs.

Layer of plates that cover shell made of a horn-like substance called keratin

RED-LEGGED
TORTOISE

SCALE

### TORTOISES

Tortoises live on land and have high, domed, or knobbly shells to protect them from predators, and perhaps to provide room for larger lungs. They have strong, thick legs to support the weight of the shell, like pillars holding up a large building.

SNAPPING
TURTLE

Neck stretches up to breathe air above surface of the water

Well camouflaged for lying in wait for prey underwater

Flattened shell for easier swimming

Strong legs with long claws to grip mud or rocks at the bottom of the water

YOUNG
HATCHING

## FACT BOX

**Family:** 13 families include Chelydridae (snapping turtles), Cheloniidae (sea turtles), Emydidae (pond and river turtles), Testudinidae (tortoises), Chelidae (Austro-American side-necked turtles)

**Habitat:** Tortoises usually live on land; turtles in the sea. Terrapins live in freshwater and on land

**Distribution:** All temperate and tropical land and oceans

**Food:** Plants, worms, shellfish; sea turtles eat fish, sponges, seaweed, and crabs

*Egg tooth drops off soon after hatching*

## SEA TURTLES

The seven kinds of sea turtle spend their lives wandering the tropical oceans of the world. Some of them, such as this green turtle, migrate long distances between feeding areas and the beaches where they lay their eggs. Most sea turtles have hard, bony shells like tortoises but leatherback turtles have tiny bony plates under a leathery skin.

GREEN TURTLE

## HATCHING OUT

Tortoises and turtles all lay eggs. The eggshells of tortoises and some turtles are hard, but those of sea turtles and some river turtles are soft. Females usually bury their eggs in a hole they dig in the sand or the soil. The young use a special sharp tooth on its snout to break through the egg.

*Star-like patterns and knobs*

## KNOBBLY SHELL

As its name suggests, the starred tortoise has star-like patterns on its shell. Like all turtles and tortoises, it has a two-part shell which covers its body like a suit of armour. The shell is made of bony plates that are fused to the tortoise's ribs and spine. The top part of the shell is called the carapace and the bottom part is the plastron.

*Back flippers used for steering when swimming*

*Powerful legs to support weight of shell*

STARRED TORTOISE

### Find out more

DEFENCE 34
FRESH WATER 70
ISLANDS 76
REPTILES 297

## DESERT TORTOISES KEEPING COOL

Desert tortoises lie in the shade or rest in burrows during the hottest part of the day. They come out in the early morning and late afternoon when it is cooler. During the hottest months they may go into a deep sleep.

*High domed shell makes it hard for an enemy to crush in its jaws or to swallow*

DESERT
TORTOISES

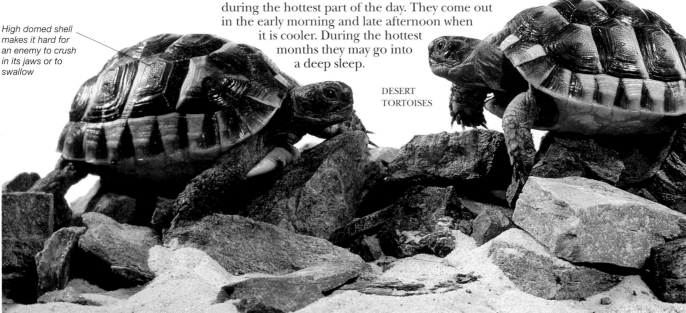

# TOUCANS

CHESTNUT EARED
ARACARI

TOUCANS ARE AMONG THE MOST unusual looking of all birds. Their giant bills are as long as the bird's body. Although the bill makes the bird look top-heavy, it is largely hollow and lightweight. It is strengthened on the inside by a network of slender struts of bone. Even so, toucans' bills are fragile and sometimes break. When roosting, it will turn its head backwards and rest its large bill on its back. Toucans live high up in the top branches of tropical rainforests.

RED-BILLED
TOUCAN

*Males often have longer and more colourful bills than females*

## TIGHT GRIP

Spending their lives in trees, toucans need to keep a strong grip on branches as they perch and move about. They have powerful feet with two toes pointing forwards and two backwards, unlike the usual three facing forwards, one facing backwards of most perching birds.

*Bill of each species has different colours and patterns to help the birds recognize one another*

## TOUCAN PLAY

One toucan may pluck a fruit in its huge bill, then toss it high in the air for a neighbour to catch. Toucans also bill-wrestle – two birds will start striking their bills together, and then clasp each other's bill. They then start pushing until one almost falls off the perch and gives up.

### FACT BOX

**Family:** Ramphastidae

**Habitat:** Tropical forests

**Distribution:** Mexico, Central and South America

**Food:** Mainly fruit, also seeds, insects, small birds and reptiles and their eggs and young

**Nest:** Tree hole, with lining of wood chips and seeds

**Eggs:** 24, white

**Size:** 33–66 cm (13–26 in) including the bill

*After grabbing food, toucan tosses its head upwards to swallow it*

*The bill has toothed edges to give it a firm grip on the food*

*Toe placement (also found on woodpeckers) ensures really strong grip*

*Sharp saw-like edges can cut through fruit*

SCALE

## PERFECT PRUNING

Like long-handled pruning tools used in orchards, the massive bill of a toucan is perfect for collecting hard-to-reach fruit. It allows the toucan to pluck fruit (or seeds) from the outermost twigs of a tree that are too slender to bear the weight of the bird's plump body.

### Find out more

BIRDS 115
RAINFORESTS 62

# VERTEBRATES

AFRICAN
WHITE-BACKED
VULTURE

ANIMALS THAT HAVE A BACKBONE are called vertebrates. This column of bones not only supports the body, it also contains and protects a spinal nerve cord. The back is made up of many separate bones, called vertebrae, which is where the name vertebrate comes from. The backbone is part of the internal skeleton. Most vertebrates have two pairs of limbs. In fish these take the form of fins, while in other vertebrates they have become legs and arms, flippers, or wings. Some vertebrates, such as snakes, have no external limbs. Along with snakes, backboned animals include very familiar creatures such as fish, frogs, birds, dogs, and humans.

## BIRDS OF A FEATHER

Fossils show that birds were once flightless reptiles, probably dinosaurs. Like reptiles, birds have scales, but apart from those on their legs and feet, the scales have evolved into feathers. No other group of animals has these lightweight structures. Feathers help make birds the greatest of all flyers. Although some birds, such as the ostrich and penguins, have lost their power of flight, they manage well without it. Like mammals, birds are warm-blooded.

HUMAN SKELETON

## ANIMALS WITH BACKBONES

All vertebrates have a skeleton – a framework, usually of bones, inside their bodies. The bones in many joints are covered with flexible cartilage and attached to muscles, for movement. The skeleton consists of three main parts: skull, backbone, and limbs. In most vertebrates, the backbone extends to the end of the tail. A vertebrate skeleton grows as the animal grows, unlike the external skeleton of an insect.

*Backbone with row of vertebrae gives main support to skeleton*

*Humans and other apes do not have a tail*

*Flexible internal skeleton supports the body and gives it shape*

*Most mammals walk on upright legs*

### FACT BOX

**Family:** Includes cartilaginous fish (Chondrichthyes), such as sharks; bony fish (Osteichthyes), such as salmon; amphibians (Amphibia) such as toads, frogs, and newts; reptiles (Reptilia) including crocodiles, lizards, and tortoises; birds (Aves) such as penguins and eagles; mammals (Mammalia) including humans, rodents, cats, whales, and seals

**Habitat:** From underground streams to mountain tops, and deserts to the ocean depths

**Distribution:** Worldwide

**Food:** Huge range of both plants and animals, including other vertebrates

LION

*Body covered in fur*

## MAMMALS

Mammals share three major features. Females suckle (feed) their young on milk produced by their mammary glands. They are "warm-blooded", producing their own heat within their bodies. Finally, almost all have hair (or fur) which helps keep them warm and may serve as a waterproof coat.

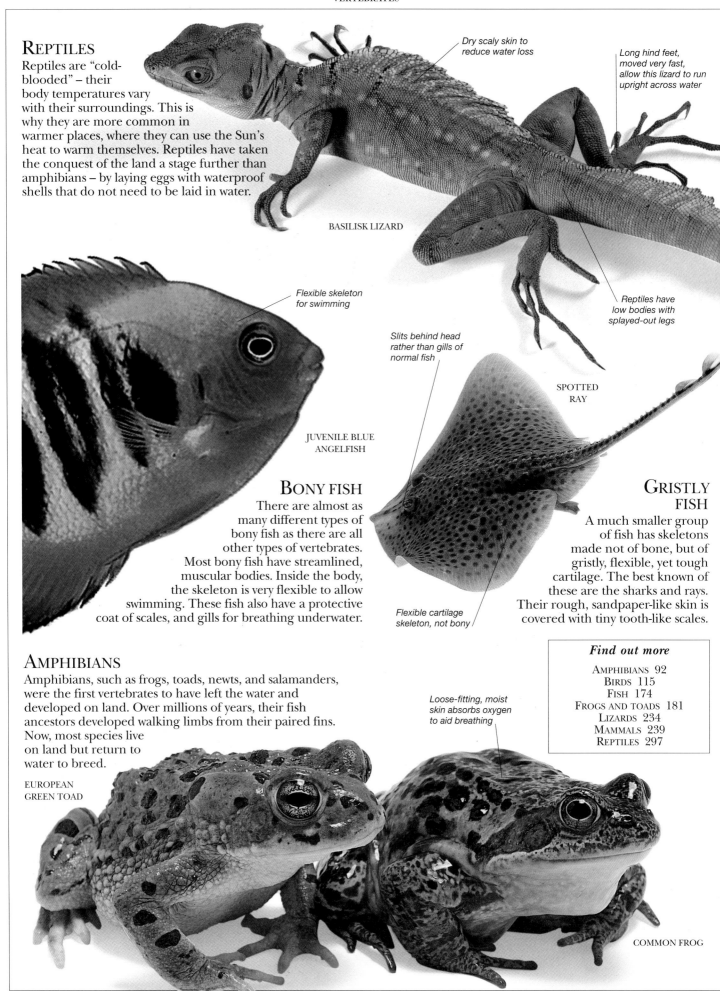

# REPTILES

Reptiles are "cold-blooded" – their body temperatures vary with their surroundings. This is why they are more common in warmer places, where they can use the Sun's heat to warm themselves. Reptiles have taken the conquest of the land a stage further than amphibians – by laying eggs with waterproof shells that do not need to be laid in water.

*Dry scaly skin to reduce water loss*

*Long hind feet, moved very fast, allow this lizard to run upright across water*

BASILISK LIZARD

*Reptiles have low bodies with splayed-out legs*

*Flexible skeleton for swimming*

*Slits behind head rather than gills of normal fish*

SPOTTED RAY

JUVENILE BLUE ANGELFISH

# BONY FISH

There are almost as many different types of bony fish as there are all other types of vertebrates. Most bony fish have streamlined, muscular bodies. Inside the body, the skeleton is very flexible to allow swimming. These fish also have a protective coat of scales, and gills for breathing underwater.

*Flexible cartilage skeleton, not bony*

# GRISTLY FISH

A much smaller group of fish has skeletons made not of bone, but of gristly, flexible, yet tough cartilage. The best known of these are the sharks and rays. Their rough, sandpaper-like skin is covered with tiny tooth-like scales.

# AMPHIBIANS

Amphibians, such as frogs, toads, newts, and salamanders, were the first vertebrates to have left the water and developed on land. Over millions of years, their fish ancestors developed walking limbs from their paired fins. Now, most species live on land but return to water to breed.

*Loose-fitting, moist skin absorbs oxygen to aid breathing*

EUROPEAN GREEN TOAD

COMMON FROG

> ### *Find out more*
> AMPHIBIANS 92
> BIRDS 115
> FISH 174
> FROGS AND TOADS 181
> LIZARDS 234
> MAMMALS 239
> REPTILES 297

# VULTURES

USING THEIR LONG, BROAD WINGS, vultures soar high in the sky, for hours on end, in search of animal corpses on the ground far below. They are birds of prey, but are unusual because they eat little else but carrion – the flesh of animals that are already dead. Generally, birds of prey are superb hunters who seize their prey live with their feet. Vultures, however, do not have the powerful feet and sharp claws needed to do this. Instead, they glide on the warm air currents or perch on trees to look out for carrion below. Some vultures rely on their sharp sense of smell to locate dead or decaying animals.

WHITE-BACKED VULTURE

*Broad, squarish wing*

*Large wing span to aid soaring*

TURKEY VULTURE

*Bald head keeps bird from getting matted with blood as it feeds*

## DEAD ANIMAL DIET
The vulture's strongly hooked, sharp-edged bill is perfect for ripping through the tough skin of carrion (dead animals) or for slicing up flesh. These birds of prey also have very rough tongues for scraping the flesh from bones. The African white-backed vulture sticks its head and neck inside a carcass to gobble up everything.

### FACT BOX

**Family:** New World vultures: Cathartidae; includes condors; Old World vultures: Accipitridae

**Habitat:** Grasslands, farmland, deserts, mountains, forests

**Distribution:** Worldwide in warm climates except Australasia

**Food:** Mainly dead animals

**Nest:** Ledges, caves, trees

**Eggs:** 1–3, mostly white, pale green, or pale brown

**Size:** 56–150 cm (22–59 in)

## CARCASS PARTS
Vultures often crowd around the same carcass, squabbling noisily as they fight for scraps. Smaller, weaker-billed vultures have to wait for the larger vultures with the strongest bills to arrive and break the carrion's skin before they can feed. Different vulture species also feed on different parts of the carcass – so a large flock of vultures can strip every shred of flesh from the body of a horse or an elephant, in an amazingly short time.

*Strong hooked beak*

*Talons (claws) not as sharp as in other birds of prey*

## TOOL USER
The Egyptian vulture is one of the very few animals known to use a tool. It seizes a stone in its bill and drops it onto an ostrich egg to break the shell and get at the food inside.

EGYPTIAN VULTURE

SCALE

*Beak can grip stone securely to help bird break open eggshell*

### Find out more

BIRDS 115
EAGLES 167

## WAITING FOR WARMTH

Vultures need undisturbed cliffs or trees for nesting and rearing their young. They also spend a good deal of time roosting at night on rocks or branches. During the morning, they rest there while they wait for the Sun to warm up the ground. Once conditions are right, they soar off on the currents of air that rise from the warm ground and go in search of food. Food for vultures is the flesh of dead animals.

# WADING BIRDS

A VARIETY OF BIRDS FROM different families spend their lives wading in shallow waters and along shores. They are wading in search of a rich supply of food containing huge numbers of small animals such as snails, worms, and shrimps. All wading birds have long, slender legs for walking into the water, long necks for reaching down to feed, and long bills for seizing prey. True waders (called shorebirds in North America), include sandpipers, which feed mainly by probing with their bills into the mud and pulling out their prey.

RED-CROWNED CRANES
IN COURTSHIP DANCE

## UP-TURNED BILL

The avocet is a graceful wader with a unique up-curved bill. It sweeps this precision tool from side to side in shallow muddy water. An avocet filters prey, such as tiny shrimps and insect larvae, out of the water using a complex series of "teeth" inside the bill.

PIED AVOCET

## DANCING CRANES

The long-legged, long-necked cranes perform amazing dances to attract mates and to communicate with one another during their courtship ceremonies. They leap in the air and display their wings to attract a mate. Male and female cranes have similar plumage, and partners stay together all their lives.

## DEADLY STALKER

Herons, including egrets, hunt mainly alone. The bird will stand still and rigid, or walk in slow-motion through the shallows until it spots a fish or frog. Then suddenly it darts out its head – the neck straightening out from its usual S-shape, like a powerful spring. The heron seizes the victim with a long, dagger-like bill.

### FACT BOX

**Family:** Herons: Ardeidae; Cranes: Gruidae; Avocets and stilts: Recurvirostridae; Sandpipers and snipes: Scolopacidae

**Habitat:** Shores and shallow fresh and marine waters

**Distribution:** Worldwide

**Food:** Snails, insects, fish, frogs, crustaceans, small mammals

**Size:** Up to 176 cm (69 in) in height (sarus, whooping cranes)

### *Find out more*

GREAT EGRET

# WALRUSES

IT IS HARD TO MISTAKE a walrus, with its wrinkly skin, droopy moustache, and big tusks. A close relative of the seals, it is well suited to life in the extreme cold of the northern seas. An excellent swimmer and diver, a walrus is capable of descending down to 80 m (260 ft), and can stay underwater for over ten minutes when searching for food on the seabed. Here, it roots about with its tough, mobile snout in the mud or gravel, like a giant pig. The walrus breeds only every two to three years. The single baby is born on the bare ice, and is fed on milk and protected by its mother for up to two years.

## FACT BOX

**Family:** Odobenidae

**Habitat:** Sea and ice; also found on beaches and rocky islands

**Distribution:** Throughout coastal waters of the far north

**Food:** Shellfish, crabs, and sea urchins. Thousands of small clams eaten in one meal

**Lifespan:** More than 40 years

**Size:** 2.7–3.6 m (9–12 ft) long

*Tusk can grow as much as 1 m (3 ft) or more, and weigh over 5 kg (11 lb)*

## WALRUS TUSK

The two tusks on a walrus tell other walruses "who's boss" and are used to drive off rivals. A walrus will hook its tusks onto the ice to help it heave its great body out of the water, or as an anchor when it sleeps in the water. The tusks also work like a pick-axe, cutting a path through the ice.

*Hind flipper bends at right angle to support walrus on land*

SCALE

ADULT WALRUS WITH TUSKS REMOVED

*Thick layer of blubber (fat) under skin keeps walrus warm in freezing water*

*Tough, wrinkled, and folded skin*

## SENSITIVE GIANT

Each walrus finds food by swimming head-first along the ocean bottom. Its 450 sensitive whiskers act like sensors in the dark, murky water. It uses its snout to bulldoze the sand, and shoots a jet of water from its mouth, to dislodge clams and other shellfish. Then it crunches them up with a battery of grinding teeth in its heavy, powerful jaws.

## POWERFUL FLIPPERS

The walrus has two pairs of flippers in place of arms or legs. It uses its hind flippers to power itself through the water, while the front flippers are used for steering. A young walrus may nestle between its mother's front flippers or cling to her neck when she dives. On land, the walrus shuffles about awkwardly on all fours.

*Undersides of flippers are rough and knobbly to help it grip onto slippery ice*

# WASPS

MANY PEOPLE FEAR WASPS MORE than any other animals, because of their painful stings. Yet not all wasps can sting. Wasps are a large family of insects related to bees and ants. More than 100,000 different types of wasp are found worldwide. Most wasps live alone, feeding on sugary liquids such as fruit, plant sap, and flower nectar. Some species, such as common wasps and hornets, live together in a large group called a colony. Each nest colony is started by a queen who lays eggs that develop into female wasps called workers. The workers feed the young and guard the nest. In late summer, new queens hatch out. They mate with male wasps called drones, and fly away to start new nests.

## SNUG AS A GRUB

Wasp eggs hatch out into legless young called grubs. They grow up snug inside six-sided cells in the nest. They become pupae and then adults. Young wasps are meat-eaters, feeding on insects and spiders that the adults bring.

SCALE

COMMON WASP

Feelers (antennae) on top of the head are the main sensing tools

Large compound eyes are good at sensing movement

### FACT BOX

**Family:** Four different families within larger Hymenoptera family, which includes ants and bees

**Habitat:** Rainforests to deserts

**Distribution:** Worldwide on land except North and South Poles

**Size:** Depending on species 0.2–6 cm (0.008–2.5 in)

**Life cycle:** involves four stages: egg, larva, pupa, and adult

Middle section (thorax)

Narrow waist

*Find out more*

ANTS 96
BEES 111
INSECTS 212

Rear section (abdomen)

Sharp spine at tip of abdomen is fed by a poison gland

## JEWEL WASPS

Named for their bright, shiny colours, jewel wasps live alone. Each female digs a little burrow, then goes hunting. She stings an insect so it cannot move and drags it back to her burrow. Then she lays an egg on it. When her grub hatches, it feasts on insect meat.

## COLOURFUL INSECT

The common wasp has a very recognizable yellow-and-black striped body. Other animals, including people, recognize these markings as a warning that the wasp is armed with a painful sting. Other wasps differ widely in colour and size. Some species are red and black, others are shiny blue, green, or black.

JEWEL WASP

# WASPS' NEST
Found all over the world, wasps build
their nests in steamy rainforests,
scorching deserts, in gardens, and even
in homes. Many kinds of wasps live
alone, but these common wasps live
together in a large paper nest made of
chewed wood fibres. This one hangs
from a tree branch. The queen starts the
nest, and the worker wasps extend it.
The young grow up in little cells inside.

# WHALES

WHALES ARE MAMMALS AND NOT fish – they are warm-blooded, breathe air through lungs, and feed their young on milk. Their tails are horizontal, not vertical as in fish, and are divided by a notch into two flukes (flaps). The tail moves up and down to power the whale through the water. Sometimes whales will power themselves to "breach" (leap out of the water). This may be to signal to other whales. Whales' bodies are almost hairless, but they have a thick layer of blubber (fat and oil) beneath their skins to keep them warm. They can grow much larger than land mammals because the water supports the weight of their bodies. Whales also live a long time, and some may survive for 100 years.

POD OF ORCAS
(KILLER WHALES)

Huge dorsal (back) fin can be as much as 1.8 m (6 ft) tall

ORCA
(KILLER
WHALE)

## SPOUTING

A whale must come to the surface every now and then to breathe air. It breathes only through its blowholes (nostrils), not through its mouth. The whale ejects a cloud of stale, used air from the lungs and water vapour high into the air. Baleen whales have two blowholes, while toothed whales, dolphins, and porpoises have only one.

## HUNTING PACK

Like other whales, orcas (killer whales) live in groups called pods. Members of a pod are closely related and hunt together most of the time. Orcas, sperm whales, and other toothed whales hunt prey, such as squid, by seizing them in their sharp, cone-shaped teeth.

SCALE

NARWHAL

Spiralled tusk can grow to 3 m (10 ft)

## SPEEDY SWIMMERS

Killer whales are fast swimmers, with a top speed of about 50 kmh (31 mph) – faster than a speedboat. Armed with 40 to 56 large sharp teeth, they prey on a wide variety of fish, squid, turtles, penguins, seals, and other dolphins and whales. Despite their name, no wild killer whale has ever been known to harm or kill a human.

### FACT BOX

**Family:** Baleen whales (without teeth) include blue and humpback whales; toothed whales include dolphins, killer and pilot whales, porpoises, narwhal, and sperm whales

**No. of species:** 77

**Habitat:** Oceans

**Distribution:** Worldwide

**Food:** From shrimp-like krill to fish, squid, and seals

**Size:** 1.2–33 m (4–108 ft) long

## SWORD FIGHTER

The male narwhal's single, long, and spiral-twisted tusk is the origin of the legend of the unicorn. Males use their tusks to compete with rivals, striking them together, like swordsmen fencing. About one in every three narwhal has a broken tusk – the tusks are hollow, and a blow can shatter one.

Up to 9.8 m (32 ft) in length

### Find out more

CONSERVATION 82
DOLPHINS 160
MAMMALS 239
OCEANS 74

## OCEAN WANDERERS
A humpback whale breaches in the waters of Alaska. Like other great whales it feeds during the short summer in the Arctic or Antarctic, when food is plentiful. It will then migrate to warmer, tropical waters to breed. Whales roam long distances across the world's oceans in search of their seasonal food of plankton and fish. Some whales travel over 20,000 km (12,500 miles) a year.

# WILDEBEEST

LARGE, CLUMSY, AND VERY NOISY, wildebeest are antelopes that live in large herds on the grassy plains of Africa. They are also called gnus, an African word which describes the loud, explosive snort that they make. Grass is their main food and they eat the leafy middle part of grass plants. Wildebeest drink every day if water is available, but can live for five days without drinking. To find enough food and water to drink, they often wander over the grasslands, sometimes covering thousands of kilometres each year. These wandering journeys, called migrations, involve crossing dangerous, fast-flowing rivers.

## LION FODDER

Lions eat a lot of wildebeest, killing them with a suffocating bite to the throat or the muzzle. One adult wildebeest can feed a whole pride (group) of lions. Cheetahs and hyenas attack young wildebeest.

## FACT BOX

**Family:** Bovidae

**Habitat:** Open grassy plains and savanna

**Distribution:** Africa, from southern Kenya to northern South Africa

**Food:** Grass

**Gestation period:** 9 months

**Lifespan:** 25–30 years

**Size:** 100–130 cm (40–50 in)

SCALE

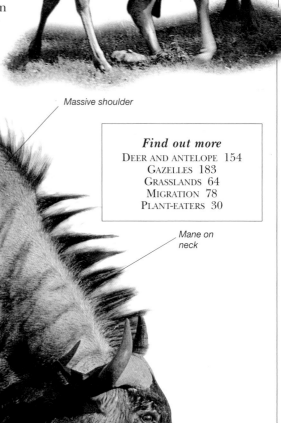

Mother licks newborn calf clean

## BORN TO RUN

Female wildebeest give birth standing up. Newborn calves can stand up three to five minutes after being born, and are licked clean by their mothers. They are up and running with the herd half an hour later. When the herd is not on the move, females and young gather in groups of 10–1,000.

Long, hairy tail

Massive shoulder

Mane on neck

### Find out more

DEER AND ANTELOPE 154
GAZELLES 183
GRASSLANDS 64
MIGRATION 78
PLANT-EATERS 30

## MASSIVE BEASTS

Both sexes have horns, as well as massive heads and shoulders. Their necks have manes (tufts of hair), and they have beards under their throats. The long, hairy tail nearly reaches down to the ground.

# WOLVES

THE WOLF IS THE LARGEST WILD member of the dog family and the ancestor of the domestic, or pet, dog. Wolves are intelligent animals that live together in packs made up of between eight and 20 family members. Each wolf knows its own place in the pack, which is usually led by the oldest male and female. By hunting together, they can kill large animals, such as deer and moose, which are up to ten times the weight of a wolf. A wolf pack patrols a territory, killing mainly sick, injured, old, or young prey.

## CUB IN THE PACK

The most dominant male and female wolf in a pack are the only ones to mate and have cubs. The cubs are suckled for about ten weeks. Then the cubs' mother and the younger wolves bring up partly digested meat for them to eat until they are old enough to hunt with the pack.

## EERIE HOWLS

Wolves howl in order to keep in touch with each other or to warn other wolves to keep out of their area. If one wolf howls, other members of the pack may join in. They often harmonise with each other to make the pack sound as large and strong as possible. Lone wolves rarely howl.

*Even wolf cubs have jaws full of sharp teeth*

WOLF CUB

*Superb senses of smell and hearing, but poor eyesight*

*There are four to seven cubs in a litter*

*Wolves have as many as 17 different facial expressions*

*Long legs enable the wolf to run fast*

*Five claws on front foot and four on back foot*

## HUNTING PREY

Wolves have long legs and walk or run on their toes. This allows them to move much faster than if they moved on the flat sole of the foot as humans do. Their long, sensitive noses and ears pick up the smells and sounds of other animals, so wolves can track their prey easily. Their long muzzles have powerful jaws with 42 sharp teeth for killing prey, chewing meat, gnawing bones, and fighting.

GREY WOLF

SCALE

## WELL-PACKED FOR WINTER

Wolves dwell in the furthest northern and colder regions of Europe, Asia, and North America. Here they inhabit the vast forests of spruce, pines, and larches. To help them survive in cold northern lands, wolves have a thick fur coat with soft, dense underfur and a layer of long fur on top. Their large feet and claws grip rocks, ice, and other slippery surfaces. Wolves have strong bodies and long, powerful legs for chasing their prey over long distances.

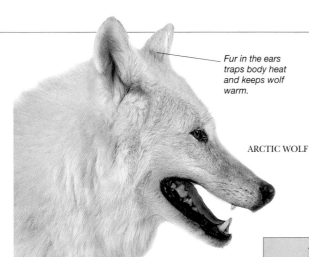

Fur in the ears traps body heat and keeps wolf warm.

Ears standing up to listen for prey or danger

ARCTIC WOLF

# MANED WOLF

Named after the dark mane of fur on its back, the maned wolf has extremely long legs to allow it to see over the tops of tall grasses. It hunts mainly at night for small animals and birds, and pounces on its prey in the same way as a fox.

MANED WOLF

# WHITE WOLF

Wolves that live in snowy Arctic lands often have white coats for camouflage in the winter. This helps them to get really close to their prey without being seen. In summer, their coats turn to grey, brown, or black. Wolves living in the forests to the south of the Arctic have grey or blackish fur.

## FACT BOX

**Family:** Canidae

**Habitat:** Forests, Arctic tundra, deserts, plains, and mountains

**Distribution:** North America, South America, Europe, Asia, Middle East

**Food:** Mammals, carrion, and plant material

**No of young:** 4–7

**Size:** Head and body length 101–152 cm (40–60 in); males larger than females

# BODY LANGUAGE

The way a wolf holds its body and behaves tells the other wolves in a pack how important it is. A dominant wolf stands tall with its ears and tail pointing upward and its teeth showing. A low-ranking, or submissive, wolf crouches down, holds it head between its legs and turns down its ears. Instead of growling, it whines.

This wolf holds its head down in a submissive or defensive position

GREY WOLF

## Find out more

# WOODPECKERS

THERE ARE ABOUT 200 DIFFERENT kinds of woodpeckers in the world. Most of these birds live among trees. A few however, such as the American flickers, live in treeless areas, feeding and nesting on the ground. Woodpeckers can hop up trunks and branches with great speed and agility. They ensure a firm grip on the vertical surface by having powerful feet, in most cases with two toes pointing forwards, one to the side, and one backwards, plus strong, sharp claws. A few smaller species have only three toes. Their beaks bore into wood like high-speed drills.

GREAT SPOTTED WOODPECKER

Built-in "shock absorber" prevents bird knocking itself out when it hammers a tree

Speckled pattern of light and dark for camouflage in woodlands

Powerful chisel-tipped bill for hacking into wood

## WING STRUCTURE
A woodpecker's short, broad wings are ideal for the bird's' quick, bounding flight from tree to tree. They are not migrating birds.

## HAMMER ACTION
You may hear a woodpecker before you see one – they make a rapid tapping or knocking noise as they swiftly bash their bills against tree trunks and branches. They do this to expose insect grubs hiding beneath the bark so they can eat them, or to chisel out their nest holes, or to attract a mate.

Very long tongue has sticky tip with tiny hooks to make sure of seizing insects

EUROPEAN GREEN WOODPECKER

### FACT BOX

**Family:** Picidae

**Habitat:** Forests, woods, some in open country, also deserts

**Distribution:** Worldwide except Australia, New Zealand, Antarctica

**Food:** Mainly insects, especially wood-boring insect larvae, ants and termites; also nuts, seeds, fruits, and tree sap

**Nest:** A tree hole or burrow

**Eggs:** 3–12, white

**Size:** 7.5–52 cm (3–20 in)

SCALE

Widely spread toes give firm grip on bark

Stiffened tail feathers pressed against bark to give extra support

## VERY LONG TONGUE
The woodpecker's tongue is so long that it has to coil it up inside its skull. Powerful muscles flick the tongue in and out of the bill with lightning speed to catch insects.

*Find out more*
BIRDS 115
WOODLAND 60

# WORMS

WORMS ARE A VARIED GROUP of long, legless creatures. There are millions of different kinds on land and in water, but they all belong to four large families. Ribbon worms live mostly in salt water. Roundworms have long, thin, threadlike bodies. They are found everywhere, even inside animals and plants. There may be more roundworms on this planet than any other animal. Flatworms include tapeworms, which live in the guts of pigs, dogs, and other animals. Segmented worms, or annelids, include earthworms and leeches, and dwell in damp earth and water.

LEECH

*Tiny bristles help worm grip soil as it burrows*

## BLOOD-SUCKING LEECHES

Leeches live in lakes, streams, and damp places. They feed on other animals', including humans', blood. The leech's flattened body has a sucker at each end. The suckers grip the flesh of a victim while the leech sucks its blood.

*Sucker grips prey's flesh*

## EARTHWORMS

There are 3,000 different species of earthworms and they live underground in most parts of the world. Like other annelids, the earthworm's body is divided up into segments (rings). It eats decaying plants, and feeds by taking in soil and digesting the plant pieces it contains.

PARCHMENT WORM

*Ring-like segment*

SCALE

## FACT BOX

**Family:** More than 20,000 species in 4 main families: flatworms, ribbon worms, roundworms, and segmented worms

**Habitat:** Salt and fresh water, on land in soil, or on or inside animals or plants

**Distribution:** Worldwide except Antarctic .

**Food:** Plant and animal matter

**Eggs:** From tens to thousands

**Size:** Microscopic to 12 m (40 ft)

## PARCHMENT WORMS

These segmented worms live inside tough, papery tubes which they make to protect them in the mud. The end of the tube sticks out of the mud on seashores. Parchment worms feed on tiny creatures which they filter from seawater.

EARTHWORM

## SEASIDE LUGWORMS

Lugworms live on muddy seashores, in U-shaped burrows. They swallow mud and absorb the tiny plants and animals it contains. Waste mud is passed to form casts on the surface. Fishermen dig where they see the casts to catch lugworms as bait.

LUGWORM

*Find out more*

ANIMAL HOMES 46
COURTSHIP AND MATING 38
DEFENCE 34

# ZEBRAS

ZEBRAS ARE ACTIVE, NOISY striped horses that live in the wild in Africa. Each zebra has its own unique set of stripes, just as each human has their own unique set of fingerprints. Zebras live in herds of between four and 20 individuals, and are believed to recognize others in the herd by their special striped markings. They spend a lot of time nuzzling and grooming each other with their front teeth. Living in herds gives zebras some safety in numbers against dangerous predators such as lions, leopards and hyenas. Zebras run away from danger but they may also bite predators with their sharp teeth, or kick out with their hooves.

ZEBRA FOAL

Mane runs from forehead to tail

ZEBRA LEG

Narrow hoof for speed

Cutaway shows how hoof fits around toe bones

## BUILT FOR SPEED

Long legs and small, narrow hooves allow a zebra to run really fast. Like a horse, a zebra has only one toe on each foot and runs on the tips of its toes. The toe bones are protected by the tough, horny hoof.

## MINIATURE ADULTS

When zebra foals are born, they are well developed and up within an hour so they can run away from danger. They have a mane (long hair) running from forehead to tail, and another patch of hair on the centre of their belly. Foals suckle for about six months and stay with their mother for up to three years.

GREVY'S ZEBRA

Shoulder height can reach 160 cm (64 in)

Stripes evenly spaced and close together

Short, stiff striped mane stands upright

Stomach digests (breaks down) grasses to get the most nutrients from the food

SCALE

## POOR GRASSY DIET

Zebras spend 60–80 per cent of each day biting off the coarse, tough tops of grasses with their sharp front teeth. The plants are less nourishing than meat so these herbivores (plant-eaters) have to spend virtually all day feeding to get enough goodness. The zebras' long muzzles enable them to break up their food with rough grinding teeth along their cheeks. Their long necks help them to reach down to the ground easily to nibble the grasses.

## GRASSLAND GALLOPERS
Galloping across the flat African grasslands and plains, zebras rely on their speed to escape from stalking cats and ravenous dogs. Living in herds also protects them as herd members can warn each other of danger, and predators find it hard to pick out individual animals from a group. In the dry season, zebras may wander great distances in search of fresh grass to graze on and water holes that have not run dry.

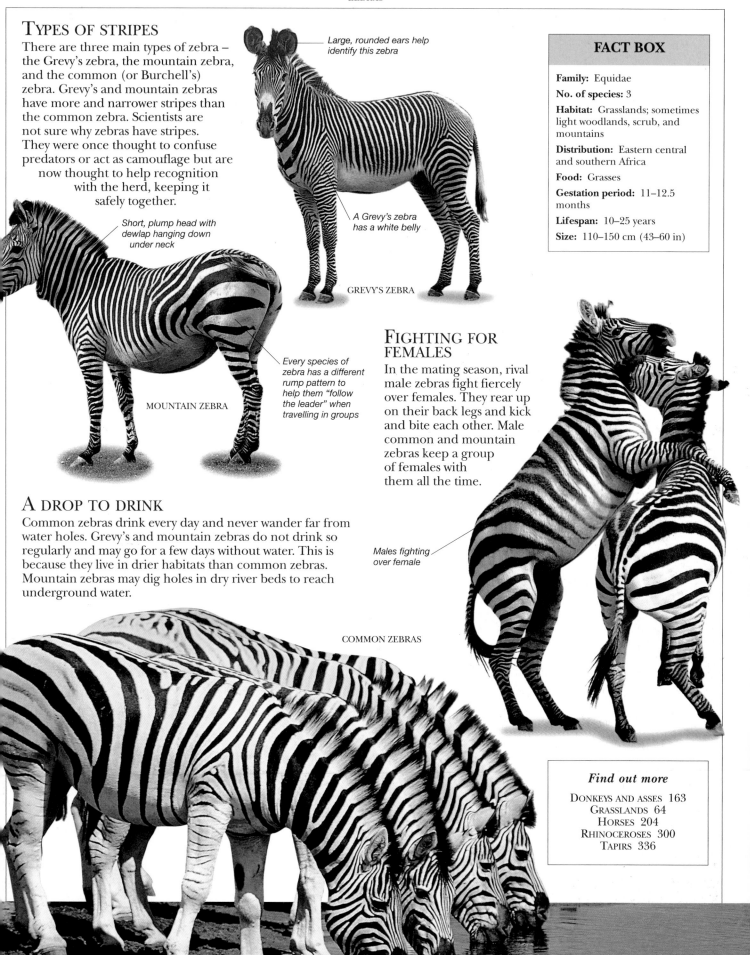

# TYPES OF STRIPES

There are three main types of zebra – the Grevy's zebra, the mountain zebra, and the common (or Burchell's) zebra. Grevy's and mountain zebras have more and narrower stripes than the common zebra. Scientists are not sure why zebras have stripes. They were once thought to confuse predators or act as camouflage but are now thought to help recognition with the herd, keeping it safely together.

*Large, rounded ears help identify this zebra*

*A Grevy's zebra has a white belly*

GREVY'S ZEBRA

*Short, plump head with dewlap hanging down under neck*

*Every species of zebra has a different rump pattern to help them "follow the leader" when travelling in groups*

MOUNTAIN ZEBRA

## FACT BOX

**Family:** Equidae

**No. of species:** 3

**Habitat:** Grasslands; sometimes light woodlands, scrub, and mountains

**Distribution:** Eastern central and southern Africa

**Food:** Grasses

**Gestation period:** 11–12.5 months

**Lifespan:** 10–25 years

**Size:** 110–150 cm (43–60 in)

# FIGHTING FOR FEMALES

In the mating season, rival male zebras fight fiercely over females. They rear up on their back legs and kick and bite each other. Male common and mountain zebras keep a group of females with them all the time.

*Males fighting over female*

# A DROP TO DRINK

Common zebras drink every day and never wander far from water holes. Grevy's and mountain zebras do not drink so regularly and may go for a few days without water. This is because they live in drier habitats than common zebras. Mountain zebras may dig holes in dry river beds to reach underground water.

COMMON ZEBRAS

### *Find out more*

# GLOSSARY

**Abdomen:** the "tummy" part of an animal's body that contains its digestive and reproductive organs. An insect's abdomen is at the rear of its three body sections.

**Algae:** simple, plant-like organisms that make their own food. They can be green, brown, red, or blue-green in colour.

**Amphibian:** a vertebrate that lives partly on land and partly in water. Amphibians depend on water in which to breed.

**Antennae:** pairs of long sensory organs (feelers) on the heads of insects and crustaceans. They detect vibrations, smells, and tastes.

**Arthropod:** An invertebrate with a jointed body case, such as an insect or a spider.

**Blubber:** a layer of fat found under the skin of animals that live in the cold. Blubber helps to keep them warm, and also acts as a food store.

**Breeding:** producing offspring by mating. In mammals and birds, breeding also involves raising the young.

**Bull:** the male of the species, as with whales, seals, and cattle.

**Burrow:** an underground tunnel dug by an animal. The animal lives in its burrow and may also bring up its young there.

**Camouflage:** the way animals escape being seen by blending in with their background.

**Canines:** long, fang-like teeth found in mammals. They are well-developed in dogs and cats, which use them to kill. Some male animals display their canine teeth to frighten off rivals.

**Carnivore:** a mammal with specially shaped teeth, mainly for feeding on meat. Carnivore can also refer to any meat-eating predator.

**Carrion:** dead or rotting animal flesh that is eaten as food by meat-eaters known as scavengers.

**Cartilage:** a tough, flexible tissue, also known as gristle, found in the skeletons of vertebrates. The skeletons of sharks and rays are almost entirely made of cartilage.

**Caterpillar:** the wingless, worm-like larva of a butterfly or moth. Caterpillars have legs and powerful jaws.

**Cephalopod:** a mollusc with a large head and a ring of arms, such as an octopus or squid.

**Cocoon:** the silk case, or pupa, that protects moths while they change from larvae into adults.

**Colony:** a large group of animals that live and/or breed together.

**Courtship:** behaviour that forms a bond between a male and a female before mating.

**Crustacean:** an invertebrate with a tough exoskeleton and jointed limbs that lives mainly in water. A few crustaceans, such as wood lice, have adapted to life on land.

**Chrysalis:** the hard case that protects butterflies while they change from larvae into adults.

**Domestic:** animals that have been tamed and then bred as farm animals, such as cows. Also refers to animals that live in the home, such as dogs and cats.

**Down:** the fluffy body feathers that keep a young bird warm.

**Echinoderm:** a marine invertebrate with a hard outer covering (the test) and a body divided into five sections.

**Echolocation:** the way in which dolphins and bats find their way. It involves sending out sound signals and then listening for the echoes that bounce back off objects in front of them.

**Embryo:** a developing baby animal before it is born or hatched.

**Environment:** the external conditions and surroundings in which a plant or animal lives.

**Exoskeleton:** a hard, outer skeleton that surrounds an animal's body and gives it shape and protection.

**Feral:** a domestic animal that has returned to live in the wild.

**Fertilize:** the process by which male sex cells are joined to female sex cells to produce new living things.

**Food chain:** a process whereby food passes along a chain of living things – usually from small ones to big ones. For example, plankton is eaten by shrimps, which are eaten by small fish, which, in turn, are eaten by large fish.

**Gills:** organs that enable animals, such as fish and certain amphibians, to breathe underwater.

**Habitat:** the natural home of an animal.

**Hibernation:** the ability of some animals to sleep or shut down their bodies for long periods of time. This generally happens in winter when food is scarce and temperatures are very low.

**Incisors:** the front teeth of mammals, which may be used to nibble or gnaw.

**Insects:** the group of hard-bodied, jointed animals that are recognized by their three body sections and six pairs of legs.

**Invertebrate:** an animal without a backbone.

**Larvae:** the young, immature stage of certain animals, such as insects and amphibians. An insect larva tends to be the feeding and growing stage in the life cycle.

**Life cycle:** the stages animals go through from birth to death, which are repeated continuously in following generations.

**Mammal:** a vertebrate animal that feeds its young on milk and has a covering of hair.

**Marsupial:** a mammal that gives birth to underdeveloped young who then complete their growth in a pouch on their mother's tummy.

**Mating:** when a male and female animal join together in order that male sex cells can fertilize female sex cells.

**Metamorphosis:** a major change in an animal's body shape during its life cycle. Caterpillars turn into butterflies or moths through metamorphosis.

**Migration:** the two-way journeys that animals make to be in the right place, at the right time, to take advantage of a seasonal supply of food.

**Mimicry:** the way animals copy other animals or objects in their environment. This may be to make them appear more fierce or poisonous than they really are, or to blend in with their surroundings.

**Mollusc:** an invertebrate animal with a head and muscular foot. Many molluscs have a shell outside or sometimes inside their bodies.

**Moult:** the shedding of the exoskeleton when crustaceans, insects, spiders, and other arthropods grow. Also applies to the loss of hair, skin, or feathers in mammals, reptiles, and birds when growing a fresh coat or plumage.

**Nocturnal:** active at night, but inactive during the day.

**Nutrients:** any material taken in by a living thing to sustain life.

**Nymph:** the immature stage of invertebrate animals, such as dragonflies and newts, that go through an incomplete metamorphosis.

**Opposable:** the thumb of a primate, including humans, capable of moving into a position facing the other digits in order to provide a firm grasp of an object.

**Parasite:** an animal that lives on, or inside, the body of another species, known as its host.

**Pedipalp:** a pair of appendages on the head of an arachnid. Pedipalps can be used for defence, digging, touch, or guiding food into the mouth. A scorpion's pedipalps are modified into claws.

**Plankton:** minute plants and animals that drift about at the surface of seas and lakes.

**Predator:** an animal that kills and eats other animals.

**Prey:** an animal that is killed and eaten by a predator.

**Pupa:** the resting, non-feeding stage in the life cycle of certain insects when they turn from larvae into adults. This is the stage at which many internal developments occur.

**Reptile:** a vertebrate animal that is covered with hard, dry scales, and moves by crawling on four legs or on its belly.

**Scales:** hard, thin flakes that form the protective skin of fish and reptiles.

**Scavenger:** an animal that feeds on the remains of dead animals or plants, such as a vulture.

**Snout:** the elongated part of an animal's head that includes the mouth and nose.

**Sonar:** system used by bats and dolphins, by which they emit high-frequency sounds and listen for the echoes so they can locate objects in the environment.

**Species:** group of plants or animals that are able to breed with each other.

**Suckling:** the act of mammal mothers feeding their young with milk from the breast.

**Tadpole:** the immature, larval, stage of frogs and toads.

**Talons:** the claw-like feet of birds of prey.

**Tentacles:** the flexible, arm-like structures lined with stinging cells on sea anemones and jellyfish. Also applies to the long, elastic appendages of squid and cuttlefish that they use to capture their prey.

**Territory:** an area of living space defended by an animal from others of its own species.

**Thorax:** the middle section in an insect's body, which has legs and wings attached and the muscles to make them work.

**Tropical:** living in the hot region that circles the world either side of the Equator between the tropics of Cancer and Capricorn.

**Vertebrate:** an animal with a backbone.

# INDEX

# Picture credits

The publisher would like to thank the following for their kind permission to reproduce their photographs:

t=top, a=above, b=below, l=left, r=right, c=centre, f=far

**Aquila Photographics:** Mick Durham 112.

**Ardea London Ltd:** Adrian Warren 140, 193; Clem Haagner 262; Eric Dragesco 158cl; Graham Robertson 277t; Jean-Paul Ferrero 186.

**Barleylands Farm Museum:** L. E. Bigley 138c, 138br.

**BBC Natural History Unit:** Anup Shah 188; G & H Denzau 340; Jurgen Freund 148.

**Biofotos:** Heather Angel 93, 171, 228, 271; Jason Venus 268.

**Birmingham Museum and Art Gallery:** 275bl.

**Bruce Coleman Ltd:** 233tr; Alain Compost 240cl; Allan G. Potts 286, 295tl; Bob & Clara Calhoun 333br; C. C. Lockwood 244bl; CB & DW Frith 263tr; Dr Eckart Pott 131ca; Erwin & Peggy Bauer 302cl; Francisco J. Erize 91b; Fred Bruemmer 312tl; George McCarthy 352; Gerald S. Cubitt 142b; Gordan Langsbury 349cl; Gunter Ziesler 236tr, 236; Hans Reinhard 280b; HPH Photography 132tr, 231cr; J. P. Zwaenepoel 341cr; Jane Burton 59tl, 59tr, 311; Jeff Foott 266c, 320br; Jen & Des Bartlett 251br; Joe McDonald 290bl; John Cancalosi 244tl, 289tr; John Markham 291b; John Shaw 357; Johnny Johnson 283cr, 296; Jorg & Petra Wegner 341b; Kim Taylor 337b; Konrad Wothe 230cl; Luiz Claudio Marigo 290tl; M. P.

L. Fogden 285tr; Mark N. Boulton 187cfrb; Michael Fogden 82tl; Pacific Stock 220; Paul Van Gaalen 136cl; Rod Williams 90t, 141b, 302t; Tero Niemi 289b; Wayne Lankinen 356tl.

**Colorific!:** Ferorelli 41tl.

**Julian Cotton Photo Library:** 116.

**Philip Dowell:** 3 (pig and zebra), 15 (zebra), 128br, 217tr, 217bc, 227bc.

**Greenpeace Inc:** Rowlands 83tc.

**Images Colour Library:** 91cr, 129, 158, 192tr, 213; Joe Cornish 205; National Geographic 167.

**Katz Pictures:** David Gordon 18clb, 18bl.

**FLPA - Images of nature:** David Hosking 253; E & D Hosking 26b; M. B. Withers 100cra; Mark Newman 98tr; Silvestris 322.

**Ingrid Mason Pictures:** William Mason 359.

**The Natural History Museum, London:** 19tl, 30tr, 33tc, 46l, 56cl, 79tr, 86cla, 86-87, 87tr, 87cr, 91cl, 113bl, 115crb, 120tr, 123cla, 153, 160cla, 169clb, 176cr, 196tl, 209b, 341t, 353clb; Colin Keates 99cl.

**Natural Science Photos:** C. Dani and I. Jeske, Milano 218; C. Jones 202; Carol Farneti Foster 217cl.

**N.H.P.A.:** A. N. T. 190cl, 282b; Alan Williams 265; Andy Rouse 227tl, 349tr; Anthony Bannister 337tl; B & C Alexander 276; B. Jones & M. Shimlock 146; Daniel Heuclin 142c, 238tr; Dave Watts 282cl, 282cr; E. Hanumantha Rao 238bl; Gerard Lacz 320tr, 321c; Jany Sauvanet 94tr; John Shaw

338; Laurie Campbell 295tr, 295b; Lutra 308tr; Martin Harvey 183c, 223c; Michael Leach 258cr; Nigel J. Dennis 137; Norbert Wu 222; Stephen Dalton 103b, 121cb, 288, 319c, 327tl, 328, 333tl; T. Kitchin & V. Hurst 107, 151, 314tl.

**Norfolk Rural Life Museum:** 191c.

**Oxford Scientific Films:** 41tr, 90bl, 111b, 127tl, 213tl, 309br; Alastair Shay 104; Anthony Bannister 101; Babs & Bert Wells 245cr; Ben Osborne 11br, 277br; Daniel J. Cox 109b, 283bl; David B. Fleetham 175, 256, 294; David W. Breed 201c; Dr E. R. Degginger 251tr; Fredrik Ehrenstrom 216b; G. I. Bernard 324; Hans & Judy Beste 223br; Hans Reinhard/Okapia 284; Karen Greer, Partridge Films 165; Konrad Wothe 244br; Mark Hamblin 187cr, 287tl; Matthews & Purdy 355tl; Max Gibbs 37br; Michael Leach 335; Micheal Fogden 332tl; Mike Hill 238br, 258l, 259, 260bl, 260r; Niall Benvie 241b; Partridge Productions Ltd 321cla; Rafi Ben-Shahar 211, 355cr; Stan Osolinski 83br, 178c, 185cr, 355cr; Steve Turner 136cra, 239cl, 245cl; Tim Jackson 251l; Tobian Bernhard 316; Victoria McCormack 110; Wendy Shattil & Bob Rozinski 191b; Zig Leszczynski 70tl, 75bl, 172tl, 306.

**Oxford University Museum:** 143cr.

**Planet Earth Pictures:** 240b, 241tr, 321tr; Adam Jones 303b; Alain Dragesco 261tl, 304c; Alex Kerstitch 43tr, 43cra, 43cr; Andre Bartschi 266b; Angela Scott 38-39; Anup Shah 258br, 339tl; Beth Davidow 290cr; Brian Kenney 26t, 286c; David Kjaer 247, 278tr;

Denise Tackett 332c; Doug Perrine 161, 242; Ed Darack 349b; Ford Kristo 243cl; Gary Bell 243tl, 263br, 329b; Georgette Douwma 203b; Jan Tove Johansson 348; John Downer 241cl, 261bl; John R. Bracegirdle 155; John Waters 304b; Jonathan Scott 233b; K & K Ammann 203tl; Ken Lucas 69tl, 197tl, 279tl, 303tl; Kurt Amsler 242l, 242t; M & C Denis-Huot 229tr, 302b; Pete Oxford 236tl; Peter Scoones 73tl; Robert Canis 286tl; Scott McKinley 264tr; Terry Mayes 300cr; Tom Brakefield 95b, 266t.

**Ian Redmond:** 172bl.

**South of England Rare Breeds Centre:** 24c, 138tr, 138cla, 166c, 184b.

**Still Pictures:** Alain Guillemont 312cr; Bergerot Robert 230tl;

David Cavagnaro 289tl; Dominique Halleux 189tr; Fritz Polking 183b, 231tl; Kevin Schafer 270l; M & C Denis-Huot/Bios 210b; Michael Gunther 139b; Norbert Wu 232; Philippe Henry 283tl; Roland Seitre 254tr, 270cr, 272tl, 314tr; W. Moller 125.

**The Stock Market:** 191.

**Tony Stone Images:** 229bl, 301, 363b; Art Wolfe 187cfr, 230br, 254b, 358b; Byron Jorjorian 272r; Chris Harvey 362; Chris Johns 363cr; Christer Fredriksson 300tr; Daniel J. Cox 308, 320l; David E. Myers 122tr; Hans Strand 97; Jake Rags 118; James P. Rowan 203tr; Kevin Schafer 312b; Manoj Shah 141cr, 201tr, 339bl; Renee Lynn 313; Rosemary Calvert 229cr; Stuart Westmorland 314b, 354; Terry Donnelly 123; Theo Allofs 300l; Tim Davis 97cr, 272bl;

Tom Bean 318b.

**University Museum of Zoology, Cambridge:** 55l.

**Weymouth Sealife Centre:** 310tr, 310ca.

**Barry Watts:** 246tl.

**Woodfall Wild Images:** John Robinson 181.

**Jerry Young:** 2 (porcupine), 15 (terrapin, alligator, and wolf), 52tl, 54–55, 67tr, 92crb, 99tr, 103tr, 105bl, 113tl, 113bc (Malayan frog beetle), 113bfl, 116bl, 123tr, 135tl, 149tr, 150tr, 157tr, 157bl, 158tl, 158cr, 179bc, 180cr, 180bl, 182tl, 185cl, 185bc, 210bl, 213tr, 231bl, 235c, 235bl, 239tr, 252bc, 254tl, 278bc, 297tl, 297bc, 305bc, 342cr, 343cl, 351c, 356cr, 356bc, 358tl, 358tr.

Jacket: **Jerry Young:** inside front crb, b; front tfrc, c; back tlc.

The photography in this book would not have been possible without the help of the following people and places:

Peter Anderson, Craig Austin, Jon Bouchier, Paul Bricknell, Geoff Brightling, Jane Burton, Martin Camm, Peter Chadwick, Gordon Clayton, Bruce Coleman, Andy Crawford, Geoff Dann, Richard Davies, Philip Dowell, Mike Dunning, Andreas von Einsiedel, Ken Findlay, Neil Fletcher, Max Gibbs, Will Giles, Steve Gorton, Frank Greenaway, Marc Henrie, Gary Higgins, Kit Houghton, Ray Hutchins, Colin Keates, Dave King, Bob Langrish, Cyril Laubscher, Bill Ling, Mike Linley, Jane Miller, Tracy Morgan, Nik Parfitt, Rob Reichenfeld, Tim Ridley, Karl Shone, Steve Shott, Michael Spencer, Harry Taylor, Kim Taylor, David Ward, Matthew Ward, Barry Watts, David Web, Dan Wright, Jerry Young

Winners and runners-up of the 1998 and 1999 DK Eyewitness/RSPCA Young Photographer Awards: Jonathan Ashcroft, Anna Brownlee, Katie Budd, Josephine Green, James Lewis, Montana Miles-Lowery, Jenny Moffat, Rebecca Noble, Celine Philibert, Keshini Ranasinghe, Raphaella Ricciardi, Kathleen Swalwell, and Oliver Thwaites

Allendale Vampire (Haven Stud, Hereford), Haras Nationale De Compeign, and Odds Farm Park

# Acknowledgements

**With special thanks to:** Chris Packham,
TV presenter and wildlife photographer, for
writing the Foreword; and Ambreen Nawaz,
Publications Assistant, Royal Society for the
Prevention of Cruelty to Animals (RSPCA)

**Editorial assistance:** Selina Wood
**Design co-ordination:** Alexandra Brown
**Design assistance:** Janet Allis, Polly Appleton,
Lester Cheeseman, Sheila Collins, Joanne
Connor, Carol Oliver, Laura Roberts

**Jacket design:** Karen Shooter
**DTP assistance:** Janice Williams
**Production assistance:** Silvia La Greca
**Index:** Lynn Bresler
**International sales support:** Simone Osborn

**Illustrators:** Martin Camm, Luciano Corbella,
Kenneth Lilly, Mick Loates,
Mallory McGregor, Richard Orr

**Model maker:** Staab Studios